PEDIGREES
OF SOME OF THE
EMPEROR CHARLEMAGNE'S
DESCENDANTS

J. Chapman sc.

CHARLEMAGNE

Publish'd as the Act directs April 1 1797.

PEDIGREES
OF SOME OF THE
EMPEROR CHARLEMAGNE'S DESCENDANTS
Volume III

Compiled By

J. ORTON BUCK

*President General of the Order of the Crown of Charlemagne
in the United States of America*

and

TIMOTHY FIELD BEARD

*Genealogist General of the Order of the Crown of Charlemagne
in the United States of America*

Including a Chapter
"A Glimpse of Emperor Lothair"

by

ALLEN CABANISS, Ph.D.

*Research Professor of History
University, Mississippi*

Published by

GENEALOGICAL PUBLISHING CO., INC.

*The eighteenth-century engraving reproduced
as the frontispiece is in the collection of
Mr. J. Orton Buck.*

CONTENTS

vii

Dedication

ROBERT ERSKINE CAMPBELL
1884-1977

The Right Reverend Robert Erskine Campbell, monk of the Order of the Holy Cross, was born into Eternal Life on the 23rd of August 1977, in the 93rd year of his birth, the 67th year of his ordination to the Sacred Priesthood, and the 51st year of his consecration as a bishop in the Succession of the Apostles in the One, Holy, Catholic, and Apostolic Church.

Robert Erskine Campbell was born into this world on the 13th of August in the Year of our Lord 1884, to the Reverend Robert Erskine Campbell and his wife, Rebecca Biddle Bishop. The birth took place in Florida, New York, where his father was the rector of the local Episcopal parish. Bishop Campbell descended on both sides from families that established themselves in this country during the colonial period. His father's people were Scotch Presbyterian plantation owners of South Carolina, while his mother's family were Philadelphia Quakers.

After graduation from Columbia University in 1906, and the General Theological Seminary three years later, Bishop Campbell as a young deacon of the Episcopal Church traveled to the mountains of Tennessee where he served as a missionary for a year. There he was ordained a priest in December of 1909. Returning to New York City, he served as a curate of St. Luke's Church. However, the mountains of Tennessee and their inhabitants held a special attraction for him; therefore, he returned as Headmaster of St. Andrew's School, Sewanee, in 1911. This school for mountain boys was established by the Order of the Holy Cross, an Episcopal monastic community, as part of their missionary outreach.

It was while he was working with the Order that Bishop Campbell became convinced that he wished to give his life to God and to his Church as a Religious, so he relinquished the position of headmaster in 1915, to become a novice of the Order at their Mother House in West Park, New York. Shortly after his life profession in 1917, he returned to St. Andrew's School, where he continued to serve until 1922. It was at this time that the Order was beginning new work in the hinterland of Liberia; Bishop Campbell's genius for leadership and organization were needed in that far-off land. There he served as Prior of their mission for three years until he was elected Bishop of Liberia, which post he held until malaria forced him to resign his diocese in 1936 and to return to Holy Cross Monastery in West Park, New York, eventually again returning to St. Andrew's School. Bishop Campbell completed his active ministry by serving the Order and the companion Order of St. Helena as their Superior from 1948 to 1954.

The Order's beautiful and busy Mount Calvary Retreat House in the hills above Santa Barbara, California, became Bishop Campbell's "retirement" home. From there he continued to serve God, the Order, and the Church in the Far West until the day his death brought to a close a very full life.

Bishop Campbell's wise and holy counsel was much sought by the Church at large — be it in the gatherings of his brother bishops of the world-wide Anglican Communion when they met every ten years at Lambeth Palace, the London residence of the Archbishop of Canterbury, or in the tri-annual conventions of the Episcopal Church in the United States of America, or at the yearly meetings of the House of Bishops of that same body, or in the many and varied church organizations which elected him to positions of leadership and trust.

As might be expected, Bishop Campbell was the recipient of many honorary degrees, decorations, and honors. Among them were a *Sacrae Theologiae Doctor* from his seminary, a *Divinitatis Doctor* from the University of the South, and a Doctor of Canon Law from the University of Liberia. The Liberian government made him a Grand Commander of the Star of Africa, and Columbia University awarded him their Distinguished Service Medal of Merit as a Missionary and Educator. He was further honored by the most ancient (1048 A.D.) of all knighthoods, the Sovereign Order of St. John of Jerusalem, who welcomed him into their fellowship. Bishop Campbell was also the Honorary

Chaplain General for the Order of the Crown of Charlemagne, the National Society: Americans of Royal Descent, the Order of the Three Crusades, and a member of the Baronial Order of the Magna Carta, the Sons of the American Revolution, and other organizations of merit.

Those who were priviliged to know Bishop Campbell will miss this strong advocate of Holy Church and the civilization which developed under her guidance in the Western world. All who knew this Christian gentleman feel a great loss, for the qualities of dignity, reserve, and graciousness which his life so beautifully exemplified are so lacking in the world of today. But, above all, we will miss the companionship of one who throughout his life was a joyous child of God.

The Reverend Frank Kenneth Barta

PREFACE

"There were those who ruled in their kingdoms and were men renowned for their power, giving counsel by their understanding . . . leaders of the people in their deliberations . . . wise in words of instruction. There were some of them who have left a name so that men declare their praise. And there are some who have no memorial, who have perished as though they had not lived."

Sirach XLIV, 3, 4, 8, 9

This is the third in the series of lineage books published by the Order of the Crown of Charlemagne in the United States of America under the title PEDIGREES OF SOME OF THE EMPEROR CHARLEMAGNE'S DESCENDANTS. Volume I compiled by the first President General of the Order, Marcellus Donald R. von Redlich, appeared in 1941 and in 1972 was reprinted by the Genealogical Publishing Company of Baltimore. Volume II compiled by Aileen Lewers Langston and J. Orton Buck was published by the Order in 1974 and is still available.

In 1975, Mr. Beard and I started this compilation of Charlemagne lineages. For the most part, they have come from the lineage papers of members of the Order. Although no proofs for any of the generations of any of the lines have been given in this book, each generation has been substantiated to the satisfaction of the Genealogist General before the member was admitted to the Order. We have again weighed all the evidence for each line and believe that at this time each line included in this book is a valid Charlemagne descent.

It is hoped that this volume will be of value to those interested in genealogy and history, and also will be a guide and source of information to others seeking a line into which their ancestry can be tied to obtain noble, royal and imperial descent. A proven descent from the Emperor Charlemagne has long been considered a genealogical achievement and is the envy of many who have not been able to achieve this distinction.

Time is the dimension which makes life a dream. Each moment of life passes and ceases to exist. At a definite point in time, Charlemagne knelt in St. Peter's at Rome. Leo III placed the imperial crown upon his head. Now all is gone, the moment, the actors in that momentous event, and even the stage, the old basilica long since razed after the ravages of time to make way for the present edifice. At any given moment in time, we find a stage and the actors playing their parts only to have the curtain drop as that moment passes into history. Some of the actors have played greater parts than others and their actions during their brief sojourn on earth have influenced the lives of many in following generations. Genealogy is the recalling of certain succeeding moments in time which are like a series of knots on a very long length of cord.

J. Orton Buck
16 November 1977

1907 Capers Avenue
Nashville, Tennessee 37212

FOREWORD

In the Foreword of Volume II, I presented a survey of genealogical sources published since Volume I had been written in 1941, which might lead the average person with little ancestral knowledge on to the possible road back to Charlemagne. I stressed the point that it is difficult to make this forty generation leap in one mad dash. The necessity of proceeding cautiously cannot be overemphasized. The gradual gathering together of documents, such as full copies of birth, marriage and death certificates; wills; deeds; Bible records; parish register entries; tombstone inscriptions and interment listings; and other personal and public papers relating to your family, may seem a bit ridiculous when you feel that you know when you were born, the names of parents, when your grandparents died, etc.; but there comes a time in this accumulating process when you start to learn things that you didn't know, such as possibly the names of a grandmother's parents, and the pieces of an enormous puzzle start to fall into place.

It was as a result of the favorable reaction to the foreword of Volume II, that I wrote *How to Find Your Family Roots* (New York, McGraw-Hill, 1977, ie. 1978) which should help all people find their origins. Many will never find a line to Charlemagne, but they may discover interesting stories about their own ancestors. They may find some forebears who fled from the oppression of the Tsars of Russia, or the military demands of the German Empire, or others who fought in our American Revolution or our Civil War. They may even reach back and find Spanish progenitors who settled in the American Southwest, or Mexico, in the 16th century, or some who came on the Mayflower to Plymouth, Massachusetts, in 1620, or settled in Jamestown, Virginia, in 1607. They may find black or white ancestors who came over in bondage and struggled for their freedom, Jewish ancestors who escaped the Inquisition, and settled in New Amsterdam, Roman Catholic ancestors who fled to Maryland from the Protestant rule in England, or French Huguenots who rejected the Roman Catholic regime of France, and founded New Rochelle, New York.

xxi

The interesting fact is that there has never been quite as diverse a country as ours, or one in which so many different ethnic groups and religious sects have lived in harmony. The accord indeed has sometimes been forced by wars and laws, but after two hundred years the citizens of the United States seem to be settling down and forming an interesting society in which genealogists can explore their past.

Genealogy as a pastime has flourished in this country since the first family history was published by the Stebbins family of Hartford in 1771, but it has had its greatest advance in times of extended peace and prosperity. The period from the end of the War of 1812 to the beginning of the Civil War saw the first serious publication of local histories with genealogical sections on families of the town and counties of this country and a number of solid genealogies, such as the *Hoyt Family* (1857) by David Webster Hoyt (1833-1921), the *Steele Family* (1859) by Daniel Steele Durrie (1819-1892), *A Genealogical Register of the Descendants of Several Puritan Families* (1859-1864) by Abner Morse (1793-1865) in 4 volumes, and *The Genealogy of the Brainerd Family in the United States* (1857) by my double great-great-great granduncle, the Rev. David Dudley Field, D.D. (1781-1867), also the author of a history of the towns of Haddam and East Haddam, Connecticut, in 1814, a history of Berkshire County, Massachusetts, in 1829, and a history of Pittsfield, Massachusetts in 1844 (see Chapter LIV for his ancestry). The great bulk of these publications were produced in New England, where the New England Historic Genealogical Society was founded at Boston in 1845, and first issued its *The New England Historical and Genealogical Register* in 1847, now the oldest genealogical periodical in the world.

Following the Civil War and until the beginning of World War I came the greatest surge of genealogical output until recent years. Printed genealogies, enormous volumes of town and county histories (many of the later so-called "mug books" were the vanity press publications of such companies as Beers, Lewis and Lippincott) which often are still the basic authorities on particular families, or families of a certain area, poured forth from all parts of the United States. The value of many of these volumes was assessed at the time of our recent Bicentennial when family associations and historical societies realized their basic worth and reprinted them in profusion. The best of these reprints had new indexes and additional chapters bringing families and local histories up to date. The period between the two World Wars continued some of the momentum of the post Civil War period, and saw the expansion of the *National Genealogical Society Quarterly* first issued in Washington, D.C. in 1912, and the establishment of Donald Lines Jacobus' *The American Genealogist,* in New Haven, Connecticut, but in the thirty year period following World War II the number of genealogical publications produced has been staggering.

Four special reasons in my opinion account for this. The first is the continued and increased interest of mobile Americans in finding their roots, the second is the interest of The Church of Jesus Christ of Latter-day Saints in genealogy, the third is the advance in quick copying and photo offset which allows more people to copy material in homes, archives and libraries and to publish their findings, in a "less" expensive manner and the fourth has been the Bicentennial which encouraged so many people to look back over the last two hundred years. Alex Haley's book, *Roots: the Saga of an American Family* (1976), was published in the Bicentennial year, and the production of this family story on television led many people both black and white to libraries and archives to search for their past.

The stumbling block for genealogists in this mobile society is often the starting point. Many people are uncertain of the place or date of death or marriage of recent ancestors. We do not have the excellent English system of central registration of vital records which has been in effect in that country since 1837. In the case, for example, of my own grandfather, Maximillian Cornelius Beard, I was lucky in knowing from family stories that he was born in Biloxi, Mississippi on 27 Nov., 1864 and even more fortunate to be able to verify it from a family Bible record, as there were no official vital records kept in Mississippi until this century. I also knew that he was married in Canandaigua, New York, 25 Sept. 1888, and I was able to verify this from some engraved wedding silver, a wedding invitation, a printed county history and an official copy of his marriage record from the New York State Department of Health, which has kept records since 1880. His death in Hartford, Connecticut, 19 Feb. 1924, was verified by a copy of his death certificate from the Connecticut State Department of Health. If I hadn't had some idea from my family about the places where these events took place and the dates, I would have been hard pressed to discover the documents.

His father's records would have been even more difficult to find, without family help, as he was born in Portsmouth, England in 1824, before central registration, he married first in Canandaigua, New York, in 1852 before vital records were kept in New York State, he married secondly in Bethlehem, Pennsylvania, in 1881 before that state kept records, and only in the end, when he died in Brookline, Massachusetts, in 1906, a state where vital records have been kept since the 17th century, did he at last have one of his vital records officially documented. The wanderings of my grandfather and great-grandfather both of whom also lived in New Orleans, Louisiana, and New York City, are not, in the least, unusual in this country, and they point up the problems faced by many genealogists, since you cannot really start serious genealogical research until you gather together the basic documents concerning your immediate forebears. Recent correspondence has also pointed up the alarming fact that many public vital records departments are rejecting the reasonable requests by genealogists for vital records. It appears that I was more fortunate than I realized to obtain a copy of my grandfather's death certificate from Connecticut, as today that state rejects all requests for vital records and says that only genealogists may look at their records. Of course they do not give you a list of genealogists, and for a person living, say, in California or Pennsylvania this poses a problem. It also seems that I applied for my grandparents' marriage record from New York State in the nick of time. Today they are telling people to write back in a year or so, and they send a form stating that you should visit libraries as you really don't need vital records. A recent letter to the Louisiana Department of Health and Human Resources for death certificates of 1898 and 1927 received a reply that this information was confidential, and only available to relatives. The Alabama State Department of Health rejected a recent request for a death certificate with a personal check enclosed and stated that they could only accept a certified check, as their drawers were full of bad ones. It seems to me that bureaucracy and bad judgment are the impediments to genealogists in these particular cases, and we can understand the problems to a certain degree. Connecticut should know that you have a right to have your grandfather's death certificate; New York should think about the money they could take in which would help pay employees, and the amount it costs to reject a request. Louisiana shouldn't care how you are related to someone who died 50 or 80 years ago, as the information could hardly be called confidential at this late date. Alabama should wait until a check clears before they process an order, and then they wouldn't have all those debts owing to them.

There are also keepers of other records such as deeds and wills who state that they are too busy to look in indexes, and that it isn't their job in the first place. Others tell you that it will cost you three to ten dollars a name to check the indexes. Some court houses may tell you that their records are private and that only lawyers can use them. Certain libraries may say that anyone *but* genealogists may use their collections. Registrars of deeds and wills who have early records in their custody should give as much attention to requests for copies of these records as those of the present day, as these are public documents of which they are the curators. If they don't want to do so, then they should deposit them in the state archives, as has been done in Maryland, for example, with most of the 18th century and some 19th century material. It is actually part of their job to look in indexes, and if a simple request comes with a stamped, self-addressed envelope, then they should reply. Rambling complicated requests are another matter, and they should have a list of researchers to whom they can refer these correspondents. Libraries that discriminate against genealogists, or anyone else, should be reported to higher authorities, or blasted with letters to the editors of the appropriate newspapers. Genealogists have as much right to use libraries as any other type of historian, stamp collectors, lawyers, financial specialists, or any other group who might be using a library for a special purpose. Genealogists should fight for certain basic rights. Any will or deed should be a public record available to all. Marriage records should be available to anyone after fifty years, birth records after seventy-two years (since the census records are open to use after this period), and all death records should be available as soon as they are filed. There is so little fraud that can be committed with these records after someone has died, or has lived, or been married for that time span. In this same vein, I feel that every adopted person has the right to know their true heritage, and that they should be able to see a full copy of their original birth record when they become an adult. There are probably thousands of descendants of Charlemagne who are prevented from knowing this line of descent by bureaucrats. If you are refused a public record by a public agency, hammer at them until you get it.

A few lineages such as those shown of the ancestry of Edward Converse, Alexander Magruder and Oliver Manwaring were not verified by me, and to my mind need further proof to cement the British connections. The Baskerville ancestry of George Beckwith which has been accepted by many genealogists in the past would seem to be tenuous in light of the concordance of Baskerville pedigrees presented by Vernon M. Norr in his *Some Early English Pedigrees Combined from Most Available Sources 1958-1968* (Arlington, Va., the author, 1968. pp. 13-19), but lines from Charlemagne could probably be developed through other Beckwith wives. Welsh descents in general and especially through Joan, the natural daughter of King John of England, and the wife of Llewellyn the Great, Prince of Wales, have problems which have been pointed out by Peter Bartrum in his *Welsh Genealogies A.D. 300-1400,* an eight volume work published in Cardiff in 1974 by the University of Wales Press for the Board of Celtic Studies. Some variant lines through such families as de Broase (Briouze, Brews, etc.) and Le Strange can circumvent these difficulties and are noted in this book. A future article by William Reitsweisner will examine descents from Joan and Llewellyn of Wales. It will be published in the first few numbers of a new periodical, *The Genealogist,* which is expected to be issued in late 1978, under the aegis of Winston DeVille and Neil Thompson, both Fellows of the American Society of Genealogists.

Happily, in this volume there are some new lines including ancestry of Charles Rodes (Rhodes) and Richard Wright, both of Virginia, and Col. James Burd of Pennsylvania which have been added to the literature of genealogy by researchers who have surmounted all the difficulties that I have pointed out above, and have found their way back through time to Charlemagne. Through the years that follow, it is hoped that many others will follow this same path and find their way back to the great Holy Roman Emperor celebrated by our order.

Timothy Field Beard
6 January 1978

ABBREVIATIONS

A.B. — Bachelor of Arts
ae. — age, aged
aft. — after
Ala. — Alabama
ante — before
Apr. — April
Ark. — Arkansas
assn. — association
asst. — assistant
assoc. — associate
atty. — attorney
Aug. — August

b. — born
B.A. — Bachelor of Arts
bapt. — baptised
B.E. — Bachelor of Engineering
Beds. — Bedfordshire
bef. — before
Berks. — Berkshire
B.S. — Bachelor of Science
bet. — between
BT. — baronet
Bucks. — Buckinghamshire
bur. — buried
B.W.I. — British West Indies

ca. — circa (about)
C.A.R. — National Society Children of the American Revolution
Calif. — California
Cambs. — Cambridgeshire
Can. — Canada
Capt. — Captain
Cdr. — Commander
Co. — County (United States)
co. — county (England)

coh. — coheir, coheress
Col. — Colonel
Colo. — Colorado
Conn. — Connecticut
cr. — created
C.S.A. — Confederate States of America

d. — died
D.A.C. — Daughters of the American Colonists
DAR — National Society Daughters of the American Revolution
dau. — daughter
D.C. — District of Columbia
D.C.W. — Daughters of Colonial Wars
D.D. — Doctor of Divinity
D.D.S. — Doctor of Dental Surgery
dec. — deceased
Dec. — December
Del. — Delaware
Dist. — District
div. — divorced
Dr. — Doctor
d.s.p. — (decessit sine prole) died without issue
d.s.p.l. — (decessit sine prole legitima) died without legitimate issue
d.s.p.m. — (decessit sine prole mascula) died without male issue
d.s.p.s. — (decessit sine prole superstite) died without surviving issue

d.v.m. — (decessit vita matris) died during mother's issue lifetime
d.v.p. — (decessit vita patris) died during father's lifetime
ed. — edition
Ens. — Ensign
E.E. — Electrical Engineering
Eng. — England
Esq. — Esquire
etc. — et cetera

Feb. — February
fl. — flourished
Fla. — Florida

Ga. — Georgia
Gen. — General
Gent. — Gentleman
Gloucs. — Gloucestershire
Gov. — Governor
grad. — graduate

h. — heir, heiress
Hants. — Hampshire
Herefs. — Herefordshire
Herts. — Hertfordshire
Hist. — Historical
Hunts. — Huntingdonshire

Ill. — Illinois
Ind. — Indiana
Inq. Post Mort. — Inquisition Post Mortem
Inst. — Institute

Jan. — January
Jr. — Junior

Kans. — Kansas
K.B. — Knight of the Bath
K.G. — Knight of the Garter
Knt. — Knight
Ky. — Kentucky

La. — Louisiana

Lancs. — Lancashire
Leics. — Leicestershire
L.I. — Long Island (New York)
lic. — license
Lieut. — Lieutenant
Lincs. — Lincolnshire
liv. — living
Lt. — Lieutenant

m. — married
M.A. — Master of Arts
Maj. — Major
Mar. — March
Mass. — Massachusetts
M.D. — Doctor of Medicine
Md. — Maryland
M.E. — Mechanical Engineer
Me. — Maine
Mgr. — Manager
Mich. — Michigan
Miss — Mississippi
Mo. — Missouri
M.P. — Member of Parliament
Mtg. — Meeting
N.C. — North Carolina
Nev. — Nevada
N.H. — New Hampshire
N.J. — New Jersey
N.Y. — New York
Northants. — Northamptonshire
Notts. — Nottinghamshire
Nov. — November
nr. — near

Oct. — October
Okla. — Oklahoma
Ont. — Ontario
Ore. — Oregon

Pa. — Pennsylvania
P.C. —Privy Coucillor
Penna. — Pennsylvania
prob. — probably
Ph. D. — Doctor of Philosophy
Phila. — Philadelphia
Pres. — President

reg. — registered
ret. — retired
Rev. — Reverend
R.I. — Rhode Island

s. — son
SAR — National Society Sons of the American Revolution
S.C. — South Carolina
Sept. — September
sen. — senior
serg. — sergeant
Soc. — Society
S.R. — Society of the Sons of the Revolution
Sr. — Senior
Staffs. — Staffordshire
subs. — subsequent to
Tenn. — Tennessee
Tex. — Texas
Twp. — Township
Treas. — Treasurer

U.D.C. — United Daughters of the Confederacy
U.S.A. — United States Army

USMC — United States Marine Corps
USN — United States Navy
USNR — United States Naval Reserve
Univ. — University

Va. — Virginia
V.I. — Virgin Islands
V.M.I. — Virginia Military Institute
Vt. — Vermont
V.P. — Vice President

Warks. — Warwickshire
Warws. — Warwickshire
Wash. — Washington
w.d. — will dated
Westm. — Westmorelandshire
wid. — widow
Wilts. — Wiltshire
Wisc. — Wisconsin
Worcs. — Worcestershire
w.p. — will proved
W.V. — West Virginia
Wyo. — Wyoming
yrs. — years

CHAPTER I

A GLIMPSE OF EMPEROR LOTHAIR

by Allen Cabaniss
Research Professor
of History
The University of Mississippi

+ IN MEMORIAM +
Hiram Kennedy Douglass

Lothair (born 795; emperor 840-855), grandson of Charlemagne, had a "bad press" in his own time; the chroniclers were not very kind to him. The annals of St. Bertin for the year 840 reported that upon the death of his father, Louis the Pious, Lothair violated the laws of nature and took up arms against his brothers, Louis the German and Charles the Bald, that he behaved with insolence, depraved cupidity, and brutality against them. The annals of Fulda for the same year attributed his accession to his father's dying whim rather than to legal right. Two years later they noted that he was continuing in his "pristine pertinacity." It is pleasant, therefore, to turn away from those vicious and gratuitous remarks to a somewhat different view of him from another source and to glance at him through less jaundiced eyes.

During the interval 851-852 a monk of Luxeuil, Angelom by name, in Holy Orders at least a deacon, began to compile a running commentary on the Biblical Song of Songs. It was not his first book (a commentary on Genesis) nor would it be his last (a commentary on I and II Samuel and I and II Kings). For some reason Angelom was permitted to leave his cloister temporarily and go to the imperial court at Aix-la-Chapelle. Since his library at Luxeuil was deficient in many volumes to which he required access, it was probably in connection with his research and writing that he went, for he stated that "at the sacred palace I was studying vigilantly under the broad mantle of instructors in the

1

liberal arts and of expositors of Holy Scripture." Although perhaps adequately trained in Latin rhetoric, he was accustomed to make the conventional deprecatory apologies about his ability. But despite his reticence, he attracted the attention of Emperor Lothair who summoned him to court to discuss Scripture with him.

Apparently Angelom had more than one session with the emperor, since he referred to intimate conversations about the heavenly life which, he stated, were accompanied by seasons of prayer. It is a delightful scene thus intimated: emperor and lowly monk chatting about Scriptural and spiritual matters, then joining in prayer. The ultimate result of those conferences was a command by Lothair that Angelom write a brief exposition of the Song of Songs. Naturally the monk demurred, protesting his meager learning, but the emperor was insistent. Rising to his full dignity and authority, Lothair came just short of threatening Angelom with dire consequences if the latter refused.

The monk stated that he was terrified, astonished, and benumbed at the weight of responsibility thus laid upon him, but he did not dare offer continued resistance. Even so he felt it needful to consult his ecclesiastical superior. That person was none other than Archbishop Drogo of Metz, illegitimate half-brother of Lothair's father, Louis the Pious. At first he, too, withheld consent, but as a true courtier, preferring harmony to disturbance, he acquiesced and enjoined the imperial task upon Angelom as an act of holy obedience. The monk understood the situation, recognizing that Drogo's position required caution and realizing that his expression of agreement was not entirely frank. Angelom, therefore, undertook the work with fourfold motivation: the emperor's order, the bishop's encouragement, divine assistance, and intercession of the saintly doctors of the church.

One must wonder why the Song of Songs was the book to be expounded. Angelom's explanation may be as good as any. Lothair had, according to Angelom, often devoted time to reading that book. It seemed to be a diversion when affairs of state were not pressing. "For a moment," the monk wrote to the emperor, "you could forget the tumultuous fortunes of empire." More recently, however, Lothair's wife, Empress Irmingard, had died. So, wrote Angelom, "you could even assuage the loss of your devout wife, now in the assembly of holy women, adorned with a white robe of blessedness." Like the legendary turtle-dove of the Song, Lothair (according to Angelom) sighed in solitude and drenched his face with a rain of tears as he poured out secret prayers not only for his own transgressions, but also for the soul of the late empress. And the Song of Songs is indeed, as Angelom so aptly put it, a song of love.

Information in the preceding paragraphs allows us to date Angelom's commentary. Irmingard, whom Lothair had married in mid-October 821, died on 20 March 851. At some time in 853 the emperor had a son by liaison with Doda, a woman from one of the royal estates. The child was baptized with the typically Carolingian name Carloman. It was also known by chroniclers that Lothair had at least one other mistress, also from a royal villa, and several other children whose names have not been preserved. So the period of mourning referred to by Angelom was not of lengthy duration. Still further Lothair and Archbishop Drogo were mentioned as alive. Both died in 855, the emperor a short time after his abdication and profession as monk at Prüm.

Angelom's expressed design was for his treatise to serve as a convenient small manual which the emperor could easily carry and read for relaxation. There would be moments, Angelom supposed, when, despite cares for supervising ecclesiastical and political affairs in his realm, Lothair might have time to ponder spiritual matters. Although he would not have leisure to explore the entire range of Scripture, he would at least be able quietly to peruse Angelom's brief exposition. And it might be enough, for in the Song of Songs, more than in any other book of the Old Testament, the union of Messiah with His church is contained, albeit veiled in mystery and allegory — so thought Angelom.

Angelom apologized that he would not annotate his commentary with exact source of each excerpt he quoted. But he insisted that he balanced his sentences with sweet and bitter alike so that Lothair would neither shudder not stiffen, but find adequate medicine for his soul, remembering that the book was not historical but metaphorical. "Search the Scriptures, most glorious emperor, and penetrate divine mysteries with understanding. Your careful wisdom will be thereby encouraged to observe, rule, and instruct fleshly desires and passions as well as all the people subject to your authority." Angelom was sufficiently

3

acquainted with the Carolingians to suspect, if not actually know, that sexual restraint was not one of their marked characteristics.

He began, perhaps pretentiously, "I am now ready to put my hand to the needs of a spiritual harmony. I am ready to write an allegorical symphony, dipping my pen in the well of speculation, unfurling the sails of history, unlocking the secret room of a house, revealing inner mysteries." As the commentary progressed, unoriginal as it was and chiefly a compilation from many sources, especially from Pope Gregory I's exposition, Angelom never forgot that he was writing for an emperor. At points he drew Lothair into his text; for example, "With humility I earnestly wish to persuade, no , to impose on Your Highness. You have received great and skillful wisdom. You have achieved the defense and consideration of holy church. You have established it by bearing arms in battle array. You have fortified it with formations of barons. You have surrounded it with squadrons of knights. You protect it against incursions of enemies from foreign nations."

Such words were expressions of gratitude for physical protection of the church. But the monastic author deemed the emperor as even more worthy of praise because he was zealous and devoted to sacred instruction and to an understanding of Holy Scripture. "You have thereby fortified holy church with a Gospel shield against malign spirits ... You can therewith defend it against those who seek to destroy not the bodies but the souls of believers." Lothair was consequently urged to occupy himself at convenient times in study of Angelom's commentary and other works. The monk hoped the emperor would not be bored by the work, but would examine it carefully to attain higher peaks of virtue and induce others to the path of rectitude.

Among the many conventional titles by which Angelom addressed Emperor Lothair, several seem to have peculiar significance. By "splendor of the Franks" and "most invincible Caesar" we are given a picture of a strong and powerful ruler who brought not only protection to his people, but also conferred on them dignity and honor. By "mild prince" and "learned prince" we are presented with a picture of one who was, when not distracted by pressure of external circumstances, a serious student, seeking to learn from the accumulated wisdom of the past. In those titles one can almost visualize the meditative brooding of the "sweet prince," Hamlet. Or so at least he must have appeared to Deacon Angelom. But the latter never forgot to reiterate Lothair's awesome imperial titles, recalling that rank and dignity which Lothair inherited and with which Angelom was profoundly obsessed. What we derive from Angelom, therefore, is only a glimpse of the emperor, but it serves in some measure to supplement what we otherwise know of him.

NOTE

The chief source of the preceding essay is Angelom's book on the Song of Songs as printed in J. P. Migne, *Patrologiae cursus completus: series Latina,* Vol. cxv, columns 551b-628d.

Copyrighted 1976

Chapter II

ASTON — COCKE — BOLLING — HALL — HINES — DIXON — YARBROUGH — MAHONE

CHARLEMAGNE, King of the Franks, Emperor of the West, b. 2 Apr. 742, d. 28 Jan. 813/4; m. (third) ca. 771, Hildegarde of Swabia, b. ca. 758, d. 30 Apr. 783,

PEPIN, King of Italy (781-810) b. 777, d. at Milan, 8 July 810,

BERNARD, King of Italy (813-817), b. 797, d. at Milan, 17 Apr. 818; m. Cunigunde, d. ca. 835,

PEPIN, Count of Senlis, Peronne and St. Quentin, b. ca. 815, d. aft. 840,

HERBERT I, Count of Vermandois, b. ca. 840, murdered, ca. 902; m. Bertha de Morvois,

HERBERT II, Count of Vermandois and Troyes, b. ca. 880-890, d. at St. Quentin, ca. 943; m. Liegarde, dau. of Robert I, King of France, and Adele, his wife,

ROBERT, Count of Vermandois, b. ca. 920, d. ca. 967/8; m. Adelaide of Burgundy,

ADELAIDE DE VERMANDOIS, b. ca. 950, d. ca. 975-78; m. (first) Geoffrey I, Grisonelle, d. 21 July 987,

ERMENGARDE DE ANJOU, m. (first) ca. 980, Conan I, Duke of Brittany, d. ca. 992,

JUDITH OF BRITTANY, b. ca. 982, d. ca. 1017; m. ca. 1000, Richard II, Duke of Normandy, d. Aug. 1027,

ROBERT I, Duke of Normandy, d. 22 July 1035, by Herleve, had,

WILLIAM I, The Conqueror, King of England, b. at Falaise, France, ca. 1027, d. at Rouen, Frances, 9 Sept. 1087; m. ca. 1053, Matilda, of Flanders, b. ca. 1032, d. 3 Nov. 1083, dau. of Baldwin V de Lille, and Adele of France,

HENRY I, Beauclerc, King of England, b, at Selby, Yorks., ca. 1070, d. in France, 1 Dec. 1135; m. (first) 11 Nov. 1100, Matilda, of Scotland, b. ca. 1079, d. 1 May 1118, dau. of Malcolm III Conmore, King of Scots, and his second wife, St. Margaret of Scotland, dau. of Prince Edward, The Aethling, and Agatha, of Hungary,

MATILDA, of England, b. ca. 1104, d. 10 Sept. 1167; m. (second) 3 Apr. 1127, Geoffrey V Plantagenet, b. 24 Aug. 1113, d. 7 Sept. 1151, Count of Anjou and Duke of Burg,

HENRY II, King of England, b. 5 Mar. 1132/3, d. 6 July 1189, at Westminster; m. (her second) 11 May 1153, Eleanor of Aquitaine, b. 1123, d. 3 Mar. 1204, dau. of William VIII, Count of Poitou, and his first wife, Eleanor de Chastellerault,

JOHN I, Lackland, King of England, b. 24 Dec. 1167, d. 19 Oct. 1216; m. (second) (her first) Isabella of Angouleme, b. ca. 1188, d. 31 May 1246, dau. of Aymer de Valence, and Alice de Courtenay,

HENRY III, King of England, b. at Winchester, 1 Oct. 1207, d. at Westminster, 16 Nov. 1272; m. 14 Jan. 1237, at Canterbury, Eleanor, of Provence, b. 1217, d. 24 Jan. 1291, at Amesbury, dau. of Raymond IV Berenger, Count of Provence, and Beatrice, of Savoy,

EDWARD I, King of England, b. at Westminster, 17 June 1239, d. nr. Carlisle, 7 July 1307, had a natural son,

JOHN DE BOTETOURT, d. 25 Nov. 1324; m. 1285-92, Maud Fitz Thomas, d. aft. 28 May 1329, dau. of Thomas Fitz Otes, of Mendelsham, Suffolk, and Beatrice, dau. of William de Beauchamp,

THOMAS DE BOTETOURT, d. 1332; m. Joan (Johanna) de Somery,

JOHN DE BOTETOURT, b. 1318, d. 1385; m. (second) ante 31 May 1347, Joyce la Zouche de Mortimer,

JOHN DE BOTETOURT, b. 1367/8, d. 12 Aug. 1420; m. (first) Sir Baldwin Freville, of Tamworth Castle, Warwick, d. 1387/8,

JOYCE DE FREVILLE, b. ante 1387; m. Sir Roger Aston, of Tixall, d. ca. 1448,

SIR ROBERT DE ASTON, High Sheriff of Staffs., 1453, d. ca. 1467; m. Isabella Brereton,

JOHN ASTON, Esq., Sheriff of Staffs. 1477 and of Warwick, 1481, d. ca. 1484; m. Elizabeth Delves,

SIR JOHN ASTON, K.B., of Heywood, Staffs., d. 28 Mar. 1523; m. Joan Lyttleton,

SIR EDWARD ASTON, b. ca. 1494, at Tixall, Staffs., d. ca. 1568; m. (second) Jane (Joan) Bolles,

LEONARD ASTON, Gent., b. at Tixall, Staffs.; m. Elizabeth (Barton) Cresswell,

WALTER ASTON, Gent., b. at Langdon, Staffs.; m. Joyce Nason, of Roughton, Warwickshire,

LT. COL. WALTER ASTON, b. at Langdon, Staffs., England, ca. 1607, bur. at Westover Parish, Charles City Co., Virginia, member Va. House of Burgesses 1642-3; m. Hannah Jordan,

MARY ASTON, m. (his second) ca. 1652, Lt. Col. Richard Cocke, b. in England, ca. 1600, d. 1665/6, member Va. House of Burgesses,

RICHARD COCKE (The Younger) of Henrico Co., Va., b. ca. 1650/60; m. Elizabeth —,

ANNE COCKE, d. ca. 1749; m. 27 June 1706, Robert Bolling, Jr., b. in Charles City Co., Va., 25 Jan. 1682/3, d. in Prince George Co., Va., w.d. 23 Jan. 1747, w.p. 3 Jan. 1748/9,

ANNE BOLLING, b. 12 Dec. 1713, d. aft. 1766; m. ca. 1730, John Hall, b. in Scotland, ca. 1710, d. aft. 1771,

HUGH HALL, b. ca. 1730, d. in Brunswick Co., Va., ca. 1771; m. ca. 1748, Mary Dixon, b. in North Carolina, ca. 1733, d. ca. 1800,

ELIZABETH HUGH HALL, b. in Dinwiddie Co., Va., 31 Dec. 1748, d. 17 Apr. 1782; m. 22 Dec. 1767, Charles Hines,

MARTHA "PATSEY" HALL HINES, b. 6 Feb./Nov. 1773, d. ante 28 July 1817; m. 19 Sept. 1793, Henry Dixon, b. 8/18 May 1771, d. 6 Apr. 1867,

MARY BACON DIXON, b. 1 July 1797, bur. at Loachapoka, Ala., 18 Apr. 1874; m. at Waverly Hall, Ga., 7 Feb. 1814, James Yarbrough, b. 5 July 1787, d. aft. 25 Dec. 1839,

ELIZABETH (ELIZA) HINES YARBROUGH, b. in Harris Co., Ga., 30 Apr. 1815, bur. at Auburn, Ala., 15 May 1850; m. 19 Sept. 1833, Marion David Mahone, b. in Harris Co., Ga., 13 Aug. 1812, d. in Macon Co., Ala., 22 July 1879,

STEPHEN WILLIAM MAHONE, b. in Harris Co., Ga., 29 Aug. 1842, bur. at Greenville, Ala., 8 Feb. 1910; m. in Bullock Co., Ala., 27 Mar. 1866, Georgia Ann (Texas) Johnson, b. at Perote, Ala., 7 July 1849, bur. at Greenville, Ala., 18 Dec. 1936,

JAMES SPAIN MAHONE, b. at Rutledge, Ala., 17 Apr. 1880, d. at Montgomery, Ala., 1 Apr. 1959; M. 20 Mar. 1904, at Montgomery, Ala., Mildred Johnson Morris, b. at Oak Bowry, Ala., 15 Aug. 1886, d. at Birmingham, Ala., 5 Jan. 1975,

GERALDINE SHERMAN MAHONE, b. at Montgomery, Ala., 31 Dec. 1916; ed. incl. Mastro John Proctor Mills Studio of Music and Berringer School of Dance, Montgomery, Ala.; member: National Society Colonial Dames of the XVII Century, Past Ala. State President, past National Chaplain General, past Corresponding Secretary General; National Huguenot Society, Ala. Society past State President; the Huguenot Society of the

Founders of Manakin in the Colony of Va., Organizing Ala. Branch President; National Society U.S. Daughters of 1812, past State President, past Chaplain National, past Corresponding Secretary National, 4th Vice President National; Order of the Crown of Charlemagne in the United States of America; the National Society Daughters of the Barons of Runnemede; DAR; DAC; Daughters of Colonial Wars; U.D.C.; m. at Montgomery, Ala., 18 Nov. 1939, Lt. Col. Ret. Gerald Jacob Laubenthal, b. at Sunflower, Ala., 3 July 1911.

Chapter III

ASTON — COCKE — BOLLING — SPRAGINS — WARFIELD

CHARLEMAGNE

(See Chapter II)

ANNE COCKE, b. in Va., d. in Va.; m. 27 Jan. 1706, in Va., Robert Bolling, Jr., b. in Charles City Co., Va., 25 Jan. 1682/3, d. in Prince George Co., Va., w.p. 3 Jan. 1748/9,

SUSANNAH BOLLING, b. in Va., 16 June 1728, d. in Va.; m. in Va., 23 Dec. 1745, Alexander Bolling, a cousin,

STITH BOLLING, b. in Va., 11 May 1753, d. in Nottoway Co., Va., 1797; m. in Sussex Co., Va., 10 Oct. 1776, Charlotte Edmunds, b. in Sussex Co., Va., bapt. 24 May 1760, d. in Va., aft. 1797,

REBECCA BROWN BOLLING, b. in Va., 16 Feb. 1778, d. in Va.; m. in Nottoway Co., Va., 27 Nov. 1794, Melchijah Spragins, b. in Halifax Co., Va., d, in Va., ante 1823,

STITH BOLLING SPRAGINS, b. in Halifax Co., Va., 1796, d. at Huntsville, Ala., 8 May 1839; m. in Mecklenburg Co., Va., 30 Dec. 1824, Eliza Aperson Green, b. in Va., 1800, d. in Mecklenburg Co., Va., 19 Dec. 1889,

STITH BOLLING SPRAGINS, JR., b. at Huntsville, Ala., 3 Oct. 1829, d. at Baltimore, Md., 5 July 1904; m. at West River, Md., 29 May 1866, Elizabeth Ann Hamilton, b. at West River, Md., 20 Feb. 1837, d. at Philadelphia, Pa., 31 Jan. 1912,

LOUYSE DUVALL SPRAGINS, b. at Baltimore, Md., 19 Nov. 1869, d. at Lower Merion Twp., Montgomery Co., Pa., 6 July 1948;

11

m. at Baltimore, Md., 26 Oct. 1898, John Ogle Warfield, D.D.,
b. in Frederick Co., Md., 12 May 1871, d. in Montgomery Co.,
Pa., 16 Mar. 1950,

JOHN OGLE WARFIELD, JR., M.D., b. at Baltimore, Md., 3 Apr.
1900, attended Chestnut Hill Academy, Phila,; St. John's
College, B.A. and M.A.; Univ. of Md. Medical School, M.D.
with Gold Medal and Hirsh Pathology Award. He is a member
of the Medical Society of D.C.; American Medical Association;
American College of Surgeons; International College of
Surgeons; Southern Surgical Congress; Medical Arts Society,
founder, Secretary, President; Pan-American Medical Society,
President; Washington Academy of Surgeons, founder, Sec'y,
Pres.; Acad. International of Med.; Kappa Alpha (Southern);
Nu Sigma Nu (medical); Cosmos Club, Washington, D.C.;
Mason 32nd degree, Knights Templar, Shriner; Society of
Colonial Wars, Md. and D.C., Governor, Deputy Gov. Gen.;
S.R. in D.C.; Baronial Order of Magna Charta; Military Order
of the Crusades, Commander Gen.; Order of the Crown of
Charlemagne in the United States of America, Chirurgeon
Gen., Nat'l Society, Americans of Royal Descent, First Vice
President General; Huguenot Society in Maryland, founder;
Order of Three Crusades; Order of First Families of Virginia.
He m. 16 Dec. 1924, at Baltimore, Md., Rachel Elizabeth
Baldwin, b. in Harford Co., Md., 5 June 1896, dau. of John
Rush Baldwin and Cora Baldwin (cousins) and have issue:

1) JOHN OGLE WARFIELD, III, b. at Washington, D.C., 8
Apr. 1930; m. 14 July 1953, at Panama City, Fla.,
Jimmie Lou Kirkland, b. 23 June 1933, dau. of James
Cliatt Kirkland, and has issue:

a) JOHN OGLE WARFIELD IV, b. at Washington,
D.C., 13 Oct. 1954, a member of the Order of the
Crown of Charlemagne in the United States of
America.

Chapter IV

ASTON — BINNS — CARGILL — MASON

CHARLEMAGNE

(See Chapter II)

LIEUT. COL. WALTER ASTON, b. at the Manor of Langdon, Staffs., Eng., ca. 1607, d. at Westover, Charles City Co., Va., 6 Apr. 1656, member Va. House of Burgesses, 1642-43; m. Hannah Jordan, w.d. 4 Oct. 1665. She m. (second) — Hill, as his second wife.

ELIZABETH ASTON, d. 1713; m. (his second) ante 6 Apr. 1656, Thomas Binns, b. ca. 1622, d. in Surry Co., Va., 1669,

THOMAS BINNS, b. ca 1658, d. in Surry Co., Va., ante 1 June 1699,

CHARLES BINNS, b. ca. 1698, d. Surry Co., Va. (w.p. 20 Mar. 1749); m. Judith Eldridge, b. Surry Co., Va., d. Surry Co., Va., 1 Aug. 1762,

LUCY BINNS, b. Surry Co., Va., ca. 1743, d. in Sussex Co., Va., 13 Dec. 1773; m. ca. 1768, Col. John Cargill III, b. at "The Glebe", Surry Co., Va., ca. 1741, d. at "Invermay", Sussex Co., Va. 2 Dec. 1777,

SARAH HARRISON CARGILL, b. at "Invermay" Sussex Co., Va. 1770, d. at "Windsor", Sussex Co., Va. (w.p. 5 Jan. 1837); m. in Brunswick Co., Va., 28 Mar. 1799, John Raines Mason, b. at "Windsor", Sussex Co., Va., 24 Apr. 1770, d. at "Windsor", in Dec. 1826,

NATHANIEL CARGILL MASON, b. at "Windsor", Sussex Co., Va., 1 Jan. 1800, d. at Reynoldsburg, Ohio, 27 Apr. 1875; m. Catherine (Kisiah) McMicken, b. in Tenn. or Ala., 1 Jan. 1804, d. at Smyrna, La., 11 Feb. 1880,

13

COL. JOHN RANDOLPH MASON, b. in Va. or Ala., 17 May 1825, d. at "Flowervale", Smyrna, La., 8 Jan. 1895; m. 20 Jan. 1852, at the residence of John A. Gamble, Smyrna, La., Nancy Amanda Gamble, b. in Wilcox Co., Ala., 30 Apr. 1832, d. at Pelican, DeSota Parish, La. 18 Apr. 1908,

DR. WILLIAM HAMILTON MASON, b. at Smyrna, La., 20 Nov. 1864, d. at Pelican, DeSota Parish, La., 6 Jan. 1939; m. at Double Churches, DeSota Parish, La., 29 June 1890, Anna Elizabeth Hart, b. at Naborton, La., 1 Jan. 1870, d. at Pelican, La. 17 Jan. 1942,

WILMER MASON, b. at Naborton, DeSoto Parish, La., 29 Apr. 1893, d. at Longview Texas, 11 Apr. 1961; m. at Baton Rouge, La., 20 Aug. 1913, Susie Evelyn Barron, b. at Welsh, La., 15 Mar. 1895, liv. 1967,

GLEN MORGAN MASON, b. at Pelican, La., 24 Aug. 1915; La. State Univ. Teachers College, B.A.; Univ. of Arizona; Harvard University; World War II, Lieut. U.S.N.R.; member: SAR; National Society, Americans of Royal Descent; Baronial Order of Magna Charta; Order of the Crown of Charlemagne in the United States of America; Order of Three Crusades, 1096-1192; Navy League of the U.S.; Kappa Phi Kappa; Delta Sigma Phi; Chapparrol Club, of Dallas; Shreveport Club; Advertising Club of Shreveport; Shreveport Country Club; Shreveport Yacht Club; Rotary International; Chamber of Commerce; Centime Club, Former President; m. 19 Feb. 1939, at Baton Rouge, La., Frances Ellen Walk, b. at Decatur, Ala., 2 Nov. 1917, and had

   1) LLOYD GLEN MASON, b. 11 July 1940, at Alexandria, La., m. Jenifer Esther Victory;

   2) KENT WALK MASON, b. at Baton Rouge, La. 15 Mar. 1945;

   3) MICHAEL HUMPHREY MASON, b. at Shreveport, La., 17 Sept. 1950;

   4) KY ELLEN SHAW MASON, b. at Shreveport, La., 2 Oct. 1956.

Chapter V

BECKWITH — RUSK — McVEIGH — BROOKS

CHARLEMAGNE

(See Chapters II, XLVI, LII)

JOHN I, Lackland, King of England,

JOAN, nat. dau., b. ante 1200, d. Feb. 1237, bur. at Llanvaes in Anglesey; m. dur. Ascensiontide, 1206, Llewellyn ap Jorwerth, Prince of Wales, d. at Aberconway, 11 Apr. 1240,

GLADYS DHU, d. 1251; m. (second) 1230, Ralph de Mortimer of Wigmore, d. 1246,

ROGER DE MORTIMER, 6th Baron Mortimer of Wigmore, b. ca. 1231, d. at Kingsland, ante 10 Oct. 1282; m. 1247, Maude de Braiose, d. ante 23 Mar. 1300/1,

SIR EDMUND DE MORTIMER, 7th Baron Mortimer of Wigmore, b. ca. 1261; m. ca. 1285, Margaret Fienes, d. 1333/4,

SIR ROGER DE MORTIMER, 8th Baron Mortimer of Wigmore, cr. Earl of March in Oct. 1328, b. 25 Apr. 1287, d. 29 Nov. 1330; m. ante 6 Oct. 1306, Joan de Geneville, b. 2 Feb. 1285/6, d. 19 Oct. 1356,

JOAN DE MORTIMER, d. 1337-51; m. (his first) ante 18 June 1330, Sir James de Audley, of Knesdale, Shropshire, M.P. 1331-86, b. 8 Jan. 1312/3, d. 1 Apr. 1386, w.d. 1385,

JOAN DE AUDLEY, b. ca. 1332; m. Sir John Tuchet of Markeaton, co. Derby, b. 25 July 1327, d. ante 10 Jan. 1361,

JOHN TUCHET, m. Margaret Mortimer,

SIR JOHN TUCHET, Lord Audley, M.P. 1406-8, b. 23 Apr. 1371, d. 19 Dec. 1408; m. (second) Isabel — , liv. June 1405,

ELIZABETH TUCHET, m. Sir John Baskerville, b. 1403, d. 1455,

— BASKERVILLE,* m. Sir William Beckwith of Clint,

THOMAS BECKWITH of Clint, d. 1495; m. a dau. of William Heslerton, Knt.,

JOHN BECKWITH, m. a dau. of Thomas Radcliffe of Mulgrave,

ROBERT BECKWITH, of Boxholm, nr. Ripley, Yorks., liv. 1469,

JOHN BECKWITH of Thorpe,

ROBERT BECKWITH, w.p. 24 Mar. 1536; m. Jennet — ,

MARMADUKE BECKWITH, m. (first) Anne Dyneley, of Bramhope, Yorks.,

THOMAS BECKWITH, of Acton, liv. 1612, bur. at Acton; m. . Frances Frost, of Acton,

THOMAS BECKWITH, of Acton, b. 1569, d. 12 Jan. 1615, at Featherstone; m. Barbara Milburn, of Hinderskelf, d. 1644,

GEORGE BECKWITH, b. at Featherstone Castle, Yorks., bapt. 29 Mar. 1606, d. at London, Eng., Nov. 1676; m. 1649, Frances Hervey (Harvey), b. at St. Joseph's Manor, Eng., d. at the family manor, Calvert Co., Md., ca. 1676,

CHARLES BECKWITH, b. in Calvert Co., Md., ca. 1669, d. in Prince George Co., Md., 18 Sept. 1712; m. 9 Oct. 1702, Anne — , d. in Prince George Co., Md., 17 Oct. 1746,

GEORGE BECKWITH, b. in Prince George Co., Md., ca. 1710,

16

BENJAMIN BECKWITH, b. in Frederick Co., Md., d. in Morgan Co., Ohio, 3 Apr. 1839; m. (second) Martha (Jones) Rogers, b. in Va., d. at Malta, Ohio, 7 Oct. 1841,

SOLOMON CRUM BECKWITH, b. in Muskingum Co., Ohio, 22 Apr. 1812, d. at Malta, Ohio, 12 Aug. 1888; m. 2 July 1834, Ann McBee, b. at Harpers Ferry, Va., 10 Sept. 1816, d. at Malta, Ohio, 14 May 1900,

SAREPTA ELIZABETH BECKWITH, b. at Malta, Ohio, 12 Mar. 1852, d. at Wheeling, W. Va., 3 Feb. 1927; m. at Malta, Ohio, 2 Sept. 1886, William A Rusk, b. at Rousseau, Ohio, 1 May 1853, d. at Malta, Ohio, 23 Sept, 1906,

ANNE BECKWITH RUSK, b. at Malta, Ohio, 22 Jan. 1892, d. in Prince George Co., Md., 9 Mar. 1966; m. at Malta, Ohio, 5 Aug. 1914, Clancy Henry McVeigh, b. in Windsor Twp., Ohio, 5 July 1891, d. at Wheeling, W. Va., 2 Jan. 1957,

AGNES JOAN MCVEIGH, b. at Wheeling, W.Va., 12 July 1922, ed.: Marietta College, Ohio, A.B. cum laude, Phi Beta Kappa; member: DAR, Nat'l. Soc. Sons and Daughters of the Pilgrims, Nat'l. Soc. New England Women (Founder President Southern Calif. Colony), Jamestowne Society, Descendants of Colonial Physicians and Chirurgiens, Descendants of Colonial Clergy, Order of the Crown of Charlemagne in the United States of America, etc.; Founder President, Editor-in-Chief, McVeigh — McVey — McVay Family Archives (Family Association with Quarterly); Daughters of the Union Veterans of the Civil War; First Families of Ohio, patriotic secretary; m. at Wheeling, W.Va., 21 June 1947, Clifton Rowland Brooks, M.D.

(See Chapter LXXI for issue)

*See Foreword

Chapter VI

BOBRINSKOY

CHARLEMAGNE, King of the Franks, 768-814, Emperor of the West, 800-814, crowned Emperor at Rome on Christmas Day, 800 by Pope Leo III, b. 2 Apr. 742, d. 28 Jan. 814; m. (third) in 771, Hildegarde of Swabia, b. 758, d. 30 Apr. 783, gr. dau. of Gottfried, Duke of Alamans,

LOUIS I, the Pious, *le Debonnaire,* King of the Franks, Emperor of the West, 814-840, b. at Garonne, Aug. 778, d. nr. Mainz, 20 June 840; m. (second) Feb. 819, Judith of Bavaria, d. 19 Apr. 843, dau. of Guelph I, Count of Altdorf (Alteroff) and Duke of Bavaria, and Edith of Saxony,

GISELE OF FRANCE, b. 820, d. 874; m. ante 840. Eberhard, Margrave of Friuli, d. 866, son of Unruoch, Count of Friuli,

BERENGER I, King of Italy, Jan. 888-894, Emperor, 915-924; b. 850, murdered at Verona, 7 Apr. 924; m. ca. 880, Bertila of Spoleto, d. Dec. 915, dau. of Suppo II, Margrave of Spoleto, Perugia, Italy,

GISELE OF ITALY, b. 880 or 885, d. aft. 910; m. aft. 900, Adalbert, Margrave of Ivrea, Turin, Italy, d. ante 923, son of Anscarius, Margrave of Ivrea, and Gisela (or Volsea),

BERENGER II, Margrave of Ivrea, King of Italy, 950-961, b. ca. 900, d. in captivity at Bamberg, 6 Aug. 961; m. ante 936, Willa of Arles, dau. of Boso, Count of Arles, and Willa of Tuscany, dau. of Boso, Margrave of Tuscany,

ADALBERT, King of Italy, b. 936, d. aft. July 968; m. Gergerga, Countess of Macon,

ODO-WILLIAM, of Italy, Count of Burgundy, b. 958/9, d. 21 Sept. 1026; m. 975/80, Ermengard, dau. of Renaud, Count of Roucy,

RENAUD I, Count of Burgundy, d. 4 Sept. 1057; m. ante 1 Sept. 1016, Alix (Adelheid, Judith), dau. of Richard II, Duke of Normandy, and Judith of Bretagne,

WILLIAM I, Count of Burgundy, d. 11 Nov. 1087; m. Stephanie, Countess of Barcelona,

MATHILDE, Countess of Burgundy; m. 1080, Odo I, Duke of Burgundy, d. 23 Mar. 1102,

HUGH II, Duke of Burgundy, b. ca. 1085, d. 1143; m. ca. 1110, Mathilda, Viscountess de Turenne,

ODO II, Duke of Burgundy, b. 1110, d. Sept. 1162; m. 1145, Maria, Countess of Champagne,

HUGH III, Duke of Burgundy, b. 1148, d. 25 Aug. 1192; m. 11 Sept. 1183, Beatrice de Vienne,

ANNE, Duchess of Burgundy, d. 1242; m. 1222, Amadeus IV, Duke of Savoy. b. 1197, d. 24 June 1253,

MARGUERITE, Duchess of Savoy, d. ante 1263; m. 9 Dec. 1235, Bonifacius III, Margrave of Montferrat, b. 1202, d. 1253 or 1255,

ALESSINA, Margravin of Montferrat, d. 6 Feb. 1285; m. 1263, Albert I, Duke of Braunschweig, b. 1236, d. 15 Aug. 1279,

MECHTILD, Duchess of Braunschweig-Grubenhagen, d. 29 Jan. 1319; m. 1292, Heinrich III, Duke of Silesia-Glogan, d. 9 Dec. 1309,

BEATRICE, Duchess of Silesia-Glogan, d. 24 Aug. 1322; m. 1309, Ludwig IV, Duke of Bavaria, Emperor of the Holy Roman Empire, b. 1 Apr. 1282, d. 11 Oct. 1347,

STEPHEN II, Duke of Bavaria, b. 1317, d. 10 May 1375; m. 27 June 1328, Elizabeth of Aragon, Princess of Sicily, d. 31 Mar. 1349,

FREDERICK, Duke of Bavaria, b. 1339, d. 4 Dec. 1393; m. 2 Sept. 1381, Magdalene Visconti, Duchess of Milano, d. 17 July 1404,

HEINRICH IV, Duke of Bavaria, b. 1386, d. 30 July 1450; m. 25 Nov. 1412, Marguerite, Duchess of Austria (House of Hapsburg), d. 24 Dec. 1447,

ELIZABETH, Duchess of Bavaria-Landshut. b. 1419, d. 1 Jan. 1451; m. 8 Feb. 1445, Ulrich V, Count of Württemberg, b. 1413, d. 1 Sept. 1480,

HEINRICH, Duke of Württemberg, b. 7 Sept. 1448, d. 16 Apr. 1519; m. 10 Jan. 1485, Elizabeth, Countess von Zweibrücken-Bitsch,

ULRICH, VI, Duke of Württemberg, b. 8 Feb. 1487, d. 6 Nov. 1550; m. 2 Mar. 1511, Sabine, Duchess of Bavaria, b. 23 Apr. 1492, d. 30 Aug. 1564,

CHRISTOPHE, Duke of Württemberg, b. 12 May 1515, d. 28 Dec. 1568; m. 24 Feb. 1544, Anne Marie, Margravin of Brandenberg-Beyreuth, b. 28 Dec. 1526, d. 20 May 1589,

ELEONORE, Duchess of Württemberg, b. 22 Mar. 1556, d. 12 Jan. 1618; m. 8 Jan. 1571, Prince Johachim Ernest von Anhalt-Zerbst, b. 21 Oct. 1536, d. 16 Dec. 1586,

PRINCE RUDOLF VON ANHALT-ZERBST, b. 28 Oct. 1576, d. 20 Aug. 1621; m. 31 Aug. 1612, Magdelena, Countess von Oldenburg, b. 6 Oct. 1585, d. 14 Apr. 1657,

PRINCE JOHANN VON ANHALT-ZERBST, b. 24 Mar. 1621, d. 4 July 1667; m. 16 Sept. 1649, Sophie Augusta, Duchess von Holstein-Gottorp, b. 5 Dec. 1630; d. 12 Dec. 1649,

PRINCE JOHANN LUDWIG VON ANHALT-ZERBST, b. 4 May 1656, d. 1 Nov. 1704; m. 23 July, 1673, Christine Eleanore von Zeutsch,

PRINCE CHRISTIAN AUGUST VON ANHALT-ZERBST, b. 29 Nov. 1690, d. 16 Mar. 1747; m. 8 Nov. 1727, Johanna Elizabeth,

20

Duchess von Holstein-Gottorp, b. 24 Oct. 1712, d. 30 May 1760,

SOPHIE AUGUSTE FREDERICKE, PRINCESS ANHALT-ZERBST, EMPRESS OF RUSSIA AS CATHERINE II, b. at Dornburg, 2 May 1729, d. at St. Petersburg, Russia, 17 Nov. 1796; had by Prince Grigori G. Orloff, b. 1734, d. 1783, a natural son,

COUNT ALEXIS G. BOBRINSKOY, b. at St. Petersburg, Russia, 22 Apr. 1762, d. at Bogoroditsk, Russia, 2 July 1813; m. at Reval, Esthonia, 27 Jan. 1796, Anne Dorothea, Baroness von Ungern Sternberg, b. at Reval, Esthonia, 20 Jan. 1769, d. at St. Petersburg, 9 Apr. 1846,

COUNT ALEXIS A. BOBRINSKOY, b. at St. Petersburg, Russia, 18 Jan. 1800, d. at Smela, province of Kiev (Russia), 16 Oct. 1868; m. at St. Petersburg, 9 May 1821, Sophia A., Countess of Samoiloff, b. 15 Oct. 1799, d. at Paris, France, 23 Nov. 1866,

COUNT ALEXANDER A. BOBRINSKOY, b. at St. Petersburg, Russia, 29 May 1823, d. at St. Petersburg. 9 Mar. 1903; m. 12 May 1850, Sophia A., Countess Schouvaloff, b. 29 July 1829, d. at Smela, 22 Sept. 1912.

COUNT ALEXIS A. BOBRINSKOY, b. at St. Petersburg, Russia, 31 May 1852, d. at Grasse (Alpes Maritimes) France, 2 Sept. 1927; m. 11 Apr. 1920, at the Russian Embassy, Constantinople, Braissa Novikoff, b. at Kiev, Russia, 20 Oct. 1894, d. 15 Apr. 1970,

COUNT NICHOLAS A. BOBRINSKOY, b. at Nice, France, 8 Feb. 1921; ed.: Russian Nobility School "Alexandrino", Nice; École Sasserno, Nice; Lycée du Park Imperial, Nice; Collége de Cannes, Cannes, France; Fine Arts School, Nice; advanced study in Paris; Fashion Institute of Technology; Designer, Director and President of Sina Studios, Inc. at Port Chester, N.Y.; member: Burr Artists, Inc.; Chamber of Commerce, Port Chester; The Veteran Corps of Artillery; Adjt. The Army and Navy Union U.S.A. since 1955; Prior and Secretary of State of the Hospitallers of the Orthodox Tradition of the Russian

Grand Priory Knights of Malta; The Sovereign Military Order of the Temple of Jerusalem, St. George Priory; Board of Directors of the Russian Nobility, U.S.A.; American-Russian Aid Society; Russian Children Welfare Society; The Russian Orthodox Theological Foundation; Order of the Crown of Charlemagne in the United States of America; Military Order of the Crusades; etc.; m. at New York, N.Y., 23 Sept. 1957, Tatiana Timasheff, b. at Berlin, Germany, 11 Sept. 1923,

1) (Countess) CATHERINE N. BOBRINSKOY, b. in New York, N.Y., 15 July 1958, member of the Order of the Crown of Charlemagne in the United States of America;

2) (Count) ALEXIS N. BOBRINSKOY, b. at New York, N.Y., 20 Apr. 1966, member of the Order of the Crown of Charlemagne in the United States of America.

Chapter VII

BOTELER — CLAIBORNE — HARRIS — CALLAWAY — HAYS

CHARLEMAGNE

(See Chapter X)

ROGER DE QUINCY, 2nd Earl of Winchester and Constable of Scotland, accompanied his father on the Fifth Crusade in 1219, d. 25 Apr. 1264; m. Helen of Galloway, d. 1245, dau. of Alan, Lord of Galloway and Constable of Scotland,

MARGARET DE QUINCY, d. ca. 12 Mar. 1280/1; m. ca. 1238, William de Ferrers, Earl of Derby, bur. 31 May 1254,

AGNES FERRERS, liv. 9 May 1281; m. Sir Robert de Muscegros, b. ca 1252; d. 27 Dec. 1280,

HAWISE DE MUSCEGROS, b. 21 Dec. 1276; d. aft. June 1340; m. (her third) Sir John Bures, d. at Bodington, 22 Dec. 1350,

CATHERINE DE BURES, b. ante 1315; liv. Oct. 1355; m. ante 21 May 1328. Sir Giles de Beauchamp, of Beauchamp's Court, d. Oct. 1361, son of Sir Walter de Beauchamp, (See Chapter XXXV, p. 113)

ROGER DE BEAUCHAMP, 1st Baron Beauchamp of Bletsoe, M.P. 1364-1380, Chamberlain to the House of Edward III, King of England, d. 3 Jan. 1379/80; m. Sybil de Patshull, dau. of Sir John de Patshull and Mabel de Grandison,

ROGER DE BEAUCHAMP, d. bef. his father,

ROGER DE BEAUCHAMP, Knt., 2nd Baron Beauchamp of Bletsoe and Lediard-Tregoz, b. 1363; d. 3 May 1406; m. Joan, dau. of William Clopton,

SIR JOHN DE BEAUCHAMP, Knt., 3rd Baron Beauchamp of Bletsoe, d. ca. 1412; m. (first) ante Jan. 1405/6, Margaret Holand, m. (second) Esther Stourton, dau. of Sir John Stourton and prob. by first wife, had,

MARGARET DE BEAUCHAMP, d. 1482; m. Sir Oliver de St. John, Knt. of Penmark, co. Gloucester, b. 1437,

SIR JOHN DE ST. JOHN, K.B., of Penmark, liv. 1488; m. Alice Bradshaw, dau. of Sir Thomas Bradshaw, of Haigh, co. Lancaster,

SIR JOHN DE ST. JOHN, K.B., of Bletsoe, liv. 1508; m. Sibyl, dau. of Morgan ap Jenkins ap Philip,

SIR JOHN ST. JOHN, of Beltsoe, M.P. for Bedfordshire, 1547-1552, by Anne Nevell, dau. of Thomas Nevell of Collerstock, co. Northampton, had a dau.,

CRESSETT ST. JOHN, m. John Boteler, Esq., of Snarnbrook, co. Bedford and Tobie, co. Essex, d. 1612/3,

JOHN BOTELER, of Little Burch Hall and Newlands Hall, Roxwell, co. Essex, m. 27 Dec. 1599, at Roxwell, Jane Elliott, bapt. 22 June 1576, dau. of Edward Elliott, of Newlands Hall, co. Essex, and Jane, dau. of James Gedge, Gent., of Shenfield, co. Essex,

ELIZABETH BOTELER, b. at Roxwell, co. Essex, England, ca. 1610-12, d. in Virginia, aft. 1668/9; m. ante Apr. 1638, Col. William Claiborne, Gent., bapt. at Crayford co. Kent, England, 10 Aug. 1600, d. ca. 1677/8,

MARY CLAIBORNE, b. ca. 1630, d. in New Kent Co., Va. ca. 1669; m. (second) Maj. Robert Harris, b. in Wales (?), ca. 1623, d. in New Kent Co., Va., 1701,

THOMAS HARRIS, b. in New Kent Co., Va., ca. 1665, killed by Indians, in Hanover Co., Va., 1725; m. ca. 1700, Mary Giles,

CLAIBORNE HARRIS, b. in Hanover Co., Va., listed in Hanover Co., 1726; d. in Granville Co., N.C., ante 1810; m. Judith —,

BENJAMIN HARRIS, b. in Granville Co., N.C., over 21 in 1784, d. in Anderson Dist., S.C., ante 26 May 1832; m. ante 1792, in Pendleton Dist., S.C., Karen Gillison, b. in N.C., ca. 1770, d. in Forsyth Co., Ga., aft. 1833,

ARCHIBALD HARRIS, b. in N.C., 20 May 1789, d. in Forsyth Co., Ga., 22 Dec. 1856; m. ca. 1816, in Pendleton Dist., S.C., Mary (Polly) Thompson, b. in Pendleton Dist., S.C., 15 May 1801, d. in Forsyth Co., Ga., 7 Sept. 1886,

WILLIAM HARRIS, b. in Anderson Dist., S.C., 1 Feb. 1820, d. in Whitfield Co., Ga., 8 Feb. 1884; m. in Forsyth Co., Ga., 18 Dec. 1842, Minerva Jane Whitsett, b. in Rockingham Co., N.C., 23 Dec. 1827, d. in Whitfield Co., Ga., 16 May 1904,

ANGIE RAY HARRIS, b. in Forsyth Co., Ga., 23 July 1858, d. at Chattanooga, Tenn., 5 Sept. 1925; m. in Whitfield Co., Ga., 16 Dec. 1880, Luke Henry Callaway, b. in Whitfield Co., Ga., 7 Oct. 1860, d. at Chattanooga, Tenn., 10 July 1929,

WILLIAM CLAUD CALLAWAY, b. in Whitfield Co., Ga., 13 Apr. 1883, d. at Chattanooga, Tenn., 24 Oct. 1958; m. at Chattanooga, Tenn., 20 June 1905, Elnora Koons, b. at Winston, Mo., 20 Aug. 1881,

MAUD ANGIE CALLAWAY, b. 4 June 1906, at Chattanooga, Tenn. ed.: Girls Preparatory School, Chattanooga; Maryville College, Maryville, Tenn.; University of Chattanooga; member: Nat. Society U.S. Daughters of 1812, past Nat'l. Recording Secretary, past 1st Vice President National, Honorary National President, Organizing President Chief Wauhatchie Chapter, Tenn. Society; Nat'l Soc. Daughters of Colonial Wars, past Recording Sec'y, 1st Vice President and President Tenn. Society; Nat'l. Society Sons and Daughters of the Pilgrims, past 1st Deputy Gov., Organizing Gov. of the Tenn. Society; Daughters of American Colonists; Dames of the Court of Honor; U.D.C.; Colonial Daughters of the XVII Century; National Society Americans of Royal Descent; National Gavel Society; Order of the Crown of Charlemagne in the United States of America; m. at Chattanooga, Tenn., 28 Sept. 1925, Cecil Theodore Hays,

1) MAJ. TED CECIL HAYS, b. at Chattanooga, Tenn., 3 July 1926; ed.: Northwestern University Music School; m. at Signal Mt., Tenn., 15 Aug. 1948, Betty Jean Brown, b. at Chattanooga, Tenn., 7 Mar. 1927,

    a) TED CECIL HAYS, Jr., b. at Chattanooga, Tenn., 20 Nov. 1949; ed.: University of Georgia Forestry School;

    b) BRUCE BROWN HAYS, b. at Atlanta, Ga., 27 Mar. 1953; ed.: University of Georgia Medical School; m. at College Park, Ga., 2 June 1973, Marilyn Payne,

        i) BRIAN CHRISTOPHER HAYS, b. at Atlanta, Ga., 20 Nov. 1975

2) DON CALLAWAY HAYS, b. at Chattanooga, Tenn., 16 Dec. 1928; ed.: University of Chattanooga; m. at Chattanooga, Tenn., 5 July 1947, Hazel Cherry, b at Chattanooga, Tenn., 22 Dec. 1927,

    a) ROBIN CALLAWAY HAYS, b. at Chattanooga, Tenn., 4 July 1965; member of the Order of the Crown of Charlemagne in the United States of America.

Chapter VIII

BOTELER — CLAIBORNE — HARRIS — JONES — BAXTER — CONWAY — WALTON — BROOKS

CHARLEMAGNE

(See Chapter VII)

MARY CLAIBORNE, b. ca. 1630, d. in New Kent Co., Va., ca. 1669: m. (second) Maj. Robert Harris, b. in Wales (?), ca. 1623, d. in New Kent Co., Va., in 1701,

CAPT. WILLIAM HARRIS, b. 1669, d. prob. in Hanover Co., Va., ante 1733; m. 2 Mar. 1697, Temperance Overton, b. in Va., 2 Mar. 1679, d. 19 Feb. 1716, bur. at "Cedar Hill", Hanover Co., Va., dau. of William Overton and Elizabeth Waters,

MAJ. ROBERT HARRIS, b. in St. Peter's Parish, Hanover Co., Va., 1698-1700, d. in Albemarle Co., Va., w.p. 8 Aug. 1765; m. 13 Jan. 1720, in Hanover Co., Va., Mourning Glenn (Glen), w.p. 1776, Albemarle Co., Va.,

CHRISTOPHER HARRIS, SR., b. 5 Feb. 1725, d. 3 Feb. 1794; m. (first) 22 Feb. 1745, Mary Dabney, b. 10 Feb. 1729, d. prob. in Madison Co., Ky.,

MOURNING HARRIS, b. prob. in Albemarle Co., Va., 4 June 1754; m. Foster Jones, d. in Madison Co., Ky., in 1814,

ELIZABETH JONES, m. Greenberry H. Baxter, settled at St. Louis, Mo., ante 1817,

MOURNING BAXTER, b. in Madison Co., Ky., 17 Jan. 1804, d. 24 Apr. 1845; m. at "Bonhomme" St. Louis Co., Mo., 28 Oct. 1824, Samuel Conway, b. at "Bonhomme", St. Louis Co., Mo., 25 July 1799, 4th son of Joseph and Elizabeth Conway,

LOUISA CONWAY, b. at "Bonhomme", St. Louis Co., Mo., 24 Apr. 1840, d. at St. Louis, Mo., 30 June 1895; m. in St. Louis Co., Mo., 3 Sept. 1861, Frederick Bates Walton, b. at "Belmont", Goochland Co., Va., 4 June 1839, d. at Winter Haven, Fla., 24 Dec. 1907.

ALLAN WALTON, b. at "Thornhill", St. Louis Co., Mo., 4 Mar. 1864, d. at Blytheville, Ark., 6 May 1919; m. 21 Oct. 1903, at Jonesboro, Ark., Virginia Warren Field, b. at Memphis, Tenn., 21 Oct. 1882, d. at Memphis, Tenn., 25 Oct. 1967,

VIRGINIA FIELD WALTON, b. at Jonesboro Ark., 6 Aug. 1904; ed. Lindenwood Jr. College, St. Charles, Mo.; member: DAR, past chapter Regent; Colonial Dames of America, Regent of Tenn.; U.D.C.; Hereditary Order of Descendants of Colonial Governors; Daughters of Founders and Patriots of America, past President, Tenn.; Order of the Crown in America; Order of the Crown of Charlemagne in the United States of America; National Society Americans of Royal Descent; Huguenot Society, Founders of Manakin, Va., Honorary Life President, Tenn.; Daughters of the Barons of Runnemede; Order of Three Crusades; Descendants of Lords of Maryland Manors; Fellow, Royal Society of St. George, London; Memphis Cotton Carnival Ass'n., Queen Mystic Society of the Memphi, 1974; Tenn. Women's Press and Authors Club, past 2nd Vice President; Nat'l League of American Penn Women, past President Tenn. and Memphis; etc.; m. at Blytheville, Ark., 27 Apr. 1929, Berry Boswell Brooks, Jr., b. at Senatobia, Miss., 2 Feb. 1902, d. 21 Jan. 1976.

1) VIRGINIA WALTON BROOKS, b. 4 June 1933; m. Allen Martin, at Katonah, N.Y., 29 June 1957.

a) ANN FIELD MARTIN, b. 1 Apr. 1959, in Westchester Co., N.Y.

28

Chapter IX

BRENT — MARSHAM — WARING — DUPUY — FISK

CHARLEMAGNE

(See Chapter XXXIII)

JOHN OF GAUNT, 1st Duke of Lancaster, K.G., King of Castile and Leon, b. at Ghent, 24 June 1340, d. at Leicester Castle, 3/4 Feb. 1398/9; m. (third) Catherine Roet, b. 1350, d. 10 May 1403, dau. of Sir Payn Roet and wid. of Sir Hugh Swynfort,

LADY JOAN BEAUFORT, b. at Beaufort Castle, d. at Howden, co York, 13 Nov. 1440; m. (his and her second) ante 29 Nov. 1396, Ralph Neville, K.G., 1st Earl of Westmoreland, b. 1364, d. at Raby, 21 Oct. 1425, son of John Neville, K.G. 3rd Lord Neville of Raby and his wife, Maud de Percy, dau. of Henry Percy, 2nd Lord Percy,

GEORGE DE NEVILLE, Lord Latimer, d. 1469; m. ante 1436/7, Elizabeth de Beauchamp,

SIR HENRY NEVILLE, Knt., Lord Latimer, m. Joan Bouchier, dau. of John Bouchier, Lord Berners,

SIR RICHARD NEVILLE, K.B., Lord Latimer, m. (first) Anne Stafford,

MARGARET NEVILLE, b. 9 Mar. 1494/5; m. by dispensation, 22 Nov. 1505, Edward Willoughby,

ELIZABETH WILLOUGHBY, Baroness Willoughby de Broke, d. 1562; m. ante 11 Apr. 1526, Sir Fulke Greville, Knt., of Beauchamp Court, High Sherrif, 1543, M.P.,

KATHERINE GREVILLE, m. Giles Reed, Lord of Tusburie and Witten, Gloucs.,

29

ELIZABETH REED, m. ante 1600, Richard Brent, Lord of Admington and Stoke,

GILES BRENT, b. in Gloucestershire, England, ca. 1600, d. in Stafford Co. Virginia, 31 Aug. 1671; m. (first) Mary Kittamaquund, b. prob. in Maryland,

KATHERINE BRENT, b. in Stafford Co., Va., ca. 1649, d. in Calvert Co., Md., ca. 1690; m. (his first) ca. 1665, Richard Marsham, who came to Md. in 1658, d. in Prince George's Co., Md., 7 May 1713,

KATHERINE MARSHAM, b. in Calvert Co., Md., aft. 1665, d. in Prince George's Co., Md., 1712; m. (his second) ante 1683, Basil Waring, b. in Calvert Co., Md., ca. 1650, d. in Calvert Co., Md., 1688,

BASIL WARING, b. in Calvert Co., Md., 1683, d. in Prince George's Co., Md., 1733; m. in Prince George's Co. Md., 31 Jan. 1709, Martha Greenfield, b. in Prince George's Co., Md., ca. 1690, d. in Prince George's Co., Md., 1758,

FRANCIS WARING, b. in Prince George's Co., Md., 1715, d. prob. in Md.; m. ante 1751, in Prince George's Co., Md., Mary Hollyday, b. in Prince George's Co., Md., ca 1720, d. in Md.,

THOMAS WARING, Judge, b. in Prince George's Co., Md., 1752, d. in Greenup Co., Ky., 15 Jan. 1818; m. ante 1774, prob. at Philadelphia, Pa., Lydia Walton, b. prob. at Philadelphia, Pa., ca. 1750, d. in Greenup Co., Ky., aft. 1784,

THOMAS TRUMAN GREENFIELD WARING, b. in Md., 1778, d. in Greenup Co., Ky., w.d. 1865; m. in Mason Co., Ky., 25 Apr. 1799, Nancy Mefford, b. in Penn., 1783, d. in Greenup Co., Ky., prob. aft 1830,

BASIL WARING, b. in Ky., ca. 1801, d. in Greenup Co., Ky., aft. 1850; m. in Ohio or Ky., ca. 1830, Mary Hollyday Waring (his cousin) b. in Ohio, 1808, d. in Greenup Co., Ky. aft. 1850,

MARTHA WARING, b. in Greenup Co., Ky., ante 1834, d. in Ky.

or Ohio, ante 1865; m. (his first) ante 1849, in Greenup Co., Ky., Richard Stephenson DuPuy, b. in Greenup Co., Ky., 10 Sept. 1825, d. in Ohio or Ky., aft. 1873,

JAMES NEWTON DU PUY, b. in Greenup Co., Ky., 15 Mar. 1851, d. in Greenup Co., Ky., aft. 1894; m. (first) in Lewis Co., Ky., 15 Oct. 1873, Nattie A. V. Garland, b. prob. in Ky., ca. 1853, d. in Greenup Co., Ky., 18 June 1888,

ELBERT STEPHENSON DU PUY, M.D., b. in Lewis Co., Ky., 20 Mar 1876, d. at Beckley, Raleigh Co., W. Va., 16 Oct. 1941; m. 10 June 1903, in Fayette Co., W. Va., Lillian Dixon, b. in Fayette Co., W.Va., 10 June 1880, d. at Beckley, W.Va., 21 Feb. 1969,

1) ELBERT NEWTON DU PUY, b. at Parral, W.Va., 19 Oct. 1904, grad. Fishburne Military School, Waynesboro, Va.; W. Va. Univ., B.S.; Duke Univ. Medical School, M.D.; graduate study, Rotunda Hospital, Dublin and University Hospital, Baltimore; Diplomat American Board of Obstetrics and Gynecology; Fellow, American College of Surgeons; Fellow, American College of Obstetricians and Gynecologists; Fellow, Royal Society of Medicine (England); Illinois State Medical Society, Past President; American Medical Association, Past Delegate; World Medical Assoc.; Swanberg Medical Assoc., Past President; Society of Academic Achievement, Past President and Founder; Assoc. of Military Surgeons; U.S. Army Medical Corps, Col. (ret.), dec. Silver Star Medal, Bronze Star Medal, Combat Medical Badge, etc.; member: Order of the Crown of Charlemagne in the United States of America; m. at Chicago, Ill., 7 May 1938, Ruth Christine Griffenhagen, b. at Chicago, Ill., 3 Oct. 1909,

a) JAMES NEWTON DU PUY, b. 26 July 1939; m. (first) 26 Jan. 1962 Sandra Jayne Castle, (second) Janet Marie Egendorf. By his first wife, had,
   i) CATHERINE ANNE DU PUY, b. 1 Nov. 1962;
   ii) ALFRED CASTLE DU PUY, b. 22 Aug. 1966.

31

b) KARL FREDERICK GRIFFENHAGEN DU PUY, b. 19 May 1942; m. Margaret Elizabeth Kepner, 14 Aug. 1972

c) WILLIAM EDWIN STUART DU PUY, b. 1 Oct. 1946.

2) SAMUEL STUART DU PUY, M.D., b. at Parral, W.VA., 10 Feb. 1912, d. at Miami, Fla., 5 Nov. 1974; m. at Morgantown, W.Va., 1 June 1940, Helen Elizabeth Baker, b. 19 Mar. 1916, in Monongalia Co., W. Va.,

a) NANCY LEE DU PUY, b. at Beckley, W.Va., 22 May 1941; B.A., Univ. of N.C.; M.A., Emory Univ.; member: C.A.R., Delta Delta Delta, Peace Corps 1966-68, National and Fla. Educational Assocs., Huguenot Society of Fla., Order of the Crown of Charlemagne in the United States of America; m. (first) at Coral Gables, Fla., 25 July 1964, William Paton Niblock (div.) m. (second) at Miami, 13 May 1973, James Edward Fisk, b. at Union City, Pa., 17 July 1932.
   i) ANDREA PATON NIBLOCK, b. 20 Aug. 1969.

b) SAMUEL STUART DU PUY, Jr., b. at Beckley, W.Va., 9 Apr. 1943; B.S., Davidson College, N.C.; M.D., Univ. of Fla. College of Medicine; intern, Mobile General Hospital; resident, urology, Charlotte Memorial Hospital, Charlotte, N.C.; member: Kappa Alpha Order, Southern Medical Assoc., Mecklenberg Co. Medical Society, N.C. Medical Soc., Capt., USAF, C.A.R., Huguenot Soc. of Fla., Order of the Crown of Charlemagne in the United States of America; m. at Coral Gables, Fla., 21 June 1969, Carla Jane Eloff, b. at Bellefontaine, Ohio, 1 May 1947,
   i) JOHN STUART DU PUY, b. 7 Jan. 1972;
   ii) JAMES DAVID DU PUY, b. 5 Sept. 1973.

c) DAVID NORRIS DU PUY, M.D., b. 10 Sept. 1944, at Beckley, W.Va.; ed.: Emory Univ., Atlanta, Ga.,

B.A.; Univ. of Miami School of Medicine, M.D.;
Major, Division Surgeon, Army Nat'l Guard;
member: Iron Arrow Leadership Society, Univ. of
Miami; Huguenot Society of Florida; Order of the
Crown of Charlemagne in the United States of
America; Mecklenburg Medical Society; m. 12
Aug. 1967, at Nashville, Tenn., Sandra Faye
Coley, b. at Nashville, 5 Mar. 1944,

   i) DAVID COLEY DU PUY, (adopted) b. 23
Sept. 1970;

   ii) CATHERINE BAKER DU PUY (adopted) b.
13 Mar. 1973;

   iii) LAURA KAY DU PUY (adopted) b. 26 Feb.
1975.

Chapter X

BROOKE — MACKALL — LOKER — KILBOURNE

CHARLEMAGNE, King of the Franks, Emperor of the West, b. 2 Apr. 742, d. 28 Jan. 813/4; m. (third) ca. 771, Hildegarde of Swabia, b. ca. 758, d. 30 Apr. 783,

PEPIN, King of Italy (781-810) consecrated King of Lombardy, 781, b. Apr. 777, d. at Milan, 8 July 810,

BERNARD, King of Italy (813-817), b. 797, d. at Milan, 17 Apr. 818; m. Cunnigunde, d. ca. 835,

PEPIN, Count of Senlis, Peronne, and St. Quentin, b. ca. 815; d. aft. 840,

HERBERT I, Count of Vermandois, Seigneur de Senlis, Peronne, and St. Quentin, b. ca. 840, murdered, ca. 902,

BEATRIX DE VERMANDOIS, m. (his second) Robert I, Duke of France, Marquis of Neustria, King of the West Franks, d. 15 June 923,

HUGH MAGNUS, Count of Paris, d. in June 956; m. (third) Hedwig, Princess of Germany, dau. of Henry I, the Fowler, Emperor of Germany,

HUGH CAPET, King of France (987-996), b. aft 939, d. 24 Oct. 996; m. ante 969, Adelaide, of Poitou, b. 945/50, d. 1004, dau. of William I, Count of Poitou, and Adele, dau. of Rollo, Duke of Normandy.

ROBERT II, the Pious, King of France (988-1031) b. 970, at Orleans, d. 20 July 1031; m. (his second) Constance, of Toulouse, d. 1033,

34

HENRY I, King of France (1031-1060), b. 1005/11, d. in Aug. 1060; m. Anne of Russia, d. 1074/5, dau. of Jaroslav I, Grand Prince of Kiev, d. 20 Feb. 1053/4, and his second wife, Inguigarde, dau. of Olaf, first Christian King of Sweden,

HUGH MAGNUS, Duke of France, Leader of the First Crusade, b. 1101; m. Adelaide de Vermandois, Countess of Vermandois, d. ca. 1120, dau. of Herbert IV, Count of Vermandois and Vexin, and Adele de Vexin, dau. of Raoul III, the Great, Count of Valois and Vexin,

ISABEL DE VERMANDOIS, Countess of Leicester, d. ante July 1147; m. (first) Robert de Beaumont, Seigner de Beaumont, Pont Audemer, Brionne and Vatteville in Normandy, Count de Meulan in the French Vexin, Earl of Leicester, b. ca. 1046, d. 5 June 1118, son and heir of Roger de Beaumont (see Chapters XXXII, XXXIX, XLIII, LXVIII)

SIR ROBERT DE BEAUMONT, knighted 1122, 2nd Earl of Leicester, Justiciar of England 1155-1168; m. aft Nov. 1120, Amice de Montfort, dau. of Ralph de Gael de Montfort, Lord of Gael and Montfort in Brittany, Earl of Norfolk, Suffolk and Cambridge, in England, and his wife, Emma Fitz Osbern, dau. of William Fitz Osbern,

SIR ROBERT DE BEAUMONT, 3rd Earl of Leicester, Crusader in 1179; b. ante 1135; d. 1190, at Durazzo, Greece; m. ca. 1155, Pernell (Petronilla) de Grantmesnil, d. 1 Apr. 1212, dau. of Hugh de Grantmesnil,

MARGARET DE BEAUMONT, d. 12 Jan. 1235/6; m. ante 1173, Saher (Saier) de Quincy, cr. Earl of Winchester by King John, 1207, Magna Charta Surety, 1215, Crusader in 1219; b. ca. 1155, d. 3 Nov. 1219, before Damietta, Egypt, bur. at Acre in the Holy Land,

ROGER DE QUINCY, 2nd Earl of Winchester and Constable of Scotland, accompanied his father on the Fifth Crusade in 1219, d 25 Apr. 1264; m. Helen of Galloway, d. 1245, dau. of Alan, Lord of Galloway and Constable of Scotland,

35

ELIZABETH DE QUINCY, d. ante Nov. 1328; m. Alexander Comyn, Earl of Buchan, Constable of Scotland and Justiciar, d. 1290, son of William Comyn and Margaret, Countess of Buchan,

ELIZABETH COMYN, d. ante 17 Feb. 1328/9; m. Gilbert de Umfreyville, Earl of Angus, b. 1244, d. ante 13 Oct. 1307, son of Gilbert de Umfreyville, and Maud, dau. of Malcolm, Earl of Angus,

ROBERT DE UMFREYVILLE, Earl of Angus, d. 2 Apr. 1325; m. (second) Alianore, d. 31 Mar. 1368,

THOMAS DE UMFREYVILLE, of Harbottle Castle, d. 1390/1; m. Joan de Roddam, dau. of Adam de Roddam

SIR THOMAS DE UMFREYVILLE, b. at Harbottle Castle, d. 1390/1; m. Agnes, d. 25 Oct. 1420,

ELIZABETH DE UMFREYVILLE, b. 1381, d. 23 Nov. 1424; m. Sir William Elmeden, of Elmeden, d. ante 28 Oct. 1447,

JOAN DE ELMEDEN, m. Thomas Forster, Esq., at Buckton, co. Durham,

THOMAS FORSTER, d. at Etherstone; m. Elizabeth de Etherstone, sister and heiress of Roger, Lord Etherstone,

THOMAS FORSTER, d. at Etherstone; m. Mary Fetherstonehaugh, b. at Stanhope Hall, co. Durham,

SIR ROGER FORSTER, m. Joan Hussey of Sussex,

THOMAS FORSTER, 2nd son, fl. 1574, d. 11 Oct. 1599, of Hunsden, co. Hertford; m. Margaret Browning of Chelmsford, co. Essex,

SIR THOMAS FORSTER, Knt., b. 1548, d. 1612, Justice of the Court of Common Pleas, knighted, 1604; m. Susan Foster, d. 3 Apr. 1625, dau. of Thomas Foster, of Iden, co. Sussex,

SUSAN FORSTER, bur. 18 Sept. 1612 (Whitechurch Register); m. Thomas Brooke, d. 13 Sept. 1612 (w.d. 11 Sept. 1612, w.p. 30

Nov. 1612) of Whitechurch, co. Northhampton, son of
Richard Brooke and Elizabeth Twyne,

ROBERT BROOKE, A.B., A.M., Wadham College, Oxford, settled
at Brooke Place Manor, Calvert Co., Md., in 1650, Acting
Governor, 1652, b. at London, England, 3 Jan. 1602, d. Calvert
Co., Md. 20 July 1655; m. (second) 11 May 1635, Mary
Mainwaring, b. at St. Giles-in-the-Field, London, Eng.; d. in
Calvert Co., Md.,

ROGER BROOKE, b. 20 Sept. 1637, at Brecknock College, Wales;
d. in Calvert Co., Md., 8 Apr. 1700; m. (first) Mary Wolsely, b.
in Staffordshire, England, d. in Calvert Co., Md.,

ANNE (BROOKE) DAWKINS, b. in Calvert Co., Md., d. in Calvert
Co., Md., 1733; m. (second) ca. 1702, James Mackall, b. in
Calvert Co., Md., in 1671 (?), d. in Calvert Co., Md., in 1717,

JAMES MACKALL, b. in Calvert Co., Md., in 1708, d. in Calvert
Co., Md., in 1751; m. Mary Howe, b. in Calvert Co., Md. 20
Feb. 1709, d. in Calvert Co., Md., in 1753,

CAPT. JOHN MACKALL, served in the War of the Revolution, b.
in Calvert Co., Md. 22 Oct. 1738, d. in St. Mary's Co., Md., 18
Aug. 1813; m. 11 Mar. 1758, at Christ Church, Calvert Co.,
Md., Margaret Gough, d. at St. Mary's City, Md., 1814,

REBECCA MACKALL, b. in Calvert Co., Md., 11 Feb. 1763; d. in
St. Mary's Co., Md., 15 Sept. 1825; m. in 1781, Thomas Loker,
b. in St. Mary's Co., Md., 1757; d. in St. Mary's Co., Md.,
1803,

THOMAS LOKER, b. in St. Mary's Co., Md., 15 Aug. 1798, d. in
St. Mary's Co., Md., 15 Dec. 1876; m. at St. Mary's City Md., 9
June 1835, Mary Elizabeth Jones, b. in St. Mary's Co., Md., 5
Sept. 1816, d. in St. Mary's Co., Md., 19 May 1897,

GEORGE CLINTON LOKER, b. in St. Mary's Co., Md., 3 Mar.
1839, d. in St. Mary's Co., Md., 6 May 1876; m. at Valley Lee,
Md., 19 Nov. 1868, Catherine Warren Gardiner, b. in St.
Mary's Co., Md., in 1845, d. in St. Mary's Co., Md., 28 Nov.
1870,

KATIE LOKER, b. in St. Mary's Co., Md., 28 Nov. 1870; d. at Stewartstown, Pa., 19 July 1923; m. at Baltimore, Md., 1 June 1904, Arthur Pritchard Kilbourne, b. at Potter Brook, Pa., 8 Dec. 1878, d. at Lawrenceville, Pa., 1 Dec. 1966,

DWIGHT ARTHUR KILBOURNE, b. at Stewartstown, Pa., 14 Feb. 1905, liv. 1975; m. at Towson, Md., 4 Apr. 1925, Olive Myrtle Hostler, b. at Woodbine, Pa., 2 May 1903, liv. 1975,

JOHN DWIGHT KILBOURNE, b. at Stewartstown, Pa., 2 Apr. 1926; ed.: College of William and Mary, Harvard University; past Curator of Pennsylvania Historical Society; member: S.R.; National Society Americans of Royal Descent, past Curator General; Order of Three Crusades, past Archivist General; Order of the Crown of Charlemagne in the United States of America.

Chapter XI

BROOKE — MACKALL — DAWSON — EVANS — BAUER

CHARLEMAGNE

(See Chapter X)

ANNE BROOKE, b. in Calvert Co., Md., in 1671, d. in Calvert Co., Md., in 1733; m. (second) ca. 1702, James Mackall, b. in Calvert Co., Md., in 1671, d. in Calvert Co., Md., in 1717,

BENJAMIN MACKALL, b. in Frederick Co., Md., w.p. Frederick Co., Md., 20 Mar. 1767; m. Mary Taylor,

REBECCA MACKALL, b. in Frederick Co., Md., d. in Beaver Co., Pa.; m. in Maryland, in 1764, Benoni Dawson, b. in Prince George Co., Md., in 1742; d. at Georgetown, Beaver Co., Pa., 6 May 1806,

BENONI DAWSON II, b. in Frederick Co., Md., 20 Aug. 1769, d. nr. Georgetown, Beaver Co., Pa., 14 Nov. 1844; m. 15 Nov. 1792, Katherine P.D. McKennon, b. at Annapolis, Md., 20 Oct. 1775, d. at Georgetown, Beaver Co., Pa., 18 Dec. 1848,

RUTH DAWSON, b. in Beaver Co., Pa., 30 July 1809, d. in Hancock Co., 22 Feb. 1891; m. 3 Nov. 1837, Isaac Evans, b. 3 Nov. 1815, d. in Hancock Co., W.Va., 8 Dec. 1893,

WILLIAM PORTER EVANS, b. at New Cumberland, W. Va., 11 Jan. 1852, d. at Pittsburgh, Pa., 27 Oct. 1929; m. 4 June 1884, Hannah Mary Wilson, b. at New Cumberland, W. Va., 14 May 1865, d. at St. Petersburg, Fla., in Aug. 1946,

RUTH E. EVANS, b. at Fairview W.Va., 9 Feb. 1896; m. 25 Nov. 1920, Dr. Brown Fulton, b. at Pittsburgh, Pa., in Jan. 1893, d. at Pittsburgh, Pa., in Dec. 1969,

JANE BROOKE EVANS FULTON, b. at Pittsburgh, Pa., 25 Aug. 1921; ed: Gardner School, Miss Glay's School and Lennox School, New York; Branksome Hall, Toronto; Academy of the Holy Names, Tampa, Fla.; Temple University, Philadelphia; U.S. Navy Waves; member: Order of Three Crusades 1096-1192, National Society Americans of Royal Descent, DAR, Royal Society of St. George, British American Society, Descendants of William the Conqueror and His Companions at Arms, National Huguenot Society of Pa., Order of First Families of Virginia 1607-1624/5, English Speaking Union, Historical Society of Pa., Order of the Crown of Charlemagne in the United States of America; m. at Chesapeake City, Md., 14 June 1954, Otto S. Bauer, b. 9 May 1908,

    1) DIANA CAROL EVANS BAUER, b. 24 Dec. 1955

Chapter XII

BROOKE — BEALL — SCOTT — ROEDER — POTTS

CHARLEMAGNE

(See Chapter X)

ROBERT BROOKE, A.B., A.M., Wadham College, Oxford, settled at Brooke Place, Calvert Co., Md., 1650, Acting Gov. of the Colony in 1652, b. at London, Eng., 3 Jan. 1602, d. in Calvert Co., Md., 20 July 1655; m. (first) in 1627, in England, Mary Baker, b. in Bettel, co. Sussex, Eng., d. at Wickham, co. Hampshire, Eng. 1634,

MAJ. THOMAS BROOKE, b. at Bettel, co. Sussex, Eng., 23 June 1632, d. at Brooke Manor, Md., 1676; m. 1658, Eleanor Hatton, b. at London, Eng., d. in Anne Arundel Co., Md., 1725,

COL. THOMAS BROOKE, b. at Nottingham, Prince George Co. (now Montgomery Co.), Md., 1659, d. at "Brookfield", Prince George Co., 1730; m. (first) Anne —,

THOMAS BROOKE, JR., b. at Nottingham, Prince George Co., Md., 1682; d. at "Brookfield", Prince George Co., Md., 1745; m. 9 May 1705, Lucy Smith, b. in Calvert Co., Md.,

ELEANOR BROOKE, b. in Prince George Co., Md., 7 Mar. 1718, d. in Washington Co., Md. 1785; m. 23 May 1734, Col. Samuel Beall, Jr., d. in Washington Co., Md., in Jan. 1788,

AMELIA JANE BEALL, b. in Md., 1747; m. 1767, Thaddeus Beall, Sr., b. in Montgomery Co., Md., 1745, d. in Warren Co., Ga., 1815,

41

THADDEUS BEALL, JR., b. in N.C., 1789, d. in Chambers Co., Ala., 1867; m. 28 Jan. 1805, Mary W. Jones, b. in Columbia Co., Ga., d. in Chambers Co., Ala., 1867,

THADDEUS SOLON BEALL, b. in Walton Co., Ga., 1835, d. in Lafayette Co., Ala., 29 May 1903; m. in Chambers Co., Ala., Sept. 1862, Carrie M. Boyd, b. in Chambers Co., Ala., 6 Feb. 1845, d. in Lafayetter Co., Ala.

LILLIE ORA BEALL, b. in Chambers Co., Ala., 25 June 1867, d. at Anniston, Ala., 17 May 1898; m. in Chambers Co., Ala., 15 Oct. 1883, Gabriel Moss Scott, Sr., b. 1 Dec. 1857, at Fort Deposit, Ala., d. at Anniston, Ala., 5 Feb. 1937,

GABRIEL MOSS SCOTT, Jr., b. at Lafayette, Ala., 21 Jan. 1887, d. at Tampa, Fla., Oct. 1960; m. at Anniston, Ala., 31 July 1905, Elizabeth M. Cate, b. at Anniston, Ala., 1 May 1890, d. at Wilmington, Del., 11 Mar. 1935,

> 1) ALCINE SCOTT, b. at Anniston, Ala., 12 Jan. 1910; member: Colonial Daughters of the XVII Century, Corresponding Sec'y., Nat'l Chairman Credentials, past 2nd V.P. Pa.; Officers Club of Penna.; DAR; U.D.C.; Order of the Crown of Charlemagne in the United States of America; m. (first) Charles William Potts, (second) 8 May 1965, at Philadelphia, Pa., Paul Roeder, M.D., b. at Reading, Pa., 25 Jan. 1900,
>
> > a) LUKEN WILLIAM POTTS, b. 3 Mar. 1939, m. Dorothy Merle Levin;
> >
> > b) DANIEL CHARLES POTTS, b. 8 Jan. 1946, m. Deborah Ann Yerkes;
>
> 2) KATHRYN SCOTT, b. at Anniston, Ala., 7 Jan. 1917; member: DAR, Colonial Daughters of the Seventeenth Century, Order of the Crown of Charlemagne in the United States of America; m. 17 May 1941, at Wilmington, Del., Everett Neville King, b. at Wilmington, Del., 20 June 1913,

3) DOROTHY FRANCIS SCOTT, b. at Anniston, Ala., 27 May 1923; member Colonial Daughters of the Seventeenth Century; U.D.C, First Vice President; Order of the Crown of Charlemagne in the United States of America; m. at Phila., Pa., 17 June 1941, James Webb Potts, b. at Phila., Pa., 8 Jan. 1918,

    a) ALCINE ELIZABETH POTTS, m. Edwin Earl Lukenbach;

    b) JAMES WEBB POTTS, Jr., m. Norma Sue Vessey,
        i) ANDREW EVERETT POTTS.

Chapter XIII

BROOKE — BEALL — NORRIS

CHARLEMAGNE

(See Chapter XII)

COL. THOMAS BROOKE, b. in Calvert Co., Md., in 1659, d. at "Brookfield", Prince George Co., Md., 7 Jan. 1730/1; m. (second) in Charles Co., Md., ante 4 Jan. 1699, Barbara Dent, b. in Charles Co., Md., d. in Prince George Co., Md., in 1754,

ELIZABETH BROOKE, b. in Prince George Co., Md., 1699, d. at Georgetown, Md., 2 Oct. 1748; m. Col. George Beall, b. in Prince George Co., Md., 1695, d. at Georgetown, Md., 15 Mar. 1780,

COL. GEORGE BEALL, JR., at Georgetown, Md., 26 Feb. 1729, d. at Georgetown, D.C., 15 Oct. 1807; m. ca. 1759, Ann — , d. at Georgetown, Md.,

ENSIGN LEVIN COVINGTON BEALL, b. at Georgetown, Md., 7 June 1760, d. in Montgomery Co., Md., ca. 1802; m. in Md., ca. 1781, Esther Best, b. in Md., d. in Montgomery Co., Md., aft. 1802,

JOHN BEALL, of Levin, Montgomery Co., Md., b. 23 Dec. 1781, in Montgomery Co., d. at Barnesville, Md., 26 Aug. 1831; m. in Md., in 1808, Charlotte Jones, b. in Md., 18 Feb. 1787, d. at Barnesville, Md., 22 Jan. 1867,

WILLIAM RUFUS BEALL, b. at Barnesville, Md., 24 Feb. 1814, d. at Dranesville, Va., 3 Jan. 1884; m. in Montgomery Co., Md., lic. dated, 20 Jan. 1839, Martha Elizabeth McAtee, b. in Montgomery Co., Md., ca 1811, d. at Barnestown, Md., 1895,

44

CHARLES EDWARD BEALL, b. at Barnesville, Md., 8 Oct. 1849, d. at Gaithersburg, Md., 6 Nov. 1913; m. 20 June 1883, at Georgetown, D.C., Mary Elizabeth Clements, b. at Barnesville, Md., 22 June 1853, d. at Gaithersburg, Md., 1 Jan. 1935,

MARY EMMA BEALL, b. at Toledo, Ohio, 22 Mar. 1884, d. at Gaithersburg, Md., 27 Aug. 1940; m. at Rockville, Md., 30 Aug. 1904, Abell Archibald Norris, b. nr. Leonardtown, Md., 20 Feb. 1875, d. at Gaithersburg, Md., 23 Oct. 1955,

ABELL ARCHIBALD NORRIS, JR., b. at Gaithersburg, Md., 30 June 1905; ed.: Mount Angel Preparatory School; B.S., Georgetown University; M. Ed., University of Md.; member: Phi Delta Kappa, Phi Kappa Phi, S.R., President of D.C. Society; Society of Colonial Wars, Sec'y D.C. Society; Montgomery Co. (Md.) Historical Society, Vice President; Society of the War of 1812 in Md., Past Director; Rockville Lions Club, Past President; The Society of the Ark and Dove; Baronial Order of Magna Charta; Military Order of the Crusades; Hereditary Order of Descendants of Colonial Governors; Maryland Historical Society; Order of the Crown of Charlemagne in the United States of America; m. in Washington, D.C., 30 June 1934, Mary Shafer Hershey, b. at Comus, Md, 9 July 1908,

1) JANET ANN NORRIS, b. 25 Aug. 1938; m. Frederick Edward Woodruff;

2) ABELL ARCHIBALD NORRIS, III, b. 6 Apr. 1940;

3) JAMES EDWARD NORRIS, b. 31 July 1941.

Chapter XIV

BROOKE — GANTT — BROOME — DORSEY — SUTTON — LAWRENCE — STEIN

CHARLEMAGNE

(See Chapter XII)

MAJ. THOMAS BROOKE, b. at Bettel, Co. Sussex, Eng., 23 June 1632, d. at Brooke Manor, Calvert Co., Md., 1676; m. 1658, in Calvert Co., Md., Eleanor Hatton, b. in London, Eng., d. in Ann Arundel Co., Md.,

COL. THOMAS BROOKE, b. in Calvert Co., Md., in 1659, d. at "Brookfield", Prince George Co., Md., 7 Jan. 1730/1; m. (second) in Charles Co., Md., ca 1685, Barbara Dent, b. in Charles Co., Md., ca. 1660, d. in Prince George Co., Md., in 1754,

PRISCILLA BROOKE, b. in Calvert Co., Md., 1685, d. in Calvert Co., ca. 1760; m. in Calvert Co., Md., 1705, Thomas Gantt, b. in Calvert Co., Md. in 1686, d. in Calvert Co., Md., 1765,

ANNE GANTT, b. in Calvert Co., Md., 1708, d. in Calvert Co., 1761; m. in Calvert Co., 1725, Col. John Broome IV, b. in Calvert Co., Md., in 1703, d. in Calvert Co., 1749,

HENRY BROOME, b. in Calvert Co., Md., ca 1730, d. in Calvert Co., in 1771; m. ante 1761, in Calvert Co., Anne Dawkins, b. in Calvert Co., Md., ante 1746, d. in Calvert Co., aft. 1773,

BARBARA BROOME, b. in Calvert Co., Md., ca. 1762, d. in Calvert Co., ca. 1818; m. in Calvert Co., ca. 1783, Philip Dorsey, Jr., b. in Calvert Co., Md., 11 Aug. 1759, d. in Calvert Co., 24 Apr. 1818,

MARTHA ANN DORSEY, b. in Calvert Co., Md., 18 Dec. 1785, d. in Anne Arundel Co., Md., 4 Apr. 1847; m. in Calvert Co., Md., 29 Oct. 1803, Rev. Lewis Sutton, b. in Northumberland Co., Virginia, 9 May 1781, d. in St. Mary's Co., Md., 28 Nov. 1850,

EMERALD SUTTON, b. in Calvert Co., Md., 1 Jan. 1806, d. at Baltimore, Md., 29 Apr. 1878; m. in Calvert Co., Md., 10 Dec. 1822, Dr. Thomas John Lawrence, b. in Calvert Co., Md., 1 July 1797, d. in Anne Arundel Co., Md., 24 Aug. 1852,

EMERALD LAWRENCE, b. in Anne Arundel Co., Md., 21 Nov. 1838, d. at Baltimore, Md., 28 Sept. 1895; m. at Baltimore, 23 Aug. 1862, Dr. Atilla Edward Stein, b. at Baltimore, 11 Sept., 1838, d. at Baltimore, 16 Nov. 1884,

JUDGE CHARLES F. STEIN, b. at Baltimore, Md., 25 Sept. 1866, d. at Baltimore, 5 May 1939; m. at Washington, D.C., 24 Mar. 1897, Ella Willson Griffith, b. 10 Aug. 1870, in Howard Co., Md., d. at Baltimore, Md., 9 Jan. 1940,

CHARLES FRANCIS STEIN, JR., b. at Baltimore, Md., 19 June 1900; A.B. and post graduate studies in Political Economy and History, Johns Hopkins University; LL.B., University of Md.; member: Society of the Cincinnati of Maryland, Assistant Secretary 1965-1968, Secretary 1968-1975, Vice-President 1975-1976, President 1976 —. Society of the Ark and the Dove; Order of the First Families of Virginia; Society of Colonial Wars Board of Governors, 1967-1970; Society of Sons of the Revolution; Society of Sons of the American Revolution, Board of Governors; Society of the War of 1812, President Md. Society 1955-1959, His. General Society; Baronial Order of Magna Charta, Surety; St. Nicholas Society of the City of New York; National Society of Descendants of Lords of Maryland Manors; Hereditary Order of Descendants of Colonial Governors, Chancellor, Vice President; National Huguenot Society, Chancellor General 1969——; Military Order of the Loyal Legion of the United States, Judge Advocate General 1969——; Swedish Colonial Society; German Society of Maryland, President 1970-1973; m. Jean Norris Renneburg at Baltimore, 14 May 1932, b. 20 Aug. 1908,

(1) CHARLES FRANCIS STEIN III, b. 9 Oct., 1933, m. at Baltimore, Md., 1 Sept. 1968, Ann Farinholt, b. Baltimore, Md., 9 July, 1936,

   a) LAURA HAMILTON STEIN, b. Baltimore, Md., 26 March, 1970.

   b) CHARLES FRANCIS STEIN IV, b. Baltimore, Md., 24 March 1971

2) JEAN ALEXANDRA STEIN, b. 16 Oct. 1936; m. William G. Kouwenhoven

   a) WILLIAM BERGEN KOUWENHOVEN, b. 19 Sept. 1961;

   b) NICHOLAS WILLSON KOUWENHOVEN, b. 9 Sept. 1964.

Chapter XV

BROOKE — SMITH — WATERS — HIGGINS — DAVIS — FITCHETT — LAMBERT — MORTON

CHARLEMAGNE

(See Chapter X)

ROBERT BROOKE, A.B., A.M. Wadham College, Oxford, settled at Brooke Place Manor, Calvert Co., Md., in 1650, Acting Gov. of the Colony in 1652, b. at London, England, 3 Jan. 1602, d. at Brooke Place Manor, 20 July 1655; m. (second) 11 May 1635, Mary Mainwaring, b. at London, England, d. at Brooke Place Manor, in Maryland,

ELIZABETH BROOKE, b. at Brooke Place Manor, Calvert Co., Md., 28 Nov. 1655, d. ante 1687; m. 29 May 1671, Capt. Richard Smith, b. in Calvert Co., Md., ca. 1653, w.p. in Calvert Co., Md. 19 Mar. 1714,

COL. JOHN SMITH, b. in Calvert Co., Md., d. in Calvert Co., Md., w.p. 25 Apr. 1738; m. Sarah Young,

MAJ. JOHN SMITH, b. in Calvert Co., Md., w.p. in Calvert Co., Md., 15 Oct. 1759; m. Mary Hamilton, d. in Calvert Co., Md.,

PHILEMON HAMILTON SMITH, b. in Calvert Co., Md., 7 July 1744, d. in Calvert Co., Md., in 1772; m. Betsey Rawlings, b. ca. 1749, d. 25 Jan. 1811,

MARGARET HAMILTON SMITH, b. in Calvert Co., Md., 11 Feb. 1769, d. in Montgomery Co., Md., 1 Feb. 1833; m. 2 June 1785, Capt. Richard Waters, surgeon in the Revolution, b. in Prince Georges Co., Md., 1759/60, d. in Montgomery Co., Md., 28 Apr. 1810;

49

RICHARD RAWLINGS WATERS, b. in Montgomery Co., Md., 14 Dec. 1794, d. in Montgomery Co., Md., 5 Jan. 1885; m. at Georgetown, D.C., 16 Dec. 1817, Jerusha Anne Shaw, b. at Georgetown, D.C., 23 Oct. 1799, d. in Montgomery Co., Md., 2 May 1879,

MARGARET REBECCA WATERS, b. in Montgomery Co., Md., 20 Oct. 1819, d. at Baltimore, Md., 2 Jan. 1902; m. in Montgomery Co., Md., 3 Aug. 1837, Jesse Thomas Higgins, b. in Montgomery Co., Md., 7 Mar. 1814, d. at Baltimore, Md., 14 Oct. 1887,

ANNE WATERS HIGGINS, b. at Rockville, Md., 15 Feb. 1843, d. at "Land of Promise", Glenarm, Baltimore Co., Md., 25 Jan. 1925; m. 22 June 1871, at Baltimore, Md., Eldred Baylor Davis, b. at Christiansburg, Va., 13 Feb. 1843, d. at Christiansburg, Va. 14 Feb. 1881,

LILIAN GLENN DAVIS, b. at Baltimore, Md., 20 July 1872, d. at "Land of Promise", Glenarm, Md., 26 Apr. 1945; m. at Baltimore, Md., 26 June 1895, Thomas Howard Fitchett, b. at Baltimore, Md., 30 Apr. 1873, d. at Fort Lauderdale, Fla., 27 Feb. 1953,

MARGARET GLENN FITCHETT, b. at Baltimore, Md., 1 Jan. 1906, d. 5 Sept. 1977, ed.: Briarcliff, Johns Hopkins Univ.; member: DAR, D.A.C., Lords of Maryland Manors, American Clan Gregor Society, Daughters of the Barons of Runnemede, U.D.C., United States Daughters of 1812, Maryland State Society of the Huguenots, Order of the Crown of Charlemagne in the United States of America; m. at Towson, Md., 19 Feb. 1927, Louis Edwin Lambert, Jr., b. at Baltimore, Md., 2 July 1905,

    1) MARGARET GLENN LAMBERT, b. at Baltimore, Md., 3 Jan. 1928, ed.: Rollins College, Univ. of Florida, member: DAR, D.A.C., secretary; Maryland Lords of Manors, State chaplain; American Clan Gregor Society; Daughters of the Barons of Runnemede; U.D.C.; United States Daughters of 1812; Maryland State Society of the Huguenots; Order of the Crown of Charlemagne in the United States of America; m. 4 June

1949, at Fort Lauderdale, Fla., Alan William Morton, b. 10 Dec. 1925, at Morristown, N.J.,

a) BRUCE ALAN MORTON, b. 23 Oct. 1951, at Miami, Fla., ed.: The Citadel, Univ. of South Florida; member: .C.A.R., SAR, Order of the Crown of Charlemagne in the United States of America;

b) DAPHNE GLENN MORTON, b. 28 July 1953, grad.: Univ. of South Florida, member: Order of the Crown of Charlemagne in the United States of America.

c) STUART SOMERSET MORTON, b. 25 Sept. 1956, at Miami, Fla., student at the University of Fla.; member: C.A.R., C.A.C., Order of the Crown of Charlemagne in the United States of America;

d) ROSALIE MARGARET MORTON, b. 19 July 1966, at Fort Lauderdale, Fla., member: CAR, C.A.C.; Order of the Crown of Charlemagne in the United States of America;

2) ROBERT LOUIS LAMBERT, b. 4 Feb. 1930, at Baltimore, Md., grad.: Univ. of Miami; member of the Order of the Crown of Charlemagne in the United States of America; m. 27 Nov. 1954, at Fort Lauderdale, Fla., Sally Hannah MacLean, b. 13 Dec. 1934, at Evanston, Ill.,

a) ROBERT FREDERICK LAMBERT, b. 17 Apr. 1957, at Miami, Fla.; ed.: Babson College;

3) THOMAS RONALD FITCHETT LAMBERT, b. 5 Feb. 1943, at Miami, Fla.; grad. Fort Lauderdale University; member: Order of the Crown of Charlemagne in the United States of America; m. (first) 20 Jan. 1962, Eileen Marie Hannah, b. at Buffalo, N.Y., 10 June 1946,

a) NANCY MARIE LAMBERT, b. 8 Nov. 1962;

b) KIMBERLY MARGARET LAMBERT, b. 7 May 1964;

c) THOMAS RONALD LAMBERT, b. 20 Apr. 1966;

m. (second) 15 Sept. 1967, Sylvia Lynch, b. at Winston Salem, N.C., 8 July 1944,

d) JULIA GLENN LAMBERT, b. 6 Mar. 1968.

4) NANCY CYNTHIA LAMBERT, b. 14 June 1946, at Miami, Fla., grad.: Fla. Atlantic Univ., member: DAR; m. at Fort Lauderdale, Fla., 15 Apr. 1967, William Lanier McGee II, b. 18 May 1944, at Charleston, S.C.,

a) WILLIAM LANIER MCGEE III, b. 12 Feb. 1974;

b) MARGARET ELIZABETH MCGEE, b. 5 July 1976.

Chapter XVI

BROOKE — HILL — BROOKE — BENNETT — WILLSON — WALLIS — PERRY — STIEFEL

CHARLEMAGNE

(See Chapter X)

GOV. ROBERT BROOKE, b. at London, Eng., 3 June 1602, d. in Calvert Co. Md., 20 July 1665; m. (first) in England, 25 Feb. 1627, Mary Baker, b. at Battel, Sussex, Eng., d. 1634, at Wickham, co. Hampshire, Eng.,

COL. BAKER BROOKE, b. at Battel, co Sussex Eng., 16 Nov. 1628, d. in Calvert Co., Md., 1679; m. in Calvert Co., Md., 1664, Ann Calvert, b. in England, 164-; d. in Md., 1713, dau. of Gov. Leonard Calvert, b. in England, 1606, d. in St. Mary's Co., Md., 9 June 1647.

BAKER BROOKE, Jr., b. in Calvert Co., Md., d. in St. Mary's Co., Md., 1698; m. Katherine Marsham,

LEONARD BROOKE, d. in Prince George's Co., Md., 1736; m. Ann — , d. in Prince George's Co., Md., 1770, w.d. 15 Dec. 1769, w.p. 2 July 1770,

LEONARD BROOKE, b. 1728, d. in Prince George's Co., Md., 1785; m. in Great Britain, ca. 1755, Elizabeth Maxwell,

ESTHER MAXWELL BROOKE, b. 1755; d. in Prince George's Co., Md., 1842; m. 23 Apr. 1780, in Prince George's Co., Md., Henry Hill, Jr.; b. in Prince George's Co., Md., 1750, d. in Prince George's Co., Md., 1832,

MARY ANN HOSKINS HILL, b. in Prince George's Co., Md., 25 Aug. 1795, d. in Kent Co., Md., 14 June 1849; m. in Prince

George's Co., Md., 25 Oct. 1814, James Brooke, b. in Charles Co., Md., 1785, d. at Annapolis, Md., 2 Feb. 1822, son of Richard Brooke and grandson of Leonard Brooke and Ann — (see above),

HENRIETTA ELEANOR BROOKE, b. in Prince George's Co., Md., 25 June 1820, d. in Kent Co., Md., 17 Apr. 1877; m. in Kent Co., Md., 13 June 1837, George Hayward Willson, b. at "Ellendale", Kent Co., Md., 25 May 1810, d. there 2 Apr. 1873, a descendant of Richard Smith and Eleanor Brooke, dau. of Gov. Robert Brooke and his second wife, Mary Mainwaring,

MARY GEORGIANNA WILLSON, b. in Kent Co., Md., 13 Feb. 1842, d. in Queen Anne's Co., Md., 10 May 1906; m. at Chesterton, Md., 26 Apr. 1864, Francis Adolphus Wallis, b. in Kent Co., Md., 28 Mar. 1828, d. at Queenstown, Md., 21 June 1904,

HENRIETTA ELEANOR WALLIS, b. in Kent Co., Md., 9 Nov. 1869, d. at Hyattsville, Md., 17 June 1959; m. at Chestertown, Md., 25 June 1895, Elton Howard Perry, b. in Talbot Co., Md., 11 Nov. 1861, d. at Queenstown Md., 11 Feb. 1923,

ELEANOR BROOKE PERRY
    (See Chapter XXXVI)

Chapter XVII

BROWNE — LANE — SMITH — EELLS — PARKER — FITLER

CHARLEMAGNE, King of the Franks, Emperor of the West, b. 2 Apr. 742, d. 28 Jan. 814; m. (third) in 771, Hildegarde, b. 758, d. 30 Apr. 783, dau. of Gerold I, Count in Vinzgau,

LOUIS I, the Pious, *le Debonnaire,* King of the Franks, Emperor of the West; m. (second) in 819, Judith, d. 19 Apr. 843,

CHARLES II, the Bald, King of the Franks 840-877, Emperor of the West 875-877, b. at Frankfort-on-Main, 13 June 823, d. at Mt. Cenis in the Alps, 6 Oct. 877; m. (first) Dec. 842, Ermentrude of Orleans, d. 6 Oct. 869,

LOUIS II, the Stammerer, King of the Franks 877-879, Emperor of the West 878-879, b. 1 Nov. 846, d. at Compeigne, 10 Apr. 879; m. (second) ca. 868-70, Adelaide, d. aft. 10 Nov. 901,

CHARLES III, the Simple, King of the Franks, b. Sept. 879, d. in prison at Peronne, 7 Oct. 929; m. (third) 918/9, Princess Eadgifu, b. in England, ca. 900, d. ca. 951, dau. of Edward the Elder, King of England, and grand dau. of King Alfred the Great,

LOUIS IV, *d'Outre-Mer,* the Simple, King of the Franks, b. ca. 919/21, d. 10 Sept. 954; m. (her second) 2 Oct. 939, Princess Gerberga of Germany, b. in Saxony, ca. 913/4, d. 5 May 984, dau. of Henry the Fowler,

CHARLES, Duke of Lower Lorraine, b. 953, d. 994; m. ante 979, Bonna d'Ardennes, dau. of Godfry the Old, Count of Verdun and Ardennes,

ADELAIDE (ADELHEID) OF LORRAINE, d. aft 1012; m. Albert I, Count of Namur, d. ca. 1011, son of Robert I, Count of Lomme,

ALBERT II, Count of Namur, b. ca. 1000, d. bet. July 1063 and July 1064; m. Regilinde de Lorraine, dau. of Gothelon I, Duke of Upper and Lower Lorraine,

ALBERT III, Count of Namur, d. 1102; m. ca. 1067, Ida (or Relinde) of Saxony, wid. of Frederick, Duke of Lower Lorraine and dau. of Bernard II, Duke of Saxony, by Bertrade, dau. of Harold II, King of Norway,

GODFREY, Count of Namur, b. ca. 1067, d. 1139; m. (first) ante 1087, Sybil, dau. of Roger, Count of Chateau Porcian,

ELIZABETH DE NAMUR, b. ca. 1090; m. Gervaise, Count of Rethel 1118-1124, d. 1124,

MILICENT DE RETHEL, b. bet. 1118 and 1124; m. Robert Marmion II, d. 1143/4,

ROBERT MARMION III, d. ca. Oct. 1181; m. Elizabeth — ,

ROBERT MARMION IV, d. ca 1218; m. (first) Maude de Beauchamp,

ROBERT MARMION V, d. ca 1242; m. Juliana de Vassy,

PHILLIP MARMION, d. ante 5 Dec. 1291; m. (first) Joan de Kilpeck,

MAZERA MARMION, d. ante 5 Dec. 1291; m. Ralph de Cromwell,

JOAN DE CROMWELL, d. 1341; m. Alexander de Freville, d. 1339,

BALDWIN DE FREVILLE, b. 1303, d. 1343,

SIR BALDWIN DE FREVILLE, b. 1317, d. 1375, m. Elizabeth de Montfort,

BALDWIN DE FREVILLE, b. 1351, d. 1387/8, m. Joyce de Botetourt, b. 1367/8, d. 12 Aug. 1420, (See Chapter II, p. 8)

BALDWIN DE FREVILLE, b. 1369, d. 1400/1; m. 1338/9, Joan Greene, dau. of Sir Thomas Greene,

MARGARET DE FREVILLE, d. 1418/9, m. Hugh Willoughby of Walloton, Notts.

ELEANOR WILLOUGHBY, m. John Shirley, b. ca 1430, d. 1486,

ROBERT SHIRLEY, b. ca. 1465, liv. 1513,

RALPH SHIRLEY, 3rd son, b. ca 1495, m. Amee Lolle,

ELEANOR SHIRLEY, b. ca. 1525, bur. 28 Apr. 1595, at Snelston, co. Derby; m. Nicholas Browne, b. prob. at Snelston, co. Derby, bur. 15 Jan. 1587,

SIR WILLIAM BROWNE, b. at Snelston, co. Derby, England, d. in the Low Countries, Aug. 1610, m. Mary Savage,

PERCY BROWNE, b. ca. 1602; m. — Rich, b. ca. 1603,

NATHIANEL BROWNE, b. prob. in England, ca. 1625, d. at Middletown, Conn., ante 26 Aug. 1658; m. at Hartford, Conn., 23 Dec. 1642, Eleanor Watts, b. ca. 1627, d. at Middletown, Conn., 28 Sept. 1703,

HANNAH BROWNE, b. at Middletown, Conn., 15 Apr. 1651; m. prob. at Middletown, 5 Nov. 1669, Isaac Lane, d. at Middletown, Conn., 18 July 1711.

HANNAH LANE, b. at Middletown, Conn., 27 Mar. 1670/1, d. at Glastonbury, Conn., 27 May 1734; m. at Hartford, Conn., 27 July 1704, Benjamin Smith, b. ca. 1652, d. at Glastonbury, Conn., 20 July 1730/1

JADUTHAN SMITH, b. at Glastonbury, Conn., 23 Oct. 1709, d. at Glastonbury 20 Nov. 1781; m. (first) ante 1733, Mary Kimberly, b. at Glastonbury, Conn., 8 June 1712, d. at Glastonbury, 6 Oct. 1751,

THOMAS SMITH, b. 1741, d. at Glastonbury, Conn., 18 Aug. 1773; m. 15 June 1768, Margaret Olcott, b. at Hartford, Conn., 1 Apr. 1745,

AURORA SMITH, b. at Glastonbury, Conn., 8 June 1773, d. at Middletown, Conn., 26 Feb. 1834; m. (his first) at Middletown, Conn., 20 July 1794, Samuel Eells, b. at Middletown, Conn., 15 May 1773, d. at Richboro, Bucks Co., Pa., Dec. 1856,

RALPH SMITH EELLS, b. at Middletown, Conn., 1 Aug. 1797, d. in Bucks Co., Pa., 1845; m. (first) 2 Nov. 1821, at Middletown, Conn., Mary Catherine Williams, bapt. at Middletown, Conn., 26 Oct. 1800, d. at Middletown, Conn., 5 Dec. 1825,

SAMUEL ROBERT EELLS, bapt. at Middletown, Conn., 26 May 1825, d. at Philadelphia, Pa., 2 Mar. 1898; m. 23 Nov. 1843, in Bucks Co., Pa., Phebe Vanartsdalen Feaster, b. at Feasterville, Pa., 21 Mar. 1824, d. at Philadelphia, Pa., 13 Apr. 1905,

WALTER GIBBS EELLS, b. at Philadelphia, Pa., 23 Nov. 1861, d. at Sea Breeze, Fla., 8 Mar. 1922; m. at Philadelphia, Pa., 27 Apr. 1887, Armenia Worrell Swint, b. at Philadelphia, Pa., 24 Nov. 1861, d. at Hot Springs, Va., 12 Oct. 1937,

ELVA SOWDEN EELLS, b. at Philadelphia, Pa., 16 Dec. 1887, d. at Philadelphia, Pa., 26 May 1946; m. at Philadelphia, Pa., 27 Apr. 1910, George Laidy Parker, Jr., b. at Philadelphia, Pa., 25 Feb. 1886, d. at Philadelphia, Pa., 16 Mar. 1965,

MABELLE ELIZABETH EELLS PARKER, b. at Melrose Park, Montgomery Co., Pa., 1 Apr. 1911; ed.: Abington Friends School, the Elwood School, grad.; The Ogontz School; member: The Genealogical Society of Penna., director, Chairman of Library Accessions; Nat'l Society of Colonial Dames of America in the Commonwealth of Pa., Bd. of Mgrs., State Registrar; Daughters of Founders and Patriots of America, state Registrar, state Vice President; Daughters of the Cincinnati; DAR; Soc. of Descendants of Colonial Clergy; Swedish Colonial Soc.; Welcome Society; Huguenot Society; National Genealogical Society; Genealogical Society of N.J.; Order of the Crown of Charlemagne in the United States of America; Historical Soc. of Penna.; Chester Co., Pa. Historical

Soc.; Bucks Co., Pa., Historical Soc.; Montgomery Co., Pa., Hist. Soc.; Salem Co., N.J. Hist. Soc.; Hist. Soc. of Delaware; Conn. Hist. Soc.; Lower Merion Hist. Soc.; m. at Elkins Park, Pa., 25 Oct. 1933, Ralston Biddle Fitler, b. at Riverton, N.J., 29 May 1909, d. at Winter Park, Fla., 7 Feb. 1968,

1) RALSTON BIDDLE FITLER, JR., b. at Philadelphia, Pa., 15 Dec. 1935, m. at Butler, Pa., 20 Apr. 1963, Mary Josephine Schneider,

   a) TAMSIN LEVIS FITLER (dau.) b. 12 Aug. 1964, at Bryn Mawr, Pa.;

   b) RALSTON BIDDLE FITLER III, b. 13 Nov. 1965, at Pittsburgh, Pa.;

   c) SUSANNA RIDGWAY FITLER, b. 24 June 1969, at Pittsburgh, Pa.

2) EDWIN HENRY FITLER, b. at Philadelphia, Pa., 16 Apr. 1938, m. at Woodstock, N.Y., 30 Dec. 1961, Adele Virginia Demville,

   a) EDWIN HENRY FITLER, JR., b. 31 Jan. 1967, at Bryn Mawr, Pa.

3) WALTER EELLS FITLER, b. at Philadelphia, Pa., 9 Jan. 1942, m. at Bryn Mawr, Pa., 1 May 1964, Margo Wistar Huey,

   a) WALTER EELLS FITLER, JR., b. at Paoli, Pa., 19 Dec. 1970;

   b) KIMBERLY DURETT FITLER (dau.), b. 22 Aug. 1973, at West Chester, Pa.

Chapter XVIII

BROWNE — LANE — CANDE — HIGBEE — RATHBONE — RUSS — CROSS

CHARLEMAGNE

(See Chapter XVII)

NATHANIEL BROWNE, b. prob. in England, ca. 1625, d. at Middletown, Conn., ante 26 Aug. 1658; m. at Hartford, Conn., 23 Dec. 1642, Eleanor Watts, b. ca. 1627, d. at Middletown, Conn., 28 Sept. 1703,

HANNAH BROWNE, b. at Middletown, Conn., 15 Apr. 1651; m. prob. at Middletown, Conn., 5 Nov. 1669, Isaac Lane, b. 1639, d. at Middletown, Conn., 18 July 1711,

SARAH LANE, b. at Middletown, Conn., 29 Sept. 1678, d. at Middletown, Conn.; 30 Sept. 1737; m. at New Haven, Conn., 19 Nov. 1702, Zaccheus Cande, b. at West Haven, Conn., 5 Jan. 1674, d. at Middletown, Conn., 29 Dec. 1743,

SARAH CANDE, b. at New Haven, Conn., 3 May 1710, d. at New Haven, Conn., 6 May 1792; m. at Middletown, Conn., 9 Mar. 1731, John Higbee (Higby) b. at Middletown, Conn., 16 July 1707, d. at New Haven, Conn., 5 Dec. 1790, w.p. 4 Apr. 1791,

SARAH HIGBEE, b. at Middletown, Conn., 4 Apr. 1739, d. at Westfield, Conn., 5 Aug. 1835; m. at Middletown, Conn., 4 May 1758, Daniel Rathbone, b. in Berkshire Co., Mass., 27 Feb. 1731, d. at Milton, N.Y., 17 Jan. 1823,

VALENTINE RATHBONE, b. at Great Barrington, Mass., 17 Mar. 1768, d. at Milton, N.Y., 20 Mar. 1844; m. Love Reddington, b. 23 Feb. 1769, d. at Milton, N.Y., 28 May 1844,

HIRAM VALENTINE RATHBONE, b. at Rock City, N.Y., in 1805, d. at Jersey City, N.J., 20 Feb. 1855; m. at New York, N.Y., 17 Dec. 1847, Margaret Wanamaker, b. at New York, N.Y., 30 Sept. 1828, d. at Chicago, Ill., 18 Jan. 1904,

ANNA AUGUSTA RATHBONE, b. at Jersey City, N.J., 9 Jan. 1849, d. at Ballston Spa, N.Y., 17 Mar. 1892; m. at Pontiac, Ill., 13 Aug. 1867, Alanson Bernard Russ, b. at Galway, N.Y., 19 June 1835, d. at Canandaigua, N.Y., 26 Feb. 1920

NELLIE HOLBROOK RUSS, b. at Ballston Spa, N.Y., 13 July 1881, d. at Mission, Kansas, 6 July 1969; m. at Chicago, Ill., 5 Oct. 1904, James Franklin Cross, b. at Mission, Kan., 20 Sept. 1869, d. at Mission, Kan., 26 Feb. 1940,

J. ALAN CROSS, b. at Chicago, Ill., 7 Dec. 1906; ed.: U.S. Naval Academy; Univ. of Miami, A.B., MEd; grad studies, Ohio State Univ., Univ. of Fla.; member: Air Force Ass'n., Chapter and State President, Nat'l Director; Lions International, Club President, District Governor; SAR, Chapter President and Nat'l Committee Chairman; Huguenot Society, Chapter Pres.; Mayflower Descendants, Chapter V.P.; Order of Founders and Patriots of America; Society of Colonial Wars; Hereditary Order of Descendants of Colonial Governors; Baronial Order of Magna Charta; Order of the Crown of Charlemagne in the United States of America; m. in Florida, 13 October 1928, Delta Deitz, b. at Richwood, W. Va., 11 Nov. 1901 (See Chapter XXX)

1) J. ALAN CROSS, Jr., b. 28 Feb. 1930; B.S., Washington and Lee Univ.; Univ. of Miami, MBA; m. Mary Elizabeth Miller,

   a) MARY ELIZABETH CROSS, b. 27 May 1955;

   b) REBECCA ANN CROSS, b. 1 May 1957;

   c) DAVID SCOTT CROSS, b. 21 June 1960;

   d) JEFFREY ALAN CROSS, b. 15 July 1962;

   e) MELINDA JEAN CROSS, b. 4 Dec. 1963.

Chapter XIX

BULKELEY — PRESCOTT — HALL — PARTRIDGE — BURDEN

CHARLEMAGNE

(See Chapter XXXVIII)

MARGARET DE CLARE, b. ca. 1292, d. 13 Apr. 1342; m. (first) 1 Nov. 1307. Piers de Gavaston, Earl of Cornwall, b. at Bearn, ca. 1284, murdered at Warwick, 19 June 1312,

AMY (ANNE) DE GAVASTON, b. aft. 6 Jan. 1312; m. ca. 1334, John de Driby, b. ca. 1312 (a descendant of Henry I),

ALICE DE DRIBY, b. ca. 1340; d. 12 Oct. 1412; m. (third) Sir Anketil Malory of Kirkby, Leicestershire, d. 23 Mar. 1393,

SIR WILLIAM MALORY, of Shawbury, 2nd son, b. ca. 1380, d. 1445,

MARGARET MALORY, b. ca. 1400, d. 1438; m. Robert Corbet, of Moreton Corbet,

MARY CORBET, m. Robert Charlton, of Apley, b. ante 1430, d. aft 1472,

RICHARD CHARLTON, of Apley, b. 1450, d. 1522; m. Elizabeth (Anne) Mainwaring, dau. of William Mainwaring, of Ightfield, Shropshire,

ANNE CHARLTON, b. ca. 1480; m. ca. 1500, Randell Grosvenor, of Bellsport, b. ca. 1480, d. 1559/60,

ELIZABETH GROSVENOR, b. ca. 1515; m. Thomas Bulkeley, of Woore, b. ca. 1515/20, bur. at Market Drayton, Shrops., 1591,

REV. EDWARD BULKELEY, b. ca. 1540, d. at Odell, Bedfordshire, 1620/1; m. ca. 1566, Olive Irby, b. ca. 1547, d. at Odell, 10 Mar. 1614/5,

REV. PETER BULKELEY, b. in England, 31 Jan. 1582/3, d. at Concord, Mass., 9 Mar. 1658/9; m. (first) at Goldington, Beds., Eng. 12 Apr. 1613, Jane Allen, bapt. at Goldington, 13 Jan. 1587/8, d. at Odell, Beds., bur. 8 Dec. 1626,

REV. EDWARD BULKELEY, bapt. at Odell, Beds., Eng., 12 June 1614, d. at Chelmsford, Mass., 2 Jan. 1695/6; m. ca. 1638, Lucy Ann —,

HON. PETER BULKELEY, b. at Concord, Mass., 3 Jan. 1640/1, d. at Concord, Mass., 24 May 1688; m. at Concord, Mass., 16 Apr. 1667, Rebecca Wheeler, b. at Concord, Mass., 6 Sept. 1645, d. at Concord, Mass., 20 Feb. 1717/8,

REBECCA BULKELEY, b. at Concord, Mass., 24 Apr. 1681; m. at Concord, Mass., 9 July 1701, Dr. Jonathan Prescott, b. 5 Apr. 1677, d. at Concord, Mass., 28 Oct. 1729,

ELIZABETH PRESCOTT, b. at Concord, Mass., 2 Dec. 1713, d. at Sutton, Mass., 7 Aug. 1803; m. at Concord, Mass., 24 June 1731, Rev. David Hall, b. at Yarmouth, Mass., 5 Aug. 1704, d. at Sutton, Mass., 7 May 1789,

DR. JONATHAN HALL, b. at Sutton, Mass., 20 Jan. 1754, d. at Pomfret, Conn., 19 Aug. 1815; m. at Pomfret, Conn., 19 Apr. 1781, Bathsheba Mumford, b. 15 Nov. 1757; d. at Pomfret, Conn., 23 July 1823,

BATHSHEBA HALL, b. at Pomfret, Conn., 4 Jan. 1788, d. at Pomfret, Conn., 13 Oct. 1864; m. at Pomfret Conn., 4 June 1806, George Washington Partridge, b. at Preston, Conn., 22 Jan. 1776, d. at Stafford Springs, Conn., in 1824,

GEORGE SIDNEY PARTRIDGE, b. at Woodstock, Conn., 7 Nov. 1807, d. at Brooklyn, N.Y., 15 May 1876; m. 11 Nov. 1830, Mary Tew, at Providence, R.I.,

GEORGE SIDNEY PARTRIDGE, JR., b. at New York, N.Y., 18 Nov. 1832, d. at Lyons, France, 20 May 1875; m. at Brooklyn, N.Y., 4 Dec. 1856, Helen Derby Catlin, b. at New York, N.Y., 11 Apr. 1834, d. at Stamford, Conn., 1906-8,

WILLIAM ORDWAY PARTRIDGE, b. at Paris, France, 11 Apr. 1861, d. at New York, N.Y., 22 May 1930; m. at Venice, Italy, 14 June 1905, Margaret Ridgely Schott, b. at Philadelphia, Pa., 5 Oct. 1872, d. at New York, N.Y., 26 Dec. 1963,

MARGARET LIVINGSTON PARTRIDGE, b. at New York, N.Y., 8 Mar. 1909; m. at New York, N.Y., 16 Feb. 1931, William Armistead Moale Burden, b. at New York, N.Y., 8 Apr. 1906,

ORDWAY PARTRIDGE BURDEN, b. at New York, N.Y., 20 Nov. 1944, A.B. Magna Cum Laude, Harvard College, 1966; M.B.A., Harvard Univ. Grad. School of Business Administration, 1968; Limited Partner, William A.M. Burden & Co.; member: Advisory Committee for International Policy, International Assoc. of Chiefs of Police; Order of the Crown of Charlemagne in the United States of America; SR; Society of Colonial Wars in the State of New York; St. Nicholas Society of the City of New York, National Society Americans of Royal Descent.

Chapter XX

BULKELEY — EMERSON — READ

Charlemagne

(See Chapter XIX)

Rev. Edward Bulkeley, bapt. at Odell, Beds., Eng., 12 June 1614, d. at Chelmsford, Mass., 2 Jan. 1695/6; m. ca. 1638, Lucy Ann — ,

Elizabeth Bulkeley, b. ca. 1638, d. at Reading, Mass., 4 Sept. 1693; m. 2 or 7 Dec. 1665, Rev. Joseph Emerson, bapt. at Bishop Stratford, Herts., Eng., 25 Jan. 1621; d. at Concord, Mass., 3 Jan. 1680,

Ebeneezer Emerson, b. at Mendon (?), Mass., d. 1751; m. 1716, Mary Boutwell, b. at Reading, Mass., 1685,

James Emerson, b. at Reading, Mass., 9 Jan. 1720; m. 28 Nov. 1744, Mary Farrar, b. in N.H.,

Kendall Emerson, b. at Reading, Mass., 31 Oct. 1745, d. 5 July 1805; m. (second) Elizabeth Pratt, b. 17 Sept. 1746, d. 5 Aug. 1823,

James Emerson, b. at Reading, Mass., 17 July 1783, d. at Greenville, Ohio, 31 Jan. 1853; m. Eve Albred, of Randolph Co., N.C., b. 3 Apr. 1788,

Joseph Pratt Emerson, b. in Drake Co., Ohio, 2 Feb. 1827, d. in Montgomery Co., N.C., 13 May 1910; m. in 1859, Alice Phillips, b. in Moore Co., N.C., 30 Nov. 1831, d. in Richmond Co., N.C., 17 Mar. 1917,

Andrew Waldo Emerson, b. 18 June 1872, d. at Savannah,

Ga., 26 Dec. 1908; m. at Augusta, Ga., 27 Jan. 1898, Violet
Lee Jordan, b. at Abbeville, S.C., 23 Nov. 1879, d. at West
Palm Beach, Fla., 29 Mar. 1928,

HELEN ELIZABETH EMERSON, b. at Augusta, Ga., 23 Mar. 1899,
grad: Georgia University Teachers College; member: DAR,
Charleston Huguenot Society, Order of the Crown of
Charlemagne in the United States of America; m. at Savannah,
Ga., 24 Aug. 1923, Thomas Carpenter Read, b. at Philadelphia,
Pa., 16 July 1901, member of the Order of the Crown of
Charlemagne in the United States of America. (See Chapter
XXXI),

1) EMERSON BRACKETT READ, b. at Dobbs Ferry, N.Y., 9
Aug. 1925; B.S. 1950, The Citadel, World War II
Aviation Cadet, Post War commission Reserve First Lt.;
member: Carolina Yacht Club, Order of the Crown of
Charlemagne in the United States of America, Society of
Colonial Wars, Charleston Kiwanis Club; m. 2 Dec.
1950, at Miami, Fla., Doris Evelyn Boyd, b. at Laurens,
S.C., 3 Jan. 1924, d. 28 May 1973; m. (second) 26 Jan.
1974, at Greenville, S.C., Patricia Davenport, b. at
Greer, S.C., 14 Nov. 1927,

a) ANNE STANDISH READ, b. 4 July 1951, at Miami
Beach, Fl.; ed.: Univ. of S.C., Columbia, S.C.;
College of Charleston, Charleston, S.C.; member:
DAR, Society of Mayflower Descendants, Order
of the Crown of Charlemagne in the United States
of America, etc.; m. 25 Nov. 1972, at Charleston,
S.C., Julian Victor Brandt III, b. at Charleston,
S.C., 22 Feb. 1950

b) ELIZABETH EMERSON READ, b. 16 Feb. 1953;

c) SUSAN LEE READ, b. 26 July 1957;

d) EMERSON BRACKETT READ, Jr., b. 25 Aug. 1958.

2) THOMAS LEE READ, b. 10 May 1930, at Dobbs Ferry,
N.Y., ed.: B.S., The Citadel, 1952; member: Charleston
Rotary Club, Order of the Crown of Charlemagne in the
United States of America; m. at Wilmington, N.C., 26

July 1952, Anne Pleasants Dosher, b. at Natchez, Miss., 18 May 1932,

    a)   ANNE PLEASANTS READ, b. 4 July 1954;

    b)   HELEN EMERSON READ, b. 12 Aug. 1955;

    c)   THOMAS LEE READ, Jr., b. 5 Aug. 1958;

    d)   WILLIAM STERLING DOSHER READ, b. 22 Sept. 1964.

Chapter XXI

BULKELEY — BROWN — TUTTLE

CHARLEMAGNE

(See Chapter XIX)

Note: The Charlemagne descent of Rev. Peter Bulkeley through the Charlton line was printed in Vol. I and Vol. II of this series and is not repeated in this volume.

REV. PETER BULKELEY, b. at Odell, Beds., Eng., 31 Jan. 1582/3, d. at Concord, Mass., 9 Mar 1658/9; m. (first) at Goldington, Beds., Eng., 12 Apr. 1613, Jane Allen, bapt. at Goldington, 13 Jan. 1587/8, bur. at Odell, Beds., Eng., 8 Dec. 1626,

THOMAS BULKELEY, bapt. at Odell, Beds., Eng., 13 Apr. 1617, d. at Fairfield, Conn., 1658; m. in Conn., Sarah Jones, b. in Eng., ca. 1620, d. at Fairfield, Conn., 1682,

SARAH BULKELEY, b. at Concord, Mass., 12 Aug. 1640, d. at New Haven, Conn., 1723; m. in Conn., Eleazer Brown, b. at New Haven, Conn., bapt. 16 Oct. 1642, d. at New Haven, Conn., 23 Oct. 1714,

GERSHOM BROWN, b. at New Haven, Conn., 9 Oct. 1665, d. at New Haven, Conn.; m. at New Haven, in 1695, Hannah Mansfield, b. in Conn., 11 Mar. 1668/9, d. in Conn., 1 Nov. 1726,

ELEAZER BROWN, b. at New Haven, Conn., 12 Jan. 1696, d. at New Haven, 21 Sept. 1768; m. in Conn., 21/25 Jan. 1725, Sarah Rowe, b. in Conn., 15 Oct. 17 ——, d. in Conn., 7 May 1779,

DANIEL BROWN, b. at New Haven, Conn., 3 Nov. 1743, d. at East Haven, Conn., 9 Oct. 1788; m. at East Haven, 24 Apr. 1770, Hannah English, b. at New Haven, 29 Nov. 1749, d. at East Haven, 2 Oct. 1829,

ANER BROWN, b. at East Haven, Conn., 13 Oct. 1785, d. at East Haven, 3 Dec. 1838; m. at East Haven, Sylvia Allen, b. in Conn., 1790, d. at East Haven (liv. 1850),

SARAH A. BROWN, b. at East Haven, Conn., 7 Jan. 1825, d. at New Haven, Conn., 5 June 1910; m. at East Haven, 14 Dec. 1846, Ruel Pardee Tuttle, b. at East Haven, 11 Oct. 1825, d. at East Haven, 15 Jan. 1913,

FREDERICK RUEL TUTTLE, b. at East Haven, Conn., 14 Jan. 1848, d. at New Haven, Conn., 15 July 1902; m. at East Haven, 31 Dec. 1870, Henrietta Frisbie, b. at Hartford, Conn., 31 July 1848, d. at New Haven, 16 Sept. 1932,

BURTON LINSLEY TUTTLE, b. at East Haven, Conn., 22 Apr. 1876, d. at New Haven, Conn., 18 Jan. 1948; m. at New Haven, 11 Oct. 1906, Alta Carter, b. at New Haven, 11 Apr. 1874, d. at New Haven, 13 July 1962,

FREDERICK BURTON TUTTLE, b. at New Haven, Conn., 12 July 1908; B.A., Yale Univ., 1930; Ph.D. Yale Univ. 1942; U. S. Marine Corps, World War II; member: Soc. of Colonial Wars; S.R.; SAR; Soc. of Founders and Patriots of America, past Gov., D.C. Soc.; Baronial Order of Magna Charta; Order of the Crown of Charlemagne in the United States of America; Hereditary Order of Descendants of Colonial Governors; Descendants of Colonial Clergy; Yale Club of Washington, D.C.; etc.; m. (first) at Jonesboro, Ark., 3 Sept. 1935, Mary Emily Armstrong, b. at Jonesboro, Ark., 15 July 1914; d. at Alexandria, Va., 15 July 1972; m. (second) 14 June 1975, Mrs. Eleanor Brooke Perry Stiefel. Children by first marriage:

1) FREDERICK BURTON TUTTLE, Jr., b. 5 Jan. 1940;

2) JAMES ARMSTRONG TUTTLE, b. 5 Sept. 1943;

3) ALLEN CARTER TUTTLE, b. 2 Dec. 1944; m. Maria Shiebler,

    a) MARIKATHRYN ALLEN TUTTLE;

4) MARGARET EMILY ALTA TUTTLE, b. 18 Sept. 1946.

Chapter XXII

BULKELEY — HOUGH — HUFF — GOVE — NICHOLSON

CHARLEMAGNE

(See Chapter XIX)

REV. EDWARD BULKELEY, D.D., b. ca. 1540, d. at Odell, Bedfordshire, England, bur. 5 Jan. 1620/1; m. ca. 1566, Olive Irby, b. ca. 1547; bur. at Odell, Bedfordshire, Eng. 10 Mar. 1614/5,

ELIZABETH BULKELEY, b. 1590, in England, d. at Cambridge, Mass., 14 Oct. 1643; m. (second) at Boston, England, 9 Jan. 1618, Atherton Hough, b. at Boston, Eng., came to Boston, Mass., 4 Sept. 1633 on "Griffin", Deputy. of the Colony of Massachusetts Bay 1637, '38; d. at Boston, Mass., 11 Sept. 1650,

FERDINANDO HOUGH, b. at Wells, Me., bet. 1633-1640, d. at Rye, N. H., aft. 1702; m. at Rye, N.H., 1665, Mary Moses, b. at Rye, N.H., 1645,

THOMAS HOUGH, I, b. at Rye, N.H., bet. 1660-1675, d. at Cape Porpoise, Me., aft. 1745; m. at Kittery, Me., 2 Jan. 1700, Grace Ferris, b. at Kittery, Me., d. at Cape Porpoise, Me., bef. 1715,

THOMAS HOUGH, II, b. at Rye, N.H., 18 Aug. 1703, d. at Cape Porpoise, Me., aft. 1765; m. (first) at Portsmouth, N.H., 8 Nov. 1729, Hepsibah Banfield, bapt at Portsmouth, N.H., in Apr. 1713, d. at Arundel, Me., bef. 1746,

GEORGE BANFIELD HOUGH, b. at Arundel, Me., 1730, d. at Edgecomb, Me., bef. 1790; m. at Wells, Me., 1759, Susanna Colby, b. at Wells, Me., 5 Sept. 1732, d. at Edgecomb, Me.,

MOSES HOUGH, b. at Arundel, Me., 30 Mar. 1764, d. at Edgecomb, Me., 6 Dec. 1849; m. at Edgecomb, Me., 1 Nov. 1786, Elizabeth Chase, b. at Edgecomb, Me., 8 Mar. 1762, d. at Edgecomb, Me., 9 June 1845,

GEORGE HUFF, b. at Edgecomb, Me., 18 Feb. 1792, d. at Edgecomb, Me., 28 Oct. 1877; m. at Edgecomb, Me., 6 Mar. 1818, Esther Gove, b. at Edgecomb, Me., 28 Dec. 1797, d. at Edgecomb, Me., 24 June 1886,

ESTHER HUFF, b. at Edgecomb, Me., 22 Mar. 1829, d. at Arrowsic, Me., 22 Feb. 1916; m. at Edgecomb, Me., 26 Jan. 1865, George Edward Gove, b. at Edgecomb, Me., 26 Jan. 1841, d. at Arrowsic, Me., 16 May 1921,

ABIEL RICHMOND GOVE, b. at Edgecomb, Me., 9 May 1869, d. at Waterville, Me., 30 Sept. 1935; m. at Haverhill, Mass., 15 Sept. 1895, Eva Cole Gove, b. at Bowdoinham, Me., 25 Aug. 1866, d. at Lewiston, Me., 28 Feb. 1918,

NETTIE APPHIA GOVE, b. at Arrowsic, Me. 8 Nov. 1905; member: D. A. C.; DAR; Mayflower Society; Order of the Founders and Patriots of America; the Society of the Descendants of the Colonial Clergy; National Society Women Descendants of the Ancient and Honorable Artillery Company, Florida Court of Assistants; National Society of the Colonial Daughters of the Seventeenth Century; National Society, Daughters of 1812; Huguenot Society; New England Women; Heritage Society of Prince Edward Island, Canada; The Piscataqua Pioneers; Order of the Crown of Charlemagne in the United States of America; m. at New York, N.Y., 22 Mar. 1930, John Bixby Nicholson, M.D., b. at Bradford, Mass., 29 Mar. 1908

   1) BARBARA JEAN NICHOLSON, b. 20 Dec. 1932; m. 26 Dec. 1960, Deal Alvin Kepple;

   2) JOHN ROBERT NICHOLSON, b. 6 Dec. 1934; m. 1 Aug. 1968, Irene Castlen.

Chapter XXIII

BULKELEY — MELLOWES — WRIGHT — HEALD — BARRETT — SPAULDING — BRYANT — ZELLER — GROSS

CHARLEMAGNE

(See Chapter XIX)

REV. EDWARD BULKELEY, b. ca. 1540, bur. at Odell, Bedfordshire, Eng., 1620/1; m. ca. 1566, Olive Irby, b. in England, ca. 1547, d. at Odell, 10 Mar. 1614/5,

MARTHA BULKELEY, b. ca. 1572; m. Mr. Abraham Mellowes, d. at Charleston, Mass., w.p. in June 1639,

OLIVER MELLOWES, b. in England, ca. 1598, d. at Braintree, Mass., 1638; m. (first) at Boston, Lincs., Eng., 3 Aug. 1620, Mary James, bapt. 13 Oct. 1597,

ELIZABETH MELLOWES, b. at Sutterton, Lincs, Eng., bapt. 10 Dec. 1625, d. at Concord, Mass., 15 Feb. 1690/1, m. (first) Thomas Barrett; m. (second) ca. 1653, Edward Wright, b. at Castle Bromwich, co. Warwick, Eng., ca. 1626, d. at Concord, Mass., 28 Aug. 1691,

MARTHA WRIGHT, b. at Concord, Mass., 18 June 1659, d. at Stow, Mass., 14 June 1746; m. Israel Heald, b. at Concord, Mass., 30 July 1660, d. at Stow, Mass., 8 Sept. 1738,

MARY HEALD, (called Hale) b. at Concord, Mass., 27 Apr. 1698, d. at Acton, Mass., 1 Sept. 1758; m. ca. 1716, Deacon John Heald, b. at Concord, Mass., 18 Aug. 1693, d. at Acton, Mass., 16 May 1775,

MARTHA HEALD, b. at Concord, Mass., 4 Apr. 1718, d. at

73

Carlisle, Mass., 26 Feb. 1795; m. at Concord, Mass., 24 May 1738, John Barrett, b. at Chelmsford, Mass., 13 Dec. 1709, d. at Chelmsford, Mass., 18 Mar. 1772,

PATTY BARRETT, b. at Chelmsford, Mass., 20 Jan. 1740/1, d. at Buckfield, Me., 4 Oct. 1819; m. at Chelmsford, Mass., 29 Nov. 1764, Benjamin Spaulding, b. at Chelmsford, Mass., 5 Feb. 1739, d. at Buckfield, Me., 14 Oct. 1811,

CAPT. LEONARD SPAULDING, b. at Chelmsford, Mass., 13 Feb. 1772, d. at Buckfield, Me., 27 Aug. 1854; m. Margaretta Warren, b. 11 Jan. 1774, d. at Buckfield, Me., 13 July 1856,

CAPT. JAMES SPAULDING, b. at Buckfield, Me., 10 June 1802, d. at Earlville, Ill., 31 Oct. 1886; m. at Buckfield, Me., 5 June 1825, Cynthia Bray, b. at Minot, Me., 25 Mar. 1802, d. at Buckfield, Me., 11 Dec. 1864,

EMMA FRANCES SPAULDING, b. at Buckfield, Me., 16 Feb, 1844, d. at Manteno, Ill., 2 May, 1901; m. at Buckfield, Me., 26 June, 1864, Col. John Emory Bryant, b. at Wayne, Me., 13 Oct. 1835, d. at New York, N. Y., 27 Feb., 1900,

ALICE EMMA BRYANT, b. at Atlanta, Ga., 15 Nov. 1871, d. at East Orange, N.J., 26, Apr., 1946; m. at Mt. Vernon, N.Y., 1 Jan. 1895, Rev. Dr. Julius Christian Zeller, b. at Spring Bay, Ill., 15 Dec. 1871, d. at Kansas City, Mo., 10 Mar., 1938,

    1) MIRIAM IRENE ZELLER, b. at Hennepin, Ill., 20 Oct., 1896; ed.: Univ. of Puget Sound, Tacoma, Wash., A.B.; Huntington College, Montgomery, Ala., M.A.; Univ. of Chicago, School of Journalism; Temple Univ., Phila., Pa.; member: U.S. Daughters of 1812, Past State President, N.J.; Women Descendants, Ancient and Honorable Artillery Co., State President, N.Y.; Nat'l. Society Daughters of Founders and Patriots of America, State President, N.J.; Order of the Crown of Charlemagne in the United States of America; m. (first) at Zelleria Plantation, Yazoo City, Miss., 26 Dec. 1917, Frank Ogden, d. 1918; m. (second) at Zelleria Plantation, 26 Nov., 1927, Russell Charles Gross, b. at

Philadelphia, Pa., 27 May, 1892; d. at East Orange, N. J., June 6, 1968. Issue by second marriage:

a) ADORA GROSS, b. 7 June, 1939, Inheritor Member of the Order of the Crown of Charlemagne in the United States of America, m. Thomas Clark Bove.

2) MARGARET LOUISE ZELLER, b. at Chebanse, Ill., 26 Nov. 1902; State Teachers College (now Mississippi Southern) Hattiesburg, Miss., member: Mayflower Society in Kansas, past Governor, Deputy Governor General, member of Nat'l. Board for Kansas; Women Descendants of the Ancient and Honorable Artillery Co., President of Kansas Court; Nat'l Huguenot Society in Kansas, past President, past State Historian; DAR; U.S. Daughters of 1812, State Registrar and President Kaw Valley Chapter; Daughters of Founders and Patriots of America, State Historian; Daughters of Colonial Wars, State Registrar; Colonial Daughters of the XVII Century, state President; Americans of Armorial Ancestry; Order of the Crown of Charlemagne in the United States of America; Order of Three Crusade, 1096-1192; The Piscataqua Pioneers; etc.; m. at Topeka, Kans., 3 June 1950, Clarence Jasper Garrett, b. at Burlington, Kans., 16 Nov. 1886; d. at Emporia, Kans., 18 Feb. 1974.

Chapter XXIV

BULKELEY — MELLOWES — WRIGHT — WOOD

CHARLEMAGNE

(See Chapter XXIII)

ELIZABETH MELLOWES, b. at Sutterton, Lincs., Eng., bapt. 10 Dec. 1625, d. at Concord, Mass., 15 Feb. 1690/1, wid of Thomas Barrett, m. (second) ca. 1653, Edward Wright, b. at Castle Bromwich, Warwick, Eng., ca. 1626, d. at Concord, Mass., 28 Aug. 1691,

SAMUEL WRIGHT, b. at Concord, Mass., 12 Apr. 1661, d. at Concord, Mass., 1 Oct. 1741; m. Mary Homer, b. 26 Apr. 1664, d. 24 Dec. 1725,

JOSEPH WRIGHT, b. at Concord, Mass., 25 Dec. 1696, d. at Concord, Mass., 5 Apr. 1755; m. ca. 1719, Elizabeth Jones, b. at Concord, Mass., 17 Oct. 1700, d. 12 Oct. 1776,

PETER WRIGHT, b. at Concord, Mass., 13 Dec. 1731, d. ante 10 Oct. 1768; m. at Littleton, Mass., 1 Apr. 1755, Ellen Chase, b. 21 Dec. 1732, d. at Littleton, Mass., 17 Feb. 1810,

STEPHEN WRIGHT, b. at Littleton, Mass., 24 May 1764, d. 16 Feb. 1857; m. at Littleton, Mass., 5 Apr. 1787, Sarah Prescott, b. 31 Mar. 1765, d. at Westford, Mass., 21 Sept. 1817,

SARAH (SALLY) WRIGHT, b. at Ashby, Mass., 16 June 1791, d. at Shelburne, Mass., 20 May 1834; m. at Westford, Mass., 7 Feb. 1815, Nathan Wright, b. at Westford, Mass., 3 July 1789, d. at Westford, Mass., 17 June 1846,

WILLIAM WALLACE (WILLIS) WRIGHT, b. at Shelburne, Mass., 13 Sept. 1820, d. at Hamburg, N.Y., 16 Nov. 1903; m. at

Brooklyn, N.Y., 23 Feb. 1851, Eleanor Herdman, b. at Belfast, Ireland, 18 Apr. 1832, d. in Montgomery Co., Md., 23 May 1913,

WILLIAM WALLACE WRIGHT, JR., b. at Auburndale, Mass., 19 Apr. 1868; d. at Alexandria, Va., 20 Oct. 1946; m. at Dallas, Texas, 27 Dec. 1902, Sarah Lucinda (Sallie Lucille) Mattison, b. at Sylvarena, Miss., 13 Apr. 1879, d. at Dadeville, Ala., 21 June 1973,

CARROLL WRIGHT, b. at Wichita, Kans., 25 Oct. 1903, liv. 1974; m. at Alexandria, Va., 1 Jan. 1925, Alice Elizabeth Barron, b. at Norfolk, Va., 28 Sept. 1905, liv. 1974,

1) EDWARD BARRON WRIGHT, b. at Alexandria, Va., 16 Apr. 1926; m. at Manassas, Va., 4 Sept. 1948, Barbara Mae Beane, b. at Catlett, Va., 24 Jan. 1926,

 a) EDWARD BARRON WRIGHT, Jr., m. Linda Finkle
  i) EDWARD BARRON WRIGHT, III;

 b) BARBARA JO WRIGHT, b. 1951;

 c) ANN CAROL WRIGHT, b. 1952;

 d) BETTY ALICE WRIGHT, b. at Washington, D.C., 19 Jan. 1954; Highland School, Warrenton, Va.; Salem Academy, Winston-Salem, N.C.; Mary Baldwin College, Staunton, Va.; member: The Jamestown Society, Order of the Crown of Charlemagne in the United States of America:

 e) JOHN STEPHEN WRIGHT.

2) ROBERT MATTISON WRIGHT, b. at Alexandria, Va., 2 Oct. 1927, liv. 1974; m. at Brookmont, Md., 23 Apr. 1949, Lois Nelle Harris, b. in Stewart Co., Tenn., 11 Mar. 1927, d. 15 Oct. 1976, at Waynesboro, Va.,

 a) MARY NELLE WRIGHT, b. in Washington, D.C., 22 Feb. 1951; West Liberty State College, W. Va., B.A. 1973; member: Order of the Crown of Charlemagne in the United States of America; m.

at Fairfax, Va., 28 Aug. 1971, Craig Herbert Wood, Jr., b. at Steubenville, Ohio, 18 Sept. 1948

    i) ERIC CRAIG WOOD, b. at Steubenville, Ohio, 28 Oct. 1976.

  b) KAREN LEE WRIGHT, b. 7 Apr. 1954, Alexandria, Va.

3) CARROLL WRIGHT, Jr., m. Laura Bell Hailey, b. March 1927/8, d. 1 Dec. 1977, at Manassas, Va.,

  a) CARROLL TILDEN WRIGHT, b. Nov. 1955;

  b) LAURA ALICE WRIGHT, b. 11 Feb. 1957.

Chapter XXV

BULKELEY — SEDAM

CHARLEMAGNE

(See Chapter XIX)

Note: The Charlemagne descent of Rev. Peter Bulkeley through the Charlton line was included in Vol. I and Vol. II of this series and is not repeated in this volume.

REV. PETER BULKELEY, B.D., b. at Odell, Beds., Eng. 31 Jan. 1582/3; d. at Concord, Mass., 9 Mar. 1658/9; m. (first) at Goldington, Beds., Eng., 12 Apr. 1613, Jane Allen, bapt. at Goldington, 13 Jan. 1587/8, bur. at Odell, Beds. Eng. 8 Dec. 1626,

THOMAS BULKELEY, bapt. at Odell, Beds., Eng., 13 Apr. 1617, d. at Fairfield, Conn., 1658; m. in Conn., Sarah Jones, b. in Eng., ca. 1620, d. at Fairfield, Conn., 1682,

JOSEPH BULKELEY, b. prob at Fairfield, Conn., ca. 1644/48, d. at Fairfield, Conn., 1719; m. Martha Beers,

PETER BULKELEY, b. at Fairfield, Conn., 21 May 1684, d. at Fairfield, Conn., 15 Oct. 1752; m at Stratford, Conn., 25 Oct. 1707, Hannah Ward, d. at Stratford, Conn., 1772,

PETER BULKELEY, bapt. at Fairfield Conn., 9 Oct. 1715, d. prob. at Fairfield, Conn., 1801; m. at Fairfield, Conn., 1 Jan. 1741, Sarah Turney, d. prob. at Fairfield, Conn., ca. 1757.

PETER BULKELEY, b. at Fairfield, Conn., 13 May 1745, d. at Redding, Conn., 1813; m. at Redding, Conn., 2 Oct. 1768, Mary Green, b. at Fairfield, Conn., 8 Aug. 1751, d. aft. 1813,

EBENEEZER GREEN BULKELY, b. 30 Dec. 1787, d. at Rockford, Ill., 11 Feb. 1871; m. aft. 1833 (her second) Emily Tone,

EMERETT MILLER BULKELEY, b. at Bergen, Genessee Co., N.Y., 24 Nov. 1842, d. prob. at Miller S.D., 1 Mar. 1930; m. prob. at Rockford, Ill., 1 Oct. 1865, Robert Tate Sedam, b. in Lycoming Co., Pa., or on way to Stephenson Co., Ill., 15 Feb. 1839, d. at Miller, S.D., 6 Sept. 1929,

JOHN ALPHA SEDAM, b. in Ogle Co., Ill., 5 Nov. 1869, d. at Porterville, California, 28 Dec. 1962; m. at St. Lawrence S.D., 23 Dec. 1896, Lillian Elizabeth Patterson, b. at Rochelle, Ill., 28 May 1877, d. 30 Dec. 1952, dau. of Thomas Patterson and his wife, Margaret C. Campbell,

MARVIN GERALD SEDAM, b. at St. Paul, Minn., 26 Apr. 1908; grad. Univ. of Minn., 1933 Metalurgical Engineering degree; President of Alloy Rods Co., Division of Chemetron Co., York, Pa.; member: York Rotary Club, Country Club of York, York Hospital (Chairman of the Board), York Area Chamber of Commerce (President), St. Paul's Lutheran Church (Treasurer), Order of the Crown of Charlemagne in the United States of America; m. at Milwaukee, Wisc., 19 Sept. 1936, Helen Ann Thoreson, b. at Vining, Minn., 1 July 1903, dau. of Syver Thoreson and his wife Carrie Halverson.

1) MARVIN GERALD SEDAM II, b. 26 Aug. 1942; member of the Order of the Crown of Charlemagne in the United States of America; m. 4 Feb. 1967, Barbara Sayford.

Chapter XXVI

BULKELEY — TREAT — HADDEN

CHARLEMAGNE

(See Chapter XIX)

Note: The Charlemagne descent of Rev. Peter Bulkeley through the Charlton line was included in Vol. I and Vol. II of this series and is not repeated in this volume.

REV. PETER BULKELEY, b. at Odell, Beds., Eng., 31 Jan. 1582/3, d. at Concord, Mass., 9 Mar. 1658/9 m. (second) in early Apr. 1635, Grace Chetwood, b. ca. 1602, d. at New London, Conn., in Apr. 1669, (See Chapter XXIX, b. 90)

REV. GERSHOM BULKELEY, b. at Cambridge, Mass., Jan. 1635/6, d. at Glastonbury, Conn., 2 Dec. 1713; m. at Concord, Mass., 6 Oct. 1659, Sarah Chauncey, b. at Ware, Eng., 13 June 1631, d. at Wethersfield, Conn., 3 June 1699,

DOROTHY BULKELEY, b. at Wethersfield, Conn., d. at Glastonbury Conn., in 1757; m. at Wethersfield, Conn., 5 July 1693, Lt. Thomas Treat, b. at Wethersfield, Conn., 12 Dec. 1668, d. at Glastonbury, Conn., 17 Jan. 1712/3, son of Richard Treat and Sarah Coleman,

REV. RICHARD TREAT, b. at Glastonbury, Conn., 14 May 1694, d. ca. 1759; m. 7 Aug. 1728, Susanna Woodbridge, bapt. 6 Feb. 1703/4, dau. of Rev. Timothy Woodbridge, of Hartford, Conn., who grad. at Harvard College, 1676, was a member of the Saybrook Synod in 1708, and d. 30 Apr. 1732, ae. abt. 80 yrs.,

ASHBEL TREAT, d. ca. 1780, at Lenox, Mass; m. Dorcas Waterman, b. ca. 1729, d. at Auburn, N.Y., 8 Aug. 1804,

MOSES TREAT, b. at Lenox, Mass., 14·Mar. 1771, d. at Throop (formerly Senett), Cayuga Co., N.Y., 7 June 1843; m. at Sharon, Conn., 4 Dec. 1791, Mahala Manrow, b. at Sharon, Conn., 7 Apr. 1776, d. at Throop, N.Y., 16 July 1846,

JULIA TREAT, b. in Vermont, 2 July 1796, d. at Throop, N.Y., 20 Sept. 1875; m. at Senett, N.Y., by 1820, Joseph Hadden, Jr., b. at Hunter, Greene Co., N.Y., 4 Sept. 1797, d. at Port Byron, N.Y., 3 June 1895,

ROBERT GRIFFIN HADDEN, b. in the Town of Mentz, Cayuga Co., N.Y., 11 May 1822, d. at Port Byron, N.Y., 23 July 1896; m. at Victory, N.Y., 1 Jan. 1846, Esther M. Rumsey, b. in the Town of Victory, 30 Sept, 1822, d. at Port Byron, 28 Aug. 1902,

DELOS D. HADDEN, b. in the Town of Mentz, Cayuga Co., N.Y., 20 Nov. 1849, d. at Port Byron, N.Y., 12 June 1911; m. at Port Byron, N.Y., 6 Dec. 1871, Helen E. Smith, b. in Lennox Twp., Madison Co., N.Y., in 1849, d. at Port Byron, N.Y., 12 Jan. 1913,

CLARENCE ADELBERT HADDEN, b. at Port Byron, N.Y., 11 Oct. 1877, d. at Camillus, N.Y., 29 Apr. 1955; m. at Weedsport, N.Y., 8 Nov. 1906, Elizabeth Permelia Kenyon, b. at Port Byron, N.Y., 14 Jan. 1878, d. at Camillus, N.Y., 6 Dec. 1966,

RAYMOND DELOS HADDEN, b. at Port Byron, N.Y., 26 Aug. 1914; B.C.S., Rider College, Trenton, N.J., 1932; Pres. Stuart Drugs Ltd., Ridgeway, Ontario, Canada; member: SR; SAR, Director Buffalo Chapter; Society of Mayflower Descendants; The Huguenot Society of N.Y.; Soc. Descendants of Colonial Clergy; Order of the Crown of Charlemagne in the United States of America; m. at Ridgeway, Ont., 16 Oct. 1948, Elizabeth Annette Stuart,

1) SHARON ROBERTA HADDEN, b. 7 Jan. 1950;

2) ROBERT JOSEPH HADDON, b. 20 Feb. 1952;

3) STUART RAYMOND HADDEN, b. 12 May 1953.

Chapter XXVII

BULKELEY — TREAT — TERRY — BAUDER

CHARLEMAGNE

(See Chapter XXVI)

DOROTHY BULKELEY, m. Lt. Thomas Treat

ISAAC TREAT, b. at Glastonbury, Conn., 5 or 15 Aug. 1701, d. at Glastonbury, Conn., 29 Aug. 1763; m. at Glastonbury, Conn., 10 Dec. 1730, Rebecca Bulkeley, b. at Wethersfield, Conn., 22 Feb. 1708/9, d. at Glastonbury, Conn., 19 Oct. 1788,

LUCY TREAT, b. at Glastonbury, Conn., ca. 1743, d. at Enfield, Conn., 29 Nov. 1831; m at Enfield, Conn., 18 Nov. 1766, Joseph Terry, b. at Enfield, Conn., 7 May 1732, d. at Enfield, Conn., 23 Apr. 1809,

DANIEL TERRY, b. at Enfield, Conn., 16 June 1783, d. at Enfield, Conn., 3 Apr. 1842; m. at Enfield, Conn., 12 Oct. 1816, Mary Pease Parsons, b. at Enfield, Conn., 25 Oct. 1787, d. at Sutton, Mass., 31 Oct. 1864,

WILLIAM TERRY, M.D., b. at Enfield, Conn., 8 June 1822, d. at Ansonia, Conn., 14 June 1908; m. at Sutton, Mass, 10 May 1848, Maria Roxanna Slocomb, b. at Sutton, Mass., in Oct. 1824, d. at Ansonia, Conn., 17 Dec. 1901,

FRANKLIN SILAS TERRY, b. at Derby, Conn., 8 May 1862, d. at Black Mountain, N.C., 23 July 1926; m. at Birmingham, Conn., 25 Apr. 1886, Grace Downes, b. at Watertown, N.Y., 31 Dec. 1864, d. at Cleveland, Ohio, 9 Jan. 1953,

JEAN TERRY, b. at Chicago, Ill., 14 June 1888, grad. Vassar College, 1911 and member of Vassar College Alumnae Council since shortly after graduation, member: Society of Colonial Dames of America, Order of the Crown of Charlemagne in the United States of America, Arizona Historical Society, Tucson Country Club, Desert Garden Club, Arizona-Sonora Desert Museum, University of Arizona Foundation and President's Club, Audubon Society, m. at Wickliffe, Ohio, 19 Oct. 1912, Paul Fleming Bauder, b. at Cleveland, Ohio 25 July 1885; d. at Tucson, Arizona, 21 Aug. 1971;

1) DORIS TERRY BAUDER, b. 7 Aug. 1913, at Cleveland, Ohio; member: Colonial Dames of America, Order of the Crown of Charlemagne in the United States of America, Arizona Historical Society, The English Speaking Union, Arizona-Sonora Desert Museum, Tucson Country Club, author of cook book for circulatory disease, CUISINE SANS CHOLESTOROL;

2) PAUL FLEMING BAUDER, JR., b. at Wickliffe, Ohio, 28 Jan. 1915, m. at Boston, Mass., 10 July 1943, Barbara Elizabeth Pidgeon, b. at Framingham, Mass., 4 Feb. 1919, dau. of George Henry Pidgeon, b. at Newton, Mass., 28 Nov. 1882, d. at Framingham, Mass., Mar. 1952; m. 6 Sept. 1910, Evadne Sewell, b. at Cambridge, Mass., 6 Nov. 1884, d. at Framingham, Mass., 9 June 1974.

Chapter XXVIII

BURD — PATTERSON — NAILE — PHELPS

CHARLEMAGNE

(See Chapter XLIII)

SIR ROBERT DE BEAUMONT II, 2nd Earl of Leicester, knighted in 1122, Justiciar of England (1155-1168), b. ca. 1104, d. 5 Apr. 1168; m. aft. 1120, Amice de Montfort, dau. of Ralph de Gael de Montfort, Lord of Gael and Montfort in Brittany, Earl of Norfolk, Suffolk and Cambridge in England and his wife Emma Fitz Osbern,

HAWISE DE BEAUMONT, d. 24 Apr. 1197; m. ca 1150, William Fitz Robert, 2nd Earl of Gloucester, d. 23 Nov. 1183,

AMICE FITZ ROBERT, Countess of Gloucester, d. 1 Jan. 1224/5; m. Richard de Clare, Earl of Clare, Hertford and Gloucester, d. ca. 28 Nov. 1217,

GILBERT DE CLARE, b. prob. ca. 1180, Earl of Gloucester and Hertford, Magna Charta Surety, d. 25 Oct. 1230; m. 9 Oct. 1217, Isabel Marshall, d. at Birkhampstead, 17 Jan. 1239/40, dau. of William Marshall, Earl of Pembroke and Isabel de Clare,

ISABEL DE CLARE, b. 2 Nov. 1226, liv. 10 July 1264; m. (his first) May 1240, Sir Robert de Brus, d. 31 Mar. 1295, son of Robert de Brus, Lord of Annandale and Isabel, dau. of David, Earl of Huntingdon,

SIR ROBERT DE BRUS, Lord of Annandale, b. July 1243, d. ante 4 Apr. 1304; m. (first) 1271, Margery, Countess of Carrick, d. ante 27 Oct. 1292, dau. of Neil, Earl of Carrick and Margaret, dau. of Walter, High Steward of Scotland,

CHRISTIAN BRUCE, d. 1356-7, sister of Robert Bruce, King of Scotland; m. in or aft. 1292, Gratney, Earl of Mar, d. ante, Sept. 1305, son of Donald, Earl of Mar and Helen, dau. of Llewellyn, Prince of North Wales,

LADY ELLEN OF MAR, m. Sir John de Mentieth of Arran, d. ante 1334, son of John de Mentieth,

CHRISTIAN MENTIETH, d. 1387/8; m. Sir Edward Keith of Synton, son of Sir Edward Kieth, Marshal of Scotland and Isabel de Synton,

JANET KIETH, wid. of Sir David Barclay; m. Sir Thomas Erskine, d. bet. 11 Nov. 1403 and 18 May 1404, of Alloa and Dun,

SIR ROBERT ERSKINE, 1st Lord Erskine, d. bet. 7 Sept. 1451 and 6 Nov. 1452; m. soon aft. 20 Dec. 1400, Elizabeth Lindsay, dau. of David Lindsay, 1st Earl of Crawford and Elizabeth, dau. of Robert II, King of Scotland,

THOMAS ERSKINE, Lord Erskine, d. in or shortly bef. 1493; m. bef. 1445, Janet Douglas, liv. Aug. 1489, dau. of James Douglas, Lord of Dalkeith and Earl of Morton and Joan Stewart dau. of James I, King of Scots and Joan Beaufort,

ALEXANDER ERSKINE, Lord Erskine, Gov. of Dunbarton Castle; m. (first) ante 9 Oct. 1466, Christian Crichton, d. bet. Nov. 1477 and Mar. 1478, dau. of Sir Robert Crichton and wid. of Sir Tobert Colville,

ROBERT ERSKINE, Lord Erskine, d. at the Battle of Flodden, 9 Sept. 1513; m. 1485, Isabel Campbell, liv. 14 Dec. 1518, 1st dau. of Sir George Campbell and his 1st wife,

JAMES ERSKINE, 1st Laird of Balgouny of Little Sauchie, co. Sterling, d. 1592-6; m. ante 1541, Christine Sterling,

ALEXANDER ERSKINE, 1st Lord of Shielfield, d. ante 20 Jan. 1580; m. Elizabeth Haliburton, dau. of Walter Halyburton and Agnes Stewart,

RALPH ERSKINE, 2nd Laird of Shielfield, d. 13 Feb. 1645; m. (first) Isabelle Cairncross,

JOHN ERSKINE, 3rd Laird of Shielfield, b. 26 Aug. 1589, d. 16 Dec. 1672; m. 28 Mar. 1617, Margaret Haliburton, b. 1593, d. 12 Dec. 1668, dau. of James Haliburton,

JAMES ERSKINE, 4th Laird of Shielfield; m. 1656, Elizabeth Carre, dau. of Thomas Carre of Cavers.

— ERSKINE, dau.; m. Patrick Haliburton, d. 29 June 1703, son of John Haliburton of Muirhouselaw and Jean Pringle,

GEORGE HALIBURTON, Lord Provost of Edinburgh, b. 1685, d. 3 Sept. 1742; m. (first) 23 Feb. 1704, Jean Clark, dau. of George Clark,

JEAN HALIBURTON, b. at Edinburgh, Scotland, 19 Apr. 1705; m. 16 Feb. 1724, Edward Burd, b. 18 Feb. 1700, son of James Burd and Margaret Brown,

COL. JAMES BURD, b. at Ormiston, Scotland, 10 Mar. 1725, d. nr. Harrisburg, Pennsylvania, 5 Oct. 1793; m. 14 May 1748, Sarah Shippen, b. at Lancaster, Pa., 22 Feb. 1730, d. 17 Sept. 1784, dau. of Edward Shippen and Sarah Plumley,

JANE (JEAN) BURD, b. 12 Aug. 1757, d. 31 Oct. 1814; m. 8 Aug. 1783, George Patterson, b. in Juniata Co., Pa., 24 July 1762, d. at Chestnut Hill, Philadelphia, Pa., 31 Oct. 1814, son of Capt. James Patterson and Mary Stuart,

GEORGE PATTERSON, b. at Juniata, Pa., 1797, d. 3 July 1871; m. (second) Lydia Ann Adams, b. 7 May 1843, d. 25 Aug. 1907, dau. of William Adams and Lydia Gamble,

EMMA JEAN (JANE) PATTERSON, b. at Pottsville, Pa., 23 Mar. 1847, d. at Morristown, Pa., 7 Sept. 1931; m. at Morristown, Pa., 1 Jan. 1867, Frederick Irvin Naile, b. at Bridgeport, Pa., 11 Oct. 1841, d. 25 May 1918,

FREDERICK RAYMOND NAILE, b. at Philadelphia, Pa., 15 June 1880, d. at Philadelphia, Pa., 5 Nov. 1937; m. 16 May 1908, at

Philadelphia, Pa., Caroline White Paulding, b. at Philadelphia, Pa., 31 Mar. 1882, d. at Washington, D.C., 7 May 1964,

ANN PAULDING NAILE, b. at Germantown, Philadelphia, Pa., 31 Jan. 1909, d. at Philadelphia, Pa., 2 May 1963; m. at Philadelphia, Pa., 14 Feb. 1931, Charles Mortimer Phelps, b. at Racine, Wisc., 9 Apr. 1903, d. at Philadelphia, Pa., 19 Nov. 1956,

ANN NAILE PHELPS, b. at Philadelphia, Pa., 8 June 1946; member: Colonial Dames of America, Chapter II; Penn. Society of Mayflower Descendants; Order of the Crown of Charlemagne in the United States of America; The Welcome Society of Penna; Acorn Club, Philadelphia; Sedgeley Club, Phila.; Philadelphia Cricket Club; Mantoloking Yacht Club, Mantoloking, N. J.; grad. Finch College, New York, N.Y., B.A. 1968.

Chapter XXIX

CHETWOOD — BULKELEY — WEBB — FOSTER — CHAPMAN — TERRY — TOMASELLO — BOVIS

CHARLEMAGNE

(See Chapters XXXVI and XXXVIII)

EDWARD I, King of England 1272-1307, b. at Winchester, 17 June 1239, d. nr. Carlisle, 7 July 1307; m. (first) 18 Oct. 1254, Eleanor of Castile, d. 29 Nov. 1290, dau. of St. Ferdinand III, King of Castile and Leon, by his second wife, Jeanne de Dammartin, Countess of Pouthieu,

PRINCESS ELIZABETH, b. at Rhudlan Castle, Carnarvon, Wales, Aug. 1282, d. 5 May 1316; m. at Westminster Abbey, 14 Nov. 1302, Humphrey de Bohun VIII, Earl of Hereford and Essex, b. 1276, d. 16 Mar. 1321/2, at Boroughbridge,

ELEANOR DE BOHUN, d. 7 Oct. 1363; m. 1327, James Butler, 1st Earl of Ormonde, b. 1305, d. 6 Jan. 1337/8,

JAMES BUTLER, 2nd Earl of Ormonde, b. at Kilkenny Castle, Ireland, 4 Oct. 1331, d. at Knocktopher Castle, Ireland, 1382; m. Elizabeth Darcy, d. 24 Mar. 1389/90,

JAMES BUTLER, 3rd Earl of Ormonde, b. aft. 1361, d. at Gowran, Ireland, Sept. 1405; m. ante 17 June 1386, Anne Welles,

JAMES BUTLER, 4th Earl of Ormonde, b. ca. 1390, d. at Ardee, Ireland, 23 Aug. 1452; m. ca. 28 Aug. 1413, Elizabeth de Beauchamp, d. nr. Shere, Aug. 1430,

ELIZABETH BUTLER, b. 1420, d. 8 Sept. 1473; m. ante Mar. 1444/5, Sir John Talbot, 2nd Earl of Shrewsbury, b. 1413, d. at the Battle of Northampton, 10 July 1460,

SIR GILBERT TALBOT, of Grafton, co. Worcester, b. 1452, d. 19 Sept. 1516; m. Audrey Cotton, of Landwade, co. Cambridge,

SIR JOHN TALBOT, of Grafton, co. Worcester, b. 1485, d. 10 Sept. 1549; m. Margaret Troutbeck, of Mobberley, co. Cheshire, b. 1492; d. aft. 1521,

ANNE TALBOT, of Grafton, co. Worcester, b. 1515; m. Thomas Needham, of Shenton, co. Salop. b. 1510, d. ante 1556,

ROBERT NEEDHAM, of Shenton, co. Salop, b. 1535, d. 18 Dec. 1603; m. Frances Aston, of Tixall, co. Stafford,

DOROTHY NEEDHAM, of Shenton, co. Salop, b. 1570, d. aft. 1629; m. Sir. Richard Chetwood, b. ca. 1560, d. aft. 1631,

GRACE CHETWOOD, b. in England, ca. 1602, d. at New London, Conn., 21 Apr. 1669; m. (his second) in England, Apr. 1635, Rev. Peter Bulkeley, b. at Odell, co. Bedford, England, 31 Jan. 1582/3, d. at Concord, Mass., 9 Mar. 1658/9 (See Chapter XXVI, p. 81)

REV. GERSHOM BULKELEY, b. at Cambridge, Mass., Jan. 1635/6, d. at Glastonbury, Conn., 2 Dec. 1713; m. at Concord, Mass., 6 Oct. 1659, Sarah Chauncey, b. at Ware, England, 13 June 1631; d. at Wethersfield, Conn., 3 June 1699,

EDWARD BULKELEY, b. at Wethersfield, Conn., ca. 1677, d. at Wethersfield, Conn., 17 Aug. 1748; m. at Concord, Mass., 14 July 1702, Dorothy Prescott, b. at Concord, Mass., 31 May 1681, d. at Wethersfield, Conn., 30 Nov. 1760,

CHARLES BULKELEY, b. at Wethersfield, Conn., 25 Mar. 1703, d. at Wethersfield, Conn., 21 Feb. 1758; m. at Wethersfield, Conn., 28 May 1724, Mary Sage, b. at Middletown, Conn., 9 Apr. 1699; d. at Wethersfield, Conn., 5 Oct. 1756,

MARY BULKELEY, b. at Wethersfield, Conn., 9 June 1725, d. at Wethersfield, Conn., 2 Dec. 1762; m. at Wethersfield, Conn., 20 May 1750, David Webb, b. at Boston, Mass., ca. 1717, d. at sea, 9 Oct. 1770,

ELIZABETH WEBB, b. at Wethersfield, Conn., ca. 1751, d. in Conn., ca. 1816; m. at Wethersfield, Conn., 4 Sept. 1769, Samuel Foster, b. at Southampton, Long Island, N.Y., 12 June 1739, d. at Rocky Hill, Conn., 13 Nov. 1797,

ELIZABETH FOSTER, b. at Wethersfield, Conn., 22 Apr. 1776, d. 8 May 1807; m. in Conn., 26 Mar. 1796, Titus Chapman, b. at Westbrook, Conn., 22 Apr. 1770, d. at Ithaca, N.Y., in 1818,

FOSTER SAMUEL CHAPMAN, b. in Conn., 21 Apr. 1797, d. at Pensacola, Florida, 1830-34; m. at Pensacola, Fla., 2 Nov. 1823, Elizabeth Sarah Moore, b. in Tennessee, ca. 1810, d. in Georgia, ca. 1850,

ELIZABETH CHAPMAN, b. at Pensacola, Fla., ca. 1824, d. at Santa Rosa, Fla., ca. 1895; m. at Columbus, Ga., 12 Nov. 1840, Sterling Terry, b. in Georgia, 19 Apr. 1818, d. at Molina, Fla., ca. 1890,

EULALIA CHAPMAN TERRY, b. at Columbus, Ga., 22 Feb. 1863, d. at Tampa, Fla., 30 Aug. 1934; m. in Santa Rosa Co., Fla., 21 Dec. 1884, Peter Tomasello, b. at Estrigno, Austria-Hungary, 10 Feb. 1861; d. at Orlando, Fla., 9 Feb. 1938,

MAMIE REGINA TOMASELLO, b. in Santa Rosa Co., Fla., 22 Sept. 1885, d. at Kissimmee, Fla., 7 Dec. 1973; m. in Santa Rosa Co., Fla., 10 Feb. 1904, John Bovis, b. at Oak Grove, Fla., 5 Oct. 1878, d. at Bay Pines, Fla., 11 Oct. 1948,

HENRY PIETRO BOVIS, b. at Bagdad, Fla., 4 Jan. 1907; m. at Okeechobee, Fla., 26 Jan. 1927, Vassie Curtis Wright, b. in Levy Co., Fla., 29 Dec. 1911,

HENRY EUGENE BOVIS, b. at Kenansville, Fla., 31 Mar. 1928; ed.: Univ. of Fla., Gainesville, B.A. cum laude, 1948, M.A., 1950; Université de Grenoble France, Certificate d'études francaise, 1951; American University, Washington, D.C., Ph.D., 1968; Foreign Service Officer (Diplomatic Service of the United States); member: International Studies Ass'n., American Foreign Service Ass'n., American Political Science Ass'n, Middle East Studies Ass'n., Middle East Institute, Phi

91

Beta Kappa, Society of Mayflower Descendants, SAR, Order of the Crown of Charlemagne in the United States of America; Baronial Order of Magna Charta; m. at Washington, D.C., 24 June 1958, Beatrice Louise Wilfong, b. in Highland Co., Va., 11 Sept. 1927,

1)   HENRY EUGENE BOVIS, JR., b. 28 Apr. 1959.

Chapter XXX

CLAYPOOLE — OSBORNE — ALDERSON — McCLUNG — DEITZ — CROSS

CHARLEMAGNE

(See Chapter XLIV)

WILLIAM III D'AUBIGNY, 3rd Earl of Sussex and Arundel, Crusader of 1218-19 (Fifth Crusade), d. at Cainell, Italy, ante 30 Mar. 1220/1; m. Mabel of Chester (See Chapter LXXXIV)

ISABEL D'AUBIGNY, m. John FitzAlan, Lord of Clum,

JOHN FITZ ALAN, Earl of Arundel, d. ante 10 Nov. 1267; m. Maud de Boteler, d. 27 Nov. 1283,

JOHN FITZ ALAN, Earl of Arundel, b. 14 Sept. 1246, d. 18 Mar 1271/2; m. Isabella Mortimer,

SIR RICHARD FITZ ALAN, Earl of Arundel, b. 3 Feb. 1266/7, d. 9 Mar. 1301/2; m. ante 1285, Alasia de Saluzzo, d. 25 Sept. 1292,

SIR EDMUND FITZ ALAN, Earl of Arundel, b. 1 May 1285, beheaded at Hereford, 17 Nov. 1326; m. Alice de Warenne, d. ante 23 May 1338,

SIR RICHARD FITZ ALAN, Earl of Arundel, b. 1306, d. 24 Jan. 1375/6; m. 5 Feb. 1344/5, Eleanor de Lancaster, d. at Arundel, 11 Jan. 1372,

SIR RICHARD FITZ ALAN, Earl of Arundel, b. 1346, d. 1397; m. Elizabeth de Bohun, d. 1385,

ELIZABETH FITZ ALAN, d. 8 July 1425; m. ante 19 Aug. 1401, Sir Robert Goushill of Hoveringham, Notts.,

ELIZABETH GOUSHILL, b. in Notts., Eng., ca. 1401-14; m. Sir Robert Wingfield, b. 1403, bur. at Letheringham, co Suffolk, ante 21 Nov. 1454,

SIR HENRY WINGFIELD, b. ca. 1439/40, d. in co. Suffolk, 6 May 1494; m. (second) ca. 1470, Elizabeth Rook (Rookes), bur. at Westthorpe, co. Suffolk,

SIR ROBERT WINGFIELD, b. at Upton, Eng., d. at Northampton, 4 Feb. 1575; m. Margery Quarles, d. aft. 14 June 1574,

SIR ROBERT WINGFIELD, b. at Upton, Eng., d. 31 Mar. 1580; m. Elizabeth Cecil, d. 6 Dec. 1611,

DOROTHY WINGFIELD, b. at Upton, Eng., d. at Norborough, Eng., 7 Nov. 1619; m. 30 Sept. 1586, Adam Claypoole, b. at Norborough, Eng., bapt. 20 June 1565, d. 1634,

SIR JOHN CLAYPOOLE, b. in England, bapt. 13 Apr. 1595, d. at Norborough, Eng., ca. 1664; m. at London, Eng., 8 June 1622, Mary (Maria) Angell, b. prob. at London, Eng., d. at Norborough, Eng. 10 Apr. 1661,

JAMES CLAYPOOLE, b. in England, 8 Oct. 1634, d. at Philadelphia, Pa., 6 Aug. 1687; m. at Bremen, Germany, Helena Mercer,

JAMES CLAYPOOLE, b. at London, Eng., 6 Dec. 1664, d. at Newcastle, Delaware, ca. 1706; m. ca 1686, Mary Cann,

JAMES CLAYPOOLE, b. in Delaware, 14 Feb. 1701, d. in Hampshire Co., Va., 7 Nov. 1789; m. Jane — , b. 1701, d. in Hampshire Co., Va. 9 Nov. 1788,

ELIZABETH CLAYPOOLE, b. in Augusta Co., Va., ca. 1739, d. in Greenbrier Co., Va., ante 1805; m. John Osborne, b. in England, 1730, d. in Greenbrier Co., Va., in 1806,

SARAH OSBORNE, b. in Greenbrier Co., Va., 1760, d. in Kanawha Co., Va.; m. 14 June 1781, in Greenbrier Co., Va., George Alderson, b. in Rockbridge Co., Va., 30 Aug. 1762, d. in Kanawha Co., Va. in 1811,

MARY ALDERSON, b. in Greenbrier Co., Va., 13 May 1787, d. at Mt. Lookout, W. Va., 13 May 1870; m. 15 Mar. 1803, in Greenbrier Co., Va., James McClung, b. in Rockbridge Co., Va., 24 Mar. 1770, d. in Greenbrier Co., Va., 24 July 1824,

SARAH LOUISA MCCLUNG, b. in Greenbrier Co., Va., 22 May 1812, d. at Mt. Lookout, W. Va., 28 Nov. 1866; m. 2 Dec. 1832, John Deitz, b. in Greenbrier Co., Va., 6 June 1809, d. in Nicholas Co., W. Va., 6 Jan. 1888,

JOSEPH DICKINSON DEITZ, b. in Greenbrier Co., Va. 17 July 1841, d. at Carl, W.Va., 13 May 1919; m. in Nicholas Co., W.Va., 2 Nov. 1865, Virginia Frances Ellis, b. in Monroe Co., Va., 20 June 1840, d. at Carl, W.Va., 1924.

EMERSON ELLIS DEITZ, b. in Nicholas Co., W.Va., 13 Dec. 1869, d. at Richwood, W.Va., 20 Jan. 1944; m. 22 Nov. 1899, in Nicholas Co., W.Va., Bessie Mae Spencer, b. in Nicholas Co., W.Va., 16 Nov. 1881, d. at Richwood, W.Va., 26 Jan. 1967,

DELTA DEITZ, b. at Richwood, W.Va., 11 Nov. 1901; A.B. Denison Univ., graduate study at Univ. of Miami; member: Genealogical Society of Greater Miami, N.E.H.G.S., DAR, U.D.C., Order of the Crown of Charlemagne in the United States of America, Kappa Kappa Gama, Women's Panhellenic Ass'n. of Miami; m. 13 Oct. 1928, in Florida, J. Alan Cross, b. at Chicago, Ill., 7 Dec. 1906 (See Chapter XVIII)

   1) J. ALAN CROSS, Jr., b. 28 Feb. 1930; m. Mary Elizabeth Miller.

Chapter XXXI

CONYERS — CONVERSE* — TOWER — READ

CHARLEMAGNE

(See Chapter X)

ROGER DE QUINCY, 2nd Earl of Winchester and Constable of Scotland, accompanied his father on the Fifth Crusade in 1219, d. 25 Apr. 1264; m. Helen of Galloway, d. 1245, dau. of Alan, Lord of Galloway and Constable of Scotland,

MARGARET DE QUINCY, d. ca. 12 Mar. 1280/1; m. ca. 1238, William de Ferrers, Earl of Derby, bur. 31 May 1254,

WILLIAM DE FERRERS, b. at Groby, co. Leicester, ca. 1240, d. 1287/8; m. Anne le Despenser, of Ryhall-Rutland,

ANNE DE FERRERS, of Groby, m. John, 2nd Lord Grey, b. at Wilton, d. 1323,

HENRY DE GREY, of Wilton, b. 28 Oct. 1282, d. 10/16 Dec. 1342; m. Anne Rockley,

REGINALD DE GREY, of Wilton, b. 1 Nov. 1311, d. at Shirland, 4 June 1370; m. ante 10 Jan. 1327, Maud Boutetourt, of Wesley, d. at Shirland, 14 Sept. 1391,

SIR HENRY DE GREY, of Wilton on Wye, d. 1394/96; m. Elizabeth deTalbot,

MARGARET DE GREY, of Wilton, d. 1 June 1454; m. John, 5th Baron d'Arcy, of Knayth, ca. 1377, d. 9 Dec. 1411,

SIR PHILIP D'ARCY, b. ca. 1398, d. 2 Aug. 1418; m. 28 Oct. 1412, Eleanor FitzHugh, of Ravensworth, d. 30 Sept. 1457,

96

MARGARET D'ARCY, b. at Ravensworth, 1 Sept. 1418, d. ante 20 Apr. 1469; m. ante 20 Nov. 1431, Sir John Conyers, Knt., of Hornsby, Yorkshire, d. 14 Mar. 1489/90,

SIR JOHN CONYERS, of Hornsby, Yorkshire, d.v.p. 1470; m. Alice Neville,

REGINALD CONYERS, of Wakerly, Northants, d. 1514; m. Anna Norwich, b. at Brampton, d. 1514,

RICHARD CONYERS, of Wakerly, Northants,

CHRISTOPHER CONYERS, bapt. at Wakerly, Northants, 27 Mar. 1552; m. 1589, Mary Halford, of Winstow, co. Lancaster (?),

EDWARD CONYERS*, b. at Wakerly, Northants, England, 30 Jan. 1590, d. at Woburn, Mass., 10 Aug. 1663, came with the Winthrop fleet, 1630, set up a ferry between Boston and Charleston, 14 June 1661, removed to Woburn, 1640 where he was deacon and a town officer; m. in England, Sarah — , d. 14 Jan. 1662,

SERGT. SAMUEL CONVERSE, bapt. at Charleston, Mass., 12 Mar. 1637/8; d. 20 Feb. 1669; m. 8 June 1660, Judith Carter, d. 1678,

SAMUEL CONVERSE, b. at Woburn, Mass., 4 Apr. 1662, d. in Thompson Parish, Killingly, Conn., ca. 1732; m. ante 1694, Dorcas Cain (Pain),

ENS. EDWARD CONVERSE, b. at Woburn, Mass., 25 Sept. 1696, d. at Thompson, Conn., (?) 9 July 1784; m. 6 Aug. 1717, Elizabeth Cooper, d. 19 Feb. 1776,

CAPT. EDWARD CONVERSE, bapt. at Killingly, Conn., 8 Nov. 1720, d. at Windsor, Conn., 9 Dec. 1800; m. Mary Davis,

SAMUEL DAVIS CONVERSE, bapt. 17 Feb. 1742, d. at Worthington, Mass., ca. 1831; m. Mahitable Harris, d. at Worthington, Mass.,

*See Foreword   97

ELISHA CONVERSE, b. ca. 1774; d. ca. 1852; m. Lucy Curtis Matthews, d. at Worthington, Mass.,

LUCY C. CONVERSE, b. 12 Nov. 1806, d. at Worthington, Mass., 21 May 1877; m. at Worthington, Mass., 12 Mar. 1832, Lyman Josselyn Tower, b. at Worthington, Mass., 29 May 1809, d. at Worthington, Mass., ca. 1885,

CAPT. ELISHA C. TOWER, b. at Worthington, Mass., 10 Dec. 1834, d. at Worthington, 7 Aug. 1886; m. at Hinsdale, Mass., 4 July 1856, Elzina Stebbins, b. at Chester, Mass., 23 Apr. 1836, d. at Pittsfield, Mass., 29 June 1906,

ROSA GEORGIANNA TOWER, b. at Worthington, Mass., 20 July 1866, d. at New York, N.Y., 13 Jan. 1920; m. at Philadelphia, Pa., 2 Oct. 1897, Harry Humphrey Read, b. at Woburn, Mass., 25 Jan. 1867, d. at Philadelphia, Pa., 5 Sept. 1933,

THOMAS CARPENTER READ, b. at Chestnut Hill, Pa., 16 July 1901; grad. Gilbert Johnson School of Law, Savannah, Ga.; studied at Beaux Arts, New York, N.Y.; grad. in Mural Painting, School of Industrial Arts, New York; member: SAR, South Carolina Society of Mayflower Descendants, Baronial Order of Magna Charta, Order of the Crown of Charlemagne in the United States of America, The Military Order of the Crusades, Charleston Lions Club, James Island Exchange Club — past President; m. at Savannah, Ga., 24 Aug. 1923, Helen Elizabeth Emerson, b. at Augusta, Ga., 23 Mar. 1899,

1) EMERSON BRACKETT READ;

2) THOMAS LEE READ.

(See Chapter XX)

Chapter XXXII

COTTER — FERRELL

CHARLEMAGNE, King of the Franks, Emperor of the West, b. 2 Apr. 742, d. 28 Jan. 814; m. (third) 771, Hildegarde of Swabia,

LOUIS I, King of the Franks, Emperor of the West (814-840), b. Aug. 778, d. nr. Mainz, Germany, 20 June 840; m. 794/5, Ermengarde, d. ca. 3 Oct. 818, dau. of Ingerman, Count of Hasbaye,

LOTHAIR I, King of Italy, Emperor of the West (840-855), b. 795, d. at Pruem, Germany, 29 Sept. 855; m. 15 Oct. 821, Ermengarde, d. 20 Mar. 851, dau. of Hugh II, Count of Orleans,

ERMENGARDE, of Lorraine, m. 846, Count Giselbert,

REGNIER I, Count of Hainaut, d. 916; m. (first) Hersent of France

GISELBERT, Duke of Lorraine, d. 939; m. Gerberga, d. 5 May 984,

GERBERGA, of Lorraine; m. Albert I, the Pious, Count of Vermandois, b. ca. 920, d. 9 Sept. 987/8, son of Herbert II, Count of Vermandois and Troyes,

HERBERT III, Count of Vermandois, b. ca. 955, d. ca. 1000; m. (her second) Ermengarde, dau. of Reinald, Count of Bar,

OTHO, Count of Vermandois, b. ca. 1000, d. 25 May 1045; m. Parvie (Pavie),

HERBERT IV, Count of Vermandois and of Valois, b. ca. 1032, d. ca. 1080; m. Adela de Vexin, dau. of Raoul III, the Great, Count of Valois, Vexin, etc.,

99

ADELAIDE (ADELHEID), Countess of Vermandois and Valois, d. ca. 1120; m. Hugh the Great, Duke of France and Burgundy, Marquis of Orleans, Count of Amiens, etc., d. 1101, son of Henry I, King of France,

ISABEL DE VERMANDOIS, Countess of Leicester, d. ante July 1147; m. (first) 1096, Robert de Beaumont, Seigneur of Beaumont, Pont-Audemer, Brionne, and Vatteville, in Normandy, Count of Meulan in French Vexin, Earl of Leicester, b. 1046; d. 5 June 1118; son of Roger de Beaumont, (See Chapters X, XXXIX, XLIII, LXVIII)

ISABEL DE BEAUMONT, m. Gilbert de Clare, Earl of Pembroke, d. 6 Jan. 1147/8,

RICHARD DE CLARE, Strongbow, 2nd Earl of Pembroke, b. ca. 1130, d. ca. 20 Apr. 1176; m. ca. 26 Aug. 1171, Eva MacMurrough, dau. of Dermot MacMurrough, King of Leinster, Ireland,

ISABEL DE CLARE, d. 1220; m. Aug. 1189, Sir William Marshall, 3rd Earl of Pembroke, Marshal of England, Regent of the Kingdom, 1216-19, b. 1146, d. 14 May 1219,

MAUD MARSHALL, d. 1248; m. (first) 1207, Sir Hugh Bigod II, 3rd Earl of Norfolk and Suffolk, a Surety for Magna Charta; b. ante 1195, d. 1224/5,

ISABEL BIGOD, m. (second) aft. 1230, Sir John FitzGeoffrey, of Shere, Farnbridge, Justiciar of Ireland, d. 23 Nov. 1258,

MAUD FITZ JOHN, bur. 7 May 1301; m. (second) ante 1270, William de Beauchamp, 9th Earl of Warwick, b. 1237, bur. 22 June 1298, son of William de Beauchamp, and his wife, Isabel de Mauduit,

ISABEL DE BEAUCHAMP, d. ca. 30 May 1306; m. Sir Patrick Chaworth, of Kidwelly, Wales, d. ca. 7 July 1283,

MAUD DE CHAWORTH, bur. at Mottis Font Priory, ante 3 Dec. 1322; m. 1298, Henry Plantagenet, b. ca. 1281, bur. at Newark

Abbey, Leics., 22 Sept. 1345, son of Edmund Plantagenet, and Blanche of Artois, his second wife,

JOAN PLANTAGENET, b. ca. 26 Feb. 1326/7, prob. d. and bur. 7 July 1349, at Byland; m. John de Mowbray, b. at Hovington, co. York, 29 Nov. 1310; d. at York, 4 Oct. 1361,

ALIANORE DE MOWBRAY, d. ante 18 June 1387; m. ante 23 July 1358, Roger de la Warre, 3rd Lord de la Warre, b. 30 Nov. 1326, d. in Gascony, 27 Aug. 1370,

JOAN DE LA WARRE, d. 24 Apr. 1404; m. 1390, Sir Thomas West,

SIR REYNOLD DE WEST, 6th Lord de la Warre, b. 7 Sept. 1395, d. 27 Aug. 1450; m. ante 17 Feb. 1428/9, Margaret Thorley, d. ante 24 Nov. 1433,

SIR RICHARD WEST, 7th Lord de la Warre, b. ca. 28 Oct. 1430, d. 10 Mar. 1475/6; m. ante 10 June 1451, Katherine Hungerford, d. 12 May 1493,

SIR THOMAS WEST, 8th Lord de la Warre, b. 1457, bur. at Broadwater, 10 Oct. 1525; m. Eleanor Copley,

SIR GEORGE WEST, of Lechlade, co. Gloucester, d. 1538; m. Elizabeth Morton,

SIR WILLIAM WEST, 10th Lord de la Warre, b. ca. 1520, d. at Wherwell, Northants, 30 Dec. 1595; m. ante 1555, Elizabeth Strange,

SIR THOMAS WEST, 11th Lord de la Warre, b. 1556, d. 24 Mar. 1601/2; m. 19 Nov. 1571, Anne Knollys,

LETITIA WEST, m. 1619, Sir Henty Ludlow, b. at Hill Deverill, Wilts., 1577, d. 16 Oct. 1639,

HENRY LUDLOW, b. 1633, at Maiden Bradley, Wilts., d. 1698; m. 1657, Catherine Webster, d. in Ireland, 1703,

STEPHEN LUDLOW, b. nr. Merthyr Tydvil, Wales, 1680, d. in Ireland, 21 Oct. 1721; m. 1702, — Lachard, b. in Wales, 1682, d. in Ireland, 1746,

ELIZABETH LUDLOW, b. and d. in Ireland; m. Rt. Hon. John Rogerson, Lord Chief Justice of King's Bench,

ARABELLA ROGERSON (CASAUBON), d. at Mallow, co. Cork, Ireland, in Apr. 1793; m. 1746, Sir Charles Cotter, Bt., of Rockforest, b. 1714, d. at Carrigtchill, Ireland, 9 June 1770,

GEORGE SACKVILLE COTTER, d. 1831; m. Margaret Rogers,

REV. JOSEPH ROGERSON COTTER, b. 2 Sept. 1790, d. 4 Feb. 1868; m. 5 Aug. 1819, Mary Purcell, d. 15 Apr. 1851,

REV. RICHARD HENRY COTTER, b. 5 Feb. 1831, d. 27 Nov. 1898, at Dublin, Ireland; m. 1 May 1861, at Ballingary, co. Limerick, Ireland, Sara Pearce Lawrenson, b. ca. 1834, d. at Dalkey, co. Dublin, Ireland,

JOSEPH ROGERSON COTTER, b. at Milan, Italy, 10 Dec. 1869, d. at Glenageary, co. Dublin, Ireland, 31 Mar. 1957; m. at Erpingham, Norfolk, England, 29 Dec. 1913, Ellen Harriett Cotter, b. at St. Helena, 2 June 1872, d. at Glenageary, co. Dublin, Ireland, 15 Sept. 1948,

JOAN JAMIESON COTTER, b. at Dublin, Ireland, 7 Aug. 1916; ed.: The Hall, Monkstown, Ireland; Trinity College, Dublin; member: Order of the Crown of Charlemagne in the United States of America, Corresponding Secretary General; Daughters of the Barons of Runnemede; Red Hill Garden Club, past Treasurer and President, 1970-72; St. Agnes School for Girls, Alexandria, Board of Governors, Recording Secretary; Board of Trustees of the Church Schools in the Diocese of Va.; Womens Auxiliary to the Alexandria Medical Society, past Treasurer; m. at Manorbier, South Wales, 20 May 1944, Henry Haskins Ferrell, Jr., M.D., b. at Danville, Va., 4 Mar. 1915 and has issue:

102

1) LESLIE COTTER FERRELL, b. 20 Jan. 1949, at Alexandria, Va.; m. 3 Aug. 1974, at Alexandria, Va., Jose Manuel Kauffmann, b. 26 Nov. 1948, at Madrid, Spain;

2) HENRY HASKINS FERRELL III, b. 12 Jan. 1951, at Alexandria, Va.;

3) JOAN PINSON FERRELL, b. 1 June 1954, at Alexandria, Va.

Chapter XXXIII

CUNYINGHAM — ROBERDEAU — PATTEN — MILLER — PIERCE — BAKER — GLASS — PAMPLIN

CHARLEMAGNE

(See Chapter VI, p. 19)

WILLIAM I, Count of Burgundy, d. 11 Nov. 1087; m. Stephanie of Barcelona, dau. of Raymond Berenger II, Count of Barcelona,

RAYMOND, Count of Burgundy, d. 26 Mar. 1107; m. in 1095, Urraca, Queen of Castile, b. 1082, d. 8 Mar. 1126, dau. and heiress of Alfonso VI, King of Castile (b. 1039, d. at Toledo, 30 June 1109) by his second wife, Constance dau. of Robert I, Duke of Burgundy,

ALFONSO VII, King of Castile, became King of Galacia in 1112 and King of Castile and Leon on the death of his mother in 1126; m. (first) in Nov. 1128, Berengeria of Barcelona, d. in Feb. 1149, dau. of Raymond Berenger III, Count of Barcelona,

SANCHO III, King of Castile, b. 1135, d. 31 Aug. 1158; m. 4 Feb. 1151, Blanche of Navarre, d. 24 June 1158, dau. of Garcia V, King of Navarre

ALFONSO VIII, King of Castile, b. 11 Nov. 1155, d. 22 Sept. 1214; m. 1170, Eleanor of England, b. 13 Oct. 1162, d. 21 Sept. 1214, dau. of Henry II, King of England and Eleanor of Aquitaine,

BERENGERIA, Queen of Castile, b. 1171, d. 8 Nov. 1244(46) succeeded her brother Henry I to the throne in 1214; m. in 1198 her cousin, Alfonso IX, King of Leon, b. 1166, d. 24 Sept. 1230, son of Ferdinand II, king of Leon and Urraca, dau.

104

of Alfonso I, King of Portugal, grandson of Alfonso VII, King of Castile,

SAINT FERDINAND III, King of Castile and Leon, b. 1200, d. 30 May 1252, (canonized 1671); m. (second) 1237, Johanna of Ponthieu, dau. of Simon, Count of Ponthieu and Aumale.

ELEANOR OF CASTILE, d. 12 Nov. 1290, at Hareby, Lincs.; m. (his first) at Burgos, Spain, in Oct. 1254, Edward I, King of England (See Chapters II and XXXVI) b. at Westminister, 17 June 1239, d. nr. Carlisle, 7 July 1307, reigned 1272-1307,

EDWARD II, King of England, 1307-1327, d. in England, 21 Sept. 1327; m. 25 Jan. 1307/8, Princess Isabella of France, d. 22 Aug. 1358, dau. of Phillippe IV, surnamed *le Bel,* King of France and Navarre,

EDWARD III, King of England, 1327-1377; m. 24 Jan. 1327/8, Philippa of Hainault, b. ca. 1312, d. 14/15 Aug. 1369, dau. of William III, Count of Hainault and Holland, and his wife Joanna (Jane) of Valois, dau. of Charles, Count of Valois, and granddau. of Phillippe III, King of France,

JOHN OF GAUNT, 1st Duke of Lancaster, K.G., King of Castile and Leon, b. at Ghent, 24 June 1340, d. at Leicester Castle, 3/4 Feb. 1398/9; m. (third) Jan. 1396/7, Catherine Roet, b. 1350, d. 10 May 1403, dau. of Sir Payn Roet and wid. of Sir Hugh Swynford,

JOHN BEAUFORT, 1st Earl of Somerset, 1st Marquis of Dorset, K.G., Lord High Admiral and Great Chamberlain of England, b. ca. 1372, at St. Catherine-by-the-Tower Hospital, d. 16 Mar. 1409/10, and bur. in Canterbury Cathedral; m. ante 28 Sept. 1397, Margaret Holland (d. 30 Dec. 1439 and bur. in Canterbury Cathedral) 3rd. dau. and co-heir of Thomas Holland, 2nd Earl of Kent by Alice FitzAlan, dau. of Richard FitzAlan, Earl of Arundel, granddau. of Thomas Holland, 1st Earl of Kent and Joan (Plantagenet) "The Fair Maid of Kent", dau. of Edmund (Plantagenet), Earl of Kent,

JOAN BEAUFORT, d. 15 July 1445; m. (first) 2 Feb. 1423/4. James

(Stewart) I, King of Scotland, b. at Dumfermline, 1394, assasinated at Perth, 21 Feb. 1436/7, son of Robert III, King of Scotland, and his wife, Annabela Drummond, dau. of Sir John Drummond of Stobhall,

JOAN STEWART (also called JOANNA) 3rd dau.; m. 1458/9, James Douglas, Lord Dalkeith, cr. Earl of Morton, 14 Mar. 1457/8, d. 1493,

JANET DOUGLAS, liv. Aug. 1489; m. (first) ante 1445, Thomas Erskine, Lord Erskine, d. in or shortly bef. 1493,

MARY ERSKINE, m. Edward Livingston, b. at Kilsyth, d. in 1482,

WILLIAM LIVINGSTON, b. at Kilsyth, d. 1540,

WILLIAM LIVINGSTON, b. at Kilsyth, d. at Flodden, 1513; m. Elizabeth Graham,

WILLIAM LIVINGSTON, b. at Kilsyth, d. ante 21 July 1545; m. Janet Bruce, dau. of Sir Robert Bruce,

MARGARET (or ELIZABETH) LIVINGSTON, b. at Kilsyth; m. Gabriel Cunyingham, b. at Craigends, d. at the Battle of Pinkie, 10 Sept. 1547,

JAMES CUNYINGHAM, b. at Ashenyeard; m. Margaret Fleming, dau. of the Laird of Barrochan,

WILLIAM CUNYINGHAM, Clerk of Signet of Edinburgh, Keeper of the Privy Seal, d. ante 1646; m. Rebecca Muirhead,

RICHARD CUNYINGHAM, b. at Glen Gannock, d. 27 Oct. 1670; m. 3 Oct. 1654, Elizabeth Heriot, d. 1672,

ROBERT CUNYINGHAM, b. 24 Mar. 1669; m. 26 Sept. 1693, Judith Elizabeth DeBonneson,

MARY CUNYINGHAM, b. at Cayon, St. Christopher (St. Kitts), B.W.I., 4 Apr. 1699, d. 13 Mar. 1771; m. at St. Christopher, B.W.I., ca. 1723, Isaac Roberdeau, b. at Rochelle, France, d. ante 1743, St. Christopher, B.W.I.,

DANIEL ROBERDEAU, b. at St. Christopher, B.W.I., 1727, d. at Winchester, Va., 5 Jan. 1795; m. 3 Oct. 1761, Mary Bostwick, b. 1741, d. 15 Feb. 1777,

MARY HORN ROBERDEAU, b. at Philadelphia, Pa., 6 May 1774, d. at Alexandria, Va., 31 Oct. 1805; m. at Alexandria Va., 14 Nov. 1793, Thomas M. Patten, b. at Roxbury, Mass., 22 July 1769, d. at Monroe, La., 6 Feb. 1820,

HARRIET ROZIER PATTEN, b. at Alexandria, Va., 12 Nov. 1803, d. at Lake Providence, La., Sept. 1853; m. at Williamsport, Md., 29 Jan. 1819, John W. Miller, b. 11 Aug. 1783, d. at Lake Providence, La., Sept. 1853,

LAURA PATTEN MILLER, b. at Winchester, Va., 4 June 1826, d. at Clinton, N.C., ca. 1910; m. 19 July 1847, Lewis H. Pierce, b. at Wilmington, N.C., 19 Aug. 1819, d. at Wilmington, N.C., 20 July 1860.

MARY RIVERA PIERCE, b. at Wilmington, N.C., 9 Nov. 1850, d. at Waynesboro, Va., 29 Dec. 1950; m. at Annapolis Junction, Md., 27 May 1874, William Hartman Baker, b. in Md., 5 Sept. 1848, d. 17 Oct. 1901,

LOUISE PATTEN BAKER, b. at Winchester, Va., 15 May 1877, d. at Winchester, Va., 29 May 1964; m. at Washington, D.C., 16 Dec. 1905, William Wood Glass, Jr., b. in Frederick Co., Va., 24 July 1874, d. at Winchester, Va., 2 Sept. 1954,

MOLLIE GLASS, b. 25 Sept., 1917, at Winchester, Va.; member: DAR, Va. State Resolutions Committee; Daughters of 1812, Chaplain National, Past State Chaplain; Colonial Dames of the XVII Century, Past State Chaplain; United Daughters of the Confederacy; Nat'l Huguenot Society, State Chaplain; Order of the Crown of Charlemagne in the United States of America; m. 23 Dec. 1941, at Washington, D.C., Jack Cole Pamplin, b. at Greensboro, N.C., 23 Sept. 1913, d. at Arlington, Va., 29 July 1974,

1) LOUISE GLASS PAMPLIN, b. 26 Aug. 1945;
2) MARY ASHBY PAMPLIN, b. 21 July 1949.

Chapter XXXIV

DAVIS — BYE — WHITE — LINTON — SMITH — BURGESS — LITTELL

CHARLEMAGNE

(See Chapters X, XXXII, XXXIX, XLIII, LXVIII)

ISABEL DE VERMANDOIS, b. ca. 1085; d. ante July 1147, Countess of Leicester; m. (second) 1119, William de Warenne, 2nd Earl of Surrey, d. 11 May 1138.

ADA DE WARENNE, d. 1178; m. 1139, Henry de Huntingdon, earl of Huntingdon and Northumberland, b. ca. 1114; d. 12 June 1152, son of David I, King of Scots, and his wife Maud of Northumberland,

MARGARET DE HUNTINGDON, d. 1201; m. (second) aft. 1171, Humphrey de Bohun, IV, d. 1182,

HENRY DE BOHUN, Earl of Hereford, b. 1176; d. in Egypt, 1 June 1220; m. Maud FitzGeoffrey de Mandeville, d. 27 Aug. 1236,

HUMPHREY DE BOHUN, V, Earl of Hereford and Essex, b. 1208, d. 24 Sept. 1275; m. (first) Maud de Lusignan, d. 14 Aug. 1241,

HUMPHREY DE BOHUN VI, d. 27 Oct. 1265; m. (first) Eleanor de Briouze (Braiose etc.) dau. of William de Braose and Eva Marshall,

HUMPHREY DE BOHUN VII, Earl of Hereford and Essex, b. ca. 1249, d. at Pleshey, 31 Dec. 1298; m. 1275, Maud de Fiennes, d. ante 1298,

HUMPHREY DE BOHUN VIII, Earl of Hereford and Essex, b. ca.

1276, d. at Boroughbridge, 16 Mar. 1321/2; m. at Westminster, 14 Nov. 1302, Elizabeth Plantagenet, b. 1 Aug. 1282, d. 5 May 1316, dau. of Edward I, King of England and Eleanor of Castile,

SIR WILLIAM DE BOHUN, K.G., Earl of Hereford and Essex, d. Sept. 1360; m. 1338 (her second) Elizabeth de Badlesmere, b. 1313, d. 1356,

SIR HUMPHREY DE BOHUN IX, K.G., Earl of Hereford and Essex and Northampton, b. 25 Mar. 1342, d. 16 Jan. 1372/3; m. aft. 9 Sept. 1359, Joanne Fitz Alan, d. 7 Apr. 1419,

ELEANOR DE BOHUN, b. ca. 1365; d. 3 Oct. 1399, m. Thomas Plantagenet, K.G., "of Woodstock", Duke of Gloucester, b. 7 Jan. 1354.5. d. Nov. 1397, son of Edward III and Philippa of Hainaut,

ANNE PLANTAGENET, b. ca., 1380, d. 16 Oct. 1438; m. (his third) 20 Nov. 1405, Sir William de Bouchier, Count of Eu, d. at Troyes, 28 May 1420,

WILLIAM DE BOUCHIER, d. ante 12 Dec. 1469; m. ante 3 Aug. 1439, Thomasine Hankford, b. 23 Feb. 1422/3, d. 3 July 1453,

FULK DE BOUCHIER, Lord FitzWarine, b. 25 Oct. 1445, d. 18 Sept. 1479; m. Elizabeth Dinham, b. ca 1450, d. 19 Oct. 1516,

JOHN DE BOUCHIER, Lord FitzWarine and Earl of Bath, K.B., P.C., b. 20 July 1470, d. 30 Apr. 1589; m. (first) ca. 1499, Cecilia Dubini (Daubeney), d. ant 1524,

DOROTHY BOUCHIER, m. John Fulford, d. 1503,

ANDREW FULFORD, b. at Stoke Gabriel, England, m. Eleanor — ,

FAITH FULFORD, b. 29 May 1561; m. at Stoke Gabriel, 29 Sept 1582, Capt. John Davis, b. 1550, d. on Malay Peninsula, Oct. 1605,

PHILIP DAVIS, m. Agnes Horton,

110

NATHANIEL DAVIS, m. Mary — ,

MARGARET DAVIS, b. in England, d. at Lahaska, Pa., 6 Oct. 1724; m. at Bermondsey, Eng., 3 July 1670, Thomas Bye VIII, b. at London, Eng., 1640, d. at Lahaska, Pa., 25 Aug. 1640,

SARAH BYE, b. at Bermondsey, Surrey, Eng., 11 Oct. 1638; m. 1 July 1702, William White,

ELIZABETH WHITE, b. at Falls, Bucks Co., Pa., 29 Sept. 1705, d. 26 Jan. 1732/3; m. (his first) 1 July 1726, Benjamin Linton, b. 30 Mar. 1703; d. 25 Jan. 1773,

JOHN LINTON, b. in Bucks Co., Pa., 15 Oct. 1727, d. 25 May 1786; m. (second) at Falls Meeting, Pa., 20 May 1772, Mary Moon, b. 8 Mar. 1736; d. 28 Nov. 1815,

ELIZABETH LINTON, b. in Bucks Co., Pa., 14 Oct. 1777, d. at Fallsington, Pa., 13 June 1844; m. at Falls Meeting, Pa., 11 Dec. 1793, Thomas Smith, b. in Bucks Co., Pa., 25 Aug. 1769; d. 6 Apr. 1847,

ELIZABETH SMITH, b. at Fallsington, Pa., 6 July 1807, d. at Baltimore, Md., 25 Feb. 1876; m. at Fallsington, Pa., 19 Nov. 1828; Amos Burgess, b. 4 Mar. 1801, d. at Baltimore, Md., 4 Jan, 1886,

THOMAS SMITH BURGESS, b. in Bucks Co., Pa., 7 July 1833; d. in Union Co., N. J., 1 Aug. 1923; m. at Philadelphia, Pa., 13 Aug. 1862, Achsah C. Allen, b. in Burlington Co., N.J., d. in Union Co., N.J., 1924,

GEORGIANNA M. BURGESS, b. at Philadelphia, Pa., 11 Aug. 1867; d. at Cedar Grove, N.J., 14 Dec. 1957; m. at Newark, N.J., 15 Sept. 1887, Abraham A. Littell, b. Sept. 1866,

HARRY ELLSWORTH LITTELL, b. at Newark, N.J., 15 May 1893; m. at Newark, N.J., 24 Nov. 1917, Emma Schnell, b. at Newark, N.J., 20 Dec. 1894, d. at Irvington, N.J., 16 Sept. 1967.

ROBERT BURGESS LITTELL, b. at Newark, N.J., 3 July 1923; ed.:
Mercer Univ., Macon, Ga.; Seton Hall Univ., So. Orange, N.J.;
Newark College of Engineering, Newark, N.J.; member: Sons
of St. George of Philadelphia; S.R.; SAR, N.J., 3rd Vice
President; Baronial Order of Magna Charta, Surety; Military
Order of the Crusades, Sec'y,; Order of the Crown of
Charlemagne in the United States of America, Councillor; St.
Nicholas Society of the City of New York; Society of Colonial
Wars; Sons and Daughters of Pilgrims, Gov., N.J.; Descendants
of the Colonial Clergy; Flagon and Trencher; Littell Family of
America, V.P.; Doane Family Assoc. of America; Bucks Co.
Historical Society; Genealogical Society of N.J.; Bergen Co.
Historical Soc.; Cedar Grove Historical Soc.; Passaic Co. Hist.
Soc.; etc.; m. 11 Feb. 1950, at East Orange, N.J., Dorothy
Clara Stagg,

1) PAMELA STAGG LITTELL, b. 6 Nov. 1951;

2) GREGORY STAGG LITTELL, b. 8 Feb. 1955;

3) VICKI STAGG LITTELL, b. 14 Aug. 1956.

Chapter XXXV

DEIGHTON — NEGUS — MEBUS

CHARLEMAGNE

(See Chapters X, XXXII, XXXIX, XLIII, LXVIII)

ISABEL DE VERMANDOIS, Countess of Leicester. d. ante July 1147; m. (second) ca. 1119, William de Warren, Earl of Surrey,

GUNDRED DE WARREN, d. aft. 1166; m. Roger de Newburgh, 2nd Earl of Warwick, d. 12 June 1151/3,

WALERAN DE NEWBURGH, 4th Earl of Warwick, b. ante 1153, d. ca. 1204; m. (second) ca. 1196, Alice de Harcourt, b. at Stanton Harcourt, co. Oxford, d. aft. Sept. 1212,

ALICE DE NEWBURGH, d. 1246-63; m. William Mauduit, Baron Mauduit of Handslope, Bucks., d. Apr. 1257,

ISABEL MAUDUIT, bur. at the Nunnery of Colehill; m. William de Beauchamp, 5th Baron Beauchamp of Elmley Castle, w.d. 7 Jan. 1268/9,

SIR WALTER DE BEAUCHAMP, of Beauchamp's Court, Steward of the Household of King Edward I, d. in 1303,

SIR GILES DE BEAUCHAMP, of Beauchamp's Court, d. Oct. 1361; m. ca. 1329, Catherine de Bures. (See Chapter VII, p. 23)

SIR JOHN DE BEAUCHAMP, d. 1378-1401; m. Elizabeth (prob. St. John), d. 1411,

SIR WILLIAM DE BEAUCHAMP, of Powyck and Alcester, d. ante 1431; m. ante Mar. 1414/5, Catherine Ufflete,

SIR JOHN DE BEAUCHAMP, K.G., Baron Beauchamp of Powyck, d. ante 19 Apr. 1475; m. ca. 1434, Margaret Ferrers,

SIR RICHARD DE BEAUCHAMP, K.B., 2nd Baron Beauchamp of Powyck, b. 1435, d. 19 Jan. 1502/3; m. 27 Jan. 1446/7, Elizabeth Stafford of Grafton, co. Worcester,

ANNE DE BEAUCHAMP, b. 1462, d. 1535; m. Sir Richard Lygon, Knt., of Arle Court, co. Gloucester,

SIR RICHARD LYGON, KNT., b. at Arle Court, co. Gloucester, d. in 1557; m. Margaret Grevelle of Arle Court, co. Gloucester,

HENRY LYGON, of Upton St. Leonard, co. Gloucester, d. ca. 1577; m. Elizabeth Berkeley, of Upton St. Leonard, co. Gloucester,

ELIZABETH (ISABEL) LYGON; m. Edward Basset of Uley, Gloucestershire, w.p. 5 Nov. 1602,

JANE BASSET, b. at Uley, co. Gloucester, d. 23 Apr. 1631; m. Dr. John Deighton, Gent., of St. Nicholas, co. Gloucester, d. 16 May 1640,

JANE DEIGHTON, bapt. at St. Nicholas, co. Gloucester, England, 5 Apr. 1609, liv. at Boston, Mass., in 1671; m. (second) ca. 1647, in Massachusetts, Jonathan Negus, b. in England, in 1602, liv. in Boston, Mass., in 1678,

CAPT. ISAAC NEGUS, b. at Boston, Mass., in Feb. 1650, d. at Swansea, Mass., 29 Nov. 1700; m. 7 Apr. 1679, Hannah Andrews, d. aft. 1702,

ISAAC NEGUS, JR., b. at Swansea, Mass., ca. 1685, d. at Freetown, Mass., liv. in 1718; m. Hannah — ,

THOMAS NEGUS, b. at Freetown, Mass., 12 May 1718, d. at Shrewsbury, N.J., 12 Apr. 1754; m. at Shrewsbury, N.J., 27 July 1748, Lavina West, b. at Shrewsbury, N.J., d. at Shrewsbury, N.J.,

JOHN NEGUS, b. at Shresbury, N.J., 13 July 1753, d. at Philadelphia, Pa., in Mar. 1823; m. in Burlington Co., N.J., 15 Feb. 1779, Mary Shreve, b. 13 Oct. 1760, d. at Philadelphia, Pa., 28 June 1811,

STEPHEN WEST NEGUS, b. at Philadelphia, Pa., 25 Apr. 1791, d. at Philadelphia, Pa., 21 Dec. 1851; m. at Philadelphia, Pa., ca. 1819/20, Eliza Rea, b. in 1798, d. at Philadelphia, Pa., 18 Mar. 1890,

ALEXANDER NEGUS, b. at Philadelphia, Pa., 17 Mar. 1834, d. at Philadelphia, Pa., 15 Dec. 1902; m. ca. 1865, at Philadelphia, Pa., Kate Rea, b. at Terre Haute, Ind., 12 Mar. 1848, d. at Philadelphia, Pa., in May 1927,

WILLIAM STEEL NEGUS, b. at Philadelphia, Pa., 26 Aug. 1868, d. at Philadelphia, Pa., 26 Apr. 1934; m. at Bustleton, Pa., 25 June 1891, Letitia Roberts Walton, b. at Abington, Pa., 30 July 1866, d. at Philadelphia 14 Feb. 1910, (See Chapter XLIV)

ESTELLE CLAXTON NEGUS, b. at Philadelphia, Pa., 8 Feb. 1901; B.A. Penn. State Univ.; member: Nat'l Society Colonial Dames of America; D.A.C.; DAR, past Regent; Daughters of Colonial Wars; Nat'l Society Sons and Daughters of the Pilgrims; Welcome Society of Pennslyvania; Order of the Crown of Charlemagne in the United States of America; m. at Glenside, Pa., 30 June 1926, George Brinker Mebus, b. at Philadelphia, Pa., 14 Apr. 1903, d. at Glenside, Pa., 13 Dec. 1972,

   1)   CHARLES FILLMORE MEBUS II, b. 15 June 1928. (See Chapter XLIV)

Chapter XXXVI

DIGGES — NEALE — HALL — WILLSON — WALLIS —
STIEFEL — McDONALD

CHARLEMAGNE, Emperor of the West, b. 2 Apr. 742, d. 28 Jan. 814; m. (third) in 771, Hildegarde, b. 758, d. 783, dau. of Gerold I, Count in Vinzgua,

LOUIS I, the Pious, Emperor of the West, b. in 778, d. 20 June 840, King of Aquitaine 781, co-regent 813, crowned Emperor at Rheims, 28 Oct. 816; m. (second) in 819, Judith, d. 19 Apr. 843, dau. of Welf, Count in Bavaria, Count of Altdorf,

CHARLES II, the Bald, Emperor of the West, b. 13 June 823, d. 6 Oct. 877, King of France, 843, King of Lorraine, 869, crowned Emperor at Rome, 25 Dec. 875; m. 14 Dec. 842, Ermentrude, d. 6 Oct. 869, dau. of Odo, Count of Orleans,

JUDITH OF FRANCE, b. ca. 843; m. (third) in 862, Baldwin I, Count of Flanders in 858, d. 879,

BALDWIN II, Count of Flanders, d. 918; m. in 884, Aelfthryth, d. 7 June 929, dau. of Alfred the Great, King of Wessex,

ARNULF I, Count of Flanders, d. 27 Mar. 964; m. Alix, d. 858/60, dau. of Herbert II, Count of Vermandois, a descendant of Charlemagne (See Chapter LXVIII)

BALDWIN III, co-Regent with his father, 958-962, d. 1 Nov. 962; m. in 961, Matilda, d. 28 May 1008, dau. of Herman Billung, Duke of Saxony,

ARNULF II, Count of Flanders, b. 961.2, d. 30 Mar. 987; m. Rosala of Ivrea, dau. of Berengar II, Marquess of Ivrea, King of Italy, a descendant of Charlemagne (See Chapter VI)

116

BALDWIN IV, Count of Flanders, b. ca. 980, d. 30 May 1036; m. 1012, Otgiva, d. 21 Feb. 1030, dau. of Frederick, Count of Luxemburg,

BALDWIN V, Count of Flanders, b. ca. 1012, d. 1 Sept. 1067; m. (her second) in 1028, Adelaide (Adele), d. 8 Jan. 1079, dau. of Robert II, the Pious, King of France, a descendant of Charlemagne (See Chapter XLVI)

MATILDA OF FLANDERS, d. 3 Nov. 1083; m. 1053, William the Conqueror, Duke of Normandy 1035, King of England 1066, b. 1027/8, d. 8/9 Sept. 1087,

HENRY I, King of England 1100-1135, b. 1068, d. 1 Dec. 1135; m. Nov. 1100, Matilda, d. 1 May 1118, dau. of Malcolm III, King of Scots and his wife, St. Margaret of Scotland,

MATILDA, dowager Empress of Germany, b. 1104, d. 10 Sept. 1167; m. (second) 3 Apr. 1127, Geoffrey V Plantagenet, Count of Anjou and Maine, b. 24 Aug. 1113, d. 7 Sept. 1151, a descendant of Charlemagne (See Chapter XXXVIII)

HENRY II, Plantagenet, King of England 1154-1189, b. 5 Mar. 1133, d. 6 July 1189; m. 18 May 1152, Eleanor, Countess of Poitou, Duchess of Aquitaine, d. 31 Mar. 1204,

JOHN I, King of England 1199-1216, b. 24 Dec. 1167, d. 19 Oct. 1216; m. (second) in 1200, Isabella, b. in 1188, d. in June 1246, dau. and heiress of Aymer Taillefer, Count of Angouleme,

HENRY III, King of England 1216-1272, b. 13 Oct. 1207, d. 15 Nov. 1272; m. 14 Jan. 1236, Eleanor, d. 25 June 1291, dau. of Raymond-Berenger IV, Count of Provence,

EDWARD I, King of England 1272-1307, b. at Winchester, 17 June 1239, d. 7 July 1307, nr. Carlisle; m. (first) 18 Oct. 1254, Eleanor of Castile, d. 29 Nov. 1290, dau. of St. Ferdinand III, King of Castile and Leon, by his second wife Jeanne de Dammartin, Countess of Ponthieu,

JOAN PLANTAGENET OF ACRE, b. in 1272, at Acre, d. 23 Apr. 1307; m. in Westminster Abbey (his second) ca. 30 Apr. 1290, Sir Gilbert de Clare, Earl of Clare, Hertford and Gloucester, b. at Christchurch, 2 Sept. 1243, d. at Monmouth Castle, 7 Dec. 1295,

ALIANORE DE CLARE, b. at Caerphilly Castle, in Oct. 1292, d. 30 June 1337; m. at Westminster, aft 14 June 1306, Sir Hugh le Despenser, 2nd Lord Despenser, Knt., hanged at Hereford, 24 Nov. 1326,

SIR EDWARD LE DESPENSER, of Buckland, Bucks., Eyworth, 2nd son, d. at the Battle of Morlaix, 30 Sept. 1342; m. at Groby, 20 Apr. 1335, Anne de Ferrers, d. 8 Aug. 1367, dau. of Sir William de Ferrers, Lord Ferrers of Groby,

SIR EDWARD LE DESPENSER, Lord Despenser, K.G., b. at Essendine, Rutland, 24 Mar. 1335/6, d. at Llanblethian, Glamorgan, 11 Nov. 1375; m. ante 2 Aug. 1354, Elizabeth de Burghersh, d. 26 July 1409, bur. at Tewkesbury Abbey, dau. and hr. of Sir Bartholomew de Burghersh, Lord Burghersh of Ewias Lacy, Hereford,

THOMAS LE DESPENSER, Lord Despenser, K.G., b. 22 Sept. 1373, d. (beheaded) 13 Jan. 1399/1400; m. ca. 1380, Constance (Plantagenet), d. 28 Nov. 1416, dau. of Edmund (Plantagenet) of Langley, Earl of Cambridge, Duke of York, son of Edward III, King of England,

ISABEL LE DESPENSER, b. at Cardiff, 26 July 1400, d. at the Friars Minoresses, London, 27 Dec. 1439; m. (her first) at Tewkesbury, 27 July 1411, Richard de Beauchamp, Lord Abergavenny, Earl of Winchester, K.B.,

ELIZABETH DE BEAUCHAMP, Baroness Abergavenny, b. at Hanley Castle, Worcester, 11 Sept. 1415, d. 18 June 1448, bur. at the Carmelites, Coventry, only dau. and hr.; m. ante 18 Oct. 1424, Sir Edward de Neville, Lord Abergavenny, K.G., d. 18 Oct. 1476, son of Ralph de Neville, 1st Earl of Westmoreland by his wife, Joan de Beaufort, dau. of John (Plantagenet) of Gaunt, Duke of Lancaster and King of Castile, son of Edward III, King of England,

118

SIR GEORGE NEVILLE, Lord Abergavenny, b. ca. 1440, d. 20 Sept. 1492, bur. at Lewes Priory, Sussex, knighted at the Battle of Tewkesbury, 9 May 1471; m. (first) Margaret Fenne, d. 28 Sept. 1485, dau. of Sir Hugh Fenne of Soulton Burdeleys, Norfolk,

SIR GEORGE NEVILLE, LORD ABERGAVENNY, K.G., b. in England, ca. 1469, d. ante 4 June 1535, bur. at Birling; m. (third) ca. 1519, Mary de Stafford, dau. of Edward de Stafford, 3rd Duke of Buckingham, K.G., and his wife, Eleanor de Percy, dau. of Henry, 4th Earl of Northumberland, by Lady Maud Herbert, his wife,

URSULA NEVILLE, m. (his first) Sir Warham St. Leger, Knt., of Ulcombe, Sheriff of Kent, 1560; President of Munster in Ireland,

ANN ST. LEGER, b. in England, 1556; d. in England, 1637; m. in England, Thomas Digges, b. in Kent, England, 1530, d. in Kent, 24 Aug. 1695; A.B. Cambridge, 1551; M.P. 1572; muster-master general of armies in Low Countries, 1586-7; son of Leonard Digges of Woton Court, Kent, and his wife Bridget Welford,

SIR DUDLEY DIGGES, b. at Chilham Castle, England, in 1583, d. 18 Mar. 1638/9, bur. at Chilham, Kent, Ambassador to Russia, 1618; member of the Virginia Company; m. Mary Kempe, d. ca. 1620, bur. at Chilham, Kent, dau. of Sir Thomas Kempe, Knt.,

GOV. EDWARD DIGGES, b. at Chilham Castle, England, in 1621, d. in Virginia, 15 Mar. 1675; m. in Va., Elizabeth Page, b. in England, d. in Va., in 1671, dau. of Col. John Page,

COL. WILLIAM DIGGES, b. at Chilham Castle, England, in 1650, w.p. Charles Co., Md., July 1697, J.P. 1671, Sheriff of co. York, 1679, came to St. Mary's Co., Md., 1680, Deputy Gov. of Md.; m. in Maryland, Elizabeth (Sewall) Wharton, b. in St. Mary's Co., Md., d. in Md., 1698,

ELIZA DIGGES, b. in Charles Co., Md., w.p. in Charles Co., in

1722; m. (his second) 1698, Anthony Neale, b. in Charles Co., Md., in 1659, d. in Charles Co., Md., in 1723,

EDWARD NEALE, b. in Charles Co., Md., in 1700; d. at "Bolingly", Queen Anne's Co., Md., 28 Dec. 1760; m. (first) Mary Lowe, b. in Prince George's Co., Md., d. in Queen Anne's Co., dau. of Col. Henry Lowe,

MARTHA NEALE, b. at "Bolingly", Queen Anne's Co., Md., in Dec. 1737, d. at "Bolingly", 31 May 1789; m. in Queen Anne's Co., Md., Francis Hall, b. in Prince George's Co., Md., in 1732, d. in Queen Anne's Co., Md. 13 Feb. 1785,

MARY TERESA HALL, b. in Queen Anne's Co., Md., in 1760, d. in Queen Anne's Co., 13 Aug. 1814; m. in Queen Anne's Co., 6 Aug. 1776, Dr. Thomas Bennett Willson, b. in Kent Co., Md., 1729, d. in Kent Co., Md., 1799,

DR. THOMAS BENNETT WILLSON, b. in Kent Co., Md., 28 Sept. 1778, d. in Kent Co., 28 Oct. 1859; m. in Kent Co., 3 June 1806, Anna Marie Smythe, b. in Kent Co., Md., 17 Oct. 1784, d. in Kent Co., 28 Apr. 1823,

GEORGE HAYWARD WILLSON, b. in Kent Co., Md., 25 May 1810, d. in Kent Co., 2 Apr. 1873; m. in Kent Co., 13 June 1837, Henrietta Eleanor Brooke, b. in Prince George Co., Md., 25 June 1820, d. in Kent Co., Md., 17 Apr. 1877,

MARY GEORGIANNA WILLSON, b. in Kent Co., Md., 12 Feb. 1842, d. in Queen Anne Co., Md., 10 May 1906; m. in Kent Co., 28 Apr. 1864, Francis Wallis, b. in Kent Co., Md., 28 Mar. 1828, d. in Queen Anne Co., Md., 21 June 1904,

HENRIETTA ELEANOR WALLIS, b. in Kent Co., Md., 9 Nov. 1869, d. in Prince George Co., Md., 17 June 1958; m. at Chestertown, Md., 25 June 1895, Elton Howard Perry, b. in Talbot Co., Md., 11 Nov. 1861, d. in Queen Anne Co., Md., 11 Feb. 1923,

ELEANOR BROOKE PERRY, b. in Queen Anne Co., Md. 9 Apr. 1906; ed.: St. Gertrude's, Ridgely, Md.; Mt. St. Agnes College,

Mt. Washington, Baltimore, Md.; member: Daughters of Founders and Patriots, President D.C. Chapter; Descendants of Lords of Maryland Manores, past President; Ark and Dove Society of Maryland, member of Board; Nat'l Society of Colonial Dames of America, Recording Sec'y; Jamestowne Society; Hereditary Order of Descendants of Colonial Governors; Daughters of the Cincinnati; Pilgrims of St. Mary's; Maryland Historical Society; Order of the Crown of Charlemagne in the United States of America, Councillor; m. (first) in Queen Anne Co., Md., 4 June 1923, Dr. Charles Valentine Stiefel, b. 11 Oct. 1894, at Washington, D.C.; m. at St. Peter's, Queen Anne Co., Md.; d. at Washington, D.C., 17 July 1967; m. (second) 14 June 1975, at Washington, D.C., Dr. Frederick Burton Tuttle, b. 12 July 1908, at New Haven, Conn., whose lineage appears elsewhere in this volume,

1) ELEANOR BROOKE STIEFEL, b. at Washington, D.C., 8 Apr. 1929; m. at Washington, D.C., 24 Apr. 1954, Cdr. Thomas Ely McDonald, USN, b. 11 Aug. 1927;

   a) ELEANOR BROOKE MCDONALD, b. 16 Aug. 1957;

   b) THOMAS HATTON MCDONALD, 7 Aug. 1959;

   c) CHARLES CALVERT MCDONALD, b. 23 Feb. 1963;

   d) MARGUERITE ELY MCDONALD, b. 17 Jan. 1965;

   e) RICHARD BENNETT MCDONALD, b. 10 Feb. 1966.

Chapter XXXVII

DRAKE — HILL — DRUMMOND

CHARLEMAGNE

(See Chapter LIV)

LOWRI FERCH GRIFFITH FYCHAN, sister of Owen Glendower, m. Robert Puleston of Emral, aged 28 on 3 Sept. 1386.

ANGHARAD PULESTON, m. Edward (Jorwerth) ap Dafydd ap Edynfed Gam, ancestor of the extinct Lords of Trevor and Viscounts Hampden, bur. Valle Crucis Abbey, 1448,

ROSE TREVOR, living 1465, m. circa 1435, Otewell Worsley, Constable of Chirk Castle, Denbigh, Wales, 1445, and a solider in the service of the Earl of Warwick, d. at Calais, 24 March 1470,

JOYCE WORSLEY, d. before 26 Apr. 1507, when her will was proved; m. before 1471 Richard Lee, Lord of the Manor of Delce in the Parish of St. Margaret's Rochester, Kent, son of Sir Richard Lee, Lord Mayor of London in 1461 and 1471 (who d. in the later year, will PCC 5 Wattys), d. 26 Sept. 1498 (as noted in his I.p.m.), and bur. at St. Stephen Walbrook, London,

RICHARD LEE of Delce, Rochester, Kent, b. circa 1474 (aged 24 in 1498), d. circa 1526 (will PCC 15 Porch); m. Eleanor, who d. circa 1552 (will PCC F 31 Powell),

GEOFFREY LEE of Delce, b. circa 1505, living 31 Henry VIII (circa 1540); m. Agnes Conyers, dau. and heiress of Leonard Conyers of Pinchingthorpe, Yorks.,

RICHARD LEE of Delce, sometime Mayor of Maidstone, Kent, living circa 1570, m. at Birchington, Kent, 19 Feb. 1551/52,

Elizabeth Crispe, dau. of John Crispe of Cleve, Isle of Thanet, Kent (bur. at Birchington, 3 Nov. 1583) and his wife, Katherine (bur. at Birchington, 9 Feb. 1544/45),

MARY LEE, living in 1609, m. Henry Drake of Frenches Manor, in the hamlet of Wiggey, near Reigate, Surrey, d. 31 Dec. 1609, and bur. at Reigate, Gary B. Roberts has pointed out that their daughter, Elizabeth Drake, the wife of James Morley, is a direct ancestress of HRH Queen Elizabeth II, since her descendant, Catherine Hoskins, the wife of William Cavendish, 3rd Duke of Devonshire, is a maternal great-great-great-great-grandmother of Queen Elizabeth, the Queen Mother.

ROBERT DRAKE, settled in Accomack Co., Virginia (in that part which is now Northampton Co., Va.) before 8 Sept. 1636, when he was noted as deceased in a patent to his son, m. at Merstham, Surrey, 16 June 1622, Joan Gawton, dau. of Thomas Gawton of Merstham, and his wife, Patience Best, dau. of Nicholas Best of Aldersted, Merstham, Surrey, bapt. at Merstham, Surrey, 10 Nov. 1607, and d. in Northampton Co., Va., in the mid-17th century (she m. secondly, circa 1636, Thomas Hunt of Accomack, who died in 1656, and had further issue),

MARY DRAKE, bapt. at Merstham, Surrey, 30 Oct. 1625, living 26 March 1688, when her husband made his will, m. circa 1645, Capt. Richard Hill of Hunting Creek, Accomack Co., Va., b. in Eng., circa 1622, d. in Accomack Co., before 21 Nov. 1694, when his will was probated,

PATIENCE HILL, b. in Northampton Co., Va., circa 1650, d. before 15 Nov. 1713, m. circa 1670, Capt. John Drummond of Accomack Co., Va., who died before 6 Jan. 1713/14, when his will was probated,

CAPT. RICHARD DRUMMOND, of Hunting Creek, Accomack Co., Va., mentioned in the will of his grandfather, Capt. Richard Hill, 26 March 1688; m. circa 1690, Ann (Tilney) Michael, widow of John Michael, and dau. of Col. John Tilney, and his wife (m. 1 March 1647), Ann Smith, dau. of Thomas and Sarah Smith of Accomack, she was living 1 Apr. 1733, and d. before 6 July 1736, when her will was probated in Accomack Co.,

123

CAPT. RICHARD DRUMMOND of Hunting Creek, d. between 9 June 1730 and 4 Apr. 1732; m. Anne Hack (m. second, Alexander Buncle of Allhallows Parish, Worcester Co., Md.), dau. of Lt. Col. George Nicholas and Ann (Wright) Hack, b. in Accomack Co., Va., circa 1695, d. in Accomack Co., Va., between 27 Sept. and 27 Nov. 1770, the dates when her will was written and probated, (see Chapter LXXVIII),

Chapter XXXVIII

DUDLEY — HUGHES — YOUNG — SMITH

CHARLEMAGNE

(See Chapters II and LXVIII)

HERBERT II, Count of Vermandois and Troyes, b. 880/90, d. at St. Quentin, ca. 943; m. Liegarde, dau. of Robert I, King of France, and Adele, his wife,

ROBERT, Count of Troyes and Meaux, b. ca. 920; d. ca. 967/8; m. (first) Adelaide, dau. of Giselbert, Count of Burgundy, and his wife, Ermengarde, of Burgundy,

ADELAIDE DE VERMANDOIS, b. 950, d. 975/8; m. (second) Geoffrey I, Grisgonelle, Count of Anjou, son of Fulk II, the Good, Count of Anjou, and his wife, Gerberga of the Gatinais,

FULK III, the Black, Count of Anjou, d. 21 June 1040; m. (second) aft. 1000, Hildegarde, d. 1 Apr. 1040, at Jerusalem,

ERMENGARDE, of Anjou, d. 21 Mar. 1076; m. (second) ca. 1035, Aubri-Geoffrey, Count of Gatinais, d. 1 Apr. 1046, son of Geoffrey III, Count of Gatinais, and his wife, Beatrice, of Macon,

FULK IV, "Rechin", Count of Anjou, b. 1043, d. 14 Apr. 1109; m. 1090/1, Bertrade, dau. of Simon I, Seigneur of Montfort l'Amauri, and his wife, Agnes d'Evreux,

FULK V, the Young, Count of Anjou, King of Jerusalem, b. 1092, d. 10 Nov. 1143, at Jerusalem; m. (first) 1110, Erembourg, d. 1126, dau. of Helias, Count of Maine,

GEOFFREY V PLANTAGENET, Count of Anjou, Duke of

Normandy, b. 24 Aug. 1113, d. 7 Sept. 1151; m. (her second) 3 Apr. 1127, Matilda (Maud), b. 1104; d. 10 Sept. 1167, dau. of Henry I, King of England, widow of Henry V, Emperor of Germany,

HENRY II, King of England (25 Oct. 1154-1189) called Curt Mantel, b. at Lemans, 5 Mar. 1133, d. at Chinon, 6 July 1189; m. (her first) 18 May 1153, Eleanor of Aquitaine, b. 1123, d. 3 Mar. 1204,

JOHN I, King of England (1190-1216) b. at Oxford, 24 Dec. 1161, d. 19 Oct. 1216; m. (second) 24 Aug. 1200, Isabella, of Angouleme, b. 1188, d. 31 May 1246,

HENRY III, King of England (1216-1272), b. at Winchester, 1 Oct. 1207, d. at Winchester, 16 Nov. 1272; m. at Canterbury, 14 Jan. 1237, Eleanor, of Provence, b. 1217, d. at Amesbury, 24 Jan. 1291, dau. of Raymond IV Berenger, Count of Provence,

EDWARD I, King of England (1272-1307), b. at Westminster, 17 June 1239, d. at Burgh-on-the-Sands, Carlisle, 7 July 1307; m. (first) 1254, Eleanor, of Castile, d. 28 Nov. 1290, dau. of St. Ferdinand III, King of Castile (1217-1252), King of Leon (1230-1252) and his second wife, Jeanne, of Ponthieu, and Aumale,

JOAN PLANTAGENET, b. at Acre, 1272, d. 23 Apr. 1307; m. (his second) 1290, Sir Gilbert de Clare, Knt., Earl of Hereford, and Gloucester, surnamed, "the Red Earl", b. at Christchurch, Hants., 2 Sept. 1243, d. at Monmouth Castle, 7 Dec. 1298,

MARGARET DE CLARE, b. ca. 1292, d. 13 Apr. 1342; m. (second) 28 Apr. 1317, Sir Hugh de Audley, Lord Audley, cr. Earl of Gloucester, 16 Mar. 1336/7, d.s.p.m., 10 Nov. 1347, son of Hugh de Audley, Lord Audley, and his wife, Isolt, dau. of Edmund de Mortimer, of Wigmore,

MARGARET DE AUDLEY, b. ante 1325, d. 7 Sept. 1349; m. ante 6 July 1336, Sir Ralph de Stafford, K.G., b. 24 Sept. 1301, d. 21 Aug. 1372,

CATHERINE DE STAFFORD, b. ca. 1340, d. ante 25 Dec. 1361; m. (his first) 25 Dec. 1357, John de Sutton III, Lord Dudley, of Dudley Castle, b. 1338, d. aft. 1369,

SIR JOHN DE SUTTON IV, of Dudley Castle, b. 6 Dec. 1361, d. 1395/6, Inq. Post Mort. 1401; m. Joan (Jane) — , Inq. Post Mort. 1409,

SIR JOHN DE SUTTON V, of Dudley Castle, b. 1379, d. 1407, Inq. Post Mort. 1407; m. Constance Blount, d. 1432, dau. of Sir Robert Blount, of Barton, co. Derby,

SIR JOHN DE SUTTON VI, K.G., Baron Dudley, Lord Lieut. of Ireland (1428-1430), M.P. (1440-1487), b. 25 Dec. 1400, d. 30 Sept. 1487; m. aft. 1422, Elizabeth Berkeley, d. ca. 8 Dec. 1478, dau. of Sir John Berkeley, of Beverstone, Gloucs., and his first wife, Elizabeth Betteshorne,

SIR EDMUND SUTTON, Lord Dudley, d. bet. 6 July 1483 and 1487; m. (second) Matilda Clifford, dau. of Thomas de Clifford, 8th Lord Clifford,

THOMAS SUTTON, d. 1530; m. Grace Threlkeld, dau. of Lancelot Threlkeld, of Yeanwith,

RICHARD SUTTON, assumed the name, Dudley, was of Yeanwith, d. 1 Jan. 1593; m. Dorothy Sanford, dau. of Edward Sanford, of Asham,

JOHN DUDLEY, of Newcastle-on-Tyne, Northumberland, m. Bridget Carre, dau. of William Carre,

SIR ROBERT DUDLEY, Knt., Collector of the Port of Newcastle, m. Ann Wood, dau. of Christopher Wood,

ROBERT DUDLEY, b. at Bristol, England; m. a sister of Edward and Richard Green,

EDWARD DUDLEY, of Bristol, b. 1602, Northampton, d. in York Co., Virginia, 1655; m. Elizabeth Pritchard, d. 1691,

COL. RICHARD DUDLEY, summoned to Orphans Court, York

127

Co., Va., 1646, d. in Gloucester Co., Va., ca. 1687; m. Mary Sewell (Seawell),

JAMES DUDLEY, soldier, b. in Va., ca. 1670; m. (second) Ann Fleet, dau. of William Fleet, of Middlesex Co., Va.,

WILLIAM DUDLEY, b. 17 Aug. 1696, in Va., d. in Va., 15 Jan. 1760; m. 21 Apr. 1721, Judith Johnson,

ROBERT DUDLEY, b. in Middlesex Co., Va., 12 Nov. 1726, d. in Spottsylvania Co., Va., 27 Dec. 1766; m. in Feb. 1746, Joyce Gale (Gayle),

COL. WILLIAM DUDLEY, b. at Fredericksburg, Va., ca. 1766, d. at Fort Meigs, Ohio, 5 May 1813; m. 23 Aug. 1792, in Fayette Co., Kentucky, Lucy Smith, b. in Spottsylvania Co., Va., 26 July 1773, d. at Lexington, Ky., 15 Aug. 1852,

DR. JEPTHA DUDLEY, b. in Fayette Co., Ky., 17 June 1802, d. at Lexington, Ky., 2 Aug. 1864; m. in Fayette Co., Ky., 2 Feb. 1824, Juliet Smith, b. in Fayette Co., Ky., 8 Aug. 1808, d. at Memphis, Tenn., 2 Oct. 1827,

MARY JANE DUDLEY, b. in Fayette Co., Ky., 15 June 1827, d. at Nicholasville, Ky., 5 July 1905; m. in Fayette Co., Ky., 23 Dec. 1845, John Barkley Hughes, b. in Jessamine Co., Ky., 4 June 1825, d. in Jessamine Co., Ky. 31 May 1858,

MARY ANN HUGHES, b. in Jessamine Co., Ky., 1 Dec. 1848, d. at Nicholasville, Ky., 23 Jan. 1918; m. in Jessamine Co., Ky., 14 Nov. 1865, David Walter Young, b. in Jessamine Co., Ky., 12 Dec. 1842, d. in Jessamine Co., Ky., 21 Feb. 1882,

MARGARET ALLEN YOUNG, b. in Jessamine Co., Ky., 25 Sept. 1866; d. at Nicholasville, Ky., 26 Aug. 1943; m. in Fayette Co., Ky., 23 Dec. 1885, Walden Rogers Smith, b. in Jessamine Co., Ky., 9 June 1862; d. at Nicholasville, Ky., 31 Jan. 1941,

LEN YOUNG SMITH, b. at Nicholasville, Ky., 20 Oct. 1901; Northwestern University, B.A. (1923), M.A. (1924), J.D. (1927); member: Chicago, Illinois State and American Bar Associations; Fellow, American Bar Foundation; Chairman,

Department of Business Law, Northwestern Univ., 1948-70, Professional Lecturer, 1970-75; Co-author twelve volumes of Business Law, latest publication, Smith and Roberson's Business Law to be published Jan. 1977; Consultant and advisor to publishers of a 40-volume series on Illinois Law and Practice; member: SAR, past President General; Huguenot Society of Illinois, past President; The National Huguenot Society, President General, 1975-7; past Vice President General, General Society of 1812, past President Illinois Society; Ancient and Honourable Order of Jersey Blues; SR; Baronial Order of Magna Charta; Order of Americans of Armorial Ancestry; National Society, Americans of Royal Descent; Military Order of the Crusades; Order of the Crown of Charlemagne in the United States of America; Order of Lafayette; Sovereign Military Order of Jerusalem; Military and Hospital Order of Sáint Lazarus of Jerusalem; Society of Colonial Wars in the State of Illinois; Filson Club; Kentucky Historical Society; Connecticut Historical Society; National Gavel Society; University Club of Chicago; Phi Beta Kappa; Order of the Coif (law); Beta Gamma Sigma (business); etc.; listed in WHO'S WHO IN AMERICA; m. at Buchanan, Mich., 7 Aug. 1930, Helen Salome Tuttle and has issue,

1) MARGARET HELEN SMITH, b. 14 Jan. 1933, at Evanston, Ill.; m. 24 Apr. 1957, at Kenilworth, Ill., Roger Dean Smith, M.D., b. 6 Oct. 1932 at Brooklyn, N.Y.,
    a) WADE RUSSELL SMITH, b. 25 Mar. 1958;
    b) CRAIG ANDREW SMITH, b. 10 July 1960;
    c) DOUGLAS DEAN SMITH, b. 19 July 1963;
    d) ROGER LEN SMITH, b. 1 May 1967.

2) WILLIAM RANSOM TUTLE SMITH, b. 20 Jan. 1938, at Evanston, Ill.; m. 7 Aug. 1960, Ruth Vivian Kumblad, b. 5 Feb. 1939,
    a) ANDREW KUMBLAD SMITH, b. 29 July 1961;
    b) WILLIAM RANSOM TUTTLE SMITH, b. 20 Jan. 1963;
    c) ALEXANDER DAVID SMITH, b. 28 Apr. 1964;
    d) NANCY RUTH SMITH, b. 17 Oct. 1966.

Chapter XXXIX

DUDLEY — SIMPSON — WILLIAMS — ANDERSON — McDONALD

CHARLEMAGNE, King of the Franks, 768-814, Emperor of the West, 800-814, crowned Emperor at Rome on Christmas Day, 800, by Pope Leo III; b. 2 Apr. 742, d. 28 Jan 814; m. (third) 771, Princess Hildegarde of Swabia, b. 758, d. 30 Apr. 783,

LOUIS, the Pious, *le Debonnaire,* King of the Franks, Emperor of the West, 814-840, b. at Garrone, Aug. 778, d. nr. Mainz, 20 June 840,

ROTRUD, b. 800, or HILDEGARDE, b. 802/4; m. Count Gerard of Auverne,

RANULF I, Count of Poitou, 839/44, b. ca 815, d. 866; m. ca. 845, a dau of Rodrick, Count of Maine,

RANULF II, Count of Poitou, Duke of Aquitaine, b. ca. 845/50, d. 5 Aug. 890,

EBLES MANCER, a natural son, Count of Poitou, 890-92, d. 932; m. (second) 911, Emiliane,

WILLIAM I, Count of Poitou, b. ca. 915, d. 963; m. 935, Gerloc (Adele), d. ca. 14 Oct. 962, dau. of Rollo, Duke of Normandy,

ADELAIDE, of Poitou, b. 945, d. ca. 1004; m. ante 969, Hugh Capet, King of France, 987-996, d. 24 Oct. 996, (See Chapter X)

ROBERT II, the Pious, King of France, b. at Orleans, 970/71, d. at Meulun, 20 July 1031; m. (second) 998, Constance, of Toulouse, d. 1033,

130

HENRY I, King of France, b. 1005/6, d. 4 Aug. 1066; m. 29 Jan. 1044, Anne of Russia, d. 1075, dau. of Jaroslav I, Grand Duke of Kiev, d. 1054, and Ingegard, dau. of Olaf III, King of Sweden,

HUGH MAGNUS, Duke of France and Burgandy, Marquis of Orleans, Count of Amiens, Chaumont, Paris, Valois, Vermandois, etc., Leader of the First Crusade, 1097, d. 1101; m. Adelaide de Vermandois, Countess of Vermandois,

ISABEL DE VERMANDOIS, Countess of Leicester, d. ante 1147; m. (first) 1096, Robert de Beaumont, Seigneur of Beaumont, Pont-Audemer, Brione and Vatteville in Normandy, Count of Meulen in French Vexin, Earl of Leicester, Companion of William the Conqueror, at the Battle of Hastings, 1066; b. 1046, d. 5 June 1118, son of Roger de Beaumont,

ROBERT DE BEAUMONT II, called le Bossu or le Goczen, Earl of Leicester, b. ca. 1104, d. 5 Apr. 1168; m. aft. 1120, Amice de Montfort, dau. of Ralph, Seigneur of Gall and Montfort, in Brittany, and grand-daughter, of Ralph, Earl of Norfolk, by Emma, dau. of William FitzOsbern,

HAWISE DE BEAUMONT, d. 24 Apr. 1197; m. ca. 1150, William FitzRobert, d. 23 Nov. 1183, Earl of Gloucester, Lord of the Manor of Glamorgan and Cardiff Castle, 1st son of Robert "de Caen", Earl of Gloucester, and his wife, Mabel, dau. of Robert FitzHamon,

AMICE FITZ ROBERT, Countess of Gloucester, d. 1 Jan. 1224/5; m. Richard de Clare, 6th Earl of Clare, Hertford and Gloucester, Magna Charta Surety, 1215, d. ca. 28 Nov. 1217, son of Roger de Clare, Earl of Hertford, and Maud de St. Hilary, dau. of James de St. Hilary,

SIR GILBERT DE CLARE, Magna Charta Surety, 1215 7th Earl of Clare, Earl of Hertford and Gloucester, b. ca. 1180, d. at Penros, Brittany, 25 Oct. 1230; m. 9 Oct. 1217, Isabel Marshall, d. at Berkhampstead, 17 Jan. 1239/40, dau. of Sir William Marshall, named in Magna Charta, 3rd Earl of

Pembroke, Marshal of England, and his wife Isabel, dau. of Richard de Clare,

SIR RICHARD DE CLARE, 8th Earl of Clare, Earl of Gloucester and Hertford, b. 4 Aug. 1222, d. 15 July 1262; m. (second) 25 Jan. 1237/8, Maud de Lacy, Countess of Lincoln, d. ante 10 Mar. 1288/9, at Lincoln,

THOMAS DE CLARE, 2nd son, Crusader, Gov. of London, Lord of Inchquin and Youghae, d. in Ireland, 1287/8; m. Juliane FitzMaurice, dau. of Maurice FitzMaurice, Lord Justice of Ireland, and Emmeline de Longespee,

MARGARET DE CLARE, b. ca. 1292, d. 13 Apr. 1342; m. (second) Lord Bartholomew de Badlesmere, hanged 1332,

ELIZABETH DE BADLESMERE, b. 1313, d. 1356; m. (first) 27 June 1316, Lord Edmund Mortimer, of Wigmore, d. 1331, son of Sir Roger Mortimer, 8th Baron of Wigmore, Earl of March, b. 25 Apr. 1282, d. 29 Nov. 1330, and Joan de Geneville, b. 2 Feb. 1285/6, d. 19 Oct. 1356,

SIR ROGER MORTIMER, 2nd Earl of March, K.G. 23 Apr. 1349, b. 11 Nov. 1328, at Ludlow, d. 26 Feb. 1359/60; m. Phillippa de Montagu, b. 5 Jan. 1381/2, dau. of William de Montagu, Earl of Salisbury,

EDMUND MORTIMER, Lord Mortimer, 3rd Earl of March, b. 1 Feb. 1352, d. 27 Dec. 1381; m. 1368, Philippa Plantagenet, grand-dau. of Edward III, King of England. She was b. 16 Aug. 1355, dau. of Lionel of Antwerp, Duke of Clarence, and Elizabeth Burgh,

ELIZABETH MORTIMER, b. at Usk, 12 Feb. 1370/1, d. 20 Apr. 1417; m. (first) ante 10 Dec. 1379, Sir Henry de Percy, Lord Percy, K.G., K.B., M.P., surnamed "Hotspur", b. 20 May 1364, at Alnwick, co. York, d. at the Battle of Shrewsbury, 14 Aug. 1403,

ELIZABETH DE PERCY, d. 26 Oct. 1427; m. 1404 John de Clifford, d. 13 Mar. 1421/3, at Meux, France, 7th Lord Clifford, K.G., M.P. 1411-21,

THOMAS DE CLIFFORD, 8th Lord Clifford, M.P. 1436-53, b. 25 Mar. 1414, slain at the Battle of St. Albans, 22 May 1455; m. aft. Mar. 1424, Joan Dacre, dau. of Thomas Dacre, Lord Dacre, of Gillesland, and Phillipa, dau. of Ralph Neville, Earl of Westmoreland, and Margaret Stafford,

MATILDA DE CLIFFORD, m. (his second) Sir Edmund Sutton, Knt. of Dudley, d. aft. 6 July 1483, son of Sir John Sutton, K.G., Lord Dudley,

THOMAS SUTTON, 5th son, d. 1530; m. Grace Threlkeld, dau. of Lancelot Threlkeld, Esq. of Yeanwith, co. Cumberland,

RICHARD SUTTON, of Yeanwith (Yeanwith Manor), took the name Dudley, d. 1 Jan. 1593; m. Dorothy Sanford, dau. of Edward Sanford, of Asham,

JOHN DUDLEY, 3rd son, of Newcastle-on-Tyne, Northumberland; m. Bridgett Carre, dau. of William Carre,

SIR ROBERT DUDLEY, Knt., Mayor of Newcastle, Collector of the Port, 1603, Knighted by King James; m. Ann Wood, dau. of Christopher Wood,

ROBERT DUDLEY, of Bristol; m. a sister of Edward and Robert Green, who mentioned Robert Dudley in their wills. In 1697, members of the Green family of Bristol visited some of their Dudley cousins in Middlesex Co., Va.

EDWARD DUDLEY, of Bristol, b. 1602 in Northampton, Eng.; m. 1626 Elizabeth Pritchard, dau. of Hester and William Pritchard, of Northampton. Came to America (Virginia) ante 19 May 1637, bringing five sons and possibly some daughters. No date of death but he was liv. in 1651 when he witnessed a deed and in 1654 when his tithes were rated in Lancaster Co., Va. Edward Dudley was the progenitor of the Dudley families of Va., N.C. and other Southern states. He first settled in York Co., Va., where he remained until 1651, when he removed to that part of Lancaster Co. lying south of the Rappahannock River which in 1773 became Middlesex County.

WILLIAM DUDLEY, eldest son, b. in Bristol, England, ca. 1621. In 1657, he patented land in Dragon Swamp, Lancaster Co., Va.. In 1666, he was a Vestryman of Christ Church Parish, Middlesex Co. and in 1668, he became Warden of Pianketank or Lower Chapel of Christ Church. He d. in 1677; m. Elizabeth Cary and had issue: James, Thomas, William, John and Christopher.

CHRISTOPHER DUDLEY, b. 1670, Gloucester Co., Va.; m. 1705, Mary Lewis, b. 1686, d. Jan. 1747, dau. of William and Mary (Smith) Lewis. They removed to Chowan Co., N.C., where he is shown as a planter in 1712. He is shown in Onslow Co., in 1731, as a Justice; d. Onslow Co., Jan. 1746.

EDWARD DUDLEY, eldest son, b. ca. 1706, Gloucester Co., Va., d. 25 Mar. 1745, Onslow Co., N.C.; m. 1726, Hasten Starkie, dau. of John and Sarah (White) Starkie; liv. 1781,

ANN DUDLEY, eldest child, b. ca. 1727, Onslow Co., N.C., d. between 1763/99; m. ca. 1746, William Simpson, liv. in Brunswick Co., 1774, d. 1799, in Chowan Co., N.C.,

MARY ANN SIMPSON, b. in New Hanover Co., N.C., 16 Jan. 1755, d. at Charleston, S.C. 17 Apr. 1840; m. Benjamin Williams, b. in Lunenburg Co., Va., 13 Nov. 1754, d. at Smithville, N.C., Lt. 2nd Reg., N.C. Continental Line, Revolutionary War.

MARY WILLIAMS, b. 4 Oct. 1776, at Smithville, N.C., d. 13 Oct. 1834, at Charleston, S.C.; m. 1794, in Brunswick Co., N.C., John Anderson, 5th, b. at Smithville, N.C., 20 Feb. 1769, d. at Charleston, S.C., 8 Apr. 1847, son of John Anderson, 3rd, b. ca. 1715, d. aft. 1790,

SUSANNA ANDERSON, b. 11 Mar. 1802, at Smithville, N.C., d. 5 Aug. 1854, at Charleston, S.C.; m. 7 Sept. 1825, at Smithville, N.C., William Henry McDonald, b. 5 Sept. 1805, at Smithville, N.C., d. 11 Sept. 1887, at Charleston, S.C., son of Isaac McDonald, b. ca. 1760, d. 1820, in Smithville, N.C.,

WILLIAM TROUT McDONALD, b. 18 June 1831, at Charleston, S.C., d. 7 Feb. 1892, at Charleston; m. 22 Jan. 1856, at

Charleston, Theresa Ann Dickinson, b. 8 Aug. 1838, at Charleston, S.C.,

WILLIAM OGIER MCDONALD, b. 1 July 1868, at Charleston, S.C., d. 18 Oct. 1930, at Gainesville, Fla.; m. 1 July 1891, at Charleston, S.C., Kate St. Clair, b. 17 Mar. 1870, at Marion, S.C., d. 8 Apr. 1953, at Ocala, Fla., dau. of James W. St. Clair of Jessamine Co., Ky., b. 1832, and Carolina M.K. Honour, b. 22 Jan. 1840, m. 9 Dec. 1866, d. 29 Mar. 1884, Fitzgerald, Ga.,

WALTER SMITH MCDONALD, b. 11 July 1900, at Charleston, S.C.; ed.: Hastoc Prep. School, Spartansburg, S.C.; Clemson Univ., Clemson, S.C.; Registered Professional Engineer; Lt. Col., U.S. Army (Engineers, Adj. Gen. Dept., and Gen. Staff Corps) 1942-46; member: Nat'l Soc. of Professional Engineers; American Soc. of Civil Engineers (Fellow) and Past State President; Georgia Engineering Society (a Founder) and Past State V.P.; Society of the Cincinnati; SAR; Society of the War of 1812; Sons of Confederate Veterans, Military Order of World Wars, Society of Military Engineers, Officers Reserve Corps, Old Guard of Georgia, Huguenot Society of S.C., Order of the Crown of Charlemagne in the United States of America, National Society Americans of Royal Descent, Society of Colonial Wars, St. Andrews Society, Clan Donald; m. 30 June 1928, Ellen Bates Clinkscales, and has issue:

1) ELLEN CLINKSCALES MCDONALD, b. 8 Sept. 1929; m. 21 Dec. 1954, Alvin Leonard Chason, Jr.,

    a) WALTER MCDONALD CHASON, b. 19 Feb. 1957;

    b) KATHERINE HONOUR CHASON, b. 25 Mar. 1959.

Chapter XL

DUNGAN — HOLDEN — WICKHAM — GARDINER — NOTTINGHAM

CHARLEMAGNE

(See Chapters XXXVI and LXX)

BALDWIN IV, Barbatus, Count of Flanders and Artois, b. 980, d. 30 May 1036; m. 1012, Otgiva (Ogive), d. 21 Feb. 1030,

BALDWIN V, the Pious, Count of Flanders, b. at Lille, 1012, d. at Lille, 1 Sept. 1067; m. ca. 1028, Adele (Adelheid) dau of Robert II, King of France, a descendant of Charlemagne (See Chapter X)

MATHILDA (MAUD) of Flanders, b. 1032, d. 3 Nov. 1083; m. 1053, William I, the Conqueror, King of England, a descendant of Charlemagne. (See Chapter LVII)

HENRY I, King of England 1100-1135, "Beauclerc", b. 1070, at Selby, Yorkshire, d. in England, 1 Dec. 1135; m. 1102, Matilda of Scotland, b. 1079, d. 1 May 1118, dau. of Malcolm III, King of Scotland,

PRINCESS MATHILDA (MAUD), b. ca. 1103/4, d. 10 Sept. 1167; m. 3 Apr. 1127, Geoffrey V, Plantagenet, Count of Anjou, b. 24 Aug. 1113, d. 7 Sept. 1151,

HENRY II, King of England, 1154-1189, "Curt Mantel", b. 5 Mar. 1132/3, at LeMans, d. at Chinon, 6 July 1189; m. 18 May 1153, Eleanore (Eleanor), Duchess of Aquitaine, and Queen of France, d. 1202, divorced wife of Louis VII, King of France,

JOHN I, King of England, 1199-1216, "Lackland", b. at Oxford, 24 Dec. 1166, d. 19 Oct. 1216, at Newark Castle,

Nottinghamshire; m. Isabel (Isabella), d. 1246, dau. of Aymer, Count d' Angoulome,

HENRY III, King of England, 1216-1272, b. 13 Oct. 1207, d. 15 Nov. 1272; m. 14 Jan. 1236, Eleanor, d. 25 June 1291, dau. of Raymond-Berenger IV, Count of Provence,

EDWARD I, King of England, 1272-1307, b. at Westminster, 17 June 1239, d. at Burgh-on-the-Sands, 7 July 1307, crowned 19 Aug. 1274; m. (second) Margaret, dau. of Philip III, King of France,

THOMAS, "of Brotherton", Earl of Norfolk and Marshal of England, b. 1 June 1300, d. 1338; m. (first) ca. 1320, Alice, dau. of Sir Roger de Hales, Coroner of Norfolk, 1303-13,

MARGARET, *suo jure,* Countess of Norfolk, cr. in Parliament in her absence, Duchess of Norfolk, 29 Sept. 1397, d. 24 Mar. 1398/9; m. (first) 1337/8, John de Segrave, Lord Segrave, d. 1353,

ELIZABETH DE SEGRAVE, *suo jure* Baroness Segrave, b. 25 Oct. 1338, d. 24 Mar. 1398/9; m. 1349, John de Mowbray, Lord Mowbray, slain by Saracens, 1368, at Thrace, while on Crusade,

ELEANOR DE MOWBRAY, b. ante 25 Mar. 1364; m. by May 1384, Sir John de Welles, 2nd Baron Welles, of Gainsby, b. at Coinsholme, Lincs., 20 Apr. 1352, d. 1422,

EUDO DE WELLES, b. at Gainsby, d. ante 1421; m. Maud de Greystoke, dau. of Ralph de Greystoke and his wife Katherine de Clifford, (See Chapter LXXVII p. 281)

WILLIAM DE WELLES, Lord Chancellor of Ireland, 1461-65; m. — Barnwell of Crickstown,

ELIZABETH WELLES, m. 1463/4, Christopher Plunket, of County Meath, 2nd Lord Killeen, d. 1467,

JANET PLUNKET, m. Nicholas St. Lawrence, Lord Howth, d. at Howth, 10 July 1526,

ALISON ST. LAWRENCE, m. Patrick Whyte of Malaffin and Flemingston,

MARGARET WHYTE, m. ca. 1547, Walter Forster, of Dublin, Ireland,

MARGARET FORSTER, d. at Dublin, Ireland, ca. 21 June 1597; m. ca. 1577, Sir John Dungan, of Castleton, Kildrought, Co. Kildare, d. at Dublin, 8 Aug. 1592,

THOMAS DUNGAN, of Lincoln's Inn, b. ca. 1584, d. in Ireland, aft. 2 Mar. 1639 and bef. 29 Nov. 1665/6; m. 1605, Mary — ,

WILLIAM DUNGAN, Perfumer, b. ca. 1607, bapt. as an adult, 15 June 1628, d. at London, England, Sept. 1636; m. at London, 27 Aug. 1629, Frances Latham, bapt. Kempston, Beds., England, 15 Feb. 1609; d. at Newport, R.I., Sept. 1677,

FRANCES DUNGAN, bapt. 12 Nov. 1632, in England, d. at Warwick, R.I., in 1697; m. in 1648, Hon. Randall Holden, b. 1612, d. at Warwick, R.I., 23 Aug. 1692, Marshall and Corp. at Portsmouth, R.I., 1638, Assistant, 1647 *et seq.,* Capt., 1664, Deputy 1666-86,

BARBARA HOLDEN, b. at Warwick, R.I., 2 July 1688, d. in R.I., 1707; m., 4 June 1690-1, Samuel Wickham, b. at Wethersfield, Conn., 16 June 1664, d. at Kingston, R.I., ca. 1712,

THOMAS WICKHAM, b. at Newport, R.I., 30 July 1700, d. at Newport, 19 Sept. 1777; m. 23 Mar. 1726, Hannah Brewer, b. at Newport, R.I., 1706 or 9 June 1700, d. at Newport, 12 Nov. 1788,

THOMAS WICKHAM, b. at Newport, R.I., 5 Apr. 1736, d. at Newport, 21 Feb. 1816; m. at Newport, 28 Dec. 1762, Elizabeth Wanton, b. at Newport, 22 Oct. 1742, d. at Newport, 25 Aug. 1814, dau. of Gov. Joseph Wanton, of R.I., and his wife, Mary Winthrop, and gr. dau. of Gov. William Wanton, of R.I., and his wife, Ruth Bryant,

ELIZABETH WICKHAM, b. at Newport, R.I., 2 Nov. 1773, d. in Somerset Co., Md., 15 Aug. 1803; m. Walter Clarke Gardiner,

b. in R.I., bapt. as an adult in 1790, d. in Northampton Co., Va., Mar. 1817,

MARY STEAD PINCKNEY GARDINER, b. at Newark, N.J., 28 Nov. 1798, d. in Northampton Co., Va., 15 Mar. 1823; m. (his second) ca. 19 June 1814, Richard Nottingham, b. in Northampton Co., Va., ca. 1783, d. in Northampton Co., Va., ca. 12 Jan. 1818,

LUTHER NOTTINGHAM, b. in Northampton Co., Va., 2 Dec. 1817, d. at Cobbs Station, Northampton Co., Va., 26 Oct. 1867; m. (second) in Northampton Co., 2 Oct. 1849, Catherine E. Dalby, b. in Northampton Co., 6 Jan. 1828, d. in Norfolk, Va., 4 Nov. 1905,

ARTHUR MCKENDREE NOTTINGHAM, b. at Eastville, Va., 17 Mar. 1856, d. at Onancock, Accomack Co., Va., 30 Aug. 1920; m. (second) at Baltimore, Md., 25 July 1900, Alice (Evans) Toulson, b. at Ewell, Somerset Co., Md., 19 Apr. 1875, d. at Westfield, Ind., 16 Jan. 1968 (See p. 111. Vol. II of PEDIGREES OF SOME OF THE EMPEROR CHARLEMAGNE'S DESCENDANTS for fuller account),

WILLIAM PROSSER NOTTINGHAM, b. at Onancock, Accomack Co., Va., 27 Apr. 1911; studied at Emory Univ., Univ. of Va. Law School, LL.B., 1934; member: Pi Kappa Alpha; Masonic Lodge, Murat Shrine Club, Indianapolis, Ind.; Indianapolis Athletic Club; Order of the Crown of Charlemagne in the United States of America, Historian General; Society of Colonial Wars, Ala.; Nat'l Society Americans of Royal Descent, Chancellor General; Military Order of the Crusades; Order of Three Crusades, Baronial Order of Magna Charta; Order of Americans of Armorial Ancestry; The Order of Colonial Lords of Manors in America; Hereditary Order of Descendants of Colonial Governors; Order of Descendants of Colonial Physicians and Chirurgeons; SAR, Indiana Chapter; Hospitaller Order of St. John of Jerusalem; m. (first) 5 Jan. 1933, at Staunton, Va., Dorothy Louise Oliver, b. 21 Mar. 1910, at Atlanta, Ga.; marriage dissolved by divorce; m. (second) 20 Dec. 1957, Gwynne Roads (Wagner) Dulin, b. 6 Oct. 1909, at Noblesville, Ind. Issue by first marriage:

1) WILLIAM PROSSER NOTTINGHAM, Jr., b. 8 Aug. 1938, at Clarksburg, W.Va.; m. (first) 1958, Ann Louise Terizian; div. aft. 1959; m. (second) 1964, Barbara (Bonner) Hansen. Issue by first wife:

   a) CATHERINE ANN NOTTINGHAM, b. 14 Feb. 1959.

   Issue by second wife:

   b) LESLIE NOTTINGHAM, b. 26 Mar. 1965,

2) JOHN OLIVER NOTTINGHAM, b. 28 July 1942, at Clarksburg, W. Va.

Chapter XLI

DUNGAN — CARRELL — CORNELL

CHARLEMAGNE

(See Chapter XL)

WILLIAM DUNGAN, Perfumer, b. ca. 1606, bapt. as an adult 15 June 1628, d. at London, England, Sept. 1636; m. at London, 27 June 1629, Frances Latham, bapt. Kempston, Beds., England, 15 Feb. 1609, d. at Newport, Rhode Island, Sept. 1677,

REV. THOMAS DUNGAN, b. at London, Eng., ca. 1632/4, bur in the churchyard at Cold Springs, Bucks Co., Pa., 1687/8; m. in 1663, prob. at Newport, R.I., Elizabeth Weaver, b. at Newport, R.I., in 1647, d. in Bucks Co., Pa., 1697, dau. of Sgt. Clement Weaver, and his wife, Mary Freeborn,

SARAH DUNGAN, b. ca. 1675-8, at East Greenwich, R.I., d. in Bucks Co., Pa., 1760; m. (first) in Pa., ca. 1697, James Carrell I, b. in Londonderry, Ireland, d. in Bucks Co., Pa., 10 Feb. 1720,

JAMES CARRELL II, b. in Bucks Co., Pa., ca. 1699, d. in Bucks Co., 17 May 1749; m. prob. in Bucks Co., 17 Aug. 1723, Diana Van Kirk, b. in Bucks Co., 1697; d. in Bucks Co., 1749,

JACOB CARRELL (KERRIL), b. in Northampton Twp., Bucks Co., Pa., 12 Dec. 1732, d. in Bucks Co., 3 July 1817; m. 12 July 1769, at Christ Church, Philadelphia, Pa., Elizabeth Jamieson, b. in Bucks Co., Pa., d. in Bucks Co., 12 July 1829, dau. of Daniel Jamieson, of Durham Twp., Bucks Co., Pa.,

ELIZABETH CARRELL, b. 7 Mar. 1790, in Bucks Co., Pa., d. 13 Mar. 1872, in Bucks Co.; m. prob. in Bucks Co., 26 Dec.

141

1817, John Cornell, b. and d. in Bucks Co., son of Cornelius and Phoebe Cornell,

JACOB CARRELL CORNELL, b. in Bucks Co., Pa., 8 Aug. 1823, d. in Bucks Co., 29 Dec. 1896; m. prob. in Bucks Co., 4 Nov. 1858, Rebecca A. Rine, b. 5 Feb. 1836, d. in Bucks Co., Pa.,

WILLIAM RINE CORNELL, b. in Bucks Co., Pa., 26 July 1867, d. at Charlotte, N.C., 24 Dec. 1934; m. at Dalton, Ga., 26 Jan. 1897, Minerei Greer, b. at Dalton, Ga., 10 Dec. 1875, liv. 1969, dau. of John Bryant Greer, and his wife, Ada Alice Atkinson,

ALYCE CORNELL, b. at Charlotte, N.C., 22 Nov. 1910; m. at Charlotte, N.C., Pickette Laney Williams, b. at Monroe, N.C., 15 Jan. 1909. She is a graduate of Wingate College, Wingate, N.C.; member: DAR, D.A.C., Nat'l Soc. Daughters of the XVII Century, Order of the Crown of Charlemagne in the United States of America, Society of the Descendants of the Colonial Clergy.

Chapter XLII

DUNGAN — CORSON — DAY — BATES

(See Chapter XL)

WILLIAM DUNGAN, Perfumer, b. ca. 1606, bur. 20 Sept. 1636; m. at London, 27 June 1629, Frances (Latham) Weston, bapt. 15 Feb. 1609, d. at Newport, R.I., Sept. 1677,

REV. THOMAS DUNGAN, b. at London, Eng. ca. 1632/4; bur. in churchyard at Cold Springs, Bucks Co., Pa. in 1687/8; m. in 1663, prob. at Newport, R.I., Elizabeth Weaver, b. at Newport, R.I., in 1647; d. in Bucks Co., Pa., in 1697,

THOMAS DUNGAN, JR., b. in R.I. in 1671; d. in Northampton, Twp., Bucks Co., Pa., 23 June 1759; m. ca. 1697, Mary Drake, b. 2 Jan. 1680 at Piscataway, N.J.,

JOSEPH DUNGAN, b. in Northampton Twp., Bucks Co., Pa., 13 Jan. 1710; d. 25 Aug. 1785; m. Mary Ohl, b. 25 Feb. 1710; d. 24 Apr. 1788,

SARAH DUNGAN, b. 25 Aug. 1742, d. 2 July 1811; m. in 1761, Benjamin Corson of Northampton, Bucks Co., Pa., b. 6 June 1743; d. 2 Oct. 1811,

JOSEPH CORSON, b. in Dublin Twp., Philadelphia Co., Pa., 15 Mar. 1764, d. in Montgomery Co., Pa., on 4 Mar. 1834; m. in 1786/7, Hannah Dickenson, b. prob. in Talbot Co., Md., ca. 1765-70, d. on 10 Dec. 1810,

HIRAM CORSON, M.D., b. at Hickory Town, Plymouth Twp., Montgomery Co., Pa., 8 Oct. 1804, d. in Bucks Co., Pa., 4

Mar. 1896; m. at Philadelphia, Pa., 26 Dec. 1833, Ann Jones Foulke, b. at Penllyn, Pa., 15 Sept. 1811, d. at Plymouth Meeting, Pa., 25 June 1888,

FRANCES STOCKTON CORSON, b. 25 Oct. 1849; m. 12 Nov. 1874, Richard Hopper Day of Philadelphia and Germantown, Pa.,

BERTHA CORSON DAY, b. at Philadelphia, Pa. 20 Aug. 1875, d. at Wilmington, Dela., 16 Dec. 1908; m. at Germantown, Pa., 17 May 1902, Daniel Moore Bates, b. at Wilmington, Dela., 18 • Apr. 1876; d. at Wilmington, Dela., 26 Feb. 1953,

CHARLES THEODORE RUSSELL BATES, b. at Wilmington, Dela., 24 July 1907, was educated at Middlesex School, Concord, Mass.; Harvard University; University of Pa.; University of Vienna; University of Dela., Graduate Economics. He is President of Arizona Society of Certified Public Accountants; Director of Great Western Bank; Director of Arizona Sonora Desert Museum; Chairman of the Board, Cold Spring Bleachery at Yardley, Pa.; Vice President and Director of Selby Motors, Tucson, Ariz.; member of Univ. of Ariz. President's Club, Delaware Society of Colonial Wars, St. Anthony Club of New York, Rotary Club of Tucson, Loyal Legion, Order of the Crown of Charlemagne in the United States of America, Wilmington Club of Wilmington, Dela., Tucson Country Club, Univ. of Ariz. Foundation. He m. 16 Dec. 1937 (her second) at Las Vegas, Nev. Lucille Alberta Weeks, and has no issue.

Chapter XLIII

ELLIS

CHARLEMAGNE, son of King Pepin and Queen Bertrada, b. 2 Apr. 742, Ingelheim, d. 28 Jan. 814, Aix-la-Chapelle; King of the Franks (768-771) and Lombards (774), crowned Emperor (800); m. (third) 771, Hildegarde, dau. of Duke Gerold of Alamannia and Imma; b. 758, d. 30 Apr. 783,

LOUIS I, the Pious, b. Aug. 778, Chasseneuil, d. nr. Mainx, 6 June 840, King of Aquitaine (781), co-emperor (813), Emperor of the West (814); m. (second) Feb. 819, at Aix-la-Chapelle, Judith, dau. of Count Welf of Alamannia and Heilwig of Saxony, b. ca. 804/6, d. 19 Apr. 843, at Tours,

CHARLES II, the Bald, b. 13 June 823, at Frankfort-on-Main, d. nr. Mt. Cenlis in the Alps, 6 Oct. 877, Duke of Alamannia, Rhaetia, and Alsace (829), King of Neustria (838), King of the West Franks (840/3), of Lorraine (869), and of Italy (875), Emperor (875); m. (first) 13 Dec. 842, Ermentrude, dau. of Count Odo of Orleans, b. ca. 830, d. 6 Oct. 869,

HERSENT, of France, dau. of Charles II prob. by his second wife, Adelaide, d. 877, m (his first) Regnier, I, Count of Hainaut, d. 916, (See Chapter XXXII)

GISELBERT, Duke of Lorraine, d. 939; m. Gerberga, dau. of Henry, the Fowler, King of Saxony, d. 5 May 984,

GERBERGA, of Lorraine, m. Albert I, the Pious, Count of Vermandois, b. ca. 920, d. 988, (See Chapter LXVIII)

HERBERT III, Count of Vermandois, b. ca. 955, d. ca. 1000; m. (her second) Ermengarde (Irmgard), dau. of Reinald, Count of Bar,

OTHO, Count of Vermandois, b. ca. 1000, d. 25 May 1045; m. Pavie (Parvie),

HERBERT IV, Count of Vermandois and Valois, b. ca. 1032, d. ca. 1080; m. Adela de Vexin, dau. of Raoul III, the Great, Count of Valois, Vexin, etc.,

ADELAIDE (ADELHEID), Countess of Vermandois and of Valois, d. ca. 1120; m. Hugh the Great, Duke of France and Burgundy, Leader of the First Crusade, Marquis of Orleans, Count of Amiens, Chaumont, Paris, Valois, Vermandois, etc.; d. 1101, son of Henry I, King of France, by Anne, dau. of Yaroslav I, of Kiev,

ISABEL DE VERMANDOIS, Countess of Leicester, d. ante July 1147; m. (first) Robert de Beaumont, Seigneur of Beaumont, Pont-Audemer, Brionne and Vatteville in Normandy, Count of Meulan in the French Vexin, Earl of Leicester, b. ca. 1046, d. 5 June 1118, son and heir of Roger de Beaumont, (See Chapters X, XXXII, XXXIX, LXVIII)

SIR ROBERT DE BEAUMONT, knighted 1122, 2nd Earl of Leicester, Justiciar of England (1155-1168); m. aft. Nov. 1120, Amice de Montfort, dau. of Ralph de Gael de Montfort, Lord of Gael and Montfort in Brittany, Earl of Norfolk, Suffolk and Cambridge in England, and his wife, Emma Fitz Osbern, dau. of William Fitz Osbern,

SIR ROBERT DE BEAUMONT, 3rd Earl of Leicester, Crusader in 1179, b. ante 1135, d. 1190, at Durazzo, Greece; m. ca. 1155, Pernell (Petronilla) de Grantmesnil, d. 1 Apr. 1212, dau. of Hugh de Grantmesnil,

MARGARET DE BEAUMONT, d. 12 Jan. 1235/6; m. ante 1173, Saher (Saier) de Quincy, cr. Earl of Winchester by King John, 1207, Magna Charta Surety, 1215; Crusader in 1219, b. ca. 1155, d. 3 Nov. 1219, before Damietta, Egypt, bur. at Acre in the Holy Land,

HAWISE DE QUINCY, m. aft. 11 Feb. 1222/3, Sir Hugh de Vere, b. ca. 1210, Earl of Oxford, Hereditary Master Chamberlain of England, son of Robert de Vere, Magna Charta Surety,

ROBERT DE VERE, b. 1240, 5th Earl of Oxford, d. ante 7 Sept. 1296; m. by 22 Feb. 1252, Alice de Sanford, d. 1285, dau. of Gilbert de Sanford,

JOAN DE VERE, d. in Surrey, 1293; m. 1283, Sir William de Warenne, b. 1256, 7th Earl of Surrey, killed in a tournament at Croydon on 15 Dec. 1286, son of John de Warenne, Earl of Surrey and Alice (Alfais) de Lusignan,

ALICE DE WARENNE, b. in Surrey, d. ante 23 May 1338; m. 1305/6, Sir Edmund Fitz Alan, Knt., b. 1 May 1285, beheaded in Hereford, 17 Nov. 1326, 8th Earl of Arundel, knighted 22 May 1306,

SIR RICHARD FITZ ALAN, b. 1306, Earl of Arundel and Warenne, d. 24 Jan. 1375/6; m. (his second) (her second) 5 Feb. 1344/5. Eleanor Plantagent, d. at Arundel, 11 Jan. 1372, dau. of Henry Plantagenet, Earl of Lancaster and Maud de Chaworth,

SIR RICHARD FITZ ALAN, K.G., Earl of Arundel and Surrey, b. at Arundel, 1346, beheaded 21 Sept. 1397; m. (her second) 28 Sept. 1359, Elizabeth de Bohun, d. 3 Apr. 1385, dau. of Sir William de Bohun, K.G. and Elizabeth de Badlesmere,

ELIZABETH FITZ ALAN, d. 8 July 1425; m. (her third) (his fourth) ante 19 Aug. 1401, Sir Robert Goushill, Knt., b. at Hoveringham, Notts.,

JOAN GOUSHILL, liv. 1460; m. Sir Thomas Stanley, K.B., b. at Lathom, 1406; d. as Lord Stanley of Lathom and Knowsley, Lord. Lt. of Ireland and Lord Chamberlain of England, 20 Feb. 1459,

MARGARET STANLEY, (her brother Sir William crowned Henry VII at Bosworth Field); m. (first) 1459, Sir William Troutbeck, Knt., b. at Dunham-on-the-Hill, co. Chester, ca. 1432, d. as Lord of Prynes Castle, 1459,

JOAN TROUTBECK, b. at Prynes Castle, co. Chester; m. (second) Sir William Griffith, Lord of Penrhyn Castle, co. Caernarvon, Wales, knighted at Bath on St. Andrew's Eve, 1489 at the

Coronation of Prince Arthur; d. as Chamberlain of North Wales,

SIR WILLIAM GRIFFITH, Lord of Penrhyn Castle, co. Caernarvon, Wales, High Sheriff of Caernarvon, 1493/4, knighted at Touraine, Christmas 1513, Chamberlain of North Wales; m. (second) at Caernarvon, 1522, Jane Puleston, b. at Caernarvon Castle, Wales,

SIBILL GRIFFITH, b. at Penrhyn Castle; m. Owen ap Hugh of Bodeon, b. at Bodeon, Anglesea, High Sheriff of Anglesea, 1563, 1578, 1580, d. 1613,

JANE OWEN, b. at Bodeon, Anglesea; m. Hugh Gwyn, b. at Penarth, Caernaronshire, Wales, High Sheriff of Caernaronshire 1600,

SIBILL (SYBILL) HUGH, b. at Penarth, Caenaronshire, Wales, d. at Gadfa, Llanwddyn; m. ante 20 Sept. 1588, at Penarth, John Powell (alias John ap Howel-Goch) b. at Gadfa, Llanwddyn, Montgomeryshire, Wales; bur. at Church of Llanwddyn, Montgomeryshire, Wales, 24 July 1636,

ELIZABETH POWELL (HOWEL-GOCH) b. at Gadfa, Llanwddyn, Montgomeryshire, Wales, d. at Llwyn-du, Llangelynin, Merionethshire, Wales, 1664/5; m. in Merionethshire, Wales, ca. 1625, Humphrey ap Hugh Howel, b. at Llwyn-du, Llangelynin, Merionethshire, Wales, d. ca. 1664, at Llwyn-du, Llangelynin, Merionethshire, Wales,

ANN HUMPHREY, b. at Llwyn-du, Llangelynin, Merionethshire, Wales, d. at Tythyn Bryn Mawr, Dyffrydan Twp., nr. Dulgelly, Wales; m. at Dulgelly, Merionethshire, 1 Jan. 1649, Ellis ap Rees Lewis (alias Ellis Price) b. at Dulgelly, liv. 1678/9; d. ante 1696, at Tythyn Bryn Mawr, Dyffrydan Twp.,

ROWLAND ELLIS (I), b. at "Bryn Mawr", Dyffrydan Twp. Dolgelly; Merionethshire, Wales, 1650, d. at Gwynedd, Pa., in July 1731; m. (second) ca. 1672/3, Merionethshire, Wales, Margaret, b. at Dyffryddan, Wales, d. ca. 1730 at Bryn Mawr, Pa., dau. of Robert ap Owen ap Lewis,

148

ROWLAND ELLIS (II), b. at Bryn Mawr, Dolgelly, Merionethshire, Wales, ca. 1673/4, d. at Merionethshire, Wales; m. ca. 1692, at Merionethshire, Wales,

ROWLAND ELLIS (III), b. at Merionethshire, Wales, ca. 1692, d. at Burlington, N.J., 1762/3 (bur. in St. Mary's Episcopal churchyard); m. at St. Mary's Church, Burlington, N.J., 17 Apr. 1715, Sarah Allison, b. at Burlington, N.J., d. at Burlington, N.J., 18 July 1769 (bur. in St. Mary's churchyard),

DANIEL ELLIS, b. at Burlington, N.J., 5 Feb. 1727, d. at Burlington, N.J., 1 Sept. 1794 (bur. in St. Mary's churchyard); m. at St. Mary's Church, Burlington, 13 Oct. 1753, Bathsheba Howe, b. at Burlington, N.J., in July 1731, d. at Burlington, N.J., 8 June 1795,

ROWLAND ELLIS (IV), b. at Burlington, N.J., 8 July 1771, d. at Elkton, Md., 5 Feb. 1844; m. at Philadelphia, Pa., 19 Mar. 1796, Elizabeth Rudulph, b. at Philadelphia, Pa., ca. 1771, d. at Elkton, Md., 5 Sept. 1815,

FRANCIS ASBURY ELLIS, b. at Elkton, Md., 29 Dec. 1806, d. at Elkton, Md., 2 Nov. 1887; m. at Trinity Episcopal Church, Elkton, 3 Oct. 1833, Eliza Ann Howard, b. at Elkton, Md., 26 Nov. 1809, d. at Elkton, 16 Aug. 1861,

HOWARD ELLIS, b. at Elkton, Md., 6 July 1834; d. at New York, N.Y., 24 Dec. 1902 (bur. at Elkton, Md.); m. at New York, N.Y., 10 Nov. 1872, Aurora Minerva Bassford Gonard, b. at New York, N.Y., 10 Dec. 1845, d. at Paterson, N.J., 24 June 1921,

RUDULPH PELL ELLIS, b. at New York, N.Y., 20 Feb. 1877, d. at New York, N.Y., 7 May 1964; m. at New York, N.Y., 7 July 1905, Minette Isabella Martinez-Hernandez, b. at New York, N.Y., 22 Feb. 1884, d. at Norwalk, Conn., 24 Apr. 1966,

HOWARD ELLIS, b. in the Borough of Brooklyn, New York, N.Y., 27 Oct. 1908; ed.; Peekskill Military, Academy; Univ. of Penna., School of Fine Arts, 1932; member: Society of Colonial Wars, N.Y.; Society of the Cincinnati, Md.; Huguenot Soc., D.C. and New England; St. Nicholas Soc. of the City of

149

N.Y.; S.R., N.Y. and PA.; SAR, Del.; The Order of Colonial Lords of Manors in America; Baronial Order of Magna Charta; Order of the Crown of Charlemagne in the United States of America; Military Order of the Crusades; Military Order of the Loyal Legion; Wilmington Country Club; m. (first) 13 June 1934, at Philadelphia, Pa., Sarah Ellen Yerger, b. at Wilmington, Del., 5 Dec. 1913, d. 30 June 1961; m. (second) New Canaan, Conn., 11 Nov. 1944, Lucile Riley, b. at Warren, Ohio, 27 July 1920; m. (third) at Christ Church, Christina Hundred, Wilmington, Del., 15 Mar. 1969, Edith Maxine (Blackington) Lees, b. at Claremont, N.H., 22 May 1924,

1) HOWARD RUDOLPH ELLIS, b. 7 Nov. 1935, at Trenton, N.J.;

2) JANE DENMAN ELLIS, b. 2 Sept. 1945, at Norwalk, Conn.;

3) ROWLAND ELLIS (V), b. 13 Apr. 1949, at Wilmington, Del., m. at London, England, 11 Aug. 1970, Sandra Watchman Storrar, b. in Nirobi, Africa,

    a) ROWLAND ELLIS (VI), b. 20 Dec. 1971, at Epsom, Surrey, England.

4) JOHN PELL ELLIS, b. 20 July 1952, at Wilmington, Del.

Chapter XLIV

FOULKE — ROBERTS — WALTON — NEGUS — MEBUS

CHARLEMAGNE, King of the Franks, Emperor of the West, b. 2 Apr. 742, d. 28 Jan. 814; m. (third) 771, Hildegarde of Swabia,

LOUIS I, King of the Franks, Emperor of the West, b. Aug. 778, d. nr. Mainz, Germany, 20 June 840, m. 794/5, Ermengarde, d. ca. 3 Oct. 818, dau. of Ingerman, Count of Hasbaye,

LOTHAIR I, King of Italy, Emperor of the West, b. 795, d. at Pruem, Germany, 29 Sept. 855; m. 15 Oct. 821, Ermengarde, d. 20 Mar. 851, dau. of Hugh II, Count of Orleans,

ERMENGARDE, of Lorraine, m. ante Mar. 846, Giselbert, Count of the Maasgau and Count of Darnan, a descendant of the Merovingian Kings of France (447-680),

RAINIER I, Duke of Lorraine and Count of Hainault, b. ca. 850, d. ante 19 Jan. 915/6; m. Alberada of Mons, d. aft. 919,

RAINIER II, Count of Hainault, b. ca 890, d. 932; m. Adelaide of Burgundy, dau. of Richard, Duke of Burgundy,

RAINIER III, Count of Hainault, d. ca. 977-87; m. Adela of Dagsbourg, d. ca. 981,

LAMBERT I, Count of Louvain, d. in battle, 12 Sept. 1015; m. ca. 990, Gerberga of Lorraine, d. aft. 27 Jan. 1018/9, dau. of Duke Charles of Lorraine, a descendant of Charlemagne,

LAMBERT II, Count of Louvain, b. ca 991, d. aft 21 Sept. 1062; m. Oda of Lower Lorraine, dau. of Duke Gothelo I,

HENRY II, Count of Louvain, b. ca. 1021, d. ca. 1078/9; m. Adelaide of Orlamunda, d. aft. 1086,

151

GODFREY I, Duke of Lower Lorraine (Brabant) and Count of Louvain, b. ca. 1060 d. 25 Jan. 1139/40; m. (first) ca. 1100 Ida of Namur, d. ca. 1117/22,

ADELIZA (wid. of Henry I, King of England) b. ca. 1103 in Brabant, d. at Afflighem, bur. 23 Apr. 1151; m. 1138, William d'Aubigny, 1st Earl of Sussex and Arundel, d. at Waverly Abbey, Surrey, 12 Oct. 1176,

WILLIAM II D'AUBIGNY, 2nd Earl of Sussex and Arundel, d. 24 Dec. 1193; m. ca. 1173/4 Maud de Saint Hilaire, wid. of Roger de Clare, 5th Earl of Clare and 2nd Earl of Hertford,

WILLIAM III D'AUBIGNY, 3rd Earl of Sussex and Arundel, Crusader of 1218-19 (Fifth Crusade), d. at Cainell, Italy, ante 30 Mar. 1221; m. Mabel of Chester, dau. of Hugh, Earl of Chester (See Chapter LXXXIV, p. 305),

NICHOLE D'AUBIGNY, d. ante 1254; m. (his first) Roger de Somery, d. on or bef. 26 Aug. 1273,

JOAN DE SOMERY, d. in 1282; m. John Lestrange IV, of Knokyn, a descendant of Alfred the Great and of Cedric, 1st King of Wessex (495-534), d. prob. by drowning, between 2 and 26 Feb. 1275/6,

JOHN LESTRANGE V, 1st Lord Strange of Knokyn, b. ca 1243, d. on or bef. 8 Aug. 1309; m. (second) Maud de Walton Deyville, liv. 30 Oct. 1309,

ELIZABETH LESTRANGE, b. 1298, liv. 1320; m. 8 July 1304, Gruffudd ap Madog Vychan, 4th Baron of Glyndyrdwy and Rhuddallt, b. 12 Nov. 1298, liv. 1343, descended from King Rhodi Mawr,

ISABEL VERCH GRUFFUDD, of Rhuddallt, m. Goronwy ap Guffudd ap Madoc, a descendant of Rhirid Flaidd and of Cunedda Wiedig, King of Gwynedd ca. 530 A.D.,

TUDOR OF PENLLYN, m. Gwenhyfar verch Howel Silyf,

152

HOWEL OF PENLLYN, liv. 1426; m. Tibot verch Einion ap Gruffudd,

DAVID LLOYD AP HOWEL,

GWEHYFAR VERCH DAVID LLOYD AP HOWEL, m. David ap Ievan Vychan of Llanuwchllyn, a descendant of Rhirid Flaidd, Lord of Penllyn,

DAVID LLOYD AP DAVID, of Llannwchllyn and Llanderfel in Penllyn, liv. 1504; m. (first) Annesta verch Griffith ap Ievan,

ROBERT AP DAVID LLOYD, of Gwern y Brechtwn and Nantfreur in Llanderfel, Penllyn, d. ante 1592; m. Mary verch Reinalltop Gruffydd, a descendant of Rhodi Mawr, great King of all Wales, 843-873, Brian Boru, High King of all Ireland 1002-14, King John of England,

THOMAS AP ROBERT LLOYD of Gwern y Brechtwn, b. ca. 1515-20, d. at Llanderfel, Wales, May 1612; m. Catherine verch Robert ap Griffith, a descendant of Marchweithian, Lord of Ireland, ca. 1100,

EVAN AP THOMAS LLOYD of Nant y Friar, b. ca. 1555, d. at Llanderfel, Wales, 1640; m. Dorothea verch Evan, d. at Llanderfel, Wales, bur. 18 Feb. 1619,

THOMAS AP EVAN LLOYD, b. in Merionethshire, Wales, ca. 1578/80, d. in Merionethshire in Nov. 1649; m. Catherine verch William David,

FOULKE AP THOMAS LLOYD, b. at Llanderfel, Wales, bapt. 14 Apr. 1623; m. Lowry verch Edward ap David,

EDWARD FOULKE (EDWARD AP FOULKE AP THOMAS LLOYD) b. in Merionethshire, Wales, 13 July 1651, d. at Gwynedd, Pa., 8 Jan. 1741/2; m. in Wales, ca. 1680, Eleanor verch Hugh ap Cadwallader, b. in Wales, a descendant of Rhodi Mawr, great King of all Wales, 843-873, d. at Gwynedd, Pa. 16 Mar. 1733. They came to Philadelphia, Pa. from Wales, 17 July 1698,

153

HUGH FOULKE, b. 6 July 1685, in Merionethshire, Wales, d. at Richland, Pa., 21 July 1760; m. at Gwyedd Mtg., Pa., 4 Apr. 1731, Ann Williams, b. in Pembrokeshire, Wales, 8 Jan. 1693/4, d. at Richland, Pa., 10 Nov. 1773,

SAMUEL FOULKE, b. at Richland, Pa., 4 Feb. 1718/9, d. at Richland, Pa., 21 Mar. 1797; m. at Richland Mtg., Pa., 20 Aug. 1743, Ann Greasley, b. in 1724, d. 12 July 1797,

ISRAEL FOULKE, b. at Richland, Pa., 2 Apr. 1760, d. at Richland Pa., 27 Nov. 1824; m. 14 Jan. 1782, Elizabeth Roberts, b. 4 July 1760, d. 17 Feb. 1831/2,

THOMAS FOULKE, b. at Richland, Pa., Feb. 1784/5, d. 4 Aug. 1832; m. 1814, Sarah Lancaster, b. at Whitemarsh, Pa., 13 June 1788, d, 1869,

LETITIA FOULKE, b. 8 June 1818, d. 6 Apr. 1896; m. 1837, Jehu J. Roberts, b. at Cheltenham, Pa., 4 Nov. 1805, d. at Cheltenham, Pa., 13 Sept. 1881,

SARAH FOULKE ROBERTS, b. at Cheltenham, Pa., 29 Sept, 1842, d. at Abington, Pa., 23 Jan. 1890; m. at Philadelphia, Pa., 19 Oct. 1865, John Hill Walton, b. at Abington, Pa., 1840, d. at Philadelphia, Pa., 29 Dec. 1915,

LETITIA ROBERTS WALTON, b. at Abington, Pa., 30 July 1866, d. at Philadelphia, Pa., 14 Feb. 1910; m. at Bustleton, Pa., 25 June 1891, William Steel Negus, b. at Philadelphia, Pa., 26 Aug. 1868, d. at Somerton, Pa., 26 Apr. 1934 (See Chapter XXXV for Negus Charlemagne descent),

ESTELLE CLAXTON NEGUS, b. at Philadelphia, Pa., 8 Feb. 1901; m. 30 June 1926, at St. Peter's Church, Glenside, Pa., George Brinker Mebus, b. at Philadelphia, Pa., 14 Apr. 1903, d at Glenside, Pa., 13 Dec. 1972,

CHARLES FILLMORE MEBUS II, b. at Abington, Pa., 15 June 1928; Penna, State University, B.S. in Chemistry, 1949, B.S. in Engineering, 1951; R.O.T.C., 1945-49; U.S. Army Reserve, 1949-62, serving overseas in Germany, 1952-53, attaining rank of Capt. in Army Corps of Engineers Reserve; 7 terms in Penn.

154

General Assembly, House of Representatives; member: Pa. Society, S.R.; The Military Order of the Crusades; Baronial Order of Magna Charta; Order of the Crown of Charlemagne in the United States of America; American Society of Civil Engineers; Consulting Engineers Council of U.S.; Nat'l. Society of Professional Engineers; American Water Works Assoc.; American Society of Testing Materials; The Franklin Institute; m. at Wyncote, Pa., 26 July 1958, Joy Campbell Robbins,

1) LISA JANE CAMPBELL MEBUS, b. 7 Aug. 1961.

Chapter XLV

FOULKE — CORSON — DAY — BATES

CHARLEMAGNE

(See Chapter XLIV)

EDWARD FOULKE, m. Eleanor Hugh(s)

THOMAS FOULKE, b. prob. in Merionethshire, Wales, d. at Gwynedd, Pa., 10 Oct. 1762; m. 27 June 1706, at Gwynedd, Pa., Gwen Evans, d. at Gwynedd, Pa., 6 Dec. 1760,

WILLIAM FOULKE, b. 3 Sept. 1708, d. 10 Aug. 1798; m. 15 Aug. 1734, Hannah Jones, b. 16 Jan. 1714, d. 10 Dec. 1798,

AMOS FOULKE, b. 5 Nov. 1740, d. at Philadelphia, Pa., 1793; m. 20 May 1779, Hannah Jones of Merion, Pa., b. 28 Oct. 1748,

EDWARD FOULKE, of Montgomery Co., Pa., b. at Philadelphia, Pa., 17 Nov. 1784, d. at Penllyn, Pa., 17 July 1851; m. 11 Dec. 1810, Tacy Jones, dau. of Isaac and Gainor Jones of Montgomery Co., Pa.,

ANN JONES FOULKE, b. at Penllyn, Pa. 15 Sept. 1811, d. at Plymouth Meeting, Pa., 25 June 1888; m. at Philadelphia, Pa., 26 Dec. 1833, Dr. Hiram Corson, b. at Nickory Town, Plymouth Twp., Montgomery Co., Pa., 8 Oct. 1804, d. in Bucks Co., Pa., 4 Mar. 1896,

FRANCES STOCKTON CORSON, b. 25 Oct. 1849; m. Richard Hopper Day, of Germantown, Pa.,

BERTHA CORSON DAY, b. at Philadelphia, Pa. 20 Aug. 1875, d. at Wilmington, Del., 16 Dec. 1908; m. at Germantown, Pa., 17

May 1902, Daniel Moore Bates, b. at Wilmington, Del., 18 Apr. 1876, d. at Wilmington, Del., 26 Feb. 1953,

CHARLES THEODORE RUSSELL BATES, b. at Wilmington, Del., 24 July 1907 (See Chapter XLII)

Chapter XLVI
FOWKE — MITCHELL — NORRIS

CHARLEMAGNE, King of the Franks, Emperor of the West, b. 2 Apr. 742, d. 28 Jan. 814; m. in 771, Hildegarde of Swabia,

LOUIS I, the Pious, *le Debonnnaire,* King of the Franks, Emperor of the West, b. Aug. 778, d. nr. Mainz, 20 June 840

ROTRUD, b. ca. 800, or HILDEGARD, b. ca. 802/4; m. Count Gerard of Auverne,

RANULF I, Count of Poitou 839-44, b. ca. 815, d. 866; m. ca. 845, a dau. of Rodrick, Count of Maine,

RANULF II, Count of Poitou, Duke of Aquitaine, b. ca. 845/50, d. 5 Aug. 890,

EBLES MANCER, a nat. son, Count of Poitou, 890-92, d. 932; m. (second) in 911, Emiliane,

WILLIAM I, Count of Poitou, b. ca. 925, d. 963; m. 935, Gerloc (Adele), d. ca 14 Oct. 962, dau. of Rollo, Duke of Normandy,

ADELAIDE OF POITOU, b. 945, d. ca 1004; m. ante 969, Hugh Capet, King of France 987-996, d. 24 Oct. 996,

ROBERT II, the Pious, King of France, b. at Orleans, 970/1, d. at Meulun, 20 July 1031; m. (second) 998, Constance of Toulouse,

ADELE OF FRANCE, d. 8 Jan. 1079; m. (second) 1028, Baldwin V de Lille, Count of Flanders, b. 1012, d. at Lille, 1 Sept. 1067 (See Chapter XXXVI),

MAUD (MATILDA) OF FLANDERS, b. 1032, d. 3 Nov. 1083; m.

1053, William I, Duke of Normandy, the Conqueror, King of England, b. at Falaise, in 1027, d. at Rouen, 9 Sept. 1087,

HENRY I, King of England 1100-1135, "Beauclerc", b. 1070, d. in England, 1 Dec. 1135; m. Matilda of Scotland, b. 1079, d. 1 May 1118,

MATILDA (MAUD), b. ca. 1103/4, d. 10 Sept. 1167; m. 3 Apr. 1127, Geoffrey V Plantagenet, b. 24 Aug. 1113, d. 7 Sept. 1151,

HENRY II, King of England 1154-99, "Curt Mantel", b. 5 Mar. 1132/3, at Le Mans, d. at Chinon, 6 July 1189; m. 18 May 1153, Eleanor of Aquitaine, divorced wife of Louis VII, King of France, b. ca 1123, d. 31 Mar. 1204,

JOHN I, King of England 1199-1216, "Lackland", b. at Oxford, 24 Dec. 1166, d. 19 Oct. 1216 at Newark Castle, Nottinghamshire,

JOAN, nat. dau., b. ante 1200, d. Feb. 1237, bur. at Llanvaes in Anglesey; m. dur. Ascensiontide 1206, Llewellyn ap Jorwerth, Prince of Wales, d. 'at Aberconway, 11 Apr. 1240,

MARGARET LLEWELLYN; m. John de Brews (Braose, Briouze etc.), Lord of Bramber and Gower, b. ante 1210, d. ante 18 July 1232,

RICHARD DE BREWS a younger son, b. ante 1232, bur. at Woodbridge Priory, ante 18 June 1292; m. ante Sept. 1265, Alice Le Rus, b. 25 Dec. 1245 or 47, or 1 Jan. 1245/6, bur at Woodbridge Priory shortly before 28 Jan. 1300/1, dau. of William Le Rus, of Stinton, co. Norfolk, Akenham, co. Suffolk,

MARGARET DE BREWS, d. ante 12 May 1335; m. Roger de Coleville, b. 1251, d. ante 6 Mar. 1287/8,

ALICE DE COLEVILLE, m. (second) in 1313, Sir John Gernon, b. ca. 1297, d. ca. 1334,

MARGARET GERNON, d. ca. 1352; m. Sir Geoffrey de Gresley, b. 1309, d. 1331/2,

SIR JOHN DE GRESLEY, liv. 1328, d. ca. 1395; m. ca. 1345, Alice de Swynnerton, d. ca. 1350, dau. of Sir Thomas de Swynnerton,

SIR NICHOLAS DE GRESLEY, b. bet. 1345-50, d. bet. 1374-89; m. ante 1364, Thomasine, d. ca. 1404, dau. of Sir Thomas de Wasteneys,

SIR THOMAS DE GRESLEY, b. 1365; d. ca. 1445; m. ca 1392, Margaret, liv. 1421, dau. of Sir Thomas le Walsh of Wanlip, co. Leicester,

SIR JOHN GRESLEY, b. occ. 1410, d. 17 Jan. 1448/9; m. ca. 1409/10, Elizabeth, dau. of Sir Thomas Clarell, of Aldwark, Yorks.,

KATHERINE GRESLEY, m. 1430, William de Peto, d. 1465,

JOHN DE PETO, of Chesterton, co. Warwick, b. 1434; d. 14 Aug. 1487; m. 1453/4, Elianore, d. 1454, dau. of Robert Mantfield,

EDWARD PETO, of Chesterton, co. Warwick, d. 14 Sept. 1487; m. Goditha, d. 1502, dau. of Sir Thomas Throgmorton, of Coughton, co. Warwick,

JOHN PETO, of Chesterton, co. Warwick, b. 1478, w.p. 1542; m. 1513, Margaret, w.d. 1554, dau. of Sir Alexander Baynham, of Westbury,

AUDREY PETO, m. John Cupper. of Glympton, co. Oxford, Chipynnorton, Powick, co. Worcester, w.d. 1584,

DOROTHY CUPPER, will and adm. 27 June 1651; m. 1614, John Fowke, w.d. 7 May 1638, w.p. 7 Oct. 1642,

ROGER FOWKE, of Brewood Parish, Gunston, co. Stafford, w.p. 30 Nov. 1649; m. Mary, dau. of Sir William Bailey, of the Lea,

COL. GERARD FOWKE, of Brewood Parish, Gunston, co. Stafford, England, d. in Virginia or Maryland in 1669; m. in Maryland, aft. 1659, Ann. b. in Va., d. in Md., aft. 1672, dau. of Adam Thorowgood, and wid. of Job Chandler,

GERARD FOWKE, b. 1662, d. 1734; m. 31 Dec. 1686, Sarah Burdett,

CAPT. CHANDLER FOWKE, d. in Stafford Co., Va., 10 Feb. 1745; m. ca. 1716, Mary Fossaker,

RICHARD FOWKE, b. in Va., 11 Dec. 1741, d. in Va., 1777; m. in St. Paul's Parish, King George Co., Va., 16 Mar. 1760, Ann B Bunbury, b. in St. Paul's Parish, 12 Nov. 1741, d. in St. Paul's Parish, 1803, dau. of Thomas and Sarah Bunbury,

ROGER FOWKE, of King George Co., Va., b. 1773, d. in Mason Co., Ky., 17 Nov. 1818; m. in Va., ante 6 Oct. 1799, Susan Hawes, of Essex Co., Va., b. ca. 1780, w.p. 1840, in Henderson Co., Ky., bur. at Charleston Bottom, Ky.,

ANN BUNBURY FOWKE, b. in Fauquier Co., Va., 18 Oct. 1800, d. in Mason Co., Ky., 17 July 1891; m. in Brown Co., Ohio, 15 Sept. 1819, Ignatius S. Mitchell, b. in Mason Co., Ky., 9 Jan. 1799, bur. in Brown Co., Ohio, 3 Mar. 1882,

GERARD POLHEMUS MITCHELL, b. in Brown Co., Ohio, in 1830, d. in Henderson Co., Ky., in 1874; m. at Aberdeen, Ohio, 9 Oct. 1849, Maria Antoinette Baker, b. in Mason Co., Ky., in 1831, d. in Henderson Co., Ky., in 1880,

ELIZABETH FRANCES MITCHELL, b. in Mason Co., Ky., 27 Aug. 1850, d. at Corydon, Ky., 30 May 1931; m. (second) in Henderson Co., 2 Mar. 1880, Dr. William Virgil Norris, b. in Jefferson Co., Ky., 27 Oct. 1843, d. at Corydon, Ky., 17 Mar. 1926,

WILLIAM VIRGIL NORRIS, Jr., b. at Corydon, Ky., 18 July 1887, d. at New York, N.Y., 14 Apr. 1951; m. at Winchester, Ky., 14 Nov. 1912, Jane Bright Robinson, b. at Winchester, Ky., 22 Sept. 1892, liv. 1978,

WILLIAM VIRGIL NORRIS, III, b. at Jacksonville, Florida, 25 June 1916, ed.: University of Florida; member: SAR; Society of Colonial Wars; The Society of the Ark and The Dove; Jamestowne Society; Order of the Crown of Charlemagne in

161

the United States of America; National Genealogical Society; The Filson Club, Louisville, Ky.; Ky. Historical Society; Md. Historical Society; N.J. Historical Society; Va. Historical Society; Northern Neck of Va. Historical Society; Eastern Shore of Va. Historical Society; Fairfax Co., Va. Historical Society; New York Historical Society; N.Y. Genealogical & Biographical Society; Va. Genealogical Society; St. Louis Genealogical Society; The Manuscript Society; Delta Sigma Pi Fraternity; etc.

Chapter XLVII

GORSUCH — MERRYMAN — BRADLEY — SMITH

CHARLEMAGNE

(See Chapters X, XXXII, XXXIX, XLIII, LXVIII)

ISABEL DE VERMANDOIS, Countess of Leicester, d. ante July 1147; m. (first) in 1096, Sir Robert Beaumont, 1st Earl of Leicester, b. ca. 1046, d. 5 June 1118,

ISABEL (ELIZABETH) DE BEAUMONT, liv. 1172, mistress of King Henry I of England; m. Gilbert de Clare, 1st Earl of Pembroke, bur. at Tintern Abbey, 14 Sept. 1148,

RICHARD DE CLARE, "Strongbow", 2nd Earl of Pembroke and Viceroy of Ireland, b. ca. 1130, d. at Dublin, 5 Apr. 1176; m. 11 Aug. 1171, Eva of Leinster, d. 1177, dau. of Dermot MacMurrough, King of Leinster and More O'Toole,

ISABEL DE CLARE, *sine jure* Countess of Pembroke, b. 1172, bur. at Tintern Abbey, 1220; m. at London, in Aug. 1189, Sir William Marshall, 3rd Earl of Pembroke, Marshal of England, Regent of the Kingdom, 1216-19, b. 1146, d. 14 May 1219, bur. in the Knights Templar's Church, London,

SIBYL MARSHALL, m. ante 14 May 1219, William de Ferrers, 5th Earl of Derby, d. at Evington, nr. Leicester, Mar. 1254,

MAUD DE FERRERS, d. 12 Mar. 1298/9; m. William de Vivonia, d. 22 May 1298/9, son of Hugh de Vivonia and Mabel Malet, dau. of William Malet, Magna Charta Surety.

CECILY DE VIVONIA, b. 1257, d. at Stoke-under-Hamden, 10 Jan. 1320/1; m. John de Beauchamp of Hatch, co. Somerset, b. ante

1249, d. at Hatch, 24 Oct. 1283, son of Robert IV de Beauchamp and Alice de Mohun,

SIR JOHN BEAUCHAMP of Hatch, co. Somerset, 1st Lord Beauchamp, Governor of Bridgewater Castle 1325, d. aft. 20 Oct. 1336; m. 1301, Joan Chenduit, d. 9 Feb. 1372,

WILLIAM BEAUCHAMP of Wellington, co. Somerset, b. ca. 1302, d. ante death of his father in 1336,

MARY BEAUCHAMP, m. John Bodulgate,

ELIZABETH (MARY) BODULGATE, m. Richard Wydville of Grafton, Seneschal of Normandy 1426, Constable of the Tower of London 1424, Lieutenant of Calais 1426, Sheriff of Northampton 1437, w.d. 29 Nov. 1441, son of John Wydville of Grafton,

JOAN WYDVILLE, d. ante 1462, sister of Richard Wydville, Earl Rivers; m. (his second) at Calais, 1429, William Haut of Bishop's Bourne, co. Kent, b. 1390, d. bet. 30 Sept. 1462 and 4 Oct. 1462, bur. in the Abbey of St. Augustine at Canterbury,

SIR WILLIAM HAUT, b. ca 1430, d. 2 July 1497; m. Johanna Horne, dau. of Henry Horne of Heron,

SIR THOMAS HAUT, K.B. 1501, Justice of the Peace, co. Kent 1502, b. ca. 1466, d. 28 Nov. 1502; m. ca. 1485, Isabel (Elizabeth) Frowick, dau. of Sir Thomas Frowick of London and Ealing, co. Middlesex, and Joan Sturgeon.

JANE HAUT, b. ca. 1486; m. (second) Robert Wroth of Enfield, co. Middlesex, d. bet. 8 May 1535 and 26 May 1536, son of John Wroth and Margaret Newdigate,

SIR THOMAS WROTH, Knt., resident of Enfield, co. Middlesex, b. 1516, d. in co. Middlesex, bet. 9 Oct. 1573 and 16 Apr. 1575; m. 1539/40, Mary Rich, dau. of Sir Richard Rich, 1st Lord Rich, Lord Chancellor of England, and Elizabeth Jenks,

MABEL WROTH, b. ca. 1542, bur. at Bishop's Bourne Church 1597; m. (first) 10 June 1560, Edward Aucher of Bishop's

Bourne, co. Kent, b. ante 1540, d. 14 Feb. 1567/8, at Bishop's Bourne, son of Anthony Aucher of Ottringden and Affra Cornwallis,

ELIZABETH AUCHER, b. 1561/2, bur. at Canterbury Cathedral, 3 Dec. 1627; m. ca. 1580/1, Sir William Lovelace, the elder, bapt. at St. Alphege, Canterbury, 30 Sept. 1561, d. at Canterbury, bet. 6-19 Oct. 1629, son of William Lovelace and Anne Lewis,

SIR WILLIAM LOVELACE, the younger, Knt., of Berthersden, co. Kent, bapt. at St. Alphege, Canterbury, England, 12 Feb. 1583/4, d. at Groll, Holland, 12 Aug. 1627; m. (her first) 1610, Anne Barne, b. bet. 1587-92, d. at London, bet. 15 May 1632 and 22 May 1633, dau. of Sir William Barne, Knt., of Woolich, co. Kent and Anne Sandys,

ANNE LOVELACE, b. in co Kent, England, prob. ca. 1610, d. in "parts beyond the seas" (Virginia) early in 1652; m. ca. 1628, Rev. John Gorsuch, Rector of Walkhorne, co. Hertford, Eng., b. ca. 1600-1609, d. at Haymow, Eng. bet. 1647-51,

CHARLES GORSUCH, bapt. at Walkern, Herts., Eng., 25 Aug. 1642, d. in Baltimore Co., Md., 27 June 1716; m. ante 13 Mar. 1677, Sarah Cole, b. in Baltimore Co., Md., d. in Baltimore Co., Md., bet. 6 July 1689 and 15 Feb. 1690, dau. of Thomas Cole and Priscilla — ,

THOMAS GORSUCH, b. in Maryland, 1678/80, d. in Baltimore Co., Md., bet. 23 Sept. 1774 and 4 Nov. 1774; m. 19 Aug. 1714, Anne Ensor, b. prob. in Baltimore Co., Md., ca. 1690, dau. of John Ensor and Jane — ,

JOHN GORSUCH, b. in Baltimore Co., Md., ca. 1730, d. in Baltimore Co., Md., 7 Aug. 1808; m. 11 Mar. 1755, Elizabeth Merryman, b. in St. Paul's Parish, Baltimore, Md., 13 June 1734, d. 2 Sept. 1795, dau. of John Merryman and Sarah Rogers,

ELEANOR GORSUCH, b. at Baltimore, Md., 30 Jan. 1774, d. at Baltimore, Md., 27 Aug. 1858; m. at Baltimore, Md., 25 Apr.

1793, Joseph Merryman, b. in St. Paul's Parish, Baltimore, Md., 15 Mar. 1760, d. at Baltimore, Md., 17 Aug. 1829,

GEORGE MERRYMAN, b. at Baltimore, Md., ca. 1810, d. at Baltimore, Md., 24 Sept. 1885; m. at Baltimore, Md., 28 Mar. 1839, Eliza Ellen Hardester Austin, b. at Baltimore, Md., 7 Apr. 1812, d. at Baltimore, Md., 27 Mar. 1898,

JOSEPH PURNELL MERRYMAN, b. at Baltimore, Md., 26 Apr. 1841, d. at Bangor, Me., 4 July 1924; m. Eleanor Jane Lucas, b. at Baltimore, Md., 22 Sept. 1840, d. at Baltimore Md., 11 Nov. 1911, dau. of James Lucas and Margaret Brown,

FLORENCE PURNELL MERRYMAN, b. at Baltimore, Md., 14 Sept. 1877, d. at Clearwater, Fla., 22 Apr. 1957; m. at Baltimore, Md., 16 Nov. 1896, Henry Russell Bradley, b. at Bangor, Me., 29 Oct. 1861, d. at Bangor, Me., 2 Aug. 1912,

MARGARET BRADLEY, b. at Bangor, Me., 1 Nov. 1898, d. at Peterborough, N.H., 22 May 1976; m. at Bangor, Me., 11 Nov. 1920, Harvey Hassall Smith, b. at Astoria, L.I., N.Y., 13 Oct. 1894, d. at Peterborough, N.H., 1 Mar. 1969,

PERRY EDWARDS HALL SMITH, b. at New York, N.Y., 3 Oct. 1935, ed.: Phillips Exeter Academy; Princeton Univ., A.B.; Harvard Univ., M.A.; Fulbright Scholar in Venice (attended Universities of Perugia and Padua), member: St. Nicholas Society of the City of New York, Society of Colonial Wars, Sons of the Revolution, Huguenot Society, Colonial Order of the Acorn, Order of the Crown of Charlemagne in the United States of America, Baronial Order of Magna Charta. Military Order of the Crusades.

Chapter XLVIII

GREENHALGHE — BOOTH — WALSH — PRYOR

CHARLEMAGNE

(See Chapters II and XXXVI)

HENRY I, KING OF ENGLAND, b. 1070, d. at Lions - le Forét, Dec. 1135, had a natural son,

ROBERT OF CAEN, EARL OF GLOUCESTER, (created 1122), b. possibly at Caen, Normandy, b. c. 1090, d. at Bristol, 31 Oct. 1147, and bur. there in the Priory of St. James; m. Maud, dau. of Robert Fitz Hammon, Lord of Glamorgan; and Lord of Crelly in Calverdos, Baron of Thoringin, by his wife, Sybil, dau. of Roger de Montgomery, Earl of Shrewsbury, d. c. 1157,

MAUD FITZROBERT, b. c. 1135, d. 24 July 1189; m. c. 1141, Ranulph de Gernons, Viscount d'Avranches, Earl of Chester, d. 16 Dec. 1153, bur. at St. Werburg's, Chester,

HUGH DE KEVELIOC, 3RD EARL OF CHESTER, b. at Kevelioc, Merioneth, 1147, d. at Leeke, Staffordshire, 1181; m. c. 1167, Bertrade of Evereux, dau. of Simon de Montfort, Count of Evereux, b. 1153, d. 1227,

HAWISE OF CHESTER, COUNTESS OF LINCOLN, b. 1180, d. bef. 3 March 1242/43; m. Robert de Quincy, brother of Saher de Quincy, 1st Earl of Winchester, Crusader, d. at London, 1217,

MARGARET DE QUINCY, (m. secondly, William Marshall, Earl of Pembroke), d. bef. 30 March 1266; m (first) bef. 21 June 1221, John de Lacy, Earl of Lincoln (created 1232), Constable of Chester, Magna Charta Surety, 1215, son of Roger de Lacy, b. 1192, d. 22 July 1240,

ALICE (IDONIA) DE LACY, b. c. 1223, m.c. 1238, Sir Geoffrey de Dutton of Nether Tabley, Crusader, b. c. 1200, d. 1248,

SIR GEOFFREY DE DUTTON of Nether Tabley, Lord of Warburton, Nether Tabley and Thelwall, b. c. 1239, living in 1275,

MARGARET DE DUTTON, heiress of Nether Tabley (m. first, Robert de Denbigh, by whom she had no issue), m. (second) c. 1276, Sir Nicholas Leycester, Lord of Nether Tabley, jure uxoris, Senechal to the Earl of Lincoln, d. in 1295,

ROGER LEYCESTER, Lord of Nether Tabley, b. c. 1278, d. c. 1349, m. Isabel,

NICHOLAS LEYCESTER, Lord of Nether Tabley, d. shortly after his father, c. 1349, m. c. 1322, Mary de Mobberley, dau. of William de Mobberley of Mobberley, and sister and co-heir of Sir Raufe de Mobberley,

ELIZABETH LEYCESTER, living 1404/05, m. (as his second wife) William Manwaring (Mainwaring) of Over Pever, Cheshire, d. 1364, (See Chapter LVII, p. 207)

RANDLE MANWARING, Lord of Over Pever, bef. 1365, d. 1456, m. 1393, Margery, widow of Richard Buckley of Chedhill, Cheshire, and dau. of Sir Hugh Venables, Baron of Kinderton, d. after 1456, and bur. with her husband at Over Pever,

JOAN MANWARING, b. probably at Over Pever, c. 1398, living in 1482, m. 1411, John de Davenport of Davenport, b. c. 1399/1400, d. c. 1475,

JOHN DAVENPORT of Davenport, d. c. 1482, m. bef. 1460, Elizabeth Savage, dau. of Sir John Savage of Clifton,

RALPH DAVENPORT of Davenport, b. c. 1461, d. c. 1511, m. 1484, Margery Davenport, dau. of Hugh Davenport of Henbury, living 1517,

JOHN DAVENPORT of Davenport, b. c. 1485, d. 25 May 1555, m.

(first) c. 1498/99, Matilda Brereton, dau. of Sir Andrew Brereton of Brereton, d. bef. 1540,

JOHN DAVENPORT of Davenport, b. c. 1505/06, d. 11 July 1582, and bur. at Swettenham, m. (first) Eleanor Holland, dau. of Thurston Holland of Denton, Lancs., d. bef. 1544,

ANNE DAVENPORT, b. probably at Davenport, b. c. 1535, m. (as his second wife) Thomas Greenhalghe of Brandlesome, Bury. Lancs., b. c. 1520-30, d. 18 July 1577,

JOHN GREENHALGHE of Brandlesome, b. c. 1550, bur. at Bury, Lancs. 19 Jan. 1615, m. Alice Holt, dau. of Robert Holt of Stubley, Lancs., b. c. 1550, bur. at Bury Lancs., 23 Aug. 1618,

JOHN GREENHALGHE, Governor of the Isle of Man, 1640-1651, b. 1597, d. 19 Sept. 1651, and bur. at Malew, Isle of Man; m. (first) circa 1615, Alice Massie, dau. of the Rev. William Massie, Rector of Wilmslow, Cheshire, b. c. 1596, bur. at Bury, Lancs., 4 June 1620,

RICHARD GREENHALGHE of Bury, Lancs., b. c. 1616, d.v.p. and bur. at Bury, 19 Jan. 1635/36,; m. at Bury, 1 Nov. 1631, Alice Rosthorne, dau. of Edward Rosthorne of Newhall, Lancs., b. c. 1616, bur. at Bury, 12 May 1634,

THOMAS GREENHALGHE of Brandlesome, bapt. at Bury, Lancs., 16 Apr. 1633, bur. at Bury, 15 Jan 1690/01,; m. c. 1665, Elizabeth Bridgeman, dau. of Dr. Henry Bridgeman, Bishop of Sodor and Man, 1671-1682, brother of Sir Orlando Bridgeman, ancestor of the Earls of Newport,

ORLANDO GREENHALGHE, 3rd son, of Middleton, Lancs., b. probably Chester, Feb. 1673, living in 1705; m. Elizabeth,

JOHN GREENHALGHE of Bury, b. probably at Middleton, c. 1696, m. at Bury, 18 Oct. 1716, Ann Shaw,

WILLIAM GREENHALGHE of Bury, bapt. at Bury, 3 March 1728; m. (second) at Bury, 2 May 1758, Mary Lomax,

169

JOHN GREENHALGHE of Bury, baptised at Bury, 11 May 1763; m. at Bury, 26 Oct. 1784, Elizabeth Wolstenholme,

RACHEL GREENHALGHE, b. at Bury, Lancs., 24 Oct. 1787, d. at Newark, N.J., 13 Aug. 1845; m. at Bury, Lancs., 15 Aug. 1808, George Booth, who settled in New Jersey in the spring of 1840, son of Joseph and Betty (Duckworth) Booth of Bury, b. at Bury, Lancs., 24 Jan. 1786, d. at Newark, N.J., 13 Feb. 1860,

ELIZABETH BOOTH, b. at Bury, Lancs., 23 Sept. 1812, d. at Newark, N.J., 18 March 1882, m. at Bolton, Lancs., 7 March 1841, Daniel Walsh, who settled in New Jersey in the spring of 1840, son of James and Sally (Hamer) Walsh of Bolton, b. at Bolton, Lancs., 14 June 1814, d. at Newark, N.J., 22 Aug. 1887,

RACHEL ANNA WALSH, b. at Bolton, Lancs., 22 Dec. 1841, d. at Newark, N.J., 27 July 1921, m. at Newark, N.J., 23 Jan. 1868, Robert Westall Pryor, who settled in the United States in 1864, son of Thomas Pryor (1819-1863), and his wife, Sarah Ann Westall (1818-1857), dau. of Robert (at Providence, R.I., July 19, 1863) and Mary (Walker) Westall of Hulme, Lancs., and paternal grandson of William Pryor (1794-c. 1863), who settled in Stockport, N.Y., in 1831 and his wife, Ann Pilkington, whom he married at the Collegiate Chapel in Manchester, Lancs., 7 Nov. 1818, b. at Oswaldtwistle, Lancs., 16 Sept. 1845, d. at Newark, N.J., 13 July 1926,

WILLIAM WALSH PRYOR, b. at Newark, N.J., 7 Sept. 1869, d. at Montclair, N.J., 30 Dec. 1947, m. at Newark, N.J., 3 Feb. 1904, Annie May Young, dau. of David Young, Sr. (b. at Alloa, Clackmananshire, Scotland 6 May 1849, d. at St. Petersburg, Fl., 6 Feb. 1939) and his wife, Mary Ella Wilson, (b. at Newark N.J., 4 Oct. 1850, d. at Towaco, N.J., 29 July 1929), dau. of Hercules Miller and Mary Jane (Bush) Wilson, b. at Newark, N.J., 5 Sept. 1872, d. at Verona, N.J., 3 June 1952

WILLIAM YOUNG PRYOR, Columbia University, 1931; J.D. New York University Law School, 1934; Mil. Serv.: World War II, U.S. Army; member of: The Saint Nicholas Society of the City of New York; The General Society, Sons of the Revolution (New Jersey); The National Society of the Sons of the American Revolution (Past Vice President General); General Society of Colonial Wars (Member of Council, N.Y., and Deputy Governor, N.J.); The Colonial Society of Pennsylvania, The Hereditary Order of the Descendants of Colonial Governors (Past Governor General); Gen. Soc. of War of 1812 (Past President, N.J.) The Huguenot Society of New Jersey (Past President); The Order of the Crown of Charlemagne in the United States of America; The Military Order of the Crusades (Commander General); Batonial Order of the Magna Charta, Washington Association of New Jersey; Sovereign Military Order of Temple of Jerusalem (Past Grand Prior); New Jersey Historical Society; Monmouth Battlefield Association; New Jersey Genealogical Society; National Genealogical Society; New York Biographical and Genealogical Society; Kane Lodge 454 New York, Princeton Club, National Gavel Club; Essex Fells Country Club, New Jersey; The New England Society, b. at Newark, N.J., 24 Oct. 1908, m. at Montclair, N.J., 29 July 1944, to Marianna Love Brand, dau. of Graton S. Brand of Montclair, N.J., and his wife, Ethel Love Poole, dau. of John Morton and Annie Florence (Love) Poole, of Wilmington, Del., member of: The National Society of the Daughters of the American Revolution; National Society, United States Daughters of 1812; National Society of New England Women; The Hereditary Order of the Descendants of Colonial Governors; National Society, Daughters of the American Colonists; National Society, Daughters of Colonial Wars; The Society of the Descendants of the Colonial Clergy (Trustee); The National Huguenot Society, b. at Wilmington, Del., 8 Apr. 1909, Issue:

1.) ANN LOVE PRYOR, b. at Montclair, N.J., 28 March 1946, educated at Vermont College, Montpelier, Vt., and Bloomfield College, Bloomfield, N.J., member of: National Society of the Daughters of the American Revolution; and the Huguenot Society.

2.) WILLIAM BRAND PRYOR. educated at St. Petersburg, Florida Junior College; Long Island University, Southampton College, member of: The General Society of the War of 1812 (Md.); The Saint Nicholas Society

171

of the City of New York; The General Society, Sons of the Revolution (N.Y.); The National Society of the Sons of the American Revolution (N.J.); General Society of Colonial Wars (N.Y.); The Society of the Descendants of the Colonial Clergy; The Huguenot Society of New Jersey; Sovereign Military Order of the Temple of Jerusalem (Commandeur), b. at Montclair, N.J., 13 Aug. 1947.

Chapter XLIX

GYE — MAVERICK — WALTON — BURNAP — STEARNS — FRANCE — WELLS — HUGO — SMITH — POPE

CHARLEMAGNE

(See Chapters X, XXXII, XXXIX, XLIII, LXVIII)

ISABEL DE VERMANDOIS, Countess of Leicester, b. ca 1076, d. ante July 1147; m. (first) Robert de Beaumont, Siegneur of Beaumont, Port Audemer, Brionne, and Vatteville, in Normandy, Count of Meulan in the French Vexin, Earl of Leicester; b. ca. 1046; d. 5 June 1118, son and heir of Roger de Beaumont,

ISABEL DE BEAUMONT, m. Gilbert de Clare, Earl of Pembroke, d. 6 Jan. 1147/8,

RICHARD DE CLARE, Strongbow, 2nd Earl of Pembroke, b. ca 1130; d. ca. 20 Apr. 1176; m. ca. 26 Aug. 1171, Eva MacMurrough, dau. of Dermot MacMurrough, King of Leinster, Ireland,

ISABEL DE CLARE, d. 1220; m. Aug. 1189, Sir William de Marshall, 3rd Earl of Pembroke, Marshal of England, Regent of the Kingdom, 1216-1219, Crusader, b. 1146, d. 14 May 1219,

SYBIL MARSHALL, d. by 1238; m. (his first) 1219, William de Ferrers, 5th Earl of Derby, b. 1190, d. 22 Sept. 1247,

MAUD DE FERRERS, d. 12 Mar. 1298/9; m. at Poitou, France, William de Vivonia, called "de Fortibus", of Chewton, d. ca. 22 May 1259,

JOAN DE VIVONIA, b. 1249, d. ante 1314; m. Reynold (Reginald) FitzPiers,

PETER FITZ REGINALD, of Chewton, b. ca. 1274, d. 18 Nov. 1322; m. Ela Martel, b. at Marston, Sussex, ae. 7 in 1280, dau. of Roger Martel,

ROGER FITZ PETER, b. at Chewton, d. ca. 1320,

HENRY FITZ ROGER of Chewton, b. ca. 1318, bur. at Chewton Mendip, 18 Feb. 1352; m. Elizabeth Holland, bur. at Chewton Mendip, 1388,

JOHN FITZ ROGER, of Chewton, b. by 1352, d. 1382; m. ca. Apr. 1369, Alice, d. 27 Mar. 1426,

ELIZABETH FITZ ROGER, b. at Chewton, 1370, d. 15 Apr. 1414, heiress of Chewton; m. ca. 1396, Richard Stucle (Stuckley) of Trent, co. Somerset, d. 1410-14,

HUGH STUCKLEY, b. at Afton, co. Devon, aft. 1398, d. 1459; m. Katherine, d. 26 Mar. 1467, dau. of John Affeton,

NICHOLAS STUCKLEY, b. at Afton, Devon, ca. 1449; m. Thomasine Cokeworthy,

SIR THOMAS STUCKELY (or Stucley) m. a dau. of Thomas Wode,

MARGARET STUCKLEY m. Charles Farringdon,

ANN FARRINGDON m. Thomas Dowrish of Dowrish House, b. ca. 1532, d. ca. 1590,

GRACE DOWRISH m. (his second) ca. 1555, Robert Guye or Gye, b. ca. 1531, d. prob. 1604-8,

MARY GYE, b. at Sanford, co. Devon, England, ca. 1580, liv. 1666 in Massachusetts; m. at Islington, co. Devon, 28 Oct. 1600, Rev. John Maverick, b. at Awliscombe, co. Devon, 27 Oct. 1578, d. at Boston, Mass., 3 Feb. 1635/6,

ELIAS MAVERICK, b. at Islington, co Devon, Eng., 1604, d. at Boston, Mass. (bur at Charlestown) 8 Sept. 1684; m. ca. 1633, Mrs. Ann Harris, b. in England in 1613, d. at Reading, Mass., 7 Sept. 1697,

SARAH MAVERICK, b. 20 Feb. 1640/1, d. at Reading, Mass., 10 June 1714; m. Samuel Walton, b. at Marblehead, Mass., 4 May 1639, d. at Reading, Mass., 22 Mar. 1717/8,

SARAH WALTON, b. at Marblehead, Mass., 1664, d. at Reading, Mass., 27 Aug. 1731; m. at Reading, Mass., 28 May 1688, Thomas Burnap, Jr., b. at Reading, Mass., 17 Jan. 1664, d. at Reading, Mass., 24 Aug. 1726,

MARTHA BURNAP, b. at Reading, Mass., 3 Apr. 1697, m. at Reading, Mass., 9 Oct. 1717, Ebenezer Stearns, b. 1690, d. at Belchertown, Mass., in 1759,

DAVID STEARNS, Sr., b. at Sutton, Mass., 25 Mar. 1729, d. at Goshen, Mass., 28 Feb. 1788; m. at Dudley, Mass., 7 Sept. 1756, Hannah Burnell, b. at Dudley, Mass., Mar. 1732, d. at Goshen, Mass., Dec. 1827,

DAVID STEARNS, Jr., b. at Dudley, Mass., 26 July 1757, d. in Clinton Co., Ohio, 5 Sept. 1836; m. at Hingham, Mass., May 1782, Susannah Beal(s), b. at Hingham, Mass., 30 May 1759, d. in Clinton Co., Ohio, 10 Mar. 1849,

MARY STEARNS, b. at Bennington, Vt., 9 Dec. 1787, d. in Tuscarawas Co., Ohio, 17 Feb. 1825; m. in Washington Co., Pa., 1801, Adam France, Jr., b. in Lancaster Co., Pa., 1783, d. in Marshall Co., Ind., Mar. 1850,

CHRISTIAN FRANCE, b. in Germany, 11 July 1802, d. 1877; m. 6 Nov. 1823, in Tuscarawas Co., Ohio, Elizabeth Jones, b. in Wales, 9 Nov. 1805, d. 26 Aug. 1863,

LOUISE FRANCE, b. in Ohio, 1 Feb. 1838, d. at Cheyenne Wells, Colorado, 24 June 1908; m. at Monona, Iowa, 3 Mar 1858, Willoughby Wells, b. at Fairfax, Vt., 14 Feb. 1832, d. at Cheyenne Wells, Colo., 21 Apr. 1907,

ANNIE MAUDE WELLS, b. at Sterling Tsp., Minn., 5 Sept. 1858, d. at Winnipeg, Manitoba, 22 June 1928; m. at Sterling Tsp., Minn., 12 July 1887, Nicholas Frederick Hugo, b. at Kingston, Ont., 15 June 1860, d. at Duluth, Minn., 22 Feb. 1921,

175

ANNIE TREVANION HUGO-SMITH, b. at Duluth, Minn., 12 Oct. 1888; m. 17 June 1913, at Duluth, Minn., Robert Duane Smith, b. at Castlewood, Dakota Territory, 16 Oct. 1886, d. at Angola, Ind., 28 June 1970,

TREVANION HUGO-SMITH, b. at Duluth, Minn., 11 Mar. 1924; ed.: Stanbrook Hall, Duluth, Minn.; Wells College, Aurora, N.Y.; B.A., B.S., University of Minnesota; member: Kappa Kappa Gamma Alumae, San Francisco, Secretary, President; Century Club of California, Corresponding Secretary, Asst. Librarian; Colonial Dames of America; Order of the Crown of Charlemagne in the United States of America; m. at Reno, Nev., 8 May 1948, John Arnold Pope, b. at Sacramento, Cal., 14 June 1914,

1) ROBERT TREVANION POPE, b. 29 Nov. 1949, at San Francisco., Cal.; ed.: Cathedral School for Boys, San Francisco; Lick-Wildmerding School, San Francisco; Whitman College, Walla Walla, Wash.; Tufts University, M.A., Economics; member: Nu Sigma Chi, American Economics Assoc., Sierra Club, Order of the Crown of Charlemagne in the United States of America.

176

Chapter L

GYE — MAVERICK — SKINNER — CONEY — CHURCH — CROSWELL — EMERSON

CHARLEMAGNE

(See Chapter XLIX)

MARY GYE, b. at Sanford, co. Devon, England, ca. 1580, liv. 1666, in Massachusetts; m. at Islington, co. Devon, Eng., 28 Oct. 1600, Rev. John Maverick, bapt. at Awliscombe, co. Devon, Eng., 27 Oct. 1578, d. at Boston, Mass. 3 Feb. 1635/6,

MOSES MAVERICK, b. in co. Devon, Eng., ca. 1610, d. at Marblehead, Mass., 28 Jan. 1686; m. ante 6 May 1635, at Marblehead, Mass., Remember Allerton, b. at Leyden, Holland, ca. 1614, d. at Salem, Mass., ante 22 Oct. 1656,

ELIZABETH MAVERICK, b. at Marblehead, Mass., bapt. 30 Sept. 1649, d. at Boston, Mass., ante 29 Nov. 1698; m. at Marblehead Mass., ante 1 May 1679, Thomas Skinner, b. 1644, d. at Boston Mass., 28 Dec. 1690,

ABIGAIL SKINNER, b. at Boston, Mass., ca. 1685, d. at Stoughton, Mass., 6 Mar. 1728; m. at Boston, Mass., 6 Sept. 1711, Nathaniel Coney, bapt. at Boston, Mass., 24 Mar. 1677, d. at Boston, Mass., 19 Nov. 1742,

SAMUEL CONEY, b. at Boston, Mass., 15 Apr. 1718, d. at Augusta, Me., 12 Apr. 1803; m. at Stoughton, Mass., 28 Jan. 1742, Rebecca Guild, b. at Dedham, Mass., 6 Sept. 1721, d. at Augusta, Me., 21 Apr. 1793,

SUSANNA CONEY, b. at Stoughton, Mass., 11 Oct. 1755 d. at Mercer, Me., 6 May 1844; m. at Shutesbury, Mass., 18 May

1778, John Church, b. at Killingly, Conn., 9 May 1753, d. at Farmington, Me., 12 Mar. 1838,

SUSANNA CHURCH, b. at Farmington, Me., 22 July 1789, d. at Mercer, Me., 3 July 1861; m. at Farmington, Me., 22 Feb. 1807, Dr. Andrew Croswell, b. at Plymouth, Mass., 9 Apr. 1778; Harvard College, 1798, d. at Mercer, Me., 4 June 1858,

EMILY COX CROSWELL, b. at Mercer, Me., 1 Dec. 1817; d. at Mercer, Me., 2 Aug. 1852 (g.s.); m. at Mercer, Me. 29 Mar. 1841, John Perley Emerson, b. at Bridgeton, Me., 16 Nov. 1812; d. at Baltimore Md., 4 Oct. 1874 (g.s.),

GEORGE DENNY EMERSON, b. at Mercer, Me., 1849; d. at Newton, Mass., 23 July 1878; m. at Boston, Mass., 19 Nov. 1874, Fannie Howard Macomber, b. at Boston, Mass., 12 Sept. 1848; d. at East Orange, N.J., 7 Apr. 1911,

HOWARD EMERSON, b. at Newton Centre, Mass., 31 Aug. 1875; d. at Newton, Mass, 4 May 1961; m. at Pittsburgh, Pa., 24 Jan. 1898, Ada Maxwell, b. at Pittsburgh, Pa., 30 July 1878; d. at Brookline, Mass 13 June 1963,

COL. MAXWELL EMERSON, b. at Newton Centre, Mass., 25 Mar. 1903; ed.: Phillips Andover Academy, Bordentown Military Institute, Dartmouth College, Memphis State University, M.A.; member: SAR, past President Tennessee Society; Society of Colonial Wars, Sec'y Tennessee Society; Mayflower Society of Tennessee, Deputy Governor General; Hereditary Order of Descendants of Colonial Governors; Descendants of Colonial Clergy; Colonial Lords of Manors, Ancient and Honorable Artillery Company of Massachusetts; Baronial Order of Magna Charta; Order of the Crown of Charlemagne in the United States of America; Military Order of World Wars; Military Order of Foreign Wars, past Commander, Tennessee; *HEREDITARY REGISTER; WHO'S WHO IN THE SOUTH AND SOUTHWEST;* m. (first) Mary Byram Millet, at New York, N.Y., 18 Aug. 1927; b. at Bridgewater, Mass., 23 Oct. 1904, dau. of Dr. Charles Sumner Millet and Elizabeth Collamore Howland; m. (second) at Memphis, Tenn., 1 Aug. 1945, Dorothy Jane Kerr, b. at Memphis, Tenn., 16 Oct. 1911;

1) DAVID MILLET EMERSON, b. 10 July 1928: m. Janet Zulauf;

   a) JANE HOWLARD EMERSON, b. 19 June 1955, Ft. Hood, Texas.

   b) SUSANNA EMERSON, b. 9 Jan. 1957, U.S. Army Hospital, Germany.

   c) PETER MAXWELL EMERSON, b. 14 June 1964 (adopted) Germany

   d) BRADFORD MAC DONALD EMERSON, b. 21 June 1965, U.S. Army Hospital, Germany.

2) JUNE ALICE EMERSON, b. 10 Oct. 1947; m. 17 Jan. 1975, Agana, Guam, Clyde Michael Dunn, b. 20 Nov. 1945.

Chapter LI

GYE — FRANCE — COX — WARREN

CHARLEMAGNE

(See Chapter XLIX)

MARY STEARNS, b. at Bennington, Vt., 9 Dec. 1787, d. in Tuscarawas Co., Ohio, 17 Feb. 1825; m. in Washington Co., Pa., 1801, Adam France, Jr., b. in Lancaster Co., Pa., 1783, d. in Marshall Co., Ind., Mar. 1850,

JACOB FRANCE, b. in Tuscarawas Co., Ohio, 8 Feb. 1825, d. in Marshall Co., Ind., 19 July 1909; m. in Holmes Co., Ohio, 25 Oct. 1846, Eliza Ann Witherow, b. in Holmes Co., Ohio, 15 May 1820, d. in Marshall Co., Ind., 9 Dec. 1870,

THOMAS BROWN FRANCE, b. in Marshall Co., Ind., 30 June 1853, d. at Pasadena, Calif., 31 Dec. 1948; m. in Starke Co., Ind., 18 Feb. 1877, Amelia Desdemona Hani, b. in Holmes Co., Ohio, 20 Jan. 1860, d. at Pasadena, Calif., 30 Sept. 1947,

MAUDE CASTELLA FRANCE, b. in Marshall Co., Ind., 11 Feb. 1878, d. in St. Joseph Co., Ind., 1 Feb. 1920; m. at Plymouth, Ind., 27 Sept. 1894, Franklin Cox, b. in Marshall Co., Ind., 27 Sept. 1875, d. in St. Joseph Co., Ind., 24 Jan. 1965,

1) HAZEL IRENE COX, b. in Marshall Co., Ind., 13 Dec. 1896; ed.: University of Southern California, Los Angeles; member: DAR, Chapter Regent, State Recording Sec'y; D.A.C., organizing Chapter Regent, State Regent (Ind.); Women Descendants of the Ancient and Honorable Artillery Company, Organizing President of Indiana Court, past Sec'y National Society; Colonial Dames of the XVII Century, past-state Historian, Indiana; Order of the Crown of Charlemagne in the

180

United States of America; m. in Marshall Co., Ind., 20 June 1915, Elza Phillip Warren, b. in Marshall Co., Ind. 26 Aug. 1890; d. at Lafayette, Ind., 8 Dec. 1966,

a) RICHARD PHILLIP WARREN, b. at South Bend, Ind., 3 Feb. 1920; m. at Frankfort, Ill., 14 Sept. 1942, Eloise Guirl, b. in South Haven Twp., Mich., 2 Mar. 1921,

    i) SUSAN CAROL WARREN, b. at South Haven, Mich., 8 Aug. 1943; ed.: Purdue University; member: Women Descendants of the Ancient and Honorable Artillery Company, Kappa Kappa Kappa, Order of the Crown of Charlemagne in the United States of America; m. in Tippecanoe Co., Ind., 25 Dec. 1965, Jack William Oliver, b. in Tippecanoe Co., Ind., 25 Nov. 1938;

    ii) SALLY ANN WARREN, b. at Lafayette, Ind., 24 June 1944; grad: Purdue University; member: Women Descendants of the Ancient and Honorable Artillery Company, Kappa Kappa Kappa, Kappa Delta Pi, Order of the Crown of Charlemagne in the United States of America:

    iii) RICHARD PHILLIP WARREN, Jr., b. 1 Nov. 1947.

2) LEAH LILLIAN COX, b. in Marshall Co., Ind., 4 Sept. 1911; ed: U.C.L.A. (Los Angeles); member: Northern Indiana Museum and Historical Society, Order of the Crown of Charlemagne in the United States of America; m. at South Bend, Ind., 30 Aug. 1952, Richard Owen Stoll, b. in St. Joseph Co., Ind., 1 Apr. 1906.

Chapter LII

HUMPHREY — PALMES — AVERY — WAL(S)WORTH — MORGAN — KINNE — CLEVELAND — CRANE — BIRCH — COLLINS

CHARLEMAGNE, King of the Franks, Emperor of the West, father of

LOUIS I, the Pious, King of the Franks, Emperor of the West; m. (first) Ermengarde (Irmgard), d. 3 Oct. 818, dau. of Ingeramun (Ingram), Count of Hasbaye,

LOTHARIUS I (LOTHAIR), King of Italy, Emperor of the West, b. ca. 795, d. 29 Sept. 855; m. (first) 15 Oct. 821, Ermengarde (Irmgard), d. 20 Mar. 851, dau. of Hugo II, Count of Tours (or of Alsace),

LOTHARIUS II, King of Lorraine (Lotharingien-Lothierregne-Lotharingia). b. ca. 835, d. 8 Aug. 869; m. (second) ca. 862, Waldrade, formerly his concubine) who died as a nun in Remiremont ca 868,

BERTHA, b. ca. 863, d. 8 Mar. 925; m. (first) ca. 879, Theobald (Thibault) Count of Arles,

BOSO, Count of Arles, 926-31, Markgraf of Tuscany, 931-36, b. ca. 885; m. Willa,

WILLA, m. ca. 936, Berenger II, King of Italy, Markgraf of Ivrea, d. 6 Aug. 966, son of Adalbert, Markgraf of Ivrea and his wife Princess Gisela, dau. of Berenger I, King of Italy, Emperor of the West,

SUSANNA, (often referred to as Rosela); m. (first) Arnolph II, *le Jeune,* Count of Flanders, son of Baldwin III, Count of Flanders and his wife, Matilda, dau. of Hermann Billung, Duke of Saxony,

BALDWIN IV, *le Barbu*, Count of Flanders, b. ca. 980, d. 30 May 1035; m. (first) ca. 1012, Ogive (Otgive) d. 21 Feb. 1030, dau. of Frederick, Count of Luxemburg,

BALDWIN V, the Pious, Count of Flanders, b. ca. 1012, d. 1 Sept. 1067; m. ca. 1028, Adele (Adelheid) d. 8 Jan. 1079, dau. of Robert II, King of France, and widow of Richard III, Duke of Normandy,

MATHILDA (or MAUD) of Flanders, b. ca. 1032, d. 2/3 Nov. 1083; m. ca. 1050/3, William I, Duke of Normandy, The Conqueror, King of England, b. 1027, d. 9 Sept. 1087,

HENRY I, *Beauclerc*, King of England, b. 1068, d. 1/2 Dec. 1135; m. (first) 11 Nov. 1100, Princess Mathilda, b. 1079, d. 1 May 1118, dau. of Malcolm III *Canmore*, King of Scotland, by his second wife, St. Margaret, dau. of Prince Edward, the Exile and his wife, Agatha,

MATHILDA (MAUD) b. 1104, d. 10 Sept. 1169, wid. of Henry V. Emperor of Germany; m. (second) 22 May 1127/8 Geoffrey V Plantagenet, Count of Anjou, b. 24 Aug. 1113/4, d. 7 Sept. 1151,

HENRY II, King of England, b. 5 Mar. 1132/3, d. 3 July 1189; m. 1 May 1152, Eleanor, Duchess of Aquitaine and Queen of France, d. 31 Mar. 1204, the divorced wife of Louis VII, King of France and dau. of William, Duke of Aquitaine and Count of Poitou,

JOHN I, *Lackland*, King of England 1199-1216, b. 24 Dec. 1166, d. 19 Oct. 1216; m. (second) 24 Aug. 1200, Isabella of Angouleme, b. 1188, d. 31 May 1246,

HENRY III, King of England 1216-1272, b. 1 Oct. 1207, d. at Westminster, 16 Nov. 1272; m. (first) at Canterbury, 1236, Eleanor of Provence, b. 1217, d. at Amesbury, 24 Jan. 1291, dau. of Raymond Berenger, Count of Provence,

183

EDMUND, surnamed "Crouchback", M.P. 1276, Earl of Lancaster, Leicester, and Derby, b. at London, 16 Jan. 1244/5, d. at Bayonne, 5 June 1295; m. (second) 1276, Blanche of Artois, d. at Paris, 2 May 1302,

HENRY PANTAGENET, b. 1281, d. 22 Sept. 1345, cr. Earl of Lancaster, 10 May 1324, M.P. 1298-9; m. 1298, Maud de Chaworth, liv. 1345, only dau. and hr. of Sir Patrick Chaworth, Knt., Lord of Kidwelly and Isabel de Beauchamp, (See Chapter XXII, p. 100)

JOAN PLANTAGENET, d. 7 July 1349; m. ca. 28 Feb. 1326/7, John de Mowbray, b. at Hovingham, Yorks., 29 Nov. 1310, d. at York, 4 Oct. 1361,

ALIANORE DE MOWBRAY, d. 18 June 1387; m. (his third) 1358, prob. Lancs., Roger de la Warre, 3rd Lord de la Warre, b. 13 Nov. 1326, d. 27 Aug. 1370, in Gascony,

JOAN DE LA WARRE, d. 24 Apr. 1404; m. 1390, Sir Thomas West, Lord West, b. 1365, d. co. Dorset, bur. 19 Apr. 1405, Christ Church Priory,

SIR REYNOLD (REGINALD) WEST, Lord de la Warre, b. 7 Sept. 1395, d. 27 Aug. 1450; m. (first) in Cornwall, ante 17 Feb. 1428/9, Margaret Thorley of Tybeste, Cornwall, d. ante 24 Nov. 1433, dau. of Robert Thorley and Anne Lisle,

SIR RICHARD WEST, 7th Lord de la Warre, b. prob. in Sussex, 28 Oct. 1430, d. 10 Mar. 1475/6; m. ante 10 June 1451, Katherine Hungerford of Meytesburg, Wilts., d. 12 May 1493, dau. of Sir Robert Hungerford and Margaret Botreaux, dau. of Sir William Botreaux, M.P., 1455-1472,

SIR THOMAS WEST, 8th Lord de la Warre, K.G., K.B., b. 1457, d. 10 Oct. 1525, bur. at Broadwater; m. (second) prob. in Sussex, Eleanor Copley, b. in Sussex, dau. of Sir Roger Copley and Anne Hoo,

SIR GEORGE WEST of Warbelton, Sussex, d. 1538; m. Elizabeth Morton, dau. of Sir Robert Morton of Lechlade, co. Gloucester,

184

SIR WILLIAM WEST, Lord de la Warre, b. ca. 1520, d. at Wherwell, Hants., 30 Dec. 1595; m. (first) ante 1555, Elizabeth Strange, dau. of Thomas Strange of Chesterton, co. Gloucester,

SIR THOMAS WEST, Lord Delaware, 11th Baron, b. ca. 1556, d. 24 Mar. 1601/2; m. 19 Nov. 1571, Anne Knollys, liv. 30 Aug. 1608, dau. of Sir Francis Knollys, K.G. and Mary Cary, Chief Lady of the Bedchamber to Queen Elizabeth I,

ELIZABETH WEST, b. at Wherwall, Hants., 11 Sept. 1573, d. at Compton Valence, co. Dorset, 15 Jan. 1632/3; m. (his second) at Wherwell, 12 Feb. 1593/4, Herbert Pelham, b. at Buxstepe, Warbleton, 1546, d. prob. at Fordington, 12 Apr. 1620,

ELIZABETH PELHAM, b. at Hellingly, England, 27 Apr. 1604, d. in co. Dorset, Eng., ante 1630; m. (her third, his second) ca. 4 Apr. 1621, at Salisbury, Eng., John Humphrey, b. at Chaldon, co. Dorset, Eng., ca. 1596, d. in England, ante 20 Apr. 1652,

ANNE HUMPHREY, bapt. at Fordington, co. Dorset, Eng., 17 Dec. 1625, d. at Swansea, Mass., 17 Dec. 1695; m. prob. in England, ca. 1642/3, William Palmes, b. in Eng. or Ireland, d. at Ardfinnan, Ireland, ante 1680,

SUSANNAH PALMES, b. in England or Ireland, ca. 1665, d. at Groton, Conn., 2 Oct. 1747; m. at Swansea, Mass., 25 Oct. 1686, Capt. Samuel Avery, b. at New London, Conn., 14 Aug. 1664, bur. at Ledyard (Northern Groton) 1 May 1723,

MARY AVERY, b. 10 Jan. 1695, d. prob. at New London, Conn., ante 23 Sept. 1742; m. (his first) prob. at New London, Conn., 16 Jan. 1720, William Wal(s)worth, b. on Fisher's Island, N.Y., Jan. 1694/5, d. at Bozrah, Conn., 17 May 1774,

MARY WAL(S)WORTH, b. prob. at Groton, 29 Sept. 1721, d. at Groton, aft. 31 Mar. 1796; m. at Groton, Conn., 1 July 1742, Deacon Solomon Morgan, b. at Groton, 5 Oct. 1708, d. at Groton, 22 Nov. 1791,

ANNA MORGAN, b. at Groton, Conn., ca. 1751, d. aft. 1824; m. 31 May 1770, at Groton, Conn., Rev. Aaron Kinne, b. at

Lisbon, Conn., 24 Sept. 1744, d. at Talmadge, Ohio, 14 July 1824,

MARY KINNE, b. at Groton, Conn., 16 Aug. 1777, d. at Winsted, Conn., 13 May 1860; m. at Barkhamsted, Conn., 25 Feb. 1805, Alexander Cleveland, b. at East Windsor, Conn., 16 Oct. 1783, d. at Winsted, Conn., 5 Sept. 1860,

RUFUS CLEVELAND, b. at Barkhamsted, Conn., 18 Dec. 1807, d. at Glastonbury, Conn., 11 June 1897 (bur. at Winsted, Conn., 14 June 1897) m. (first) 9 Dec. 1830, at Winchester, Conn., Sally Ann Burnham, b. at Colebrook, Conn., 29 Mar. 1803, d. at Barkhamsted, Conn., 17 Apr. 1854,

CAROLINE ELIZABETH CLEVELAND, b. at Barkhamsted, Conn., 3 Apr. 1840, d. at New York, N.Y., 23 Nov. 1924; m. at Barkhamsted, Conn., 10 Oct. 1865, Warren Cady Crane, b. at West Granville Conn., 18 July 1841, d. at New York, N.Y., 23 Apr. 1943,

ELLEN CLEVELAND CRANE, b. at Brooklyn, N.Y., 26 Oct. 1869, d. at Woburn, Mass., 12 Apr. 1961; m. at New York, N.Y., 25 July 1900, John Harvey Birch, b. at Peekskill, N.Y., 1866, d. at Woburn, Mass., 11 July 1950,

EMILY VIRGINIA BIRCH, b. at Cranford, N.J., 10 Feb. 1904; m. at New York, N.Y., 23 Feb. 1923, Wortham Alexander Collins, b. at Paris, Texas, 13 Apr. 1894, d. at Rye, N.Y., 4 Sept. 1969,

WILLIAM WORTHAM COLLINS, b. at Dallas Texas, 20 Feb. 1931; B.A., Amherst College, 1953; U.S. Naval Reserve, 1951-55; Chairman, Associates of Fine Arts. Amherst College; Donor, Collins Print Room, Amherst College Art Museum; Senior Warden, Christ's Church, Rye, N.Y.; Honorary Trustees Committee, American Association of Museums; member: Order of the Crown of Charlemagne in the United States of America; Nat'l Society, Americans of Royal Descent; Society of Colonial Wars; Order of Americans of Armorial Ancestry; Society of Mayflower Descendants; The Society of Descendants of Colonial Clergy; m. at Haines Falls, N.Y., 14 July 1962, Ann Drewry Kindred, b. at New York, N.Y., 4 Oct. 1936,

1) WILLIAM WORTHAM COLLINS, JR., b. 23 Mar. 1964, at Greenwich, Conn.;

2) CHRISTOPHER RAGLAND COLLINS, b. 23 Mar. 1966, at Greenwich, Conn.;

3) PAMELA CRANE COLLINS, b. 10 July 1969, at Greenwich, Conn.

Chapter LIII

HUMPHREY — PALMES — AVERY — WALSWORTH — WILLIAMS — METCALF — HARPER — CROZER

CHARLEMAGNE

(See Chapter LII)

MARY AVERY, b. 10 Jan. 1695, at Groton, Conn., d. at Groton, Conn., 17 May 1739; m. (his first) prob. at Groton, Conn., 16 Jan. 1720, William Walsworth II, b. on Fishers Island, N.Y. (nr. Groton, Conn.) Jan. 1694/5, d. at Bozrah, Conn., 17 May 1774,

LUCY WALSWORTH, 4th dau., b. at Groton, Conn., 3 Dec. 1732, d. at Lebanon, Conn., 10 Aug. 1795; m. at Groton, Conn., 12 Oct. 1753, Capt. Veach Williams, who commanded troops in the Colonial and Revolutionary Wars, b. at Lebanon, Conn., 23 Apr. 1727, d. at Lebanon, Conn., 11 Sept. 1804,

EUNICE WILLIAMS, 5th dau., b. at Lebanon, Conn., 13 Feb. 1775, d. at Cooperstown, N.Y., 28 Feb. 1844; m. at Lebanon, Conn., 6 July 1793, Hon. Arunah Metcalf, b. at Lebanon, Conn., 14 Feb. 1771, d. at Cooperstown, N.Y., 15 Aug. 1848,

NATHAN WILLIAMS METCALF, b. at Otsego, N.Y., 12 Apr. 1794, d. at Chicago, Ill., 19 Nov. 1873; m. at Darien, N.Y., 4 Dec. 1816, Jerusha Clark, b. prob. at Darien, N.Y., ca. 1796, d. at Chicago, Ill., 31 Dec. 1883,

LYDIA ELECTA METCALF, b. in Otsego Co., N.Y., 25 Feb. 1818, d. at Pittsburgh, Pa., 28 Jan. 1904; m. prob. in Otsego Co., N.Y., 4 June 1836, John Harper, b. at Donegal, Ireland, 5 Dec. 1811, d. at Pittsburgh, Pa., 5 Apr. 1891,

CHARLES SPANG HARPER, Esq., b. at Pittsburgh, Pa., 5 Mar. 1853, d. at Philadelphia, Pa., 5 Apr. 1911; m. at Cleveland, Ohio, 26 Oct. 1882, Julia Azuba Murfey, b. at Cleveland, Ohio, 25 Dec. 1856, d. at Yonkers, N.Y., 17 Mar. 1909,

LYDIA HARPER, b. at Pittsburgh, Pa., 9 Aug. 1883, d. at Bryn Mawr, Pa., 2 June 1974; m. at New York, N.Y., 5 Dec. 1906, George Knowles Crozer, Jr., b. at Upland, Pa., 9 Dec. 1875, d. at Haverford, Pa., 26 Nov. 1936,

CHARLES HARPER CROZER, b. at Upland, Pa., 22 Nov. 1913; B.A. with Honors, Princeton University; member: Baronial Order of Magna Charta, Order of the Crown of Charlemagne in the United States of America, S.R., The Military Order of the Loyal Legion. The Society of Mayflower Descendants, The Philadelphia Cricket Club, The Merion Cricket Club; m. (second) at St. Croix, V.I., 12 Sept. 1972, Mary Therese Gillen, b. at Atlantic City, N.J., 20 Feb. 1923.

Chapter LIV

LLOYD — EATON — MORRISON — TALLMAN — DUDLEY — FIELD — FINLEY — BEARD

CHARLEMAGNE

(See Chapters II and XXXVI)

KING JOHN OF ENGLAND, b. at Beaumont Palace, Oxford, 24 Dec. 1167, d. at Newark Castle, 19 Oct. 1216, was the father of a natural daughter, Joan, possibly by Constance, Duchess of Brittany,

JOAN, d. at Aber, 2 Feb. 1236/37, bur. at Llanfaes; m. circa 1205/06, Llewelyn Fawr (the Great) ap Jorwerth, Prince of North Wales, d. at Aberconway, 11 April 1240, and bur. at the Abbey there,

ANGHARAD FERCH LLEWELYN, m. Maelgwn Fychan, Lord of Cardigan Is-Ayron, son of Maelgwn ap Rhys, Lord of Ceredigion (c. 1170-1230), d. 1257,

ELLEN FERCH MAELGWN, m. Meredith ap Owen, Lord of Cardigan Uch-Ayron, son of Owen ap Griffith (d. 1235), and grandson of Griffith ap Yr Arglwydd Rhys, by his wife, Matilda, dau. of William de Braose, d. 1265,

OWEN AP MEREDITH, LORD OF ANHUNOG, CAERWEDROS, etc., of Iscoed, Ceredigion, d. 15 Aug. 1275; m. his first cousin, Angharad ferch Owen, dau. of Owen ap Meredith, Lord of Cedewen (d. 25 Sept. 1255, bur. Strata Florida Abbey), and his wife Margaret ferch Maelgwn, sister of Ellen ferch Maelgwn, above),

LLEWELYN AP OWEN, LORD OF CAERWEDROS, of Iscoed,

Ceredigion, d. 1309; m. perhaps the dau. of Sir Robert de Valle, Lord of Trefgarn in Pembrokeshire,

THOMAS AP LLEWELYN, Lord of a quarter of Gwynnioneth and half of Iscoed, d. by 14 Aug. 1343, m. his niece, Elinor dau. of Meredith ap Llewelyn and Llencu, dau. of Llewelyn ap Owen.

ELLEN FERCH THOMAS, m. Griffith Fychan, Lord of Glendower, and they were the parents of Owen Glendower (1359-c. 1416), (See Chapter LXXXIV, p. 305)

LOWRI FERCH GRIFFITH, sister of Owen Glendower, m. Robert Puleston of Emral, aged 28 on 3 Sept. 1386,

JOHN PULESTON, of Emral, will dated 20 Feb. 1442/43 and proved 17 Apr. 1444, m. Angharad Hanmer, dau. of Griffith Hanmer of Hanmer, Flintshire,

MARGARET PULESTON, m. David ap Evan ap Einion, Constable of Harlech Castle, 1461-1468,

ANGHARAD FERCH DAVID, m. William ap Griffith of Cochwillan, Caernarvonshire, Sheriff of Caernarvonshire, 1485, d. circa 1500,

MAUD FERCH WILLIAM, (m. second Evan ap Griffith ap Meredith), m. as her first husband, Reynold Conwy. of Bryn Euryn, Llandrillo in Rhos, Denbighshire,

HUGH CONWY of Bryn Euryn (m. second Ellen Griffith, dau. of Sir William Griffith of Penrhyn, Caernarvonshire), left a will dated 1540, m. as his first wife, Annes, dau. of Owen ap Meyrick of Anglesey, by his wife, Ellen ferch Robert ap Meredith,

JANET CONWY, m. Meredith Lloyd of Beaumaris, Anglesey, son of John Lloyd, and his wife, Margaret Gethin, dau. of Maurice Gethin of Voelas, Denbighshire, and his wife, Anne Middleton, dau. of David Middleton of Chirk Castle, Denbigh, Receiver-General of Wales during the War of the Roses,

THE RIGHT REV. GEORGE LLOYD, Bishop of Chester, 1604-1615, educated at Jesus College, Cambridge, D.D., 1598, consecrated Bishop of Sodor and Man in 1600, d. 1 Aug. 1615, bur. Chester Cathedral; m. Ann Wilkinson, dau. of John Wilkinson of Norwich near Chester,

ANNE LLOYD, widow of Thomas Yale of Plas Grono, Wrexham, Denbighshire, Wales (whom she m. at Chester by license dated 13 Apr. 1612), returned to England on the death of her husband, Gov. Eaton, taking with her, Elihu Yale, her grandson, later benefactor of Yale College, and her daughter, Hannah Eaton, and d. at London, in 1659, m. (second) circa 1627, Theophilus Eaton; son of the Rev. Richard Eaton, (Lincoln College, Oxford, 1586) vicar of Great Budworth, Cheshire; Deputy Governor of the Eastland or Baltic Company of London, who organized the settlement of the New Haven Colony with the Rev. John Davenport, and arrived at Boston on the "Hector", 26 June 1637, with his family and a "goodly company", purchased the land at "Quinnipac", now New Haven, from the Indians in the summer of 1637, and settled there, 30 March 1638, where he served as Governor of the Colony until his death, b. at Stony Stratford, Bucks., Aug. 1591, d. at New Haven, Conn., 7 Jan. 1657/58,

HANNAH EATON, baptised at St. Stephen's, Coleman St., London, 6 Oct. 1632, d. at New Haven, Conn., 4 May 1707, m. at London, 14 July 1659, William Jones, Deputy Governor of the New Haven Colony, 1664, Deputy Governor of Connecticut, 1691-1697, son of David and Jane Jones, bapt. at St. Martin's in the Fields, London, 20 March 1624, d. at New Haven, Conn., 17 Oct. 1700, where he and his wife are buried in the Center Church Cemetery, on either side of Governor Eaton, with the epitaph, for all three on the same stone, being, "Eaton, so faimed, so wise, so meek, so just/The Phoenix of the world here hides his dust/Forget this name New England never must/T' attend you sir, beneath these framed stones/are come your honored son and daughter Jones/On each hand to repose their weary bones." The tombstone has been moved to the Jones plot in the Grove St. Cemetery, New Haven,

SARAH JONES, b. at New Haven, Conn. 17 Aug. 1662; m. (second) John Dudley of Guilford, Conn.; m. (first) at New

Haven, Conn., 21 Oct. 1687, Andrew Morrison, a merchant of Scottish birth, who d. at New Haven, bef. 30 Jan. 1702/03,

ANNA MORRISON, b. at New Haven, Conn., 4 Nov. 1693, d. at Guilford, Conn., 4 Oct. 1773; m. at Guilford, Conn., 17 June 1714, Dr. Ebenezer Tallman, son of Dr. Peter and Ann (Wright) Tallman of Guilford, and grandson of Peter Tallman, General Solicitor of Rhode Island in 1661, and his first wife, Ann Hill,

MARY TALLMAN, b. at Guilford, Conn., circa 1724, d. at Guilford, Conn., 26 March 1778, aged 54; m. at Guilford, Conn., 17 Feb. 1741/42, Deacon David Dudley, son of Caleb and Elizabeth (Buck) Dudley, b. at Guilford, Conn., 27 Nov. 1718, d. at North Guilford (now Madison), Conn., 17 Feb. 1807, and buried with his wife in the West Cemetery, Madison, Conn.,

ANNA DUDLEY, b. at North Guilford, Conn., 13 Apr. 1752, d. at Madison, Conn., 7 Oct. 1819; m. at Guilford, Conn., 25 Nov. 1767, Capt. Timothy Field; son of Ensign David Field, and his third wife, Abigail (Tyler) Stone, widow of Jedediah Stone, and dau. of Isaac and Abigail (Pond) Tyler of Branford, Conn.; he answered the Lexington Alarm in April 1775; in 1776, he joined the Seventh Regiment raised in Connecticut for the defense of the State, and was appointed its sergeant-major, during this period he was with the army of Gen. Washington stationed on the upper part of Manhattan, and he fought at the Battle of White Plains. In 1780 he was a Lieut. in the Seventh Regiment of the Conn. Militia under Col. William Worthington, and on 10 Apr. 1781, he was appointed a Lieut. in Capt. Peter Vail's Co., Conn. Coast Guard, and promoted to Capt. 18 June 1781. He was b. at East Guilford, Conn., 12 Mar. 1743/44, d. at Madison, Conn. 1 Jan. 1818, (They were also the parents of the Rev. David Dudley Field, D.D., 1781-1867)

THE REV. TIMOTHY FIELD, educated at Yale College, class of 1797, Pastor of the First Congregational Church, Canandaigua, N.Y., 1799-1807, Pastor of the Congregational Church of Westminster West, Vt., 1807-1844, b. at East Guilford, Conn., 28 Sept. 1775, d. at Brattleboro, Vt., 23 Feb. 1844; m. (first) at

Madison, Conn., 3 Jan. 1801, Wealthy Ann Bishop, b. at Guilford, Conn., 9 July 1773, d. at Westminster West, Vt., 17 Apr. 1814, dau. of Josiah Bishop of Madison, Conn. and his wife, Anne Crampton, dau. of James and Mary (Coe) Crampton of Guilford, Conn.,

ALFRED BISHOP FIELD, merchant, of Canandaigua, N.Y., b. at Avon, N.Y., 6 Oct. 1806, d. at Canandaigua, N.Y., 23 Feb. 1858; m. (second) at Canandaigua, N.Y., 7 March 1833, his first cousin, Ann Field Beals, dau. of Thomas Beals, banker, of Canandaigua, N.Y., and his wife, Abigail Field, dau. of Capt. Timothy and Anna (Dudley) Field, and paternal granddaughter of Samuel and Rebecca (Wilkinson) Beals of Boston, Mass., educated at the Emma Willard School, Troy, N.Y., b. at Canandaigua, N.Y., 4 Dec. 1805, d. at Detroit, Mich., 5 Jan. 1896,

LOUISE HOWELL FIELD, educated at the Maplewood Academy, Pittsfield, Mass., b. at Canandaigua, N.Y., 23 Oct. 1845, d. at Canandaigua, N.Y., 3 Apr. 1917; m. at Canandaigua, N.Y., 4 Oct. 1866, Horace Marshall Finley, photographer and musician, son of Marshall Finley of Canandaigua, author in 1849 of one of the first books dealing with photography in the United States, and his wife, Ann Eliza Bailey, dau. of James and Ann (High) Bailey of Jackson, Mich., b. at Bristol, N.Y., 23 Jan. 1838, d. at Canandaigua, N.Y., 17 July 1901,

GERTRUDE FIELD FINLEY, educated at the Granger Place School, Canandaigua, b. at Canandaigua, N.Y., 18 June 1869, d. at Sheffield, Mass., 20 Apr. 1941, m. at Canandaigua, N.Y., 25 Sept. 1888, Maximillian Cornelius Beard of Canandaigua and New York City, educated at the University of Louisiana (now Tulane), and the Stevens Institute, Hoboken, N.J., son of Dr. Cornelius Collins Beard of New Orleans, La., and Brookline, Mass., and his first wife, Philadelphia Stuart-Menteth, dau. of Capt. Thomas Loughnan and Isabella Maria (Tobin) Stuart-Menteth of Menteth's Point, Canandaigua Lake, N.Y., sister and heiress, in her issue, of Sir James Stuart-Menteth, 3rd Baronet, of Mansfield Park, Ayrshire, Scot., and Mentheth's Point, Canandaigua Lake, N.Y. (see Volume II, p. 272),

STUART-MENTETH BEARD II, educated at the Horace Mann School, New York City, 1900-1912, Williams College, class of 1916, and the University of Toulouse, France, served in World War I, 11 May 1917-20 July 1919, as a First Lieutenant with the 4th Field Artillery of the 1st Division, banker with the U.S. Mortgage and Trust, New York City in the 1920's, owner and manager of the Sheffield Inn, Sheffield, Mass., 1929-1955, b. at Canandaigua, N.Y., 28 Nov. 1893, d. at Sheffield, Mass., 8 Sept. 1955; m. at Asbury Park, N.J., 30 June 1921, Natalie Sudler Turner, dau. of Henry Clay Turner of Wilmington, Del., and his wife, Elizabeth Ellen Sudler, dau. of Dr. James Selby Sudler of Bridgeville, Del., educated at Swarthmore College, class of 1912, b. at Wilmington, Del., 20 Dec. 1888, d. at Great Barrington, Mass., 7 Jan. 1957 (See Chapter XXXVIII) Issue:

1.) STUART-MENTETH BEARD III, educated at the Berkshire School, Sheffield, Mass., Swarthmore College, and Cornell University, entered in the U.S. Army 1942, discharged as a First Lieutenant in 1946, after serving in the Pacific Theatre, member of the Order of Colonial Lords of Manors in America, b. at Spring Lake, N.J., 16 Oct. 1922, d. at Gainesville, Fla., 8 July 1970, m. at Baltimore, Md., 20 June 1955, Alice Hopkins Warner, dau. of James Potter Warner (d. at Baltimore, 1957) and his wife, Anne Hopkins Moore (d. at Clearwater, Fla., 30 Aug. 1975), b. at Baltimore, Md., March 3, 1920, Issue:

   a) ANNE STUART-MENTETH BEARD, member of the Order of Colonial Lords of Manors in America, b. at Clearwater, Fla., 10 Aug. 1957.

2.) HENRY SUDLER BEARD, educated at the Berkshire School, Sheffield, Mass., the United States Naval Academy, Annapolis, Md., and Cornell Law School, partner in Anderson and Beard Attorneys at Law, Westfield, Mass., b. at Yonkers, N.Y., 25 March 1924, d. at Springfield, Mass., 7 Nov. 1966, m. at Armonk, N.Y., 13 June 1953, Faith Johnson, now living in Blandford, Mass., dau. of Walter Haynes Johnson, Jr. (d. at Stamford, Conn., 4 Oct. 1973) and his first wife,

Marinde Hamill (d. N.Y.C., 13 Apr. 1957), dau. of David La Rose Hamill of Buffalo, N.Y., educated at the Abbott Academy, Andover, Mass., Smith College and the University of Massachusetts, b. Buffalo, N.Y., 12 Feb. 1932, Issue:

a) JAMES SUDLER BEARD, educated at the Lenox School, Lenox, Mass., and the University of Massachusetts, member of the Order of Colonial Lords of Manors in America, b. at Springfield, Mass., 10 Jan. 1955.

b) WALTER JOHNSON BEARD, educated at the Lenox School, Lenox, Mass., the Wooster School, Danbury, Conn., member of the Order of Colonial Lords of Manors in America, b. at Springfield, Mass., 15 Nov. 1955.

c) SARAH BEARD, educated at Berkshire Junior College, and Smith College, member of the Order of Colonial Lords of Manors in America, b. at Springfield, Mass., 14 Sept. 1957.

d) STUART-MENTETH BEARD IV, educated at the Darrow School, Junior Member, Sons of the Revolution in the State of New York, member of the Order of Colonial Lords of Manors in America, Inheritor Member of the Order of the Crown of Charlemagne in the United States of America, b. at Springfield, Mass., 29 Dec. 1960.

e) PHILADELPHIA BEARD, member of the Order of Colonial Lords of Manors in America, b. at Springfield, Mass., 12 Dec. 1962.

3.) TIMOTHY FIELD BEARD, Fellow American Society of Genealogists, graduated from the Indian Mountain School, Lakeville, Conn., in 1946, the Berkshire School, Sheffield, Mass., in 1949, Williams College, Williamstown, Mass., in 1953 with a B.A. in History, and Columbia University in 1962 with an M.S. in Library Science, since 1962 he has been a librarian in the Local History and Genealogy Division of the New

196

York Public Library, member: The Order of the Crown of Charlemagne in the United States of America, Genealogist General; Sons of the Revolution in the State of New York; Society of Colonial Wars in the States of New York, and New Jersey, Genealogist, N.Y.; St. Nicholas Society of the City of New York, Genealogist; the Order of Colonial Lords of the Manor in America, Registrar; the Saint Andrews Society of the State of New York; the Baronial Order of Magna Charta; Hereditary Order of the Descendants of Colonial Governors; Order of Descendants Colonial Physicians and Chirurgiens, Genealogist; Society of the Cincinnati of Maryland; Military Order of the Crusades; National Society of Americans of Royal Descent, Genealogist; the Society of Genealogists, London; the Delaware Historical Society; and Maryland Historical Society; the Worcester County (Md.) Historical Society; the Irish Genealogical Research Society; the Dumfriesshire and Galloway Natural History and Antiquarian Society; the Norfolk and Norwich Genealogical Society; the Mendelssohn Glee Club; The Church Club of New York; served in the U.S. Air Force in Bordeaux, France from 1954 to 1956, when he was honorably discharged as a First Lieutenant, b. at Great Barrington, Mass. Dec. 19, 1930, m. at New York City, Sept. 12, 1963, Annette Knowles Huddleston, daughter of the late William Eugene Huddleston, Jr., of Clanton and Tuskeegee, Alabama, and his wife, the former Alma F. Robinson, now of Destin, Florida, educated at the University of Alabama, member of the John Jay Chapter NSDAR, New York City, through descent from George Dawson of Maryland and Georgia, Regent, 1976-1978, and The Church Club of New York, b. Montgomery, Alabama, Sept. 20, 1933.

197

Chapter LV

LYNDE — LORD — LATHROP — BROCKWAY — REED — GLOVER

CHARLEMAGNE

(See Chapters X, XXXII, XXXIX, XLIII, LXVIII)

ISABEL DE VERMANDOIS m. (second) William de Warenne, 2nd Earl of Surrey,

ADA DE WARENNE, d. 1178; m. 1139, Henry de Huntingdon, Earl of Huntingdon and Northumberland, b. 1114, d. 12 June 1152,

DAVID DE HUNTINGDON, Earl of Huntingdon, b. 1144, d. at Yardley, 17 June 1219; m. 26 Aug. 1190, Maud of Chester, b. 1171, d. 1233, dau. of Hugh, Earl of Chester,

MARGARET DE HUNTINGDON, m. 1209, Alan, Lord of Galloway, hereditary Constable of Scotland, d. 1234,

DEVORGILLA, of Galloway, d. 28 Ian. 1289/90; m. 1233, John de Baliol, of Barnard Castle, d. 1269,

CECILY DE BALIOL, d. ante 1273; m. Sir John de Burgh, Baron of Lanvallei of Walkern, d. ante 3 Mar. 1279/80, son of John de Burgh. b. 1210, d. 1275, knighted 1239, and Hawise de Lanvallei (dau. of William de Lanvallei, d. 1217, Magna Charta Surety 1215),

HAWISE DE BURGH, b. 1256, d. subs. 1282; m. Sir Robert de Grelle, 7th Baron of Manchester, b. 1252, d. 15 Feb. 1282,

JOAN DE GRELLE, d. Mar. 1352/3; m. subs. 19 Nov. 1294, John de la Warre, 2nd Baron de la Warre, d. 9 May 1347, son of Sir Roger de la Warre and Clarice de Tregoz,

CATHERINE DE LA WARRE, d. 9 Aug. 1361; m. (second) 1328, Sir Warin de Latimer, Lord Latimer, b. ca. 1300, d. 13 Aug. 1349, son of Thomas, Lord Latimer and Lora, dau. of Henry de Hastings,

ELIZABETH DE LATIMER, m. Thomas Griffin, through whom the Latimer title descended,

RICHARD GRIFFIN, d. 1411; m. Anna, dau. of Richard Chamberlain,

NICHOLAS GRIFFIN, d. 1436; m. Margaret Pilkington, dau. of Sir John Pilkington,

NICHOLAS GRIFFIN, Lord Latimer, Sheriff of Northamptonshire, 1473, b. 5 June 1426, at Brixworth, d. 6 June 1482; m. (first) Catherine, dau. of Richard Curzon,

CATHERINE GRIFFIN, m. Sir John Digby, of Eye Kettleby, Leicestershire, knighted at Bosworth Field, d. ca. 1533, son of Everard Digby, M.P. and Sheriff of Rutlandshire, and Jacquelle, dau. of Sir John Ellis,

WILLIAM DIGBY, Esq., of Kettleby and Luffenham, Leics., d. ante 1 Aug. 1529; m. (first) Rose Prestwich, dau. of William Prestwich of Lubenham and his wife, dau. of Sir Thomas Poultney,

SIMON DIGBY, of Bedale, co. York, executed in March 1570; m. Anne Grey, dau. of Reginald Grey of York, attainted 1569, executed 28 Mar. 1570,

EVERARD DIGBY, m. Katherine Stockbridge, dau. of Mr. Stockbridge de Vanserschaff Theuber de Newkirk,

ELIZABETH DIGBY, b. ca. 1584, d. at London, 1669; m. at Hackney, 25 Oct. 1614, Enoch Lynde, a Netherlands shipping merchant, d. at London, 23 Apr. 1636,

HON. SIMON LYNDE, bapt. at London, Eng., June 1624, d. at

Boston, Mass., 22 Nov. 1687; m. at Boston, Mass., 22 Feb. 1652/3, Hannah Newgate,

HON. NATHANIEL LYNDE, b. in Mass., 22 Nov. 1659, d. at Saybrook, Conn., 5 Oct. 1729; m. 1683, Susannah Willoughby, b. at Charleston, Mass., 10 Aug. 1664, d. at Saybrook, Conn., 21 Feb. 1709/10 (See Chapter LXXVII)

ELIZABETH LYNDE, b. 2 Dec. 1694, d. at Lyme, Conn., 22 June 1778; m. 11 July 1720, Hon. Richard Lord, b. at Lyme, Conn., 1690, d. at Lyme, Conn., 6 Aug. 1776,

SUSANNA LORD, b. at Lyme, Conn., 16 Jan. 1724, d. at Chelsea, Mass. (?), 3 Feb. 1808; m. 23 Jan. 1745/6, Elijah Lathrop, b. at Norwich, Conn., 4 Sept. 1720, d. at Norwich, Conn., 13 Mar. 1814,

EUNICE LATHROP, b. at Norwich, Conn., 13 Sept. 1753, d. at Clinton, N.Y., 10 Sept. 1823; m. 8 Dec. 1772, Rev. Thomas Brockway, b. at Lyme, Conn., 20 Jan. 1744/5, d. at Columbia, Conn., 5 July 1807,

EUNICE BROCKWAY, b. at Lebanon, (now Columbia), Conn., 20 Nov., d. 23 Jan. 1859; m. at Hebron or Lebanon, Conn., 29 Aug. 1799, Ebenezer Reed, b. at Lebanon, Conn., 29 Aug. 1774, d. at Chili, Monroe Co., N.Y., 15 May 1831,

AUSTIN BROWN REED, b. at Hebron, Conn., 23 Mar. 1804, d. in Monroe Co., N.Y., 10 Apr. 1852; m. at Ellington, Conn., 20 Oct. 1824, Mary Richardson, b. in Conn., 28 Sept. 1803, d. at Paw Paw, Mich., 4 Feb. 1891,

WILLIAM ASA REED, b. at Ogden, Monroe Co., N.Y., 10 Feb. 1829, d. at Dryden, Mich., 9 June 1888; m. in Monroe Co., N.Y., 20 July 1856, Weltha Sholes, b. in Monroe Co., N.Y., 17 Jan. 1839, d. at Dryden, Mich., 6 Jan. 1924,

AUSTIN BROCKWAY REED, b. at Dryden, Mich., 5 Oct. 1857, d. at North Branch, Mich., 9 Jan. 1931; m. at Metamora, Mich., 20 Apr. 1879, Phoebe Evaline Tainter, b. at Metamore, Mich., 25 Apr. 1859, d. in Attica Twp., Lapeer Co., Mich., 5 June 1936,

FRANCES ADA REED, b. at Arcadia, Lapeer Co., Mich., 15 July 1895; ed.: Lapeer Co. Teachers Normal, Detroit Conservatory of Music; member: DAR; Daughters of 1812, past 1st. V.P., Nat'l New England Women; Mayflower Descendants; Colonial Daughters of the XVII Century, State President; Daughters of Founders and Patriots; Order of Americans of Armorial Ancestry, Councillor; Sons and Daughters of the Pilgrims, Honorary Governor General; Children of the American Colonists, Honorary President General; Daughters of the Union 1861-65, Honorary President General; First Families of Virginia; Jamestowne Society; Founders of Hartford Soc.; Old Plymouth Colony Descendants; Flagon and Trencher; Nat'l Presidents Association; Nat'l Gavel Society; Nat'l Society Americans of Royal Descent; Order of the Crown of Charlemagne in the United States of America; Daughters of the Barons of Runnemede, Nat'l Pres.; Dames of the Court of Honor, Honorary Pres. Gen.; Women Descendants of the Ancient and Honorable Artillery Co., Hon. Pres. Nat'l.; Daughters of Colonial Wars, past Nat'l 1st V.P.; Order of Three Crusades, 1096-1192, Councillor; Nat'l Huguenot Soc., past Registrar Gen.; Historical Memorials Society in Detroit; Midland Co., Historical Soc., past Pres.; etc.; m. 18 Feb. 1918, Hugh Wallace Glover, b. 18 Feb. 1895, at North Branch, Mich. and has issue:

1) JANET RAE GLOVER, b. 8 Aug. 1923, at Brown City, Mich.; m. 25 Mar. 1945, at Midland, Mich., Laurence Claude Lang, b. 3 Oct. 1925, at Brunswick, Ga., son of Dr. Nathaniel Hawthorne Lang and Beatrix Brock, his wife,

   a) STEPHEN GLOVER LANG, b. 30 Dec. 1949, at Midland, Mich., Medical Student, West Germany;

   b) LAURENCE CLAUDE LANG III, b. 17 Apr. 1953, at Midland, Mich., Dental Student, University of Detroit;

   c) JANET REED LANG, b. 10 Mar. 1957, at Midland, Mich., Student Michigan Central University, Mt. Pleasant, Mich.

Chapter LVI

MAGRUDER* — MARQUIS — ALLEN — REASOR — WHEELER

CHARLEMAGNE

(See Chapters X, XXXII, XXXIX, XLIII, LXVIII)

ISABEL DE VERMANDOIS, b. in France, ante 1085; d. in England, ante 1147; m. 1096 (first) Robert I de Beaumont, 1st Earl of Leicester and Count of Meulan, b. in Normandy, ca. 1046; d. 5 June 1118, bur. at Preaux, Normandy,

SIR ROBERT II DE BEAUMONT, knighted in 1122, 2nd Earl of Leicester, Justiciar of England, 1155-1168, b. 1104; m. aft. 1120, Amice de Gael de Montfort, dau. of Ralph de Gael de Montfort, Lord of Gael and Montfort in Brittany, Earl of Norfolk, Suffolk and Cambridge, in England, and his wife, FitzOsbern, dau. of William FitzOsbern,

HAWISE DE BEAUMONT, d. 24 Apr. 1197; m. ca. 1150, William FitzRobert, 2nd Earl of Gloucester, a descendant of Charlemagne, Alfred the Great and William the Conqueror, d. 23 Nov. 1183, bur. at Keynsham,

AMICE OF GLOUCESTER, d. 1 Jan. 1224/5; m. ca. 1173/6, Richard de Clare, Earl of Clare and Hereford and a Magna Charta Surety, b. 1150; d. bet. 30 Oct. and 28 Nov. 1217,

GILBERT DE CLARE, Earl of Clare and Hereford and Gloucester, and a Magna Charta Surety, b. ca. 1180, d. at Penros, Brittany, 25 Oct. 1230; m. 9 Oct. 1217, Isabel Marshall, d. at Berkhampstead, 11 Jan. 1239/40, dau. of William Marshall, Earl of Pembroke, and Regent of England, 1216-1219, and Crusader,

ISABEL DE CLARE, b. 2 Nov. 1226, d. ante May 1275; m. 2 Nov.

1226, Sir Robert de Brus, Lord of Annandale, a descendant of Charlemagne, d. at Lochmaben Castle, 31 Mar. 1295,

SIR ROBERT DE BRUCE (or Brus) Lord of Annandale and 1st Lord Brus, b. in July 1243, d. ante 4 Apr. 1304, bur. at Holm Cultram; m. (first) at Turnberry Castle, in 1271, Margery (or Marjory, or Margaret) Countess of Carrick, d. ante Oct. 1292,

KING ROBERT I BRUCE, of Scotland, b. at Writtle, Essex, 11 July 1274; d. at Cardross, Scotland, 7 June 1329; m. (first) ca. 1295, Isabel, b. at Mar, Aberdeen, ca. 1276, d. ante 1302, dau. of Donald, Earl of Mar,

PRINCESS MARJORIE (or Mary) of Scotland, b. at Dundonald, Ayr, ca. 1296, d. 2 Mar. 1315/6; m. ca. 1315, Walter Stewart, 6th High Steward of Scotland, b. at Dundonald, Ayr, 1293, d. 9 Apr. 1326,

KING ROBERT II, of Scotland, b. at Dundonald, Ayr, 2 Mar. 1315/6, d. at Dundonald Castle, 19 Apr. 1390; m. (first) by Papal Dispensation, 22 Nov. 1347, Elizabeth Mure, b. at Kilmarnock, ca. 1320, d. ante May 1355,

ROBERT STEWART, 1st Duke of Albany, Regent of Scotland 1404-1420, b. ca. 1340, d. at Stirling Castle, 3 Sept. 1420; m. (first) 9 Sept. 1361, Margaret Graham, Countess of Monteith, b. in Perthshire, ante 1334, d. bet. 21 July 1372 and 4 May 1380,

MARJORY (MARCELLINA) STEWART, b. at Lorne, Argyll, ca. 1372, d. ante 1432; m. (his first) 6 Feb. 1392, Duncan Campbell, 1st Lord Campbell of Lochow, Argyll, b. ca. 1370, d. in 1453, bur. at Kilmun

ARCHIBALD (or CELESTIN) CAMPBELL, of Lochow, Master of Campbell, b. ca. 1393, d. bet. 24 Apr. 1431 and March 1440; m. (first) Elizabeth Somerville, dau. of John Somerville, 3rd Lord Somerville,

COLIN CAMPBELL, 1st Earl of Argyll, d. 10 May 1493; m. ante 9 Apr. 1465, Elizabeth (or Isabel) Stewart, d. at Dumbarton, 26 Oct. 1510, dau. of John Stewart, 2nd Lord Lorne,

ARCHIBALD CAMPBELL, 2nd Earl of Argyll, b. ca. 1466, d. at the Battle of Flodden, 9 Sept. 1513; m. Elizabeth Stewart, dau. of the 1st Earl of Lennox,

DONALD CAMPBELL, fourth son, became Abbot of Coupar in May 1559, Keeper of Privy Seal under Earl of Arran for Mary, Queen of Scots, b. 1492, d. 1562; m. Margaret Gordon, who d. ante 1559,

SIR JAMES CAMPBELL, of Kiethock, Laird of Aberchiel and Kiethock, m. Mary Montifex,

MARGARET CAMPBELL, wid. of Andrew Drummond, 4th Laird of Balliclove, b. in Perthshire, Scotland, ca. 1580, d. in Perthshire; m. in Perthshire, ca. 1605, Alexander Magruder, b. in Perthshire, in 1569, d. in Perthshire,

ALEXANDER MAGRUDER*, b. in Perthshire, Scotland, in 1610, came to Calvert Co., Md., in 1651, d. in Prince George's Co., Md., 1677; m. (second) ante 1660, in Calvert Co., Md., Sarah — , b. in Prince George's Co., Md., ca. 1630; d. in Prince George's Co., Md., 1671,

SAMUEL MAGRUDER, b. in Prince George's Co., Md., ca. 1660, d. in Prince George's Co., Md., in Mar. 1711; m. in Prince George's Co., Md., ca. 1684, Sarah Beall, b. in Scotland, in 1669, d. in Prince George's Co., Md., in Apr. 1734,

NINIAN MAGRUDER, b. in Prince George's Co., Md., ca. 1686; d. in Prince George's Co., Md., w.p. June 1751; m. Elizabeth Brewer, b. at Annapolis, Md., 26 Oct. 1690; d. in Prince George's Co., Md.,

JOHN MAGRUDER, b. in Prince George's Co., Md., 11 Nov. 1709, d. in Montgomery Co., Md., w.p. 11 Nov. 1782; m. Jane Offutt, b. in Md., w.p. in Montgomery Co., Md. 4 July 1787,

ELEANOR MAGRUDER, b. in Md. 1746, liv. in Shelby Co., Ky., 1813; m. William Kidd Marquiss, b. in Md., ca. 1744, d. in Shelby Co., Ky. ca. 1812/3,

MARY MARQUIS, b. in Md., 2 Jan. 1773, d. May 1861; m. in

Nelson Co., Ky., 30 Aug. 1792, James Allen, b. in Pa., 9 Jan. 1766, d. in Shelby Co., Ky., 17 Jan. 1818,

ELIZABETH ALLEN, b. 2 Sept. 1793, d. in Spencer Co., Ky., 14 Mar. 1869; m. at Taylorsville, Ky., 14 Dec. 1809, Josiah Reasor, b. in Frederick Co., Va., 2 Apr. 1789, d. in Spencer Co., Ky., 6 Nov. 1868,

JAMES ALLEN REASOR, b. in Spencer Co., Ky., 16 Aug. 1821, d. in Indiana, 16 Sept. 1876; m. in Spencer Co., Ky., Mary Carlin, b. in Spencer Co., Ky., 5 Mar. 1823, d. in Jefferson Co., Ky., 11 Sept. 1869,

SARAH ANN REASOR, b. in Jefferson Co., Ky., 24 July 1847, d. in Jefferson Co., Ky., 20 Nov. 1926; m. in Jefferson Co., Ky., 2 Oct. 1866, Christopher Columbus Wheeler, b. in Jefferson Co., Ky., 21 Dec. 1836, d. in Jefferson Co., Ky., 11 Sept. 1911,

BUFORD MINOR WHEELER, b. in Jefferson Co., Ky., 9 Mar. 1876, d. at Dawson Springs, Ky., 5 May 1921; m. at Louisville, Ky., 14 Nov. 1900, Gertrude Frances Riley, b. at Waterford, Ky., 14 Dec. 1876, d. at Louisville, Ky., 19 Sept. 1955,

HOWARD RAYMOND WHEELER, b. in Jefferson Co., Ky., 10 Feb. 1911; Ed.: University of Louisville; member: Baronial Order of Magna Charta; Order of the Crown of Charlemagne in the United States of America; American Clan Gregor Society; Filson Club, Louisville; Kentucky Historical Society; a Kentucky Colonel; m. at Jeffersonville, Ind., 16 July 1931, Elva Lois Moore, b. at Louisville, Ky., 30 May 1913,

1) JANICE RAE WHEELER, b. in Jefferson Co., Ky., 28 Apr. 1938; Georgetown College; m. Jefferson Co., Ky., 28 Jan. 1961, Clarence Ray Jones, b. 9 Apr. 1939, in Pendleton Co., Ky.; Georgetown College; son of Rufus Jones and his wife, Frances Wigglesworth

   a) REBECCA RAE JONES, b. 7 Nov. 1964;

   b) RICHARD LEN JONES, b. 23 Nov. 1967.

*See Foreword

205

Chapter LVII

MANWARING* — PALMER — SHEPARD — FENN — MITCHELL — COOKE — LEAPER

CHARLEMAGNE, King of the Franks and Emperor of the West, b. 2 Apr. 742, d. at Aix la Chapelle (Aachen) 28 Jan. 814; m. 771 the Swabian Princess, Hildegarde, b. 758, d. 30 Apr. 783,

PEPIN, King of Italy and of Lombardy, b. Apr. 777, d. at Milan, 8 July 810. He had a son,

BERNARD, King of Italy, b. 797, d. at Milan, 17 Apr. 818; m. Cunigunde, d. ca. 835,

PEPIN, Count of Senlis, Peronne and St. Quentin, b. ca. 815, d. aft. 840,

HERBERT I, Count of Vermandois, Seigneur of Senlis, Peronne and St. Quentin, b. ca. 840, murdered ca 902; m. Bertha de Morvois, dau. of Guarri, Count of Morvois,

HERBERT II, Count of Vermandois and Troyes, b. 880-890, d. at St. Quentin, 943; m. Liegarde, dau. of Robert I, Duke of France, and Adele, his first wife,

ROBERT, Count of Vermandois, b. ca. 920, d. ca. 967-8; m. Adelaide of Burgundy, dau. of Giselbert, Count of Burgundy, and his wife, Ermengarde,

ADELAIDE DE VERMANDOIS, b. 950, d. 975-8; m. (first) Geoffrey I, Grisgonelle, Count of Anjou, d. 21 July 987, son of Fulk II, "the Good", Count of Anjou, and his wife Gerberga,

ERMENGARDE OF ANJOU, m. 980, Conan I, Duke of Brittany, d. 992,

JUDITH OF BRITTANY, b. 982, d. 1017; m. 1000, Richard II, "the Good", Duke of Normandy

ROBERT I, Duke of Normandy, d. 22 July 1035, had a son,

WILLIAM I, King of England (1066-1087), The Conqueror, b. at Falaise, France, 1027, d. at Rouen, France, 9 Sept. 1087; m. (her second), 1053, Matilda of Flanders, b. 1032, d. 3 Nov. 1083,

HENRY I, King of England; 1100-1135, b. 1070; d. in England, 1 Dec. 1135,

ROBERT DE CAEN, natural son, "The Consul", Earl of Gloucester, 1122-1147, b. ca. 1090; d. at Bristol, 31 Oct. 1147; m. Maud, dau. of Robert Fitz Hamon, Lord of Crelly in Calverdos, Baron of Thoringi, and Sybil, dau. of Roger de Montgomery, Earl of Shrewsbury,

MAUD, d. 29 July 1189; m. ca. 1141, Ranulf de Guernan, Count d'Avranches, Earl of Chester, d. 16 Dec. 1153, son of Ranulph de Meschines, Earl of Chester, and Lucy,

HUGH OF KEVELIOC, Earl of Chester, b. 1147; d. 1181; m. 1169, Bertrade d'Evreux de Montfort, dau. of Simon, Count of Montfort,

AMICIA, m. Sir Ralph de Masnilwaring, Knt., Justice of Chester, temp. Richard I,

ROGER MANWARING, of Warmincham, in Chester; m. Christian de Birtles,

WILLIAM MANWARING, of Over Peover, temp. Henry III,

WILLIAM MANWARING, of Over Peover, liv. 10 Edward II; m. Mary, dau. of Henry Davenport,

WILLIAM MANWARING, of Over Peover; m. (second) Elizabeth, dau. of Nicholas Leycester, and a sister of John Leycester, of Nether Tabley (See Chapter XLVIII, p. 168),

RANDLE MANWARING, of Over Peover; m. Margery, wid. of Richard Buckley, and dau. of Hugh Venables, Baron of Kinderton,

RALPH MANWARING, of Kermincham, Chester, 3rd son; m. Margery Savage, wid. of Sir John Maxwell,

WILLIAM MANWARING, of Nantwich, Chester, 5th son; m. — Titley, dau. of William Titley, of Titley, Shropshire, armiger,

GEORGE MANWARING, of Exeter, 3rd son; m. Juliana, dau. of Thomas Spurway, mayor of Exeter, 1540,

OLIVER MANWARING,

OLIVER MANWARING, Benefactor of Exeter and Dawlish, d. 1672; m. 1618, Prudence, bapt. 23 Dec. 1599, dau. of Henry Esse or Eshe, Gent., bur. at Sowton, Devon, 8 June 1640,

OLIVER MANWARING*, bapt. at Dawlish, Devon, Eng., 16 Mar. 1633/4, d. at New London, Conn., 2 Nov. 1723; m. Hannah Raymond, bapt. at Salem, Mass., Feb. 1643, d. at New London, Conn., 18 Dec. 1717,

MARY (MERCY) MANWARING, bapt as an adult, 25 Oct. 1702, d. at New London, Conn., Mar. 1739; m. at New London, Conn., 1 Dec. 1706, Jonathan Palmer, b. at Stonington, Conn., 7 Aug. 1668; d. at Stonington, Conn., 1726, w.d. 24 June, w.p. 21 Oct. 1726,

LOVE PALMER, b. at Stonington, Conn., 26 Feb. 1719; m. at Stonington, Conn., 23 Dec. 1736, Jonathan Shepard I, of Coventry and Stonington, Conn.,

JONATHAN SHEPARD II, b. 6 Jan. 1739/40; liv. at Tinmouth, Vt., 1790; m. Hanna Benjamin, in Conn.,

ELISHA SHEPARD, b. 1758, d. aft. 1820 when he applied for a Revolutionary War pension; m. Mary — ,

*See Foreword

208

PAMELIA SHEPARD, b. 1796, d. in 1854; m. 22 Nov. 1812 Ethan Fenn, b. in Vt., in 1790/4, d. in Vt., 24 Nov. 1844,

RHODA PAMELIA FENN, b. at Rutland, Vt., 27 July 1816, d. at Colon, Mich., 27 Mar. 1865; m. ca. 1832, George Baltimore Mitchell, b. at Royalton, N.Y., 15 June 1810, 2nd Count de Royalton, d. at Royalton, 26 Mar. 1838,

GEORGE MARVIN MITCHELL, 3rd Count de Royalton, b. at Royalton, N.Y., 6 Aug. 1836, d. 7 Mar. 1883; m. 5 July 1853, at Middleville, Mich., Mary-Alice (von) Walrath, b. in Herkimer Co., N.Y., 23 Dec. 1834, d. at Sturgis, Mich., 3 Sept. 1901,

CORA MAY MITCHELL, 4th Countess de Royalton, b. at Middleville, Mich., 4 Oct. 1864, d. at Goshen, Ind., 14 Aug. 1949; m. (second) in Barry Co., Mich., 29 Dec. 1886, Joseph Robert George Cooke, b. in Barry Co., Mich., 7 July 1858; d. in Sturgis, Mich., 4 Apr. 1910; m. (third) 25 June 1925, Bishop Hovey Schriber, of St. Paul, Minn., d. 1925, issue by second husband: (See Vol. II, PEDIGREES OF SOME OF THE EMPEROR CHARLEMAGNE'S DESCENDANTS for other descendants of her first and second husbands)

ROBERT GEORGE COOKE, B.A. (St. Thomas College) b. at Sturgis, Mich., 31 Oct. 1906, 7th Baron de Montjoye, 5th Count de Royalton; Knight Commander of Justice, Royal Yugoslavian Hospitaller Order of St. John of Jerusalem, Prior and Bailliff of the North; Knight of the Equestrian Order of St. Agatha of the Republic of San Marino; Member: Order of the Crown of Charlemagne in the United States of America, Honorary President General; Baronial Order of Magna Charta; The Military Order of the Crusades; Order of Three Crusades 1096-1192, First Vice President General; Order of St. Elizabeth (Philippines); National Society Americans of Royal Descent, past Registrar General; Order of Americans of Armorial Ancestry; Society of Colonial Wars in the State of Alabama; Hereditary Order of Descendants of Colonial Governors; SAR; m. at North St. Paul, Minn., 1 Aug. 1935, Helen Marie Mullery, b. at Duluth, Minn., 18 Feb. 1910, dau. of Valentine J. Mullery and his wife Mary Reinhart; Lady of

Honor and Devotion, Royal Yugoslavian Hospitaller Order of
St. John of Jerusalem, and Lady of the Order of St. Elizabeth
(Philippines) and has issue:

1) MARY-ALICE WALDORF COOKE, B.A. (Goucher
College), b. at St. Paul, Minn., 7 Sept. 1936; Lady of
Honor and Devotion, Royal Yugoslavian Order of St.
John of Jerusalem; Order of the Crown of Charlemagne
in the United States of America; National Society
Colonial Daughters of the 17th Century, etc.; m. at St.
Paul, Minn., 14 Sept. 1957, Percy Faraday Leaper, B.S.
(Johns Hopkins), Knight of Grace, Royal Yugoslavian
Hospitaller Order of St. John of Jerusalem; b. at
Waterbury, Conn., 23 Jan. 1935, only child of Col.
Percy Joshua Leaper, U.S.A., who d. at Philadelphia,
Pa., in 1956, and his wife, Rosina Gradidge. Issue:

   a) CARRIE ANN LEAPER, b. 30 July 1958, at
   Baltimore, Md., Member: Order of the Crown of
   Charlemagne in the United States of America,
   National Society Americans of Royal Descent;
   student at Wooster College, Ohio; m. 25 June
   1978, Penninton, N. J., Thomas Clifford
   Schmierer;

   b) SCOTT ROBERT FARADAY LEAPER, b. 30 Jan.
   1961, at Oak Park, Ill., Member: Order of the
   Crown of Charlemagne in the United States of
   America, Baronial Order of Magna Charta;

   c) LAURA MARIE LEAPER, b. 15 Feb. 1963, at Oak
   Park, Ill., Member: Order of the Crown of
   Charlemagne in the United States of America,
   Order of Three Crusades 1096-1192.

Chapter LVIII

MORE — DUTCH — KNOWLTON — PRESTON — CLARK — MORGAN — DOW

CHARLEMAGNE

(See Chapters X, XXXII, XXXIX, XLIII, LXVIII)

ISABEL DE VERMANDOIS, Countess of Leicester, d. ante July 1147; m. (second) William de Warenne, Earl of Surrey, d. 11 May 1138,

ADA DE WARENNE, d. 1178; m. 1139, Henry de Huntingdon, b. ca. 1114; d. 12 June 1152,

DAVID, EARL OF HUNTINGDON, d. at Yardley, Northants., 17 June 1219; m. 26 Aug. 1190, Maud of Chester,

ADA DE HUNTINGDON, m. Sir Henry de Hastings, of Ashill, co. Norfolk, d. ante 9 Aug. 1250,

SIR HENRY DE HASTINGS, of Ashill, co. Norfolk, d. ante 5 Mar. 1268/9; m. Joan de Cantelou,

SIR JOHN DE HASTINGS, of Abergavenny, b. 1262, d. 1312/3; m. Isabel de Valence,

ELIZABETH DE HASTINGS, m. Sir Roger de Grey, of Ruthin, co. Denbigh, d. 1352/3,

JULIANE DE GREY, d. 29 Nov. or 1 Dec. 1361; m. ante 14 Feb. 1329/30, John Talbot, of Richard's Castle, co. Hereford, d. 20 Sept. 1355,

JOHN TALBOT, of Richard's Castle, co. Hereford, bapt. 3 May 1337, d. 18 Feb. 1374/5; m. Katherine, d. ante 9 Apr. 1381 (m. 2nd., Sir John Seint Clare),

ELIZABETH TALBOT, d. in Devon, 3 Aug. 1407; m. Sir Warin l'Arcedeckne,

ELEANOR L'ARCEDECKNE, d. 20 July 1447; m. ante May 1385, Sir Walter Lucy, of Newington, co. Kent. d. 4 Oct. 1444,

ELEANOR LUCY, of Newington, Kent, m. Thomas Hopton, of Hopton, co. Salop,

ELIZABETH HOPTON, of Hopton, co. Salop, b. 1426/7, d. 22 June 1498; m. Sir Roger Corbet, of Moreton Corbet, co. Salop, d. 1467,

JANE CORBET, m. Thomas Cresset, of Upton Cresset, co. Salop, w.d. 20 Aug. 1520,

RICHARD CRESSET, of Upton Cresset, co. Salop, liv. 19 Henry VIII; m. Jane Wrottesley, of Wrottesley, co. Stafford,

MARGARET CRESSET, m. Thomas More, of Larden, co. Salop,

JASPER MORE, of Larden, co. Salop, w.p. 25 May 1614; m. Elizabeth Smalley,

KATHERINE MORE, b. 1587, liv. 1620; m. Samuel More, of Linley; by Jacob Blakeway, liv. 1618, had an illegitimate son,

RICHARD MORE, bapt. at Shipton, co. Salop, Eng., 23 Nov. 1614, was a passenger on the Mayflower, 1620; d. at Salem, Mass., ca. 1697; m. (first) at Plymouth, Mass., 30 Oct. 1636, Christian Hunt,

SUSANNA MORE, bapt. at Salem, Mass., 12 Mar., 1652, d. aft. 24 Aug. 1728; m. ca. 1676, Samuel Dutch, d. ante 19 Mar. 1693/4,

SUSANNA DUTCH, bapt. 25 Sept. 1683; d. aft. 18 Aug. 1762; m. at Wenham, Mass., 26 Dec. 1705, Benjamin Knowlton, b. at Ipswich, Mass., d. at Ipswich, Dec. 1764,

BENJAMIN KNOWLTON, JR., bapt. at Ipswich, Mass., 23 Nov. 1718, d. at Ipswich, Mass., 3 Apr. 1789; m. at Ipswich, Mass., 28 Feb. 1738, Susanna Potter, bapt. at Ipswich, Mass., 18 Oct. 1719, d. at Ipswich, Mass., ante Apr. 1756,

EZRA KNOWLTON, bapt. at Ipswich, Mass., 29 July 1739, d. at Hamilton, Mass., Dec. 1814; m. at Ipswich, Mass., 11 Feb. 1762, Abigail Dodge, b. at Beverly, Mass., 8 Apr. 1735, d. at Hamilton, Mass., 28 Oct. 1812,

ABIGAIL KNOWLTON, b. at Hamilton-Wenham, Mass., 22 Apr. 1771, d. at Beverly, Mass., 21 Feb. 1870; m. at Wenham, Mass., 9 Feb. 1795, Benjamin Preston, bapt. at Beverly, Mass., 7 July 1771, d. at Beverly, Mass., 11 Aug. 1849,

ABIGAIL (NABBY) PRESTON, b. at Beverly, Mass., 3 Sept. 1797, d. at Beverly, Mass., 17 Mar. 1841; m. at Beverly, Mass., 24 May 1819, Peter Clark, Jr., b. at Beverly, Mass., 15 Apr. 1797, d. at Beverly, Mass., 12 Oct. 1880,

PETER ELLINGWOOD CLARK, b. at Beverly, Mass., 3 May 1830, d. at Beverly, Mass., 19 Sept. 1922; m. at Beverly, Mass., 6 June 1850, Lydia Augusta Creesy, b. at Beverly, Mass., 20 Apr. 1830; d. at Beverly, Mass., 19 Apr. 1909,

SUSAN AUGUSTA CLARK, b. at Beverly, Mass., 2 Aug. 1856; d. at Beverly, Mass., 31 Jan. 1944; m. at Beverly, Mass., 1 Jan. 1885, William Carroll Morgan, b. at Beverly, Mass., 20 July 1858; d. at Beverly, Mass., 27 Jan. 1928,

NETTIE CLARK MORGAN, b. at Beverly, Mass., 19 July 1885, d. at Beverly, Mass., 1 Oct. 1964; m. at Beverly, Mass., 21 Aug. 1907, Waldo Hayward Dow, b. at Danvers, Mass., 28 July 1882, d. at Danvers, Mass., 9 July 1973,

LYDIA ROPES DOW, b. at Beverly, Mass., 18 Apr. 1912; member: DAR, past chapter Regent, Mass. Ex-Regents Club; Daughters of 1812, Hon. State President; Society of Mayflower Descendants; Hereditary Order of Descendants of Colonial Governors; Daughters of the Founders and Patriots of America, Old Plymouth Colony Descendants; D.A.C.; Dames of the Court of Honor; Sons and Daughters of the First Settlers of Newbury, Mass.; Women Descendants of the Ancient and Honorable Artillery Company, State Recording Sec'y; Descendants of Colonial Clergy; Flagon and Trencher; Order of the Crown in America; Order of the Crown of Charlemagne in the United States of America; Peabody Historical Society, Recording Sec'y.; Danvers Historical Society; Beverly Historical Society; N.E. Historic Genealogical Society; etc; m. at Pelham, N.H., 27 Feb. 1937, Christopher Alonzo Finlay, b. at Quebec, Canada, 24 Feb. 1905, d. at Peabody, Mass., 3 Jan. 1975,

1) SUSAN CAROLINE FINLAY, b. 12 Mar., 1942 at Melrose, Mass.; m. at Danvers, Mass., 29 Nov. 1975, William Homer Watkins, b. at East Cleveland, Ohio, 12 Apr. 1941;

2) CAROL JOHANN FINLAY, b. 27 Apr. 1950, at Peabody, Mass.; m. at South Sudbury, Mass., on 23 Feb. 1974, Richard Burton Schrafel, b. at Mineola, N.Y. on 24 June 1950.

Chapter LIX

NEWBERRY — MOSELEY — POMEROY — DEWEY — BUSH — CADWELL — PHEATT — HUBBELL — SMALLWOOD

CHARLEMAGNE

(See Chapters X, XXXII, XXXIX, XLIII, LXVIII)

ISABEL DE VERMANDOIS, Countess of Leicester, d. bef. July 1147; m. (first) 1096, Sir Robert de Beaumont, b. 1049; d. June 5, 1118; Lord of Beaumont, First Earl of Leicester, Companion to William the Conqueror at Hastings 1066,

ISABEL DE BEAUMONT, m. Gilbert de Clare, Earl of Pembroke, d. 6 Jan. 1147/8,

RICHARD DE CLARE, Strongbow, 2nd Earl of Pembroke, b. ca. 1130; d. ca. Apr. 20, 1176; m. ca. 26 Aug. 1171, Eva MacMurrough, dau. of Dermot MacMurrough, King of Leinster, Ireland,

ISABEL DE CLARE, d. 1220; m. Aug. 1189, Sir William Marshall, 3rd Earl of Pembroke, Marshal of England, Regent of the Kingdom, 1216-19; b. 1146; d. 14 May 1219,

EVA MARSHALL, d. bef. 1246; m. William de Braose (Brews, etc.) 6th Baron Braose, 14th Lord of Abergavenny (1228-1230), d. 2 May, 1230,

EVA DE BRAOSE, d. bef. 28 July, 1255; m. aft. 25 July, 1238 and bef. 15 Feb. 1247, William de Cantelou, Baron of Abergavenny, of Calne, Wiltshire and Ashton Cantelou, co. Warwick; d. Sept. 25, 1254, a descendant of Charlemagne,

215

MILICENT DE CANTELOU, d. abt. 1299; m. Eudo la Zouche of Haryngworth; d. 1295,

ELIZABETH LA ZOUCHE, m. by 20 Jan. 1287/8 as a child, Sir Nicholas de Pyntz, (See Chapter LXXIX, p. 293)

HUGH DE POYNTZ, b. Hoo, Kent, pro. ae. 12 Feb. 1318/7, d. shortly bef. 2 May 1337; m. by 1 June 1330, Margaret, prob. dau. of Sir Walter Paynel of Brooke, Wilts.

NICHOLAS DE POYNTZ, b. North Okenden, Essex, ae. 17 in 1337, d. by Michaelmas 1376; m. by 13 Oct. 1333, Eleanor Erleigh, dau. of Sir John Erleigh,

MARGARET POYNTZ, m. ca. 1370, John de Newburgh, b. ca. 1340, d. Bindon Abbey, 4 June 1381,

JOHN NEWBURGH, b. ca. 1370, d. soon aft. Feb. 1438/9; m. by 1400 Joan Delamere, dau. of Sir John Delamere of Dorset.

JOHN NEWBURGH, b. ca. 1400, d. in Dorset, 1 Apr. 1484; m. (2) ca. 1435, Alice, wid. of John Westbury, dau. of William Carent of Toomer, co. Somerset,

THOMAS NEWBURGH, b. ca. 1445, 3rd and youngest son, received manor of Berkley from his mother; d. 15 March 1512/13; m. ca. 1484, Alice, who m. (2) Thomas Kyrton, and d. 1525,

WALTER NEWBURGH (NEWBOROUGH), 2nd son, b. ca. 1487, d. 12 Aug. 1517; m. ca. 1512, Elizabeth Birport, who m. (2) ca. 1520, George Strangeways and d. 1570/1,

RICHARD NEWBOROUGH (NEWBURGH), only son, b. ca. July 1517, held manors in Dorset, d. at Othe Fraunces, Dorset by 30 Jan. 1568/9; m. ca. 1552, Elizabeth dau. of William Horsey of Binghams, who mar (2) one Woodshaw after his death,

RICHARD NEWBERRY (NEWBURGH), 2nd son, b. ca. 1557, d. ca. 1629 at Yarcombe, Devon; m. 15 Jan. 1580/1, Grace Matthew, dau. of John Matthew. She bur. Yarcombe 18 Dec. 1632,

THOMAS NEWBERRY, 4th son, b. Yarcombe, 10 Nov. 1594, to Dorchester, Mass. Apr. 1634, where d. Dec. 1635; m. (1) ca. 1619 Joan, b. ca. 1600, dau. of Christopher Dabinott of Yarcombe, d. England ca. 1629,

BENJAMIN NEWBERRY, b. 1624, Yarcombe, Devon, d. 11 Sept. 1689, Windsor, Conn.; m. 11 June 1646 at Windsor, Mary Allyn, dau. of Matthew Allyn and Margaret Wyatt, also of royal descent, b. ca. 1628 Braunton, Eng., d. 14 Dec. 1703, Windsor, Conn.

MARY NEWBERRY, b. 10 Mar. 1647/8 Windsor, Conn.; m. 14 Dec. 1664, Windsor, Conn., John Moseley, b. 1638, son of John and Cecily Moseley, d. 18 Aug. 1690, Windsor, Conn.

JOSEPH MOSELEY, b. 21 Dec. 1670, d. 1719; m. 13 Sept. 1696 Abigail Root, b. 26 June 1668, Northampton, Mass., dau. of Thomas Root and Abigail Alvord,

RACHEL MOSELEY, b. 1715, d. 1 Feb. 1797, Northampton, Mass.; m. 4 Nov. 1736 Daniel Pomeroy, b. 27 Mar. 1709, Northampton, Mass., d. 8 Sept. 1755 in Battle of Lake George; son of Ebenezer Pomeroy and Sarah King,

ELEANOR POMEROY, b. 20 Oct. 1752, Northampton, Mass., d. 6 Nov. 1823, Turin, N.Y., m. 12 Aug. 1771, Noble Dewey, b. 15 June 1752, Westfield, Mass., d. 23 Dec. 1830, Westfield, son of Israel Dewey and Joanna Noble,

ELECTA DEWEY, b. 16 Nov. 1772, Westfield, Mass., d. 8 Feb. 1849, Turin, N.Y.; m. 8 Jan. 1796, Oliver Bush, b. 13 Aug. 1770, d. 9 Apr. 1844, Turin, N.Y., son of Zachariah Bush and Mary Falley,

JULIA BUSH, b. 29 July 1802, Turin, N.Y., d. 14 Apr. 1843, Turin, N.Y.; m. 7 Jan. 1827, Turin, N.Y., Joseph Cadwell, b. 24 Jan. 1796, Lisle, N.Y., d. 2 Aug. 1865, Cape Vincent, N.Y., son of Joseph Cadwell and Chloe Kellogg,

SARAH AMANDA CADWELL, b. 17 Feb. 1832, Turin, N.Y., d. 27 Aug. 1903, Toledo, Ohio; m. 21 May 1867, Cape Vincent, N.Y., Zebulon Converse Pheatt, b. 21 Dec. 1832, Cape

Vincent, N.Y., d. 7 July 1901, Toledo, Ohio, son of Isaac
Tichenor Pheatt and Ermina Frink,

ERMINA CADWELL PHEATT, b. 28 Dec. 1869, Toledo, Ohio, d. 9
Feb. 1956, Washington, D.C.; m. 12 Feb. 1895, Toledo, Ohio,
Edward Parmelee Hubbell, b. 7 Feb. 1869, Buffalo, N.Y., d. 8
Aug. 1951, Wash. D.C., son of William Butler Hubbell and
Mary Eliza Parmelee.

DOROTHY HUBBELL, b. 17 Dec. 1895, Toledo, Ohio; m. 12 Mar.
1918, Washington, D.C., Graeme Thomas Smallwood, b. 2
Aug. 1897, Revere, Mass., d. 25 Apr. 1947, Washington, D.C.
son of George Thomas Smallwood and Della Grahame
Robinson,

1.) GRAHAME THOMAS SMALLWOOD, JR., b. at Toledo,
Ohio, 26, Feb. 1919; College Moderne, Geneva,
Switzerland; Lycee de St. Giles, Brussels, Belgium;
member: The Ancient and Honorable Artillery
Company of Boston; National Society of Americans of
Royal Descent, Honorary President General; Order of
Americans of Armorial Ancestry, Past President; Order
of the Crown of Charlemagne in the United States of
America, Vice President General; Order of the
Founders & Patriots of America, Past Governor
General; Order of Descendants of Colonial Governors,
Past Governor General; Order of Three Crusades
1096-1192, Registrar General, Past Vice President
General; Military Order of the Crusades, Keeper of the
Exchequer; Order of the Crown in America, Registrar
General; Order of the First Families of Virginia; Society
of Colonial Wars, Past Asst. Registrar, D.C. Society;
Society of the War of 1812, Vice President Pa.-Soc.,
past Vice Pres. D.C. Soc.; Society of Mayflower
Descendants, Deputy Governor Pa. Soc.; Sons of the
Revolution, D.C. and Pa.; S.A.R., Past Librarian
General, Past President D.C. Society, Genealogist,
Phila-Continental Chapter; Baronial Order of Magna
Charta, Past Marshal; Nat. Huguenot Society, Past Vice
President General, Past President, D.C. Society,
Registrar, Pa. Society; The Saint Nicholas Society of the
City of New York; Netherlands Society of Philadelphia,

membership Chairman; Dutch Colonial Society of Delaware, Genealogist; The Dutch Settlers Society of Albany; The Colonial Society of Pa., Treasurer; Society of the Sons of St. George of Philadelphia, Treasurer; The National Gavel Society, Treasurer; Hereditary Order of Descendants of Loyalists & Patriots of the American Revolution, Treasurer General; Order of Descendants of Colonial Physicians and Chirurgiens, Registrar General; Nat. Society Children of the American Revolution, Past. Sr. Nat. Vice President; National Genealogical Society, Past Vice President; Genealogical Society of Pa., Board Member; Military Order of the Loyal Legion; American Friends of Lafayette, Past National President; National Society Sons and Daughters of the Pilgrims, Past Counsellor General, Past Governor, D.C. Branch; Colonial Order of the Acorn; N.Y. Genealogical and Biographical Society; The New England Historic Genealogical Society; Connecticut Society of Genealogists, Inc.; Utah Genealogical Association; Society of the Friends of St. George and the Descendants of the Knights of the Garter, Windsor Castle; St. Andrews Society of Philadelphia; Society of the Friendly Sons of St. Patrick of Philadelphia; The Welsh Society of Phila.; The Athenaeum of Philadelphia; The Union League of Philadelphia; The Poor Richard Club; Knight of the Military and Hospitaller Order of Saint Lazarus of Jerusalem; Descendants of Colonial Tavernkeepers; Royal Society of St. George, London; Sons & Daughters of the Founders of Newbury, Massachusetts; The Penn Club of Philadelphia; Philadelphia Society for the Preservation of Landmarks; National Trust for Historic Preservation; Independence Hall Association; Friends of Independence National Historical Park; Honorary Order of Kentucky Colonels; Military Order of Foreign Wars, Pa. Commandery; The Griswold Family Association; Historical Soc. of Pa.; Swedish Colonial Society of Pa.; The English Speaking Union, Phila. Branch; The Alliance Francais of Philadelphia; Jr. Chamber of Commerce, Life Senator; Almas Shrine Temple, Washington, D.C.; Lodge 51 Masonic, Phila. Nat. Counter-Intelligence Corps, Life Member; Boy

219

Scouts of America, National Board, Member-at-Large, Philadelphia Council, Finance Committeeman; Christ Church, Philadelphia, Vestryman; Bailiff of the Hospitaller Order of St. John of Jerusalem; Knight of the International Constantinian Order; The Order of Lafayette.

2.) ELIZABETH ANN SMALLWOOD, (twin) b. 26 Feb. 1919, Toledo, Ohio, d. at Bethesda Naval Hospital, 2 Nov. 1972; bur. in Arlington National Cemetery; m. at Washington, D.C., 9 Sept. 1949, Cdr. Richard Austin Wier USN. Issue:

a) MARGARET ANN WIER, b. in London, Eng., 19 July 1953; m. 30 June 1975, Charles Jernigan.

b) JEAN STUART WIER, b. at Jacksonville, Fla., 27 Oct. 1954, m. 20 Dec. 1971, Ottaviano Passarella. Issue:

i GINA DANIELA PASSARELA, b. 14 Oct. 1974

3.) ELEANOR WARREN SMALLWOOD, b. at Washington, D.C. 28 Sept. 1921; m. (first) at Washington, D.C., 17 Feb. 1942, William Neiter Beasley, deceased. m. (second) at Arlington, Va. 30 June 1955, Paul Milton Niebell. Issue by first marriage:

a) DOROTHY ANN BEASLEY, b. at Washington, D.C., 18 Nov. 1945, m. at Bowie, Md., 20 Mar. 1965, Gary Bruce Burkholder. Issue:

i JANET LYNN BURKHOLDER, b. 14 Dec. 1967

ii KAREN ANN BURKHOLDER, b. 28 Sept. 1971

b) BARBARA LEE BEASLEY, (twin) b. at Washington, D.C. 18 Nov. 1945; m. (first) at Upper Marlboro,

220

Md., 21 Oct. 1967, Jason Wetzel, div., m. (second) William Henry Sweeney, Jr., Issue:

    i WILLIAM HENRY SWEENEY, III, b. Dec. 18, 1972

    ii DARREN MICHAEL SWEENEY, b. 27 Jan. 1975

Children by second marriage:

c) PAULA NIEBELL, b. at Washington, D.C., 8 June 1956

d) NANCY NIEBELL, b. at Washington, D.C., 12 July 1958

e) PAUL MILTON NIEBELL, JR., b. at Washington, D.C., 27 Apr. 1960

Chapter LX

NEWBERRY — CLAPP — LYMAN — HOLBROOK — STICKLE — SHULTZ

CHARLEMAGNE

(See Chapter LIX)

THOMAS NEWBERRY, b. at Yarcombe, co. Devon, England, 10 Nov. 1594, d. at Dorchester, Mass., Dec. 1635; m. (first) ca. 1619, Joan, b. ca. 1600, d. ca. 1629, in England, dau. of Christopher Dabinott, of Yarcombe,

CAPT. BENJAMIN NEWBERRY, b. in England, ca. 1624, d. 11 Sept. 1689, at Windsor, Conn., m. 11 June 1646, at Windsor, Conn., Mary Allyn, b. at Braunton, co. Devon, England, ca. 1628, d. 14 Dec. 1703, at Windsor, Conn., dau. of Matthew Allyn and Margaret Wyatt,

SARAH NEWBERRY, b. at Northampton, Mass., 14 June 1650, d. 3 Oct. 1716; m. 4 June 1668, Preserved Clapp, b. at Dorchester, Mass., 23 Nov. 1643, d. at Northampton, Mass., 20 Sept. 1720,

ROGER CLAPP, b. in Mass., 24 May 1684, d. in Mass., 1762; m. Elizabeth Bartlett, d. at Northampton, Mass., 9 Aug. 1767,

JONATHAN CLAPP, b. at Northampton, Mass., 1713, d. at Easthampton, Mass., 10 May 1782; m. Submit Strong,

BENJAMIN CLAPP, b. at Easthampton, Mass., 16 Dec. 1738, d. at Southampton, Mass., 8 Nov. 1815; m. ca. 1765, Phoebe Boynton, b. 23 Nov. 1750, d. at Easthampton, Mass., 30 Nov. 1847,

SALLY CLAPP, b. in Mass., 15 Nov. 1780, d. in Mass., 9 Jan.

1844; m. in Mass., 30 Dec. 1806, Lt. Daniel Lyman, b. at Easthampton, Mass., 3 Sept. 1777, d. in Mass., 23 Sept. 1853,

LAUREN DWIGHT LYMAN, b. at East Hampton, Mass., 20 June 1820, d. at Easthampton, Mass., 21 Oct. 1902; m. in Mass., 29 Nov. 1848, Charlotte Root Stearns, b. at Southampton, Mass., 13 May 1823, d. in Mass., 6 Feb. 1861,

SARAH ELIZABETH LYMAN, b. at Easthampton, Mass., 23 Sept. 1856, d. at Delmar, N.Y., 2 May 1934; m. at Easthampton, Mass, 23 Aug. 1883, Charles Werden Holbrook, b. at Abington, Mass., 1856, d. at East Haven, Conn., 18 Dec. 1933,

ANNE MARY HOLBROOK, b. at Mapumulo Station, Natal, So. Africa, 19 Oct. 1889, d. at Newton, N.J., 22 Aug. 1963; m. at East Haven, Conn., 4 Mar. 1925, John Miller Stickle, b. in Sussex Co., N.J., 11 Oct. 1885, liv. 31 Mar. 1977,

JEAN LYMAN STICKLE, b. at Morristown, N.J., 5 June 1926; ed.: B.S., University of Pittsburgh; member: DAR, Society of Mayflower Descendants, Order of the Crown of Charlemagne in the United States of America, National Society Daughters of Founders and Patriots of America, Nat. Soc. Women Descendants of the Ancient and Honorable Artillery Company, The Society of the Sons and Daughters of the Pilgrims; m. at Newton, N.J., 19 Nov. 1960, Robert Charles Shultz, b. at Harrisburg, Pa., 2 Mar. 1917,

    1) JEANANNE HOLBROOK SHULTZ, b. 9 Nov. 1968.

Chapter LXI

NEWBERRY — CLAPP — WELLER — DOUGLAS — BRIGHTMAN — KINGSBURY — BEITER — YOUNG

CHARLEMAGNE

(See preceding chapter)

ROGER CLAPP, b. at Dorchester, Mass., 24 May 1684, d. at Northampton, Mass., 9 Jan. 1762; m. Elizabeth Bartlett, b. at Northampton, Mass., d. at Northampton, Mass., 9 Aug. 1767, dau. of Samuel Bartlett and Sarah Baldwin,

ASABEL CLAPP, b. ca. 1717, d. at Northampton, Mass., 20 Jan. 1777; m. Sarah Wright, b. at Northampton, d. at Northampton, Sept. 1751,

SARAH CLAPP, b. at Northampton, Mass., 5 Dec. 1743, d. at Westfield, Mass.; m. Solomon Weller, b. at Westfield, Mass., d. at Westfield, Mass., son of Nathan Weller and Rhoda Mosely,

RHODA WELLER, b. at Westfield, Mass., 8 Dec. 1773, d. at Westfield, Mass., 4 Mar. 1831; m. at Westfield, Mass., 8 Jan. 1792, Sperry Douglas, II, b. at New London, Conn., 8 Jan. 1770, d. at Westfield, Mass., 4 Dec. 1831,

GEORGE DOUGLAS, b. at Westfield, Mass., 25 July 1794, d. at Elyria, Ohio, 5 Nov. 1829; m. at Peru, Ohio, 8 Feb. 1820, Pearly Clary, b. at Deerfield, Mass., 4 Mar. 1796, d. at Peru, Ohio, 7 Apr. 1866,

PAMELIA CLAPP DOUGLAS, b. at Elyria, Ohio, 26 Dec. 1822, d. at Norwalk, Ohio, 5 Nov. 1906; m. at Peru, Ohio, 8 Dec. 1842, Alvin Brightman, b. at Scipio, Cayuga Co., N.Y., 11 Jan. 1818, d. at Peru, Ohio, 1 Sept. 1875,

ANNA ELIZABETH BRIGHTMAN, b. at Peru, Ohio, 4 Dec. 1855, d. at Norwalk, Ohio, 15 Apr. 1931; m. at Peru, Ohio, 25 June 1873, Edwin Jay Kingsbury, b. at Peru, Ohio, 1 Oct. 1848, d. at Norwalk, Ohio, 15 June 1917,

EURETTA PAMELIA KINGSBURY, b. at Bronson, Huron Co., Ohio, 13 May 1883, d. at Sandusky, Ohio, 1 Sept. 1958; m. at Norwalk, Ohio, 30 Sept. 1911, John Ross Beiter, b. at Malvern, Ohio, 6 Feb. 1880, d. at Canton, Ohio, 30 June 1936,

RUTH BEITER, b. at Canton, Ohio, 21 July 1914; ed.: Ward Belmont, Nashville, Tenn.; Lake Erie College, Painesville, Ohio; Flora Stome Mather, Cleveland, Ohio; Kent State, Kent, Ohio, B.A. in Education; member: DAR, D.A.C., Colonial Daughters of the XVII Century, National Society Mayflower Descendants, Daughters of 1812; Hon. Pres. General, Women Descendants of the Ancient and Honorable Artillery Company; Order of the Crown of Charlemagne in the United States of America; National Huguenot Society; Alden Kindred; Founders of Hartford; Daughters of the Barons of Runnemede; Order of Americans of Armorial Ancestry; Sons and Daughters of the Pilgrims; Daughters of Colonial Wars; New England Women; National Gavel Society; etc.; m. at Norwalk, Ohio, 16 June 1926, Britton Dennis Young, b. at Norwalk, Ohio, 24 June 1912, d. at Norwalk, Ohio, 8 Aug. 1966,

1) BRITTON DENNIS YOUNG, b. 27 May 1937, m. Nancy Fox,

  a) BRITTON DENNIS YOUNG III;

  b) MATTHEW YOUNG;

  c) DON J. YOUNG IV.

2) ANNA PAMELIA YOUNG, b. 11 Dec. 1940, member: Order of the Crown of Charlemagne in the United States of America, m. Lynn Edward Knorr, no issue.

3) ROSS BEITER YOUNG, b. 14 Mar. 1942, unmarried.

4) STEPHEN MARVIN YOUNG IV, b. 31 Aug. 1951, unmarried.

Chapter LXII

NEWBERRY — CLARK — PINNEY — EDSON — LOWELL — BUCK — WILLIAMS

Charlemagne

(See Chapter LIX)

THOMAS NEWBERRY, bapt. at Yarcombe, Eng., 10 Nov. 1594, d. at Dorchester, Mass., in Dec. 1635; m. (first) in England, ca. 1619, Joan Dabinott, b. at Yarcombe, Eng. ca. 1600, d. in Eng., ca. 1629, dau. of Christopher Dabinott,

MARY NEWBERRY, bapt. in Eng. 22 Oct. 1626; m. (his first) 13 June 1644, in Conn., Hon. Daniel Clark, b. nr. Kenilworth, Eng., in 1622, d. at Windsor, Conn., 12 Aug. 1710,

SARAH CLARK, bapt. 9 Aug. 1663; m. (first) ca. 1685, Sergt. Isaac Pinney, b. 24 Feb. 1663, d. aboard a vessel to Windsor from Albany during Queen Anne's War, 24 Oct. 1709,

ISAAC PINNEY (Jr.), b. at Suffield, Conn., 17 Jan. 1686/7, d. 12 Aug. 1717; m. 26 Jan. 1709/10. Abigail Filley, b. at Suffield, Conn., 29 Dec. 1685,, d. Nov. 1761,

JUDGE ISAAC PINNEY III, b. prob. at Windsor, Conn., 15 Jan. 1716, d. at Stafford, Conn., Sept. 1791; m. in Conn., Susannah Phelps, b. at Hebron, Conn., 23 Sept. 1731, d. at Stafford, Conn., 13 Sept. 1795,

SARAH PINNEY, b. prob. at Windsor, Conn., 25 Dec. 1756, d. at Randolph, Vt., 16 Dec. 1805; m. at Stafford, Conn., 1 July 1779, Col. Josiah Edson, b. at Stafford, Conn., 1758, d. at Randolph, Vt., 27 Oct. 1819,

DANIEL SHERWOOD EDSON, b. at Randolph, Vt., 10 Mar. 1799, d. at Ware, Mass., ca. 1850; m. at Ware, Mass., ca. 1820, Dorothy Goodell (Goodale) Pease, b. 1788, d. at Grand Ledge, Mich. 1878,

DOROTHY ANN EDSON, b. at Ware, Mass., 27 Oct. 1826, d. at Wacousta, Mich., 29 Mar. 1896, m. at Huntington, Mass., 6 June 1853, George W. Lowell, b. at Port Henry, N.Y., 6 Dec. 1824, d. at Wacousta, Mich., 22 June 1909,

ANNA GOODELL LOWELL, b. at Grand Ledge, Mich., 6 Mar. 1857, d. at Java, N.Y., 9 May 1932; m. at Grand Ledge, Mich., 19 June 1880, Oscar Allen Buck, b. at Java, N.Y., 22 Dec. 1850, d. at Arcade, N.Y., 9 Mar. 1943,

DAWN MABEL BUCK, b. at Java, N.Y., 8 July 1884, member: DAR, Chapter Regent two terms; Central Pa., Regents Club; D.A.C., Chapter Regent, Vice State Regent; Women Descendants of the Ancient and Honorable Artillery Co.; Society of Mayflower Descendants; Colonial Daughters of the XVII Century, past Corres. Sec'y. General; National Society of New England Women; Order of the Crown of Charlemagne in the United States of America, past Asst. Chaplain General; National Society, Colonial Dames of America; National Society of the Daughters of Founders and Patriots of America; Order of the Crown in America; Order of Americans of Armorial Ancestry; National Society Americans of Royal Descent, past Corres. Sec'y. General; National Society, Daughters of the American Colonists; Order of the Three Crusades, 1096-1192, past Corres. Sec'y. General; National Huguenot Society; m. at Sardinia, N.Y., 28 Jan. 1912, Howard Joseph Williams, b. at Sardinia, N.Y., 10 Feb. 1881, d. at Java, N.Y., 6 Sept. 1956,

1) LOWELL WHARTON WILLIAMS, b. 25 Dec. 1918, member: Order of the Crown of Charlemagne in the United States of America, Asst. Chaplain General; Order of Three Crusades 1096-1192; National Society Americans of Royal Descent, past Treasurer General; Order of Americans of Armorial Ancestry; Society of Mayflower Descendants; SAR, past Pres. Continental Congress Chapter; Military Order of the Crusades;

227

Lafayette Club of York (Pa.); Country Club of York; Phi Sigma Kappa; Union League of Philadelphia; m. at York, Pa., 6 July 1946, Marie Lydia Lesh, b. at Easton, Pa., 2 Dec. 1923,

a) DOROTHY SILENCE WILLIAMS, b. at York, Pa., 24 May 1951, member: DAR, Order of the Crown of Charlemagne in the United States of America; Colonial Daughters of the XVII Century; National Society of New England Women; National Society Americans of Royal Descent; Junior League; Country Club of York, Pa.;

b) LOWELL WHARTON WILLIAMS, JR., b. at York, Pa., 22 Mar. 1954, member: SAR, Order of the Crown of Charlemagne in the United States of America, National Society Americans of Royal Descent, Lambda Chi Alpha, Country Club of York.

Chapter LXIII

NEWBERRY — CLARK — PINNEY — PHELPS — MILLS — BAXTER

CHARLEMAGNE

(See Chapter LXII)

ISAAC PINNEY (Jr.), b. at Suffield, Conn., 17 Jan 1686/7, d. 12 Aug. 1717; m. 26 Jan. 1709/10. Abigail Filley, b. at Suffield, Conn., 29 Dec. 1685, d. Nov. 1761,

ANNE (ANNA) PINNEY, b. 24 Jan. 1712/3, at Hebron, Conn., d. at Hebron, Conn., 28 Jan. 1789; m. at Torrington, Conn., Asahel Phelps, b. at Hebron, Conn., 9 Nov. 1704, d. 18 Oct. 1787,

URSULA PHELPS, b. at Hebron, Conn., 16 Jan. 1740, d. at Nelson, Ohio, 20 July 1819; m. at Hebron, Conn., 1762, Deacon Ezekiel Mills, b. at Simsbury, Conn., 12 Apr. 1740, d. at Nelson, Ohio, 7 May 1809,

ISAAC MILLS, b. at West Simsbury, Conn., 11 Nov. 1780, d. at Nelson, Ohio, 5 Oct. 1826; m. 27 Nov. 1805, at Becket, Mass., Mary Adams, b. at Becket, Mass, 10 Apr. 1790, d. in Wisc., bur. in Junction Cemetery, 1854,

ISAAC EDWIN MILLS, b. at Nelson, Ohio, 22, Mar. 1811, d. at Ringgold, Ga., 18 Oct. 1889; m. at Warren, Ohio, 19 Sept. 1838, Angeline King, b. at Glasgow, Scotland, 17 Dec. 1821, d. at Nelson, Ohio, 30 Apr. 1898,

MARTHA GLENN MILLS, b. at Nelson, Ohio, 29 May 1845, d. at Glendale, Calif., 10 Mar 1927; m. at Nelson, Ohio, 17 Feb. 1863, Erskine Baxter, b. at Southington, Ohio, 9 Dec. 1834, d. at Warren, Ohio, 14 Nov. 1920,

EDWIN OTIS BAXTER, b. at Southington, Ohio, 20 Oct. 1869, d. at Warren, Ohio, 12 Nov. 1945; m. at Southington, Ohio, 16 Dec. 1896, Elma C. Haughton, b. at Southington, Ohio, 10 Dec. 1875, d. at Red Champion Heights, Ohio, 11 Feb. 1956,

FRANCIS HESS BAXTER, b. at Southington, Trumbull Co., Ohio, 17 June 1901; B.S.Ed., Kent State Univ.; member: SAR, past President John Stark Chapter; Founders and Patriots of America; Society of Mayflower Descendants; Baronial Order of Magna Charta; Military Order of the Crusades; Order of the Crown of Charlemagne in the United States of America; Scottish Rite Masons; Shriner; m. at Warren Ohio, 28 Aug.

1926, Blanche Edna Teeple, b. at Justus, Ohio, 29 Apr. 1903,

1) LT. ROBERT BRUCE BAXTER, b. at Massillon, Sraek Co., Ohio, 16 Nov. 1936 m. at Esmond, R.I., 12 May 1962, Linda Brook, b. at Providence, R.I., 13 Dec. 1939,

    a) BROOK ANN BAXTER, b. at Providence, R.I., 14 Aug. 1967;

    b) LEE ROBERT BAXTER, b. at Providence, R.I., 18 Jan. 1970.

Chapter LXIV

PALGRAVE — ALCOCK — WILLIAMS — SANDS —
HULL — HAZARD — ROBINSON — DONNELL — WARD

CHARLEMAGNE

(See Chapters II and XXXVI)

EDWARD I, King of England 1272-1307, b. at Westminster, 17
June 1239, d. nr. Carlisle, 7 July 1307; m. (first) Oct. 1254, at
Burgos, Spain, Elinore of Castile, d. at Grantham, England, 28
Nov. 1290, dau. of St. Ferdinand III, King of Castile
1217-1252, King of Leon 1230-1252, and his second wife,
Jeanne of Ponthieu and Aumale,

ELIZABETH PLANTAGENET, wid. of John, Count of Holland, was
b. at Rhudlan Castle, Carnavon, in Aug. 1282, bur. at Walden
Abbey, co. Essex, 5 May 1316; m. at Westminster, 14 Nov.
1302, Humphrey de Bohun VIII, Earl of Hereford and Essex,
b. 1276, slain at Boroughbride, bur. at Friars Chapel, York, 16
Mar. 1321/2,

SIR WILLIAM DE BOHUN, K.G. (1349) fought at Drecy, Earl of
Northampton, b. ca. 1312, bur at Walden Abbey, Essex, 16
Sept. 1360; m. (second) in 1335, Elizabeth de Badlesmere, wid.
of Edmund de Mortimer, b. 1313, d. in June 1356,

ELIZABETH DE BOHUN, bur. at Lewes, 3 Apr. 1385; m. (contract)
28 Sept. 1359, Sir Richard FitzAlan, K.G. (1386), Earl of
Arundel and Surry, b. 1346, beheaded at Cheapside and bur. at
London, 21 Sept. 1397,

ELIZABETH FITZ ALAN, Duchess of Norfolk, b. ca. 1374, d. 8
July 1425; m. ante 19 Aug. 1401, Sir Robert Goushill/Gousell
of Heveringham, Notts., d. at the Battle of Shrewsbury, 21
July 1403,

231

ELIZABETH GOUSHILL/GOUSELL of Heveringham, Notts., b. ca. 1402, liv. 1414; m. Sir Robert Wingfield of Letheringham, Suffolk, b. 1403, bur. at Letheringham, Suffolk, 21 Nov. 1451/4,

ELIZABETH WINGFIELD, d. 28 Apr. 1496/7; m. ante Jan. 1462, Sir William Brandon, Marshal of Marchelsea, b. in co. Norfolk, ca. 1425/30, d. 4 Mar. 1491,

ELEANOR BRANDON, m. (her second) John Glemham of Glemham Parva, Suffolk,

ANNE GLEMHAM, m. Henry Pagrave of Little Pagrave, Northwood, Barningham and Thruxton, Norfolk, b. 1470, bur. at Barningham, Northwood, son of John and Margaret (Yelverton) Pagrave,

THOMAS PAGRAVE, gent., of Thruxton, Norfolk, b. 1505-10; m. Alice Gunton, dau. of Robert Gunton of Thruxton, Norfolk,

REV. EDWARD PALGRAVE, Rector of Barnham Broom 1567-1623, bapt. at Thruxton, Norfolk, 21 Jan. 1640/1, w.p. at Norwich, 20 Dec. 1623,

DR. RICHARD PALGRAVE, b. at Wymondham, co. Norfolk, England, 1580-85, d. at Charlestown, Mass., in 1651; m. Anna — , b. 1593, bur at Roxbury, Mass., 17 Mar. 1668/9,

SARAH PALGRAVE, b. in England, 1621, d. at Roxbury, Mass., 29 Nov. 1665; m. 1648, Dr. John Alcock, b. in England, 1 Jan. 1626/7, d. at Boston, Mass., 27 Mar. 1667,

ANNE ALCOCK, bapt. at Roxbury, Mass., 26 May 1650, d. 27 June 1723; m. 24 Feb. 1669/70, John Williams, b. at Boston, Mass., 15 Aug. 1644, d. at Newport, R.I., Apr. — Oct. 1687,

MARY WILLIAMS, b. at Boston, Mass., 2 Oct. 1670, d. 1708; m. 1690-93, at Newshoreham, R.I., Edward Sands, b. on Block Island, R.I., 1672, d. on Block Island, R.I., 14 June 1708,

SARAH SANDS, b. at Newshoreham, R.I. 1692-94; m. rec. 28 May

1711, Newport/Jamestown, R.I., Tiddeman Hull, b. at Jamestown, R.I., 26 Mar. 1690,

ROBERT HULL, b. at Jamestown, R.I., 9 Oct. 1718, d. 24 Dec. 1768; m. at Newshoreham, R.I., 13 Nov. 1738, Thankfull Ball, b. at Newshoreham, R.I., 26 Oct. 1721,

EDWARD HULL, b. at Newshoreham, R.I., 1 Mar. 1714/5, d. on Block Island, R.I., 11 Sept. 1804; m. at Jamestown, R.I., 18 Nov. 1762, Mary Weeden, b. at Jamestown, R.I., 15 Sept. 174-,

JANE HULL, b. at South Kingston, R.I., 24 Sept. 1781, d. at Wakefield, R.I., 13 Apr. 1862; m. at South Kingston, R.I., 13 May 1807, George C. Hazard, b. at So. Kingston, R.I., 13 Apr. 1763, d. there 29 Sept. 1829,

LAURA HAZARD, b. at So. Kingston, R.I., 4 Nov. 1819, d. at Wakefield, R.I., 12 Mar. 1915; m. at Wakefield, R.I., 17 Mar. 1841, Attmore Robinson, b. at Philadelphia, Pa., 23 Apr. 1804, d. at Wakefield, R.I., 2 Aug. 1890,

GEORGE HAZARD ROBINSON, b. at Wakefield, R.I., 20 Apr. 1847, d. at New York, N.Y., 5 Sept. 1919; m. at New York, N.Y., 14 June 1869, Sarah Delamater, b. at New York, N.Y., 12 Dec. 1846, d. at New York, N.Y., 20 Dec. 1929,

RUTH ROBINSON, b. at New York, N.Y., 28 Mar. 1870, d. at New York, N.Y., 22 May 1949; m. at New York, N.Y., 10 Oct. 1894, Harry Ellingwood Donnell, b. at Portland, Me., 2 May 1867, d. at New York, N.Y., 25 Feb. 1959,

SARAH DELAMATER DONNELL, b. at New York, N.Y., 16 Oct. 1906, d. at New York, N.Y., 25 June 1962; m. at Northport, L.I., N.Y., 28 Aug. 1933, Francis Xavier Ward, b. at New York, N.Y., 14 July 1904, liv. 1977 at Gardiner, Me.,

NICHOLAS DONNELL WARD, b. at New York, N.Y., 30 July 1941; ed.: Trinity School, New York; Columbia College, New York, B.A.; Georgetown University Law Center, Washington, D.C., L.L.B.; member: American Bar Association; Bar Association of D.C.; American Judicature Society; Selden

233

Society; American Society For Legal History; Washington, D.C. Estate Planning Council; Barrister Inn, Phi Delta Phi (President, 1977-78); Ancient and Honorable Artillery Co. of Massachusetts; The Saint Andrew's Society of Washington, D.C.; The Saint George's Society of Philadelphia; The Veteran Corps of Artillery, State of New York; The Military Society of the War of 1812; New England Society of the City of New York; General Society of the War of 1812 (D.C. and Md.) (President D.C. 1976-78); The Saint Nicholas Society of the City of New York; Aztec Club of 1847 (Vice President 1976-); Military Order of the Loyal Legion of the United States (Recorder, D.C. 1974 -, Chancellor-in-Chief, 1977-); General Society, Sons of the Revolution (N.Y. and D.C.) (2nd Vice President, D.C. 1976-, Secretary, D.C. 1973-, General Secretary 1976-); Sons of Union Veterans of the Civil War (Vice Commander, Lincoln-Cushing Camp #2, 1975-77); The Huguenot Society of America; Sons of the American Revolution (President, D.C. 1976-77); The Netherlands Society of Philadelphia; General Society of Colonial Wars (D.C. and N.Y.) (Secretary, D.C. 1973-); Colonial Order of the Acorn; Military Order of Foreign Wars of the United States (Registrar, D.C., 1976-77); The Colonial Society of Pennsylvania; The Order of the Founders and Patriots of America (Treasurer, D.C., 1974-); Sons of Confederate Veterans (Judge Advocat, Jefferson Davis Camp #305, 1977-, Aid-de-camp to Commander-in-Chief, 1976-77); The Hereditary Order of the Descendants of Colonial Governors (Third Deputy Governor General, 1976-78); General Society of Mayflower Descendants (Deputy Governor; D.C., 1974-78); The Order of the Crown in America (Councillor, D.C., 1976-); The Baronial Order of Magna Charta (Committee on Magna Charta Day Award, 1974-); Order of Americans of Armorial Ancestry; National Society Americans of Royal Descent; The Dutch Settlers Society of Albany; The Society of the Descendants of the Colonial Clergy (Chancellor General, 1975-77); The Military Order of the Crusades (Keeper of the Exchequer, 1977-); Order of Three Crusades 1096-1192; The Order of the Stars and Bars (Commander, Jefferson Davis Chapter, 1975-78); Order of the Crown of Charlemagne in the United States of America (Advisory Council, 1974-); The National Huguenot Society (President, D.C., 1975-77, Curator General, 1975-77); The Order of Lafayette; Dutch Colonial

234

Society of Delaware; Flagon and Trencher; Descendants of Colonal Tavern Keepers (Mine Host, 1977); The Hereditary Order of Descendants of the Loyalists and Patriots of the American Revolution (Chancellor General, 1973-); Order of Descendants Colonial Physicians and Chirurgiens (Chancellor, 1977-); Grand Cross, Sovereign Military Order of the Temple of Jerusalem (Prior, Priory of St. King Charles the Martyr, 1975-; Grand Avocat, 1976-); Officer, The Military and Hospitaller Order of Saint Lazarus of Jerusalem; The Society of the Friends of St. George's and The Descendants of the Knights of the Garter; American Revolution Roundtable of D.C., Editor, Newsletter (1975-1977); Vice President, 1977-1978); Civil War Roundtable of D.C.; Rhode Island Historical Society; Maine Historical Society; The Barristers; The Metropolitan Club of the City of Washington; The Cosmos Club; The University Club of Washington; The Union Club of the City of New York, Inc.; Alpha Delta Phi; m. 6 Sept. 1968, at Washington, D.C., Elizabeth Reed Lowman, b. 12 Nov. 1944, at Takoma Park, Md., dau. of Roy Melton Lowman, and Elizabeth Marsh Reed.

Chapter LXV

PELHAM — WINSLOW — WARREN — SEVER —
O'REILLY

CHARLEMAGNE

(See Chapters X, XXXII, XXXIX, XLIII, LXVIII)

ISABEL DE VERMANDOIS, Countess of Leicester, d. ante 1147; m. (first) 1096, Sir Robert de Beaumont, 1st Earl of Leicester, b. ca. 1049, d. 5 June 1118,

ISABEL DE BEAUMONT, m. Gilbert de Clare, Earl of Pembroke, d. 6 Jan. 1147/8,

RICHARD DE CLARE, "Strongbow", 2nd Earl of Pembroke, b. ca. 1130, d. ca. 20 Apr. 1176; m. ca. 26 Aug. 1171, Eva MacMurrough, dau. of Dermot MacMurrough, King of Leinster, Ireland,

ISABEL DE CLARE, d. 1220; m. in Aug. 1189, Sir William Marshall, 3rd Earl of Pembroke, Marshal of England, Regent of the Kingdom 1216-19, b. 1146, d. 14 May 1219,

MAUD MARSHALL, d. 27 Mar. 1248; m. bef. Lent 1207, Hugh le Bigod, 3rd Earl of Norfolk, Magna Charta Surety 1215, d. Feb. 1224/5, son of Roger le Bigod, 2nd Earl of Norfolk, Lord High Steward of England and a Surety for Magna Charta,

ISABEL LE BIGOD, m. ante 12 Apr. 1234, Sir John FitzGeoffrey, Justiciar of Ireland, d. 23 Nov. 1258,

MAUD FITZ JOHN, bur. at Worcester, ca. 18 Apr. 1301; m. ante 1270, William de Beauchamp, 9th Earl of Warwick, b. 1237, d. at Elmley, Worcs., bur. 22 June 1298,

ISABEL DE BEAUCHAMP, d. ca. 30 May 1306; m. Sir Patrick Chaworth of Kidwelly, Wales, d. ca. 7 July 1283,

MAUD DE CHAWORTH, bur. at Mottis Font Priory, ante 3 Dec. 1322; m. 1298, Henry Plantagenet, b. ca. 1281, bur. at Newark Abbey, Leics., 22 Sept. 1345, son of Edmund Plantagenet and Blanche of Artois,

PRINCESS JOAN PLANTAGENET, b. ca. 26 Feb. 1326/7, prob. d. and bur. at Byland, 7 July 1349; m. John de Mowbray, b. at Hovington, Yorks., 29 Nov. 1310, d. at York, 4 Oct. 1361,

ALIANORE DE MOWBRAY, d. ante 18 June 1387; m. ante 23 July 1358, Roger de la Warre, 3rd Lord de la Warre, b. 30 Nov. 1326, d. in Gascony, 27 Aug. 1370,

JOAN DE LA WARRE, d. 24 Apr. 1404; m. in 1390, Sir Thomas West, 3rd. Baron West of Oakhanger, Northampton, son of Sir Thomas West and Alice Fitz Herbert,

SIR REYNOLD WEST, 1st Baron de la Warre, b. 7 Sept. 1395, d. 27 Aug. 1450; m. (first) ante 17 Feb. 1428/9, Margaret Thorley, d. ante 24 Nov. 1433, dau. of Robert Thorley and Anne Lisle,

SIR RICHARD WEST, 2nd Baron de la Warre, b. ca. 28 Oct. 1430, d. 10 Mar. 1475/6; m. ante 10 June 1451, Katherine Hungerford, d. 12 May 1493, dau. of Sir Robert Hungerford and Margaret Botreaux,

SIR THOMAS WEST, K.G., 3rd Baron de la Warre, b. 1457, bur. at Broadwater, 10 Oct. 1525; m. Eleanor Copley, dau. of Sir Roger Copley, M.P., K.G., and Ann Hoo of Roughway, Sussex,

SIR GEORGE WEST of Warbelton, Sussex, d. in 1538; m. Elizabeth Morton, dau. of Sir Robert Morton of Lechlade, co. Gloucester,

SIR WILLIAM WEST, 1st Lord Delaware, b. ca. 1520, d. at Wherwell, Northants., 30 Dec. 1595; m. ante 1555, Elizabeth Strange, dau. of Thomas Strange of Chesterton, Gloucs.,

SIR THOMAS WEST, 2nd Lord Delaware, b. ca. 1556, d. 24 Mar. 1601/2; m. 19 Nov. 1571, Anne Knollys,

PENELOPE WEST, b. 9 Sept. 1582, d. ca. 1619; m. ca. 1599. Herbert Pelham, b. in England, ca. 1580, d. at Boston, Lincs., 20 July 1624,

PENELOPE PELHAM, bapt. at Bures, Suffolk, Eng., in 1633, d. at Marshfield, Mass., 7 Dec. 1703; m. in 1657 Josiah Winslow, b. at Plymouth, Mass., 1629, d. at Marshfield, Mass., 18 Dec. 1680,

ISAAC WINSLOW, b. at Marshfield, Mass., in 1670, d. at Marshfield, Mass., 6 Dec. 1738; m. 11 July 1700, at Boston, Mass., Sarah Wensley, b. at Boston, Mass., in 1673, d. 16 Dec. 1753,

PENELOPE WINSLOW, b. at Marshfield, Mass., 21 Dec. 1704, d. at Plymouth, Mass., 24 May 1737; m. at Marshfield, Mass., 30 Jan. 1724, James Warren, b. at Plymouth, Mass., 14 Apr. 1700, d. at Plymouth, Mass., 2 July 1757,

SARAH WARREN, b. at Plymouth, Mass., 13 May 1730, d. at Kingston, Mass., 15 Mar. 1797; m. at Kingston, Mass., 2 Dec. 1755, William Sever, b. at Kingston, Mass., 12 Oct. 1729, d. at Kingston, Mass., 15 June 1809,

JOHN SEVER, b. at Kingston, Mass., 7 May 1766, d. at Kingston, Mass., 7 Nov. 1803; m. at Kingston, Mass., 24 May 1790, Nancy Russell, b. at Plymouth, Mass., 1767, d. at Kingston, Mass., 4 May 1848,

CHARLES SEVER, b. at Kingston, Mass., 9 Apr. 1795, d. at Plymouth, Mass., 17 Oct. 1834; m. at Kingston, Mass., 15 Jan. 1827, Jane Amarinthia Elliott, b. at Waynesborough, Ga., 30 July 1805, d. at Boston, Mass., 10 Mar. 1871,

CHARLES WILLIAM SEVER, b. at Plymouth, Mass., 1 July 1834, d. at Kingston, Mass., 19 July 1904; m. 29 Oct. 1862, at Watertown, Mass., Mary Caroline Webber, b. at Watertown, Mass., 24 Feb. 1841, d. at Cambridge, Mass., 7 Aug. 1923,

JANE ELLIOTT SEVER, b. at Cambridge, Mass., 29 Nov. 1876, d. at University City, Missouri, 7 May 1956; m. 20 June 1906, at Kingston, Mass., James Archer O'Reilly, b. at St. Louis, Mo., 24 Sept. 1879, d. at St. Louis, Mo., 5 Dec. 1947,

NOEL SEVER O'REILLY, b. at University City, Mo., 25 Dec. 1909; Harvard College, S.B.; Harvard Business School, M.B.A.; member: Society of Mayflower Descendants, Order of the Crown of Charlemagne in the United States of America, Society of Colonial Wars, Harvard Club of Chicago; Captain SC, USNR, Ret.; m. at Golf, Ill., 2 Nov. 1940, Nancy Steele Cockrell, b. at Kansas City, Mo., 3 Aug. 1916,

    1) NICHOLAS SEVER O'REILLY, b. at Bryn Mawr, Pa., 1 July 1946;

    2) ALEXANDER COCKRELL O'REILLY, b. at Toledo, Ohio, 13 Oct. 1949; m. at Chicago, Ill., 27 Aug. 1975, Sarah Bornstein, b. at Philadelphia, Pa., 3 Nov. 1947,

        a) KEVIN BERNARD O'REILLY, b. at Evanston, Ill., 13 May 1977.

239

Chapter LXVI

QUALEY — QUALLEY

CHARLEMAGNE

(See Chapter LXX)

ANNE TOVSDATTER MIDBØN, b. at Brunkeberg, Norway, in 1809, d. at Flatdal, Norway; m. at Brunkeberg, Norway, in 1837, Gregar Rue, b. at Flatdal, Norway, d. at Flatdal, Norway, in 1870,

ANNE GREGARSDATTER RUE, b. at Flatdal, Norway, in 1837, d. at Flatdal, Norway; m. at Flatdal, Norway, Einar Steinarson Kvaale, b. at Flatdal, Norway, in 1828 and d. Flatdal, Norway,

STEINAR EIVIND QUALEY, b. at Flatdal, Norway, 3 Sept. 1858, d. at Mansfield, Minnesota, 25 Oct. 1921; m. at Albert Lea, Minn., 27 May 1881, Ingeborg Johanna Kittleson, b. at Mansfield, Minn., 6 Apr. 1866, d. at Mansfield, Minn., 22 Dec. 1950,

CORNELIUS STEINER QUALEY, b. at Mansfield, Minn., 14 Sept. 1887, d. at Albert Lea, Minn., 5 Oct. 1958; m. 25 Jan. 1910, at Wadena, Minn., Mathilda Christine Olson, b. at Mansfield, Minn., 7 Jan. 1890, d. at Albert Lea, Minn., 14 May 1948,

GEORGE THOMAS QUALLEY, b. at Nevis, Minn., 22 Feb. 1928; ed.: Univ. of Minn.; Simpson College, Indianola, Iowa, B.A.; Drake Law School, Des Moines, Iowa, J.D.; grad. studies at Georgetown Univ., Washington, D.C. and at Univ. of S.D.; U.S. Navy 1946-7; member: Iowa, Nebraska, D.C., S.D. and American Bar assocs.; Delta Theta Phi; Sons of Norway; International Platform Assoc.; Masons; Nobles of the Mystic Shrine; Order of the Crown of Charlemagne in the United States of America; m. 8 Aug. 1969, at Washington, D.C., Bonita Ann Lemek, b. at Sioux City, Iowa, 13 Oct. 1946.

Chapter LXVII

RODES (RHODES) — THOMSON — GARRETT — DOUGLAS — SHACKELFORD — KENNEDY — NEWMAN

CHARLEMAGNE

(See Chapter LXV)

ISABEL DE CLARE, d. 1220, m. Aug. 1189, Sir William Marshall, 3rd Earl of Pembroke, Marshal of England, Protector, Regent of the Kingdom 1216-19, b. 1146, d. 14 May 1219, Buried in Temple Church, London, son of John Marshall,

EVE MARSHALL, d. ante 1246, m. William V. de Braose (Briouze, Brews, etc.) a descendant of Griffith, King of Wales, 6th Baron Braose, 14th Lord of Abergavenny (1228-1230), d. 2 May 1230,

EVE DE BRAOSE, d. ca. 28 July 1255, Calstone, Wilts.; m. ca. 13 Feb. 1247/8, William de Cantelou, Baron of Abergavenny, Calne, Wiltshire, and Ashton Cantelou, co. Warwick, d. 25 Sept. 1254, son of William de Cantelou of Calne, Wilts.,

MILICENT DE CANTELOU, b. in co. Warwick, ca. 1253, d. at Haryngworth, England, ca. 7 Jan. 1298/9; m. ca. 13 Dec. 1273, Eudo (Eon) la Zouche of Haryngworth, b. at Ashby, Co. Leicester, d. bet. 28 Apr. and 25 June 1279,

SIR WILLIAM LA ZOUCHE, Knt., M.P. (1308-1348); Lord la Zouche, b. at Haryngworth, Eng., 18/21 Dec. 1276, d. 11/12 Mar. 1351/2, at Haryngworth; m. ca. 15 Feb. 1295/6, Maude Lovel, dau. of John 1st Lord Lovel of Titmarsh, b. at Thorp Arnold, co. Leicester, ca. 1280, d. ca. 1346,

MILICENT LA ZOUCHE, d. 22 June 1379; m. ca. 26 Mar. 1326, Sir

William Deincourt, b. ca. 1300, d. 2 June 1364, Lord Deincourt of Blankney, Co. Lincoln, son of John Deincourt.

MARGARET DEINCOURT, d. 2 Apr. 1380; m. Sir Robert de Tibetot, b. at Nettlestead, co. Suffolk, bapt. 11 June 1341, d. in Gascony, 13 Apr. 1372.

ELIZABETH DE TIBETOT, b. in Notts., ca. 1371, d. at Ipswich, Eng., ante 1424; m. ca. 1385, Sir Philip le Despenser, Knt, of Goxhill, Camoys Manor, b. at Goxhill, co. Lincoln, ca. 1365, d. at Goxhill, Lincs., ca. 20 June 1424,

MARGERY LE DESPENSER, *de jure suo jure*, Baroness le Despenser, b. ca. 1400, d. at Nettlestead, co. Suffolk, 20 Apr. 1478; m. at Hemingsborough, Yorks., ca. 25 June 1423, Sir Roger Wentworth, Knt., b. at North Elmsall, co. York, Eng., ca. 1390, d. at Nettlestead, co. Suffolk, 24 Apr. 1452.

AGNES WENTWORTH, b. at Nettlestead, co. Suffolk, ca. 1440, d. 20 Apr. 1496; m. ca. 1460, Sir Robert Constable, Knt., b. at Flamburgh, in co. Ebor., Eng., ca. 1430, d. 23 May 1488,

SIR WILLIAM CONSTABLE High Sheriff of Yorkshire, b. at Caythorp, Eng. ca. 1480, d. at Rudston, Eng., 22 July 1526; m. ca. 1500, Joan Fullthorpe, b. ca. 1470, d. at Rudston, w.p. 18 Dec. 1540.

MARMADUKE CONSTABLE, ESQ., b. at Wassand, co. York, ca. 1501, d. at Goxhill, Lincs., 23 Jan. 1558; m. ca. 1545, Elizabeth Stokes, b. at Byckerton, Yorks., ca. 1525, d. at Goxhill, Lincs. 1560,

MARMADUKE CONSTABLE, b. at Wassand, Yorks., ca. 1546, d. at Goxhill, Lincs., bur. 11 July 1568; m. ca. 1561, Catherine Holme, b. at Holme, Yorks., ca. 1544, d. at Goxhill, Lincs., bur. 9 June 1634,

FRANCES CONSTABLE , b. at Holderness, Yorks., bapt. 12 Sept. 1568; m. ca. 1584, Sir John Rodes, Knt., b. in Derbyshire, ca. 1562, d. at Barlborough, co. Derby, 16 Sept. 1639, Knighted at the Tower of London, 15 Mar. 1603,

SIR FRANCIS RODES, Knt., b. at Barlborough, co. Derby, ca. 1585, Knighted at Whitehall, 9 Aug. 1641., d. in Eng., Feb. 1645; m. ca. 1614, Elizabeth Lascelles, b. at Sturton, Notts., 1595, d. in Eng., 1666, sole Heiress of Sir George Lascelles, Knt.

JOHN RODES, ESQ., b. at Barlborough, co. Derby, ca. 1620; m. ca. 1660, Elizabeth Jason, b. at Edial, co. Staffs., ca. 1640, daughter of Simon Jason, Esq., Edial, co. Staffs.

CHARLES RODES. ESQ., b. at Sturton, Notts., Eng., 24 Mar. 1661, d. in New Kent Co., Va., aft. 1719; m. ca. 1695, Frances — ca. 1677, d. aft. 1705, a member of Saint Paul's Parish, New Kent Co., Va.

JOHN RODES, ESQ., b. in New Kent Co., Va., 6 Nov. 1697, d. in Albemarle, Co., Va., 3 May 1775; m. Sept. 1723, Mary Crawford b. in New Kent Co., Va., Mar. 1703, d. in Albemarle Co., Va. 5 May 1775.

ANN RODES, b. in Louisa Co., Va., 26 Dec. 1734, d. at Georgetown, Ky. 29 July 1802; m. in Louisa Co., Va., 25 Jan. 1752, William Thomson, b. in Louisa Co., Va., 13 Aug. 1727, d. in Louisa Co., Va., 27 Apr. 1778.

RODES THOMSON, ESQ., b. in Louisa Co., Va., 14 Oct. 1754, d. in Fayette Co., Ky., aft. 1780; m. ca. 1776, in Orange Co., Va., Sally Vivian, b. in Orange Co., Va., ca. 1756, d. in Fayette Co., Ky., ca. 1781.

NANCY (ANN) THOMSON, b. in Louisa Co., Va., 11 July 1780, d. in Greenup Co., Ky., 17 Apr. 1876; m. ca. 1800, Thomas Johnson Garrett, b. in Louisa Co., Va., 1777, d. in Greenup Co., Ky., 1855.

SOPHIA GARRETT, b. at Mt. Sterling, Ky., 27 Feb. 1812, d. at Bellfontaine, Ohio, aft. 1879; m. at Mt. Sterling, Ky., ca. 1836, Erskine Douglas, b. at New London, Conn., 26 Apr. 1812, d. at Bellfontaine, Ohio, aft. 1879, a Mayflower Descendant.

EMMA JANE DOUGLAS, b. at Richmond, Mo., 11 Nov. 1843, d. at San Francisco, Calif., 3 Feb. 1937; m. at Union Furnace, Ohio, 15 May 1867, Col. George Taliaferro Shackelford, b. at Springfield, Ill., 28 Feb. 1837, d. at Denver Colo., 21 Sept. 1912.

LENA PRICILLA SHACKELFORD, b. at La Grange Furnace, Tenn., 9 Aug. 1868, d. at Los Angeles, Calif., 2 Feb. 1961; m. (1st) at Denver, Colo., 1 Sept. 1888, Henry S. Kennedy, M.E., b. ca. 1860, date and place of death unknown. m. (2nd) at Denver, Colo., 24 Nov. 1898, Edouard Gregory Hesselberg, "D'Essenelli" b. at Riga, Latvia, 3 May 1870, d. 12 June 1935, Los Angeles, Calif.

CLIFTON DOUGLAS KENNEDY, E.E. b. at Denver, Colo., 4 July 1889, d. at Los Angeles, Calif., 7 May 1925; m. at Philadelphia, Pa., 2 July 1918, Mary Elizabeth (Davenport) Schneider, b. at Shamokin, Pa., 27 Dec. 1894, d. at Warminster, Pa., 12 July 1976. A descendant of the Royal Hohenzolleren Family.

JOSEPHINE (JOELLE) DOUGLAS KENNEDY, b. at Los Angeles, Calif., 15 Feb. 1924; m. (1st) in Cecil Co., Md., 14 June 1941, George Henry Newman, also a descendant of Charlemagne, b. at Philadelphia, Pa., 31 Mar. 1921, m. (2nd) at New York City, N.Y., 11 Apr. 1947, Harry Clayton Kuser, E.E., b. at Philadelphia, Pa., 19 June 1924.

GEORGE FREDERICK NEWMAN, b. at Philadelphia, Pa., 4 Aug. 1942; B.S. Temple Univ.; A.S.C., Temple Univ.; also attended Drexel Univ. and Univ. of Delaware; member: German Philatelic Society, Chapter 2, (Past President and Director); American Philatelic Society; Arbeitsgemeinschaft der Sammler Deutscher Kolonialpostwertzeichen; S.R.; The Society of the War of 1812; Military Order of the Loyal Legion of the U.S.; The Sons of the Union Veterans of the Civil War, Camp 200; Society of Mayflower Descendants; The Huguenot Society of Penna.; The Denison Soc. Inc. of Mystic, Conn.; Baronial Order of the Magna Charta; The Military Order of the Crusades; Order of the Crown of Charlemagne in the United States of America; Mennonite Historical Society; Lancaster County Historical Society; Stamford Historical Society;

Stamford Genealogical Society; The Historical Society of Pa.; The Genealogical Society of Pa.; author: "A Postal History of German East Africa"; "A Preliminary Report of the European Aebi-Eby Family"; "Ein Vorlaeufiger Bericht ueber die Europaeischen Familie Aebi-Eby."; "Imperial German Naval Ship Post in Turkey 1914-1918"; co-author: "The Eby Report", Volume I, Number 1, and Number 2; "Some Descendants of Col. George Shackelford"; m. in Cecil Co., Md., 11 July 1964, Ann Louise Pachuta, b. at Philadelphia, Pa., 8 Feb. 1944. Issue:

1) DIETER EBY NEWMAN, b. 14 Nov. 1967.

Chapter LXVIII

SHERBURNE — TILTON — EMERSON — ROBIE — KNIGHT — FOSTER — PILKINGTON — VAN RIPER

CHARLEMAGNE, King of the Franks, Emperor of the West, b. 2 Apr. 742, d. 28 Jan. 813/4; m. (third) ca. 771, Hildegarde of Swabia, b. ca. 758, d. 30 Apr. 783,

PEPIN, King of Italy 781-810, b. Apr. 777, d. Milan, 8 July 810,

BERNARD, King of Italy 813-817, b. 797, d. at Milan, 17 Apr. 818; m. Cunigunde, d. ca 835,

PEPIN, Count of Senlis, Peronne and St. Quentin, b. ca. 815, d. aft. 840,

HERBERT I, Count of Vermandois, Seigneur de Senlis, Peronne and St. Quentin, b. ca. 840, murdered ca. 902; m. Bertha de Morvois,

HERBERT II, Count of Vermandois and Troyes, b. 880/890, d. at St. Quentin, ca. 943; m. Liegarde, dau. of Robert I, King of France and Adele, his wife,

ALBERT I, the Pious, Count of Vermandois, b. ca. 920, d. 987/8; m. Gerberga, dau. of Giselbert, Duke of Lorraine and his wife Gerberga, dau. of Henry I, the Fowler, King of Saxony (See Chapter XXXII)

HERBERT III, Count of Vermandois, b. ca. 955, d. ca. 1000; m. (her second) Irmgard (Ermengarde) dau. of Reinald, Count of Bar,

OTHO (OTTO, EUDES) Count of Vermandois, b. ca. 1000, d. 25 May 1045; m. Parvie,

246

HERBERT IV, Count of Vermandois and Valois, b. ca. 1032, d. ca. 1080; m. Adele de Vexin, dau. of Raoul III, the Great, Count of Valois and Vexin,

ADELAIDE (ADELHEID) Countess of Vermandois and Valois; m. Hugh the Great, Duke of France and Burgundy, Marquis of Orleans, Count of Amiens, Chaumont, Paris, Valois, Vermandois, etc., Leader of the First Crusade, son of Henry I, King of France and Anne, dau. of Yaroslav I, Grand Prince of Kiev,

ISABEL DE VERMANDOIS, Countess of Leicester, d. bef. July 1147; m. (second) William de Warenne, 2nd Earl of Surrey, d. 11 May 1138 (See Chapters X, XXXII, XXXIX, XLIII)

ADA DE WARENNE, d. 1178; m. 1139, Henry de Huntingdon, b. 1114, d. 12 June 1152, son of David I, King of Scots, and his wife, Maud of Northumberland,

WILLIAM, THE LION, King of Scots (9 Dec. 1165-1214) b. 1143, d. 4 Dec. 1214, at Stirling,

ISABEL, natural dau. by a dau. of Richard Avenal, m. (second), 1191, Robert de Ros, Magna Charta Surety, Knight Templar, Fourth Lord of Hamlake, 1183, Ambassador to King William the Lion of Scotland, 1199-1200, Sheriff of Cumberland, 1213, b. at Helmsley in Holderness, co. York, ca. 1172, d. bef. 23 Dec. 1226,

SIR WILLIAM DE ROS, of Helmsley, accompanied the King to Nance in 1230, served in Scotland and Wales (1257-1258), d. 1264/5; m. Lucy FitzPiers, dau. of Piers FitxHerbert of Brecknock, Wales, and his wife, Alice FitzRoger,

SIR WILLIAM DE ROS, of Ingmanthorpe, 3rd son, d. ça. 28 May 1310; m. in 1268, Eustache, dau. and hr. of Ralph FitzHugh,

LUCY DE ROS, m. Sir Robert Plumpton, Knt., b. at Plumpton, co. York, fl. 1307, d. 1325,

SIR WILLIAM PLUMPTON, b. at Plumpton, co. York, d. 1362; m. (second) by 1338, Christianna, wid. of Richard de Emildon, d. 1333,

ALICE DE PLUMPTON, liv. 21 Mar. 1400; m. 1351/2, Sir Richard de Sherburne, Knt., b. at Aighton, Lancs., d. 1361,

MARGARET DE SHERBURNE, b. at Aighton, Lancs.; m. ca. 1377, Richard de Bayley, b. at Stonyhurst, Lancs., ca. 1358; d. at Stonyhurst, by 1388/9,

RICHARD (formerly DE BAYLEY) DE SHERBURNE, b. at Stonyhurst, Lancs., 12 Oct. 1381, d. at Stonyhurst, 29 May 1441; m. Agnes Stanley, b. at Hooten, co. Chester, dau. of William Stanley, of Hooten,

RICHARD DE SHERBURNE, b. at Stonyhurst, Lancs., d. 25 May 1441; m. Alice Hamerton, b. at Wicklisworth, Yorks.,

ROBERT DE SHERBURNE, b. at Stonyhurst, Lancs., 1431-2, d. at Stonyhurst 29 Aug. 1492; m. Joan Ratcliff, b. at Wimmersley,

SIR RICHARD DE SHERBURNE, Knt., b. at Stonyhurst, Lancs., ca. 1450, d. at Stonyhurst, 3 Aug. 1513; m. in 1472, Joan Langton, dau. of Henry de Langton, Esq., of Walton in le Dale, by special dispensation (for they were related to each other) issued by Philip Calandrini Cardinal Bishop of Porto, dated 19 Feb. 1472.,

HUGH SHERBURNE, of Stonyhurst, b. ca. 1473; d. 6 June 1528; m. 7 July 1491, Anne, dau. of Sir Thomas Talbot,

RICHARD SHERBURNE, of Baily Hall and Haighton, 2nd son, b. ca. 1492, w.d. 25 Dec. 1580; w.p. 1581; m. Anne, dau. and coheir of Evan Browne of Ribbleton,

HUGH SHERBURNE, of Haighton, b. ca. 1516/7, sold his estate at Haighton in the beginning of Queen Elizabeth's reign (aft. 1558),

HENRY SHERBURNE, Gent., b. at Haighton, ca. 1541/2, d. 1598; m. (second) Joan, dau. of — Acton, of the City of Oxford and sister of Thomas Acton, of Oxford, a descendant of the family of Acton of Worcestershire. Henry Sherburne left Lancs. and settled at Oxford, ca. 1560 "in the Parish of St. John the Baptist over against Morton College Church in a house by him new-built, formerly called Byham (but commonly) Beam Hall".

JOSEPH SHERBURNE, b. at Oxford, England, d. at Odiham, Hants., Eng.

HENRY SHERBURNE, bapt. at Odiham, Hants., Eng., 28 Mar. 1611, d. at Portsmouth, N.H., bef. 8 Sept. 1681; in 1640, Warden of the Church of England at Portsmouth; in 1644, Gov. Bellingham appointed him Judge at Portsmouth; in 1651, the General Court of Massachusetts appointed him Associate Judge of "Strawberry Bank"; in 1660, served as Deputy to the General Court at Boston; m. (first) 13 Nov. 1637, Rebecca Gibbons, b. prob. in England, 1620; d. in New Hampshire, 3 June 1667, dau. of Ambrose Gibbons,

CAPT. SAMUEL SHERBURNE, b. at Portsmouth, N.H., 4 Aug. 1638, killed by Indians in King William's War, at Casco Bay, Maine, 4 Aug. 1691; m. 15 Dec. 1668, Love Hutchins, b. at Haverhill, Mass., 16 July 1647, d. at Kingston, N.H., Feb. 1739, dau. of John Hutchins of Haverhill,

MARGARET SHERBURNE, b. at Hampton, N.H., 15 Feb. 1678/9, d. in N.H., 1 July 1717; m. at Hampton, N.H., 26 Dec. 1698, Capt. Joseph Tilton, b. at Hampton, N.H., 19 Mar. 1677, d. at Kensington, N.H., 24 Oct. 1744,

SHERBURNE TILTON, b. at Hampton, N.H., 19 Nov. 1699, d. at Kensington, N.H., 11 Feb. 1784; m. 14 Apr. 1726, Ann Hilliard,

SARAH TILTON, b. at Kensington, N.H., 27 June 1743, d. at Candia, N.H. 14 Jan. 1814; m. 15 Nov. 1764, Lt. Col. Nathaniel Emerson, fought in Battle of Bennington, during the Revolution, under Col. Stark; b. at Chester, N.H., 2 May 1741, d. at Candia, N.H., 30 Mar. 1824,

SARAH EMERSON, b. in Rockingham Co., N.H., 4 Dec. 1771, d. at Corinth, Vt., 22 Sept. 1850; m. ca. 1787/89, in N.H., Edward Williams Robie, b. at Candia, N.H., 22 June 1767, d. at Corinth, Vt., 1 Apr. 1814,

SUSAN ROBIE, b. at Corinth, Vt., 7 Feb. 1794, d. prob. at Sun Prairie, Wisc., 7 Oct. 1846; m. at Corinth, Vt., 20 Oct. 1817, Benjamin Knight, b. at East Corinth, Vt., 26 Mar. 1796, d. prob. at Sun Prairie, Wisc., son of Joseph Knight and Hannah Hale,

MARY HALE KNIGHT, b. at Corinth Vt., 10 July 1833, d. at Sun Prairie, Wisc., in 1882; m. (first) at Sun Prairie, Wisc., 25 Mar. 1856, Jonathan Eaton Foster, b. at Ashby, Mass., 11 Sept. 1819, d. at Sun Prairie, Wisc., 26 Mar. 1864, son of Jonathan Foster and Lydia E. Cowdry,

CARL DEKALB FOSTER, b. at Sun Prairie, Wisc., 17 Sept. 1862, d. at Seattle, Wash., 27 Dec. 1929; m. (second) at Little Rock, Ark., 6 May 1903, Mary Estelle Gulley, b. at Philadelphia, Ark., 26 Jan. 1874; d. at Nashville, Tenn., 7 Oct. 1952, dau. of Col. Ransom Gulley, C.S.A., served on staff of Gen Braxton Bragg in the War Between the States, member of Arkansas Constitutional Convention, 1874, represented Izard Co., 1893-95 in Arkansas House of Representatives, State Treasurer 1895-99; and his wife, Louanna Jane Gardner,

1) CARL DEKALB FOSTER, b. 29 Aug. 1904, at Hardy, Ark., d. at Reno, Nv., 25 Mar. 1956; graduate of University of Washington, and the Chicago Art Institute, under the name of Michael Foster, author of AMERICAN DREAM, TO REMEMBER AT MIDNIGHT, HOUSE ABOVE THE RIVER, THE DUSTY GODMOTHER, other novels and many short stories; m. (first) Pamela Leonard of Seattle,

   a) PETER MICHAEL FOSTER, b. Seattle, Wash., 20 Oct. 1930;

   b) GARETH ANN FOSTER, b. Seattle, Wash., 6 Mar. 1933.

2) NANCY (BAB) GULLEY FOSTER, b. at Hardy, Ark., 21 Feb. 1907; ed. by private tutors and at Univ. of Washington, Seattle; member: DAR, chapter regent; N.Y. Colony, New England Women; Order of Americans of Armorial Ancestry; Colonial Daughters of the 17th Century, Penn. Chapter; Washington Headquarters Association — Jumel Mansion, New York City; Order of the Crown of Charlemagne in the United States of America; Dame of the St. George Priory, Order of the Temple of Jerusalem; d. at Nashville, Tenn., 14 July 1977, bur. in Rock Creek Cemetery, Washington, D.C.; m. 19 Apr. 1947, at New York, N.Y., James Orton Buck, b. 1 July 1913, Bridgeport, Conn., (See Vol. II of PEDIGREES)

a) CLARE BOWEN BUCK, b. 7 Sept. 1950, at New York, N.Y., grad. Rhodes School, studied at N.Y. Univ., American Academy of Dramatic Arts; member: DAR; N.Y. Junior League; Colonial Daughters of the 17th Century, Charter Member of the Florida Chapter and Member of the Council; Order of the Crown of Charlemagne in the United States of America, Recording Sec'y General; National Society Americans of Royal Descent; The Order of Descendants of Colonial Physicians and Chirurgiens; m. at New York, N.Y., 29 June 1970, David Maurice Morrison D'Alva, b. at New York, N.Y., 20 Oct. 1943, son of Maurice David D'Alva and Dorothy Landers Morrison.

3) MARY LUANNA FOSTER, b. 29 July 1914, at Wenatchee, Wash.; member: DAR, Order of the Crown of Charlemagne in the United States of America, Order of Americans of Armorial Ancestry; m. (second) at New York, N.Y., 11 Dec. 1937, Edward Copelan Evans, b. at Greensboro, Ga., 1 Apr. 1913, d. at Nashville, Tenn., 9 Feb. 1948, son of James Williams Evans and Leila Copelan; m. (third) 19 Dec. 1953, at Nashville, Tenn., James Penn Pilkington, b. 3 May 1923, at Marianna, Ark., son of George Henry Pilkington and Myrtie May Brown,

251

a) MARY LUANN EVANS, b. 12 Mar. 1940, at Atlanta, Ga., grad. cum laude Radcliff College, member of the Order of the Crown of Charlemagne in the United States of America; m. 11 Sept. 1961, at New York, N.Y., David MacRae Landon, b. 16 Feb. 1938, at New York, N.Y., son of the Rev. Canon Harold Landon and Jean MacRae;

b) SUSAN FOSTER EVANS, b. 27 Sept. 1941, at Little Rock, Ark.; m. at Nashville, Tenn., 27 Dec. 1965, David Norris Van Riper, b. 15 May 1941, at Honolulu, Hawaii, son of John Van Riper and Helen Turner,

  i) RANSOM VAN RIPER, b. 16 Nov. 1966, at Sharon, Mass.

c) LOUISE PENN PILKINGTON, b. at Nashville, Tenn., 7 Dec. 1954.

Chapter LXIX

SHERBURNE — INGALLS — SWEETSER — BURDELL

CHARLEMAGNE

(See Chapter LXVIII)

JOSEPH SHERBURNE, b. at Oxford, England, d. at Odiham Hants, Eng.,

JOHN SHERBURNE, of Little Harbor and New Castle, N.H., bapt. at Odiham, Hants., Eng., 13 Aug. 1615, w. d. 12 Nov. 1691, w.p. 27 Nov. 1693, was at Portsmouth, 1642, member Portsmouth-Hampton boundary committee, 1660, Sergt. 1675, King Philip's War; m. Elizabeth Tuck, dau. of Robert Tuck, of Hampton,

CAPT. JOHN SHERBURNE, of "the Plains", Portsmouth, N.H., b. ca. 1650, w.d. 17 Dec. 1723, w.p. 16 Feb. 1730/1; selectman, 1694-96, 1702, 1703; m. (first) in N.H., ante 20 May 1700, Mary Jackson,

DEACON SAMUEL SHERBURNE, of "the Plains", Portsmouth, N.H., b. 10 Aug. 1698, d. in N.H., 14 Nov. 1760; m. 27 Feb. 1726, Mercy Wiggin, b. 1709, d. 1776, in N.H.,

ANDREW SHERBURNE, Sr., b. 22 May 1738, d. at Rye, N.H., 1780; m. 4 Dec. 1760, Susanna Knight, of Kittery, Me.,

SARAH SHERBURNE, b. at Portsmouth, N.H., 1 Aug. 1779, d. 10 Aug. 1845; m. 8 Apr. 1800, David White Ingalls, b. at Standish, Me., 20 Nov. 1776, d. 1 Oct. 1835,

MARIA INGALLS, b. at West Baldwin, Me., 15 Aug. 1814, d. at Novato, California, 27 May 1876; m. in Maine, 1 June 1836,

Joseph Bryant Sweetser, b. at Lynnfield, Mass., 8 Aug. 1813, d. at Switzerland, Fla., 13 Apr. 1886,

JOHN ROBERT SWEETSER, b. at Westbrook, Me., 7 June 1840, d. at Novato, Calif. 21 Mar. 1904; m. at Westbrook, Me., 17 May 1867, Frances Ellen Johnston, b. at Falmouth, Me., 10 Dec. 1840, d. at Novato, Calif., 27 Aug. 1927,

MARIA JOSEPHINE SWEETSER, b. at Novato, Calif., 13 Sept. 1874, d. at Petaluma, Calif., 29 July 1964; m. at Novato, Calif., 29 Dec. 1892, James Black Burdell, b. at San Francisco, Calif., 18 Nov. 1869, d. at Burdell's (Novato, Calif.), 20 Sept. 1933,

JAMES BLACK BURDELL, Jr., b. at Burdell's (Novato, Calif.), 1 Jan. 1898, d. at Riverside, Calif., 22 June 1950; m. at Palo Alto, Calif., 15 Mar. 1922, Irma Blanche Aspey, b. at Mt. Ephraim, N.J., 6 Aug. 1897, d. at Petaluma, Calif., 19 Jan. 1958,

CHARMAINE ASPEY BURDELL, b. at San Francisco, Calif., 18 Sept. 1928; member of Society of Mayflower Descendants, Calif.; DAR; Los Californianos; Daughters of the California Pioneers; Order of the Crown of Charlemagne in the United States of America; Marin County Historical Society, past Vice President; m. at Napa, Calif., 25 Apr. 1961, Anthony Calhoun Veronda.

Chapter LXX

SMEDAL

CHARLEMAGNE, King of the Franks, Emperor of the West, b. 2 Apr. 742, d. 28 Jan. 814; m. (third) 771, Hildegarde, b. 758, d. 30 Apr. 783, dau. of Gerold I, Count in Vinzgau,

LOUIS I, the Pious, *le Debonnaire*, King of the Franks, Emperor of the West; m. (second) 819, Judith, d. 19 Apr. 843,

CHARLES II, the Bald, Emperor of the West, b. 13 June 823, d. 6 Oct. 877, King of France 843, King of Lorraine 869, crowned Emperor at Rome, 25 Dec. 875; m. 14 Dec. 842, Ermentrude, d. 6 Oct. 869, dau. of Odo, Count of Orleans.

JUDITH OF FRANCE, b. ca. 843; m. (third) in 862, Baldwin I, Count of Flanders, d. 879,

BALDWIN II, Count of Flanders, d. 918; m. 884, Aelfthryth, d. 7 June 929, dau. of Alfred the Great, King of Wessex,

ARNULF I, Count of Flanders, d. 27 Mar. 964; m. Alix, d. 958/60, dau. of Herbert II, Count of Vermandois, a descendant of Charlemagne (See Chapter LXVIII)

BALDWIN III, Co-Regent with his father 958-962, d. 1 Nov. 962; m. 961, Matilda, d. 28 May 1008, dau. of Herman Billung, Duke of Saxony,

ARNULF II, Count of Flanders, b. 961/2, d. 30 Mar. 987; m. Rosala of Ivrea, dau. of Berengar II, Margrave of Ivrea, King of Italy, a descendant of Charlemagne (See Chapter VI)

BALDWIN IV, Count of Flanders, b. ca. 980, d. 30 May 1036; m. (first) Eleanor of Normandy, dau. of Richard I. Duke of Normandy and Rosala of Italy,

JUDITH OF FLANDERS, b. in Flanders; m. 1051, Tostig Godwinson, b. in England, d. at Stamford Bridge, 25 Sept. 1066,

SKULE TOSTIGSON, d. in Norway; m. Gudrun Nevsteinsdatter, b. in Norway,

AASULF SKULESON, b. at Rein, Norway; m. Tora Skoftesdatter, b. at Giske Sunmore, Norway,

GUTHORM ASSUFSSON, b. at Rein, Norway; m. Sigfrid Torkellsdatter, b. at Jugl, Norway,

BAARD GUTHORMSSON, b. at Rein, Norway, d. 1194; m. Ragnfrid Erlingsdatter, b. at Kvie, Vang i Valdres, Norway,

INGEBJOR BAARDSDATTER, b. at Rein, Nord-More, Norway, d. 1226; m. Alf Erlingsson, b. at Tornberg, Norway (Ringerike),

ERLING ALFSSON, the Younger, b. at Tornberg, Norway, d. 1283; m. Kristina,

ALF ERLINGSSON, Earl, b. at Tornberg, Norway, d. 1290,

KRISTINA ALFSDATTER, SPENELSKO, d. ante 1348; m. Rane Jonsson, Knight, b. at Gjorslev, Sjaelland, Denmark, d. 1294,

EYVIND RANESSON of Sodheim, b. at Komnes, Norway, ca. 1280; m. a dau. of Peter Jakobsson, b. at Halland, Denmark,

RANE EYVINDSSON, Knight, b. at Tunesberg, Norway, liv. 1349-1362; m. Aasa Salmundsdatter of Selvik, b. at Herset, Ostfold, Norway; liv. 1396,

LIV RANESDATTER i TUNSBERG, liv. 1390; m. Steinulf Nikulasson of Sodheim,

RANE STEINULFSSON, of Sodheim, b. at Sodheim, Norway,

TORSTEIN RANESSON, of Sodheim, b. at Sodheim, Norway, d. 1465; m. Gunvor Arnfinnsdatter,

LIV TORSTEINSDATTER, of Sodheim, b. at Sandsver, Norway, (inherited Sodheim in 1466); m. Rolf Erlingsson,

TORSTEIN ROLFSSON, of Sodheim and Reine. b. and d. at Komnes, Sandsver, Norway; m. Torny of Lindheim, b. at Nesherad, Norway,

ROLF TORSTEINSSON, of Lindheim and Klevar, b. at Sauherad, Norway, d. at Sauherad, Norway, ca. 1570; m. Karin Nilsdatter Mathisson, b. at Skjerven i Lardal, Norway,

AMUND ROLFSSON, of Klevar and Lindheim, b. at Sauherad, Norway, d. at Sauherad, Norway, in 1603; m. at Sauherad, Norway, Gunhild Petersdatter, b. at Bergenn i Nes, Norway, d. at Sauherad, ca. 1575,

ROLV (ROLF); AMUNDSSON pa Klevar, b. at Sauherad, Norway, d. at Sauherad, Norway, ca 1645; m. at Sauherad, Dorothe Mattson, b. and d. at Sauherad, Norway,

BIRGIT (BIRGITTA) ROLVSDATTER KLEVAR, b. at Sauherad, Norway, d. at Bø, Telemark, Norway, in 1685; m. ca. 1623, at Sauherad, Tor Steinarson Fjaagesund, b. at Kvitseid, Norway, d. ca. 1640, at Kuitseid, Norway,

STEINAR TORSON FJAAGESUND, b. at Kvitseid, Norway, d. 1695, at Seljord, Telemark, Norway; m. at Kvitseid, Norway, Egeleiv Olavsdatter,

TOR STEINARSON FJAAGESUND, b. at Kvitseid, Norway, 1665, d. at Kvitseid, ca. 1717; m. at Bø, Telemark, Norway, in 1684, Aslaug Halvorsdatter Borga, b. at Bø, Norway, in 1661, d. at Kvitseid, Telemark, Norway, in 1729,

HALVOR TORSON BERGE i FJAAGESUND, b. in 1694, at Kvitseid, Norway, d. at Kvitseid; m. in 1719, at Kvitseid, Barbro Olavsdatter Austana, b. at Kvitseid, Norway, in 1702, d. at Seljord, Norway, in 1781,

ASLAUG HALVORSDATTER FJAAGESUND, b. in 1729, at Kvitseid, Norway, d. at Seljord, Norway; m. in 1743, at Kvitseid,

Ginleik Torson Nordgarden, b. at Seljord, Norway, in 1721, d. at Seljord, in 1772,

HALVOR GUNLEIKSON BERGE (i Fjaagesund), b. in 1746, at Kvitseid, Norway, d. in 1782, at Brunkeberg, Norway; m. in 1773, at Øyfjell, Norway, Anne Anversdatter Berge, b. at Øyfjell, in 1753, d. at Kvitseid, in 1834,

GUNHILD HALVORSDATTER HEGGTVEIT, b. and d. at Brunkeberg, Norway; m. at Brunkeberg, in 1796, Tor Egilson Midbøen, b. in 1758, at Brunkeberg, d. in 1831, at Brunkeberg,

ANNE TOVSDATTER MIDBØEN, b. at Brunkeberg, Norway, in 1809, d. at Flatdal Norway; m. in 1837, at Brunkeberg, to Gregar Rue, b. at Flatdal, d. at Flatdal, Norway, in 1870,

GUNHILD RUE, b. at Flatdal, Norway, 29 Dec. 1843, d. at 31 Oct. 1931, at Albert Lea, Minnesota; m. at Flatdal, Norway, in 1871, Aslak Olavson Smedal, b. at Aamotsdal, Norway, 3 Apr. 1842, d. at Flatdal, Norway, 14 Aug. 1911,

HAROLD ASLAKSON SMEDAL, b. at Flatdal, Norway, 15 Sept. 1876, d. at Madison, Wisc. 13 Nov. 1936; m. at Stoughton, Wisc., 24 Nov. 1897, Aasne Evans, b. at Rauland, Norway, 20 Jan. 1873, d. at Madison, Wisc., 1 Mar. 1955,

1) ERLING ARNOLD SMEDAL, b. at McFarland, Wisc., 26 Mar. 1899, d. 1 Sept. 1977; ed.: University of Wisconsin, B.A.; Rush Medical College, Univ. of Chicago, M.D.; Resident Physician, Chicago; Rush Medical College, post graduate work in Ophthalomology; Diplomate American Board of Ophthalomology; Diplomate International College of Surgeons, Certified Member; American Academy of Ophthalomology and Otolaryngology, Senior Fellow; American Assoc. of Ophthalomology; American Medical Assoc.; Ohio State Ophthalomological Society; Masonic Order; American Legion; Amvets; Order of the Crown of Charlemagne in the United States of America; m. 20 July 1931, at Chicago, Ill., Erma Kathleen Houston, b. 10 Mar. 1902, at Mansfield, Ohio.

2) MAGNUS INGVALD SMEDAL, b. at McFarland, Wisc., 20 Apr. 1905; ed.: Univ. of Wisc., B.A.; Harvard Medical School, M.D.; General Intern., Harper Hospital, Detroit, Mich.; Resident in Radiology, Boston City Hospital, Boston, Mass., 1931-33, Asst. Resident VI Surgical (Bone & Joint) Service, 1933; A.U.S. Maj. M.C. Jan. 1942; Lt. Col. Dec. 1942; Col. July 1946; member: American Board of Radiology, Diplomate; American College of Radiology, Fellow; American Roentgen Ray Society; Radiological Society of North America; American Radium Society; American Medical Association; New England Roentgen Ray Society, past President; New England Cancer Society; Masonic Order; Order of the Crown of Charlemagne in the United States of America; m. at Boston, Mass., 9 Nov. 1933, Eunice Anne Whitmore, b. at Pembroke, Ont. Canada, 24 Mar. 1910.

   a) HARALD ALBERT SMEDAL, b. at Boston, Mass., 26 Aug. 1936; m. at Litchfield, Conn., on 30 Aug. 1958, Constance (Davis) Dean, b. at Portland, Me. 21 Apr. 1939;

   b) MARI ANNE SMEDAL, b. at Boston, Mass. on 16 July 1938; m. at Madison, Wisc., on 4 June 1961, Arthur L. Morsell, III, b. at Milwaukee, Wisc. on 2 Apr. 1933.

3) ELAINE ALVINE GUDRUN SMEDAL, b. at McFarland, Wisc., 6 Oct. 1922; ed.: Univ. of Wisc., B.S., M.S., Art Education; member: Phi Mu, Sigma Lambda, Delta Phi Delta, Pi Lambda Theta, American Assoc. of University Women, Order of the Crown of Charlemagne in the United States of America; m. at McFarland, Wisc., 4 Sept. 1948, Burton Elmer Quant, b. at New London, Wisc., 17 Oct. 1918,

   a) ROBERT STEVEN QUANT, b. at Stoughton, Wisc., 3 Oct. 1953; m. at Oshkosh, Wisc., on 30 Dec. 1972, Sonja Stein, b. at Bad Nawtheim, Germany on 16 Dec. 1953.

b) WENDY SUE QUANT, b. 19 Dec. 1958, at Stoughton, Wisc.;

c) BARBARA ANN QUANT, b. 31 July 1961, at Madison, Wisc.

Chapter LXXI

THROCKMORTON — ASHTON — STEVENS — McKNIGHT — SMITH — ARLINGTON — BERWICK — BROOKS

CHARLEMAGNE

(See Chapter LXVIII)

SIR WILLIAM DE ROS, of Helmsley, accompanied the King to Nance in 1230, served in Scotland and Wales 1257-58, d. 1264/5; m. Lucy Fitz Piers, dau. of Piers Fitz Herbert of Brecknock, Wales, and his wife Alice Fitz Roger,

SIR ROBERT DE ROS, of Helmsley and Belvoir, co. Leicester, 1st Baron Ros of Belvoir, M.P. 1261, 1265; m. ante 17 May 1246, Isabel d'Aubigny, d. 15 June 1301, dau. of William d'Aubigny of Belvoir Castle and Albrada Biset, and grand dau. of William d'Aubigny, Magna Charta Surety, d. 1236,

ISABEL DE ROS, m. (first) Walter de Faucomberge, d. 31 Dec. 1318,

JOHN DE FAUCOMBERGE, Lord Faucomberge, d. 18 Sept. 1349; m. Eva, prob. dau. of Ralph, Lord Bulmer,

JOAN DE FAUCOMBERGE, m. 1376/7, Sir William de Colville of Arncliffe, d. ca. 1380/1,

SIR JOHN COLVILLE, of Arncliffe and Dale, beheaded with his wife 20 Aug. 1405, at Durham; m. Alice d'Arcy, dau. of John Lord d'Arcy,

ISABEL DE COLVILLE, liv. 1442/3; m. (first) John Wandesford, of Kirklington, d. ca. 1400, son of John de Wandesford,

THOMAS WANDESFORD, a merchant in London, Sheriff of London, d. 13 Oct. 1448; m. Idonea — ,

ALICE WANDESFORD, co-heiress; m. William Mulso of Creatingham, co. Suffolk, d. 1495,

ANNE MULSO,. m., Thomas Louthe, M.P., of Sawtry, Hunts, d. 1533,

EDMUND LOUTHE, d.v.p. (killed in 1522); m. Edith Stukeley, dau. of Stukeley of Stukeley, Hunts.,

ANNE LOUTHE, d. 1577; m. Simon Throckmorton of Earsham, co. Suffolk, d. 10 July 1527,

LIONEL THROCKMORTON, of South Elmham and Bungay, co Suffolk, d. 1599; m. (second) 1560, Elizabeth Blennerhasset, dau. of John Blennerhasset of Barsham and his (first) wife Elizabeth Cornwallis,

BASSINGBOURNE THROCKMORTON, Esq., Alderman of Norwich, b. 1564, d. 21 Sept. 1638; m. (first) Mary Hill, d. 1615, dau. of William Hill, gent., of Bury St. Edmunds, and his wife, Joan Annabel,

JOHN THROCKMORTON, bapt. 8 May 1601, d. 17 Mar. 1683/4-25 Apr. 1684, at Middletown, N.J.; m. Rebecca Covill, b. in England,

DELIVERANCE THROCKMORTON, b. ca. 1640, at Providence, R.I., d. at Middletown, N.J.; m. Rev. James Ashton, Jr., b. in England, ca. 1639, d. at Middletown, N.J., ca. 1705,

JOHN ASHTON, b. in Monmouth Co., N.J.; m. Patience — ,

RACHEL ASHTON, d. 14 May 1740; m. Richard Stevens, d. 1745,

ELIZABETH STEVENS, b. in Upper Freehold Twp., N.J., 1 May 1730; m. in Monmouth Co., N.J., Rev. Charles McKnight, b. at Antrim, Ireland, ca. 1720, d. at New York, N.Y., 1 Jan. 1776 (bur. in Trinity Churchyard).

DR. CHARLES MCKNIGHT, b. at Cranbury, N.J., 10 Oct. 1750, d. at New York, N.Y., 16 Nov. 1791 (bur. in Trinity Churchyard); m. prob. at New York, N.Y., 22 Apr. 1778, Mary Morin (Scott) Litchfield, b. at New York, N.Y., 17 July 1753, bur. in Trinity Churchyard, New York, N.Y., in 1796,

MARY SCOTT MCKNIGHT, b. at New York, N.Y., 29 Jan. 1779, d. at Eastchester, N.Y., 29 Oct. 1815; m. at Presbyterian Church in New York, N.Y., 23 Nov. 1795, Samuel Smith, b. at Haverstraw, N.Y., 2 June 1774, d. at Eastchester, N.Y., 15 Mar. 1834,

JULIANA MARIA SMITH, b. at Haverstraw, N.Y., 29 June 1801, d. at Norwalk, Conn., 30 July 1885; m. at New York, N.Y., Rev. Martin Arlington, b. in New Jersey,

ANN ELIZABETH ARLINGTON, b. at Tarrytown, N.Y., 20 Sept. 1833, d. at Norwalk, Conn., 25 Dec. 1887; m. at New York, N.Y., Robert Rooke Berwick, b. in Yorks., England, 24 Nov. 1829, d. at Superior, Wisc., 23 Oct. 1904,

CLARA LOUISE BERWICK, b. at Norwalk, Conn., 2 Nov. 1863, d. at Rochester, Minn., 9 Jan. 1947; m. at Superior, Wisc., 9 Aug. 1892, George LeMont Brooks, b. at Butternuts, N.Y., 21 May 1846, d. at Superior, Wisc., 15 Mar. 1917,

HERBERT BERWICK BROOKS, b. at Superior, Wisc., 18 May 1893, d. at Louisville, Ky., 9 Sept. 1959; m. at Louisville, Ky., 1 Jan. 1920, Ella Tatum Rowland, b. at Louisville, Ky., 13 Jan. 1894, d. at Tacoma Park, Md., 16 Dec. 1963,

CLIFTON ROWLAND BROOKS, b. at Louisville, Ky., 8 May 1923; ed.: Univ. of Wisc., B.S., M.D.; U.C.L.A., M. of Public Health; Lt. Cdr., USNR, World War II and Korean War; Lt. Col. USAFR (Flight Surgeon) Korean War and Vietnam War; member: SAR, Surgeon Calif. Society; S.R.; Calif. Society of Colonial Wars, Surgeon; Nat'l Society Sons and Daughters of Pilgrims, 2nd Deputy Gov. General, Gov. of Calif. branch; Descendants of Colonial Clergy, member of Council; Huguenot Society of Calif., Treasurer; Ancient and Honorable Artillery Co. of Mass.; New Jersey Blues; Descendants of Founders of Hartford; Dutch Settlers Society of Albany;

General Society of the War of 1812; Descendants of Colonial Tavern Keepers; Descendants of Colonial Physicians and Chirurgens, Surgeon General; Veteran Corps of Artillery, State of N.Y.; Sons of Union Veterans; Sons of Confederate Veterans; Hereditary Order of Patriots and Loyalists; Order of the Crown of Charlemagne in the United States of America; Reserve Officers Assoc.; Nat'l Rifle Assoc.; etc.; m. at Wheeling, W.Va., 21 June 1947, Agnes Joan McVeigh, b. at Wheeling, W. Va., 12 July 1922 (See Chapter V)

1) CAPT. CLIFTON ROWLAND BROOKS, Jr., b. 27 Oct. 1948, at Norfolk, Va., ed.: V.M.I., B.A. (Distinguished Military Graduate); The Basic School, Marine Corps Schools, Quantico, Va.; member: Ancient and Honorable Artillery Co. of Mass., N.J. Blues, The Jamestowne Society, Descendants of the Founders of Hartford, Dutch Settlers Society of Albany, Veteran Corps of Artillery of N.Y., SAR, S.R., Society of Colonial Wars, Gen. Soc. War of 1812, Military Order of the Loyal Legion, Military Order of Foreign Wars, Military Order of the World Wars, Descendants of: Colonial Clergy; Colonial Tavern Keepers; Colonial Physicians and Chirurgiens, The Huguenot Soc. of Calif. Nat'l Soc. Sons and Daughters of the Pilgrims, Order of the Crown of Charlemagne in the United States of America, U.S. Naval Institute, the Nat'l Rifle Assoc., The Morgan Horse Assoc., etc.; m. 28 May 1977, at Pittsfield, Mass., Amy Elizabeth Spratlin.

2) DANIEL RUSK BROOKS, b. 12 Apr. 1951; m. 26 May 1972, at Mead, Nebraska, Paula Joann Scoles,

3) LUCIEN DOUGLAS BROOKS, b. 21 July 1952.

4) DUNCAN MCVEIGH BROOKS, b. 3 Oct. 1953.

5) GORDON BERWICK BROOKS, b. 8 Dec. 1955; m. 21 Aug. 1976, at Wausa, Nebraska, Jean Ann Gunderson.

6) PHILIP HENRY BROOKS, b. 31 Aug. 1957.

Chapter LXXII

von RANTZOW — JACOBS — DANIELSEN — BERG — BARTA

CHARLEMAGNE

(See Chapter XVII)

LOUIS IV, *d'Outremer*, King of France, b. ca. 919/21, d. 10 Sept. 954; m. (her second) 2 Oct. 939, Princes Gerberga, of Germany, b. in Saxony, ca. 913/14, d. 5 May 984, dau. of Henry the Fowler,

PRINCESS MATILDA, of France, b. ca. 943, d. 25 Nov. 982/991; m. ca. 964, Conrad I, King of Burgundy, d. 19 Oct. 993, son of Rudolph I, King of Burgundy,

PRINCESS GERBERGA, of Burgundy, b. 965, d. 1016; m. (second) ca. 988, Herman, II, Duke of Swabia, d. 4 May 1003,

GISELA, of Swabia, b. ca. 993, d. 14 Feb. 1043; m. (his third) end of 1016/17, Conrad II, the Salic, Holy Roman Emperor, b. 990, d. 4 June 1039,

HENRY III, the Black, Duke of Bavaria and Swabia, King of Burgundy, Holy Roman Emperor, b. 28 Oct. 1017, d. at Bodfeld, 5 Oct. 1056; m. (second) 21 Nov. 1043, Countess Agnes, of Poitou, b. ca. 1020, d. 14 Dec. 1077, dau. of William II, Count of Poitou,

HENRY IV, Duke of Bavaria, Holy Roman Emperor, b. 11 Nov. 1050, d. 7 Aug. 1106, a Liege, Belgium; m. (first) 13 July 1066, Countess Bertha, of Savoy, b. 21 Sept. 1051, d. 27 Dec. 1087, dau. of Otto, Count of Maurienne, and Adelaide, his wife,

PRINCESS AGNES, b. 1074/5, d. 24 Sept. 1143; m. 1089, Frederick I von Hohenstaufen, Duke of Alsace and Swabia, b. ca. 1050, d. 6 Apr. 1105,

FREDERICK II von HOHENSTAUFEN, Duke of Swabia, b. ca. 1090, d. 4 Apr. 1147; m. Judith, of Bavaria, b. 1130, d. 22 Feb. - , dau. of Henry I, Duke of Bavaria, and Wulfhilda, his wife,

FREDERICK I, BARBAROSSA von HOHENSTAUFEN, Duke of Swabia and Holy Roman Emperor, b. 1122, d. at Cilicia (Asia Minor) 10 June 1190; m. 10 June 1156, Countess Beatrix, of Burgundy, b. 1143/4; d. 15 Nov. 1184, dau. of Renaud III, Count of Macon, and Burgundy,

HENRY VI, von HOHENSTAUFEN, Duke of Swabia, King of Sicily, Holy Roman Emperor, b. in Nov. 1165; d. at Messina, 28 Sept. 1197; m. 27 Jan. 1186, Princes Constance, of Sicily, d. 27 Nov. 1198,

FREDERICK II von HOHENSTAUFEN, King of Sicily and Jerusalem, Holy Roman Emperor, b. at Jesi, 26 Dec. 1159, d. at Fiorentino, 30 Dec. 1250; m. Bianca, dau. of Manfred Lancia,

MANFRED von HOHENSTAUFEN, Prince of Torentum, King of Sicily, b. ca. 1232, d. nr. Benevento, 26 Feb. 1266; m. 1248/9, Countess Beatrice, of Savoy, d. 10 May —,

PRINCESS CONSTANCE, of Sicily, b. 1249, d. 1301/2; m. 13 June 1262, Peter III, King of Aragon and Sicily, d. 11 Nov. 1285,

JAMES II, King of Aragon and Sicily, b. 1262, d. 5 Nov. 1327; m. 1 Nov. 1295, Princess Blanca, of Naples, d. 14 Oct. 1310.

ALFONSO IV, King of Aragon, b. 1302, d. 24 Jan. 1336; m. 10 Nov. 1314, Therese, of Urgel, d. 18 Oct. 1327,

PETER IV, King of Aragon, b. 5 Sept. 1319, d. 5 Jan. 1387; m. 13 June 1349, Princess Eleanore, of Sicily, d. 10 June 1374,

PRINCESS ELEANORE, of Aragon, b. 1358, d. 13 Aug. 1382; m. 18 June 1375, John I, King of Castile, b. 20 Aug. 1358, d. 9 Oct. 1390,

FERDINAND I, of Antequera, King of Aragon, b. 27 Nov. 1380, d. at Ygualada, Catalonia, 2 Apr. 1416; m. 1393, Princess Eleanore, of Albuquerque, b. 1374, d. in Dec. 1435,

JOHN II, King of Aragon, Sicily and Navarre, b. 28 June 1397, d. 19 Jan. 1479; m. in July 1447, Juana Enriquez de Cordova V Senora de Casarrubios del Monte y Arroyo Molino, b. ca. 1425, d. 13 Feb. 1468,

FERDINAND, the Catholic, King of Aragon, Sicily and Navarre, b. at Sos, Aragon, 10 Mar. 1452, d. at Madrigalejo, Estremadura, 23 Jan. 1516; m. at Valladolid, 19 Oct. 1469, Isabel, the Catholic, Queen of Castile and Leon, b. at Madrigal, 22 Apr. 1451, d. at Medina del Campo, 26 Nov. 1504,

JUANA, Princess of Castile and Aragon, b. at Toledo, 6 Nov. 1479, d. at Tordesillas, 13 Apr. 1555; m. in Flanders, 21 Aug. 1496, Philip, the Handsome (von Hapsburg) Archduke of Austria, and Duke of Burgundy, b. at Bruges, 22 June 1478, d. at Burgos, 25 Sept. 1506,

FERDINAND I, von HAPSBURG, Archduke of Austria, King of Bohemia and Hungary, Holy Roman Emperor, b. at Alcala de Henares, 10 Mar. 1503, d. at Vienna, 27 July 1564; m. at Linz, 25 May 1521, Anna, Princess of Bohemia, b. 23 July 1503, d. 27 Jan. 1547,

MARIE von HAPSBURG, b. 15 May 1531, d. 11 Dec. 1581; m. 18 July 1546, Wilhelm, Duke of Julich-Kleve-Berg, b. 28 July 1516, d. 5 Jan. 1592,

MARIE ELEANORE von JULICH-KLEVE-BERG, b. 15 June 1550, d. 23 May 1608; m. 14 Oct. 1573, Albrecht Friedrich von Brandenburg, Duke of Prussia, b. 29 Apr. 1553, d. 18 Aug. 1618,

MAGDELENE SIBYLLE von PRUSSIA, b. 9 Jan. 1587, d. 22 Feb. 1659; m. 12 July 1607, John George I, Prince-Elector of Saxony, b. 15 Mar. 1585, d. 18 Oct. 1656,

AUGUSTUS, Duke of Saxe-Weissenfels, b. 13 Aug. 1614, d. 4 June 1680; m. 23 Nov. 1647, Anna Marie von Mecklenburg-Schwerin, b. 1 July 1627, d. 11 Dec. 1669,

MAGDELENE SIBYLLE von SAXE-WEISSENFELS, b. 2 Sept. 1648, d. 7 Jan. 1681; m. 14 Nov. 1669, Friedrich I, Duke of Saxe-Gotha, b. 15 July 1646, d. 2 Aug. 1691,

ANNA SOFIE von SAXE-GOTHA, b. 22 Dec. 1670, d. 28 Dec. 1728; m. 15 Oct. 1691, Ludwig Friedrich I, Prince of Schwarzburg-Rudolstadt, b. 19 Oct. 1667, d. 24 June 1718,

PRINCE WILHELM LUDWIG von SCHWARZBURG-RUDOLSTADT, b. 15 Feb. 1696, d. 26 Sept. 1757; m. 4 May 1726, Henrietter Caroline, Baroness von Brockenburg, b. 5 June 1706, d. 9 Mar. 1784,

LOUISE HENRIETTE, Baroness von Brockenburg, b. 7 Sept. 1732, d. at Bremen, Germany, 5 Mar. 1788; m. 30 July 1757, Count Christoph Ferdinand Anton von Rantzow, b. at Wolffenbuttel, Germany, 26 Mar. 1711, d. at Holzminden, Germany, 7 Dec. 1758,

COUNT JULIUS FRIEDRICH LUDWIG von RANTZOW, b. at Delmenhorst, Oldenburg, 2 Aug. 1770, d. at Christiansted, St. Croix, Danish West Indies, 18 Aug. 1820; m. at Christiansted, St. Croix, D.W.I., 16 Jan. 1792, Elizabeth (Rebecca) de Windt, b. at St. Croix, D.W.I., 9 Aug. 1769, d. at Christiansted, St. Croix, D.W.I., 12 July 1832,

COUNTESS JULIETTE MARIE ELIZABETH von RANTZOW, b. at Copenhagen, Denmark, 19 Mar. 1801, d. at Christiansted, St. Croix, D.W.I., 19 July 1870; m. at Christiansted 14 Oct. 1817, Dr. William Stephen Jacobs, b. at Brussels, Belgium, in 1770, d. at Christiansted, St. Croix, D.W.I., 30 Dec. 1843,

MARIE LOUISE RANTZOW JACOBS, b. at Christiansted, St. Croix, D.W.I., 14 Oct. 1824, d. at St. Thomas, D.W.I., 10 Sept. 1884; m. at Christiansted, St. Croix, D.W.I., 27 Apr. 1854, Benton Danielsen, b. at St. Croix, D.W.I., in Jan. 1827, d. at Puerto Rico, aft. 1880,

JOSEPHINE ALMA DANIELSEN, b. at Christiansted, St. Croix, D.W.I., 1 Apr. 1866, d. at Brooklyn, N.Y., 24 Jan. 1953; m. at St. Thomas, D.W.I., 14 Apr. 1888, Carl Conrad Berg, b. at Copenhagen, Denmark, 11 Oct. 1845, d. at Brooklyn, N.Y., 1 Aug. 1911,

AGNES MARIE LOUISE BERG, b. at St. Thomas, D.W.I., 13 July 1903, d. at Newport Beach, California, 7 Mar. 1960; m. at St. Thomas, U.S. Virgin Islands, 27 June 1921, Louis Joseph Barta, Cdr. (SC) USN, b. at New Prague, Minn., 5 Nov. 1897, d. at Newport Beach, Calif., 15 May 1966,

1) FRANK KENNETH BARTA, b. at St. Thomas U.S. Virgin Islands. 5 Apr. 1924. As his father was a career naval officer, Fr. Barta's schooling was accomplished in Virginia, California, and New York. His education was interrupted by a tour of service in the U.S. Naval Intelligence (1943-1946) during World War II. Upon discharge from the Navy, he resumed his studies in history and political science, graduating from Stanford University in 1950. Three years at the Church Divinity School of the Pacific followed where he earned a Master of Divinity in theology.

After his ordination to the Diaconate at St Paul's Cathedral in Los Angeles, Fr. Barta returned to St. Thomas to serve as Curate of All Saints' Anglican Church. Here he was Priested in December of 1953, in the church he had been baptized in as an infant and in which five generations of his family had worshiped.

Father Barta served the Church in Jacksonville, Florida, El Monte and Fillmore, California, before becoming a chaplain in the Veterans Administration hospital system in 1968. He is also a Chaplain (Major) in the U.S. Army Reserves and a Knight of Justice and Chaplain of the Sovereign Order of St. John of Jerusalem. Fr. Barta is unmarried being a member of the Society of the Oblates of Mount Calvary, an Episcopal clerical fellowship associated with the Order of the Holy Cross.

Being especially interested in the Virgin Islands, Fr. Barta is a member of the Danish West Indian Society of Copenhagen, Denmark, and the St. Croix Landmarks

Society, St. Croix, U.S. Virgin Islands. He is also a member of the Reserve Officers Association, the Military Chaplains Association, and his alumni associations. His present home is in Palo Alto, California, where Father Barta is a chaplain in the VA Hospital.

2) AGNES DOROTHY BARTA, b. at Charleston, S.C., 25 Sept. 1926; ed.: University of Southern California, Los Angeles; member: Delta Delta Delta, Key and Scroll (Junior Women's Honorary); Colony Club, New York; North Country Garden Club (Garden Club of America); East Woods School, Oyster Bay, N.Y., Trustee; Nature Conservancy, Long Island Chapter; Order of the Crown of Charlemagne in the United States of America; listed in New York Social Register; m. 22 Jan. 1927, at Jacksonville, Fla., Curtis Cushman, b. at New York, N.Y., 26 Mar. 1927,

   a) SUSAN CUSHMAN, b. 22 Sept. 1962;

   b) JONATHAN CURTIS CUSHMAN, b. 22 Jan. 1964.

3) JOHN JOSEPH BARTA, b. at San Diego, California, 4 Nov. 1937; B.A., Claremont Men's College; member: Knight of Justice, Sovereign Order of St. John of Jerusalem; Order of the Crown of Charlemagne in the United States of America; Balboa Bay Club, Newport Beach, Cal.; Orange Co. (Cal.) Philharmonic Society; m. at Fillmore, Cal., 16 Nov. 1962, Betsy Alice Beman, b. at Los Angeles, Cal., 16 June 1941,

   a) JOHN BEMAN BARTA, b. 26 July 1964;

   b) JENNIFER ANN BARTA, b. 3 Apr. 1966.

Chapter LXXIII

WELBY — FARWELL — SPALDING (SPAULDING) — DAVIDSON — WILLES — DUNHAM — ROBIE — GRUNWELL

CHARLEMAGNE

(See Chapter XIX)

REV. EDWARD BULKELEY, b. ca. 1540, bur. at Odell, Bedfordshire, 5 Jan. 1620/1; m. ca. 1566, Olive Irby, b. ca. 1547, bur. at Odell, 10 Mar. 1614/5,

FRANCES BULKELEY, m. ca. 1595, Richard Welby (Welbie),

OLIVE WELBY (WELBIE) bapt. at Moulton, England, ca. 1604, d. at Chelmsford, Mass., 1 Mar 1691/2; m. 16 Apr. 1629, at Boston, England, Henry Farwell, b. in England, ca. 1605, d. at Chelmsford, Mass., 1 Aug. 1670,

OLIVE FARWELL, b. at Concord, Mass., ca. 1645; m. 30 Oct. 1668, at Chelmsford, Mass., Benjamin Spalding, b. at Braintree, Mass., 7 Apr. 1643, d. ante 1708,

EDWARD SPALDING, b. at Chelmsford, Mass., 18 June 1672, d. at Canterbury, Conn., 29 Nov. 1739/40; m. ca. 1695, Mary Adams, b. ca. 1676, d. 20 Sept 1754,

JONATHAN SPALDING, b. at Canterbury, Conn., 15 Apr. 1704, d. aft. 6 Mar. 1761; m. ca. 1725, Eunice Woodward, b. at Preston, Conn., 8 Mar. 1707, d. aft. 8 Mar. 1761,

EUNICE SPAULDING (SPALDING) b. at Windham, Conn., 18 Feb. 1736/7, d. 1801; m. at Mansfield, Conn., 7 Feb. 1754, Oliver Davidson, b. at Mansfield, Conn., 17 June 1734, d. aft. 15 Dec. 1761,

EUNICE DAVIDSON, b. at Mansfield, Conn., 13 June 1757, d. at Potsdam, N.Y., 29 June 1849; m. at Windham, Conn., 29 Mar. 1781, Sylvanus Willes, b. at Windham, Conn., 26 Mar. 1756/7, d. at Potsdam, N.Y., 18 Aug. 1841,

ELIZABETH (BETSEY) WILLES, b. at Windham, Conn., 20 Aug. 1786, d. at Chicago, Ill., 30 May 1871; m. at Royalton, Vt., 3 May 1808, Nathaniel Dunham, b. at Hardwick, Mass., 18 Dec. 1780, d. at Potsdam, N.Y., 2 Aug. 1848,

LOUISA WILLES DUNHAM, b. at Milton, Vt., 20 Aug. 1809, d. at Paterson, N.J., 8 June 1880; m. at Burlington, Vt., 19 May 1830, Jacob Carter Robie, b. at Concord, N.H., 4 Aug. 1808, d. at Binghampton, N.Y., 15 Apr. 1887,

EDWARD DUNHAM ROBIE, b. at Burlington, Vt., 11 Sept. 1831, d. at Washington, D.C., 7 June 1911; m. at Lisle, Broome Co., N.Y., 3 June 1858, Helen Adams, b. at Killawog, N.Y., 21 Aug. 1834, d. at Washington, D.C., 22 Nov. 1919,

LAURA ADAMS ROBIE, b. at Marathon, N.Y., 14 July 1876, d. at Tampa, Fla., 24 July 1934; m. at Washington, D.C., 30 Apr. 1902, Albert Gilbert Grunwell, b. at Arlington, Va., 1 May 1873, d. at Beaufort, S.C., 18 Sept. 1949,

JANE ELIZABETH GRUNWELL, b. 23 Dec. 1909, at Washington, D.C., ed.: Miss Mason's School, The Castle; Weylister Jr. College; George Washington Univ.; member: DAR, organizing Vice Regent and past Regent, Big Cypress Chapter, Naples, Fla.; Society of Mayflower Descendants, organizing member and Secretary, Myles Standish Colony, Naples Fla.; Nat'l Huguenot Soc. of Fla.; Order of the Crown of Charlemagne in the United States of America; American Foreign Service Association; Diplomatic and Consular Officers, Retired; member of both the Executive and Steering Committees of the Collier Co. (Fla.) Bicentennial Committee (1974-1976).

Chapter LXXIV

WELBY — FARWELL — SPALDING — SPAULDING — DAVIDSON — WILLES — DUNHAM — ROBIE — GOFF — PRATT — GARDNER

CHARLEMAGNE

(See Chapter LXXIII)

LOUISA WILLES DUNHAM, b. at Milton, Vt., 20 Aug. 1809, d. at Paterson, N.J., 8 June 1880; m. at Burlington, Vt., 19 May 1830, Jacob Carter Robie, b. at Concord, N.H., 4 Aug. 1808, d. at Binghamton, N.Y., 15 Apr. 1887,

ELLEN CARTER ROBIE, b. at Binghamton, N.Y., 1 Jan. 1834, d. at Buffalo, N.Y., 6 Jan. 1920; m. at Binghamton, N.Y., 27 Dec. 1855, Henry Augustus Goff, b. at Chatham, Conn., 20 Aug. 1834, d. at Binghamton, N.Y., 20 Apr. 1903,

LILLIE BELLE GOFF, b. at Binghamton, N.Y., 3 Feb. 1857, d. at Ithaca, N.Y., 8 Aug. 1910; m. at Binghamton, N.Y., 15 Aug. 1878, Charles Clarence Pratt, b. at New Milford, Pa., 23 Apr. 1854, d. at Binghamton, N.Y., 27 Jan. 1916,

HELEN LEE PRATT, b. at New Milford, Pa., 9 July 1897; grad.: Mrs. Scoville's Classical School, New York City; New York School of Fine and Applied Art; m. 15 Oct. 1930, at Ithaca, N.Y., Leland Grisier Gardner, b. at Bryan, Ohio, 15 Jan. 1892,

1) GEOFFREY LELAND GARDNER, b. 20 Apr. 1933, m. Susan Anne Whitener;

2) HENRY PRATT GARDNER, b. 15 Oct. 1934, m. Arden Dunning;

273

3) NANCY ELIZABETH GARDNER, b. 29 May 1936, m. Alan Cassels;

4) LELAND GRISIER GARDNER, b. 4 Nov. 1939, d. 3 Dec. 1963.

Chapter LXXV

WELBY — FARWELL — GATES — WHEELER — MERRIAM — HOWELL — ROWLAND — SETTLE

CHARLEMAGNE

(See Chapter LXXIII)

OLIVE WELBY (WELBIE) bapt. at Moulton, co. Lincoln, England, 1604, d. at Chelmsford, Mass., 1 Mar. 1691/2; m. 16 Apr. 1629, at Boston, co. Lincoln, Eng., Henry Farwell, b. in England, ca. 1605, d. at Chelmsford, Mass., 1 Aug. 1670,

ENSIGN JOSEPH FARWELL, b. at Concord, Mass., 26 Feb. 1640/1, d. at Dunstable, Mass., 31 Dec. 1722; m. 25 Dec. 1666, at Chelmsford, Mass., Hannah Learned, b. 25 Aug. 1649, d. aft. 1722,

WILLIAM FARWELL, b. at Chelmsford, Mass., 15/21 Jan. 1688, d. 27 July 1756; m. 20 July 1710, Elizabeth Soldine, b. at Dunstable, Mass., 6 Mar. 1685, d. at Harvard, Mass., dau. of John and Elizabeth (Usher) Soldine,

ELIZABETH FARWELL, b. at Groton, Mass., 2 Nov. 1713, d. at Groton, Mass.; m. 12 Jan. 1730, Jonathan Gates, d. at Harvard, Mass., 24 Dec. 1772,

JOHN GATES, b. at Harvard, Mass., 31 Oct. 1749; m. 28 Feb. 1773, at Ashburnham, Mass., Catherine Coolidge, b. at Ashburnham, Mass., 3 May 1755,

BETTY (GATES) WHEELER, b. at Ashburnham, Mass., 18 Dec. 1780; m. (second) 4 May 1809, Joseph Merriam, Jr., b. at Bedford, Mass., 19 Aug. 1785, d. 11 Oct. 1850,

NANCY KEYES MERRIAM, b. at Chesterfield, N.H., 26 Oct. 1819, d. at Oxford, Miss., 25 Nov. 1896; m. at Baltimore, Md., 20 June 1843, Benjamin Prosser Howell, b. in Gloucester Co., N. J., 10 Sept. 1810, d. at Oxford, Miss., 25 Feb. 1892,

THE REV. FRANK MERRIAM HOWELL, b. at Memphis, Tenn., 24 June 1849, d. at Somerville, Tenn., 21 Oct. 1878; m. at Oxford, Miss., 14 May 1872, V. Fredonia Shive, b. in Lafayette Co., Miss., 1848, d. at Oxford, Miss., 11 May 1885,

NANNIE EMMALINE HOWELL, b. at Princeton, Ark., 16 Feb. 1873, d. at Arkadelphia, Ark., 21 June 1909; m. at Oxford, Miss., 19 Jan. 1893, William Thomas Rowland, M.D., b. at Arkadelphia, Ark., 17 Mar. 1870, d. at Arkadelphia, Ark., 26 Nov. 1939,

1) FREDONIA ROWLAND, b. at Arkadelphia, Ark., 24 June 1894; ed.: Henderson-Brown College, Arkadelphia, Ark.; member: DAR, past Regent of two chapters, organizing Treasurer of the Arkadelphia Chapter; Huguenot Society of Washington, D.C., past Vice President; Nat'l Soc. Colonial Daughters of the XVII Century, two terms as Nat'l Councillor, President of Jamestown Chapter, 1951-57; D.C.W. in Commonwealth of Va., 3rd and 2nd V.P.; Order of the Crown of Charlemagne in the United States of America; National Society Colonial Dames of America; m. at Arkadelphia, Ark., 20 Aug. 1917, Henry Jefferson Richardson, b. at Maynard, Ark., 31 Mar. 1895.

2) WILLIAM THOMAS ROWLAND, JR., b. at Arkadelphia, Ark., 20 Apr. 1896, d. at Lexington, Ky., 9 July 1949; m. at Fordyce, Ark., 20 Jan. 1919, Della May Thomas, b. at Wilmer, Miss., 26 Mar. 1898,

a) FRANCES ROWLAND, b. at Searcy, Ark., 15 Nov. 1923; University of Ky., B.A.; served as President of the Junior League of Lexington, Ky.; member: Order of the Crown of Charlemagne in the United States of America; m. at Lexington, Ky., 16 May 1944, Robert Eulace Settle, Jr., b. at Elizabethtown, Ky., 20 July 1921,

i) ROBERT EULACE SETTLE III, b. 8 Aug. 1947 at Lexington, Ky.; m. at Rome, Ga., 15 Nov. 1969, Karen Sue Boggs, b. at Rome, Ga., 18 Feb. 1947,

    1) ROBERT EULACE SETTLE, IV, b. at Atlanta, Ga., 21 Oct. 1974.

Chapter LXXVI

WELBY — FARWELL — FLINT — HARSHMAN

CHARLEMAGNE

(See Chapter LXXIII)

OLIVE WELBY (WELBIE) bapt. at Moulton, co. Lincoln, England, 1604, d. at Chelmsford, Mass., 1 Mar. 1691/2; m. 16 Apr. 1629, at Boston, co. Lincoln, Eng., Henry Farwell, b. in England, ca. 1605, d. at Chelmsford, Mass., 1 Aug. 1670,

ENS. JOSEPH FARWELL, b. at Concord, Mass., 26 Feb. 1640/1, d. at Dunstable, Mass., (So. Nashua, N.H.) 31 Dec. 1722; m. 25 Dec. 1666, at Chelmsford, Mass., Hannah Learned, b. 25 Aug. 1649, d. aft. 1722,

JOSEPH FARWELL, b. at Chelmsford, Mass., 24 July 1670, d. at Groton, Mass., 20/21 Aug. 1740; m. at Chelmsford, Mass., 23 Jan. 1695/6, Hannah Colburn of Chelmsford, Mass., liv. 10 Mar. 1740/1,

DANIEL FARWELL, b. at Groton, Mass., 20 May 1717, d. at Fitchburg, Mass., 15 Jan. 1808; m. at Andover, Mass., 3 July 1739, Mary Moor, b. at Andover, Mass., 10 July 1718,

ISAAC FARWELL, b. at Groton, Mass., 28 Mar. 1744, d. at New Ipswich, N.H., ante 27 May 1786; m. at Groton, Mass., 6 Dec. 1770, Lucy Page, b. at Groton, Mass., 1 June 1750, d. at Groton, Mass., 27 Dec. 1814,

LUCY FARWELL, b. at New Ipswich, N.H., 3 Nov. 1771, d. in Washington Co., Ohio, 24 July 1849; m. at Fitchburg, Mass., 30 Dec. 1790, Porter Flint, b. at North Reading, Mass., 6 Sept. 1763, d. in Washington Co., Ohio, in July 1834,

LUTHER FLINT, b. at Dorset, Vt., 25 Apr. 1815, d. in Brown Co., Ind., 13 Jan. 1903; m. in Washington Co., Ohio, 10 Dec. 1835, Mary R. Edwards, b. in Washington Co., Ohio, 22 May 1815, d. in Brown Co., Ind., 23 Feb. 1871,

JAMES P. FLINT, b. in Washington Co., Ohio, 13 Apr. 1843, d. at Morgantown, Ind., 22 Oct. 1921; m. Washington Co., Ohio, 5 Sept. 1863, Isabelle Livingston, b. in Belmont Co., Ohio, 12 Jan. 1846, d. at Morgantown, Ind., 14 Oct. 1918,

ALBERT MAYWOOD FLINT, b. in Brown Co., Ind., 18 June 1870, d. at Havre, Mont., 10 Sept. 1930; m. at Monticello, Ill., 27 Apr. 1889, Maud Elizabeth Crabb, b. in Brown Co., Ind., 5 Oct. 1872, d. at Whittemore, Mich., 26 Dec. 1952,

LIDA ISABELL FLINT, b. at Sandusky, Ohio, 16 Feb. 1900; ed.: Omaha Univ., Nebraska; member: Ohio Genealogical Society, past President, past Chairman of the Board; DAR; D.A.C., past State General Records Chairman; Huguenot Society; Daughters of Founders and Patriots of America; Nat'l Society of New England Women; Order of the Crown of Charlemagne in the United States of America; m. at Charleston, S.C., 7 Sept. 1918, Willard Almon Harshman, b. at Mineral Ridge, Ohio, 4 Jan. 1894,

1) MARY CATHERINE HARSHMAN, b. 1 Apr. 1936; m. (first) David L. Behrendt (div.), (second) Harold Provence (dec.);

2) CYRIL ALBERT HARSHMAN, b. 25 Mar. 1937;

3) CORA ELIZABETH HARSHMAN, b. 28 July 1938; m. Lester C. Bartholow, Jr.;

4) VERN ROSS HARSHMAN, adopted son, b. 15 Sept. 1938; m. Mary Harden.

Chapter LXXVII

WILLOUGHBY — LYNDE

CHARLEMAGNE

(See Chapter X)

ROGER DE QUINCY, 2nd Earl of Winchester, Constable of Scotland, accompanied his father on the Fifth Crusade, 1219, d. 25 Apr. 1264; m.˙Helen of Galloway, d. 1245, dau. of Alan, Lord of Galloway, Constable of Scotland,

ELENA DE QUINCY, d. ca. 20 Aug. 1296; m. Sir Alan la Zouche, d. 1260/70, Baron Zouche of Ashby la Zouche, co. Leicester, Constable of the Tower of London,

EUDO LA ZOUCHE, of Haryngworth, d. 1295; m. Milicent de Cantelou, d. ca. 1299,

EVA LA ZOUCHE, d. 15 Dec. 1314; m. in 1289, Sir Maurice de Berkeley, Lord Berkeley of Berkeley Castle, b. 1281, d. May 1326 (both were under 8 years of age at their marriage, both were gr. grand children of Roger de Quincy and Helen of Galloway),

ISABEL BERKELEY, d. 25 July 1362; m. in June 1328, Robert de Clifford, Lord Clifford, b. 5 Nov. 1305, d. 20 May 1344, 5th in descent from William Longspee, Earl of Salisbury, named in Magna Charta, natural son of Henry II and Ela, Countess of Salisbury,

SIR ROGER DE CLIFFORD, Lord Clifford, Sheriff of Cumberland, Gov. of Carlisle Castle, 1377, b. 10 July 1333, d. 13 July 1389; m. Maud de Beauchamp, dau. of Thomas de Beauchamp and Katherine de Mortimer, dau. of Sir Roger de Mortimer, Earl of March, who m. 6 Oct. 1306, Joan de Geneville,

KATHERINE CLIFFORD, d. 23 Apr. 1413; m. Ralph de Greystoke, Lord Greystoke, b. 18 Oct. 1353, d. 6 Apr. 1418,

MAUDE DE GREYSTOKE, m. Eudo de Welles, (See Chapter XL, p. 137)

SIR LIONEL DE WELLES, K.G., Baron Welles, Gov. of Ireland, 1438-1442, d. at Towton, 29 Mar. 1461; m. ca. 1426, Joan de Waterton, dau. of Robert de Waterton of Yorkshire,

CICELY DE WELLES, m. Sir Robert Willoughby, of Eresby, d. 1466, son of Sir Thomas Willoughby, of Eresby, and Joan, dau. of Sir Richard FitzAlan, Knt., who d. 3 June 1419,

SIR CHRISTOPHER WILLOUGHBY, K.B., of Eresby, b. 1453; w.p. 13 July 1499; m. Margaret, dau. of Sir William Jenny, Knt., of Knolleshall, co. Suffolk,

SIR THOMAS WILLOUGHBY, Chief Justice of the Common Pleas; w.d. 20 July 1544, w.p. 5 Nov. 1545; m. Bridget, dau. of Sir Robert Read, Knt., Chief Justice of the Common Pleas, of Blore Place, co. Kent,

CHRISTOPHER WILLOUGHBY, of St. George the Martyr, Southark, co Surrey, w.p. 11 Jan. 1586; m. Margery Tottishurst,

CHRISTOPHER WILLOUGHBY, of Chiddingstone, co. Kent, d. ante 1633; m. Martha — ,

COL. WILLIAM WILLOUGHBY, of London and Portsmouth, England, Commissioner of the Royal Navy, b. ca. 1588; m. Elizabeth — ,

DEP. GOV. FRANCIS WILLOUGHBY, of London, M.P., Commissioner of the Royal Navy, came to New England in 1638, was selectman, deputy, magistrate 1650-54, Deputy Gov. of Massachusetts, 1665-67, 1668-70; w.d. 4 June 1670, w.p. 10 Apr. 1671, m. (third) ca. Aug. 1658/9, Margaret (Locke) Taylor,

SUSANNA WILLOUGHBY, b. 10 Aug. 1664, at Charlestown, Mass., d. at Saybrook, Conn., 21 Feb. 1709/10; m. 1683, Nathaniel Lynde, b. 22 Nov. 1659, d. at Saybrook, Conn., 5 Oct. 1729, son of Hon. Simon Lynde (a descendant of Charlemagne) and his wife Hannah Newdigate. (See Chapter LV)

Chapter LXXVIII

WRIGHT — HACK — DRUMMOND — SELBY — GARRISON — SUDLER — TURNER

CHARLEMAGNE

(See Chapter XXXVIII)

ADELAIDE DE VERMANDOIS, b. 950, d. 975/8; m. m. (second) Geoffrey I Grisgonelle, Count of Anjou,

ERMENGARDE OF ANJOU, m. 980 Conan I, Count of Brittany, d. 992,

GEOFFREY, COUNT OF BRITTANY, b. c. 980, d. 20 Nov. 1008; m. 996, Hawise of Normandy, d. 21 Feb. 1034, dau. of Richard I, "The Fearless," Duke of Normandy,

EUDES, COUNT OF BRITTANY, b. 999, d. 7 Jan. 1079,

BARDOLF, natural son of Eudes, and brother of Bodin who held Ravensworth, Mickleton, Romanlkirk, and other lands in Richmondshire, at the time of William the Conqueror's Domesday Survey, 1086,

AKARIS FITZ BARDOLF, of Ravensworth,

HERVEY FITZ AKARIS of Ravensworth, forester of the New Forest and Arkengarthdale, Yorks., living circa 1200,

HENRY FITZ HERVEY of Ravensworth, living 16 May 1212; m. Alice, dau. of Randolf Fitz Walter of Greystoke,

RANDOLPH FITZ HENRY of Ravensworth, d. before 13 Jan. 1242/43, m. Alice, dau. of heir of Adam de Staveley, Lord of Staveley, by Alice, dau. of William Percy of Kildale,

SIR HENRY FITZ RANDOLPH, d. 1262, and buried in Jervaulx Abbey,

SIR HUGH FITZ HENRY of Ravensworth, d. Berwick-on-Tees, 12 March 1304/05, and buried in the church of Romaldkirk, Richmondshire; m. Aubrey, widow of Sir William de Steyngrave, and she was buried at Jervaulx Abbey, 25 Jan. 1302/03.

SIR HENRY FITZ HUGH, 1st BARON FITZ HUGH, d. at Ravensworth, 1356; m. (first) Eve de Bulmer, dau. of Sir John de Bulmer of Wilton in Cleveland and Bulmer, Yorks., by Tiphaine de Morewike, dau. of Sir Hugh de Morewike of Morwick, Northumberland,

ANNABEL FITZ HUGH, d. before 9 Dec. 1353; m. circa 1326/27, Sir Henry le Vavasour of Hazelwood, d. before 27 Nov. 1349,

SIR WILLIAM LE VAVASOUR of Hazelwood, b. 1334, d. between 15 Aug. and 8 Sept. 1369; m. Elizabeth Cressy, dau. of Sir Hugh Cressy, and she d. shortly before 8 Nov. 1404,

SIR HENRY LE VAVASOUR of Hazelwood, Esquire to the body of King Henry IV in 1399, d. 27 March 1413; m. Margaret Skipwith, d. 1 July 1415, dau. of Sir William Skipwith of Ornesby, Lincoln, Lord Chief Justice of England,

MARGARET LE VAVASOUR, m. Hamon Sutton of Burton-by-Lincoln, M.P. for County Lincoln 1434, living in 1452,

HAMON SUTTON, living in 1452, but died in his father's lifetime,

HAMON SUTTON of Burton-by-Lincoln, heir to his grandfather, d. 22 Dec. 1501; m. Margaret Sheffield (will dated 1 Oct. 1525), dau. of Sir Robert Sheffield of Butterwick, Lincoln, ancestor of the Dukes of Buckingham,

HAMON SUTTON, of Washingborough, Lincoln (will proved 2 March 1556/57); m. Emlyn Disney (will proved 5 Jan. 1557/58), dau. of Richard Disney of Fulbeck, Lincoln,

MARY SUTTON, m. Thomas Yorke of Ashby de la Launde, Lincoln, d. 7 Sept. 1574,

MARY YORKE, d. 27 Feb. 1596/97, buried in Lincoln Cathedral; m. Thomas Randes of Nettleham, Lincoln, d. 17 Feb. 1608(09, son of Henry Randes, D.D., Bishop of Lincoln, 1547,

MARY RANDES, d. at York between 26 Feb. 1629/30 and 13 Oct. 1630; m. George Merriton, D.D., educated at St. John's College, Cambridge, Rector of Hadleigh, Suffolk, 1599 Dean of York, 1617 Chaplain to Queen Anne, wife of King James I of England, d. 23 Dec. 1624, bur. in York Cathedral,

ANNE MERRITON, d. 19 March 1670; m. in Yorkshire, 1626, Francis Wright *(Paver's Marriage Licenses)* of Bolton-upon-Swaile, Yorks., son of Francis Wright and his wife, Grace Beckwith, dau. of Roger Beckwith of Aldborough, Yorks., d. 1665,

RICHARD WRIGHT, 4th son, settled in Northumberland County, Virginia, early in 1655, where he served as a justice of the county from 1657 until his death, he had a patent for 2,200 acres in Westmoreland County, Virginia, along the Potomac River, dated 7 Oct. 1658, which included land left to his wife by her father, b. probably in Yorkshire, circa 1633, d. at Chickacone (Chickacoan), Northumberland Co., Va., shortly before 10 Dec. 1663 when his will was proved; m. at Northumberland Co., Va., 1656, Anne Mottrom, dau. of Col. John Mottram of Chickacone (d. 1655), b. circa 1639, d. after 1680, [she married secondly, before 16 Oct. 1665, David Fox, Sr., a justice of Lancaster Co., Va. (d. before 6 Jan. 1669/70, and thirdly, Col. St. Leger Codd (bur. St. Paul's Parish, Kent Co., Md., 9 Feb. 1707/08) a burgess for Lancaster and Northumberland counties, and had issue by all her husbands.]

ANNE WRIGHT, b. Northumberland Co., Va. circa 1660, d. Accomack Co., Va., before 20 March 1704/05; m. Lt. Col. George Nicholas Hack of Accomack Co., Va., son of Dr. George (Joris) Hack, by his wife, Anna Varleth, dau. of Casper and Judith (Taintenier) Varleth of Utrecht, Netherlands and New Amsterdam, d. Accomack Co., Va., between 20 March 1704/05 and 4 Apr. 1705,

285

ANNE HACK, b. in Accomack Co., Va., circa 1695, d. in Accomack Co., Va., between 27 Sept. and 27 Nov. 1770, as the widow of Alexander Buncle of Allhallows Parish, Worcester Co., Md.; m. (first) at Accomack Co., Va., after 18 Feb. 1711, Capt. Richard Drummond of Hunting Creek, Accomack Co., Va., son of Capt. Richard and Ann (Tilney) Drummond, d. at Accomack Co., Va., between 9 June 1730 and 4 Apr. 1732, (See Chapter XXXVII)

ANN DRUMMOND, d. at Snow Hill, Worcester Co., Md. before June 14, 1799, m. Capt. John Selby of Snow Hill, Md., son of Parker Selby (d. 1747) of Worcester Co., Md., and his wife, Mary Watts, dau. of Capt. John and Priscilla (White) (Layfield) Watts of Accomack Co., Va., shipbuilder, Judge of Worcester Co., d. at Worcester Co., before 10 Dec. 1790,

JAMES SELBY, of Worcester Co., Md., d. before 8 Dec. 1802; m. Mary (Polly, Molly) Sturgis, dau. of Capt. Outten Sturgis of Worcester Co., by his wife, Martha Purnell, dau. of Major John Purnell (d. 1742/43) of Mattapany, Worcester Co., and his third wife, Martha Bowen, dau. of William Bowen of Somerset Co.; d. Worcester Co., Md., before 9 June 1835,

NANCY (ANNE) SELBY, b. in Worcester Co., Md., circa 1789, d. at Greenwood, Sussex Co., Del., 28 July 1855, as the widow of David Pennewill (Md. 21 Oct. 1763-Greenwood, Del., 21 Oct. 1831), whom she had married as his 4th wife, on 31 Oct. 1814 (they were the grandparents of Simeon Selby Pennewill, Governor of Delaware from 1909 to 1913), m. (first) in Worcester Co., Md., by license dated 19 Aug. 1806, Jonathan Garrison of Accomack Co., Va., son of Archibald Garrison of Accomack Co., and his wife, Kesiah Floyd, dau. of Berry Floyd of Hogg Island, Northampton Co., Va., and his wife, Esther Dalby, dau. of Branson Dalby, b. in Accomack Co., va., 4 Dec. 1774, d. in Worcester Co., Md., circa 1812,

MARY ANN GARRISON, b. in Accomack Co., Va., circa 1808, d. at Bridgeville, Sussex Co., Del., 21 Oct. 1834; m. at Greenwood, Sussex Co., Del., 22 Apr. 1828, Dr. John Ralston Sudler, son of Joseph Sudler of Milford, Kent Co., Del., and his wife, Sarah Benn Ralston, dau. of John Ralston, Esq. of Milford, grandson of Capt. Emory Sudler (d. 1797) of Chestertown, Md.

who served in the American Revolution, and his wife, Martha Smyth (d. 1799), a descendant of Augustine Herman, 1st Lord of Bohemia Manor, Cecil Co., Md., educated at the University of Pennsylvania, b. at Milford, Del., 21 Aug. 1797, d. at Bridgeville, Del., 3 Apr. 1871,

JAMES SELBY SUDLER, M.D., of Bridgeville, Del., educated at Jefferson College, Philadelphia, b. at Bridgeville, Del., 12 July 1831, d. at Bridgeville, Del., 1 Aug. 1863; m. at Laurel, Del., 24 July 1856, Sarah Ann Hitch, dau. of State Sen. William Hitch of Hitch's Mills, Laurel, Del., and his wife, Miranda S. Short, dau. of Philip Short of Sycamore, Del., by his wife, Nancy Hill, dau. of Elzey Hill, granddaughter paternally of Levin Hitch of Laurel Del., and his wife, Nancy Bacon, dau. of Dudson Bacon (d. 1783), b. at Laurel, Del., 22 June 1835, d. at Asbury Park, N.J., 11 Oct. 1924, as the widow of Frank E. Smith, whom she had m. secondly, 17 Oct. 1866, and by whom she had further issue,

ELIZABETH ELLEN SUDLER, b. Laurel, Del. 14 June 1863, d. New York City, 7 Feb. 1905 (as the wife of David A. Himaidi, whom she had m. at Brooklyn, N.Y., 10 Dec. 1900); m. (first) at Wilmington, Del., 27 March 1883, Henry Clay Turner, the son of Jane Elliott, and adopted son of Capt. Brooke Turner of Wilmington, educated at St. Mary's College, Wilmington, admitted to the Bar of New Castle Co., Del., 24 May 1875, partner in the firm of Turner and Sharpley (Harry Sharpley), City Solicitor of Wilmington, 1881-July 1887, b. at Wilmington, Del., 7 July 1848, d. at Wilmington, Del., 3 Dec. 1897, Issue:

1.) JOSEPH M. TURNER, educated at Syracuse University and New York Law School, served as a New Jersey Supreme Court Commissioner, Master in Chancery and City Attorney of Asbury Park, N.J., b. at Wilmington, Del., 7 Jan. 1884, d. at Interlaken, N.J., 16 Feb. 1946; m. at Richmond, Va., 18 Dec. 1916, Kate Chamberlain Taylor, dau. of Wirt Edwin and Kate Evans (Chamberlain) Taylor of Richmond, Granddau. of James Marshall and Isabelle de Leon (Jacobs) Taylor of Richmond, educated at St. Catherine's School,

287

Richmond; Oldfield, Glencoe, Md., b. at Richmond, Va., May 20, 1893, d. at Red Bank, N.J., 29 Oct. 1959, Issue:

a) JOSEPH SUDLER TURNER, educated at Phillips Exeter Academy, Exeter, N.H., Rutgers University, New Brunswick, N.J., and the Parsons School of Design, N.Y.C., served in the U.S. Army in World War II, member of the Order of Colonial Lords of Manors in America, b. at 1201 Sunset Ave., Asbury Park, N.J., Jan. 3, 1918;

b) EDITH CHAMBERLAIN TURNER, educated at the University of North Carolina, Greensboro, N.C., member of the Order of Colonial Lords of Manors in America, b. at 1201 Sunset Ave., Asbury Park, N.J., 20 July 1919; m. Houston, Texas, 22 Feb. 1954, Feargus Michael O'Connor, son of Peter Francis O'Connor (1865-1950) and his wife, Agnes Thomasina Clunan (1878-196-), dau. of Michael Clunan (1826-1882) of Cork, Ire., and his wife, Alice, dau. of James Daniel of Carlisle, Northumberland, Eng., grandson of James O'Connor (d. 23 May 1913), and his wife, Margaret Henry, formerly of Houston, Texas, now of Daphne, Alabama, Issue:

> i) FEARGUS MICHAEL O'CONNOR, educated at Tulane University, New Orleans, La., b. at Houston, Texas, 18 Sept. 1954.

> ii) PETER FRANCIS O'CONNOR, educated at Duke University, b. at Houston, Texas, 18 Sept. 1954.

> iii) JAMES JOSEPH O'CONNOR, educated at Texas Agricultural and Mechanical University, b. at Houston, Texas, 4 May 1956.

> iv) KATE CHAMBERLAIN O'CONNOR, educated at the Ethel Walker School, Simsbury, Conn., b. at Houston, Texas, 19 Dec. 1957.

v) MOIRA O'CONNOR, b. at Houston, Texas, 23 June 1959.

c) SARAH ANN TURNER, educated at the University of North Carolina, Greensboro, N.C., Bouve, Boston, Mass. and Katherine Gibbs, N.Y.C., b. at the Ann May Hospital, Spring Lake, N.J., 30 Sept. 1920, m. at Little Silver, N.J., 12 Aug. 1944, John Charles Pistell, son of Clarence Kerr and Hazel (Cook) Pistell of Rumson, N.J., educated at the Taft School, and Yale University, b. Buffalo, N.Y., 14 Sept. 1920, Issue:

    i) JOHN CHAMBERLAIN PISTELL, educated at the Rumson Country Day School, Rumson, M.J.; St. Andrew's School, Middletown, Del; Hobart College, Geneva, N.Y. and the University of California at Berkeley, b. at Long Branch, N.J., 31 Jan. 1949; m. at St. Luke's in the Fields, N.Y.C., 4 Dec. 1976, Anne Louise Fleckenstein, dau. of William Owen and Jean (Swarts) Fleckenstein of Colts Neck, N.J., educated at Cornell University, Ithaca, N.Y., the University of California at Berkeley, and Columbia University, N.Y.C., b. Morristown, N.J., 14 Sept. 1953.

    ii) LAURENCE TURNER PISTELL, educated at the Rumson Country Day School, Rumson, N.J.; St. Andrew's School, Middletown, Del.; Brentwood School, Brentwood, Essex, Eng.; Trinity College, Hartford, Conn.; The University of Dublin, Dublin, Ire.; The University of Chicago; and the Fletcher School of Diplomacy, Mass., b. at Long Branch, N.J., 28 March 1951.

    iii) JOSEPH KERR PISTELL, educated at the Rumson Country Day School, Rumson, N.J.; St. Andrew's School, Middletown, Del.; Tufts College, Medford, Mass. (studied in London in his junior year), b. at

289

Long Branch, N.J., 6 Nov. 1952, m. at St. Mark's Episcopal Church, Louisville, Ky., 13 Aug. 1977, Frances Powell Heyburn, dau. of Henry Reuter Heyburn and his wife, Frances Powell Starks, dau. of the late Franklin Fergusson Starks of Louisville, b. at Louisville, 22 Dec. 1952.

iv) ANNE ELIZABETH PISTELL, educated at the Rumson Country Day School, Rumson, N.J.; St. Catherine's School, Richmond, Va.; Rumson High School; The University of Colorado and the University of New Hampshire, b. at Long Branch, N.J., 15 Apr. 1954.

d) ALICE MARSHALL TURNER, educated at the Francis Robinson Duff Dramatic Academy, N.Y.C., b. at the Ann May Hospital, Spring Lake, N.J., 5 Apr. 1922, m. at New York City, 7 Aug. 1948, Roland (Paul) Werner Anderson, son of Adrian Werner Anderson of Goteborg, Sweden and Rensselaerville, N.Y. and his wife, Oscaria Jacobson, dau. of Gustave Jacobson of Goteborg, educated at Middlebury College, Middlebury, Vt., and Fordham University, Bronx, N.Y., b. at Rosslindale (Boston), Mass., 22 Dec. 1917, Issue:

i) CHRISTOPHER TAYLOR ANDERSON, educated at Middlebury College, Middlebury, Vt., and the University of Virginia, Charlottesville, Va., b. at Long Branch, N.J., 15 Aug. 1951.

ii) CRAIG MARSHALL ANDERSON, educated at the University of Virginia, Charlottesville, Va., b. at Long Branch, N.J., 12 June 1955.

2) NATALIE SUDLER TURNER, educated at Swarthmore College, Swarthmore, Penn., b. at Wilmington, Del., 20 Dec. 1888, d. at Great Barrington, Mass., 7 Jan. 1957; m. at Asbury Park, N.J., 30 June 1921, Stuart-Menteth

Beard II, b. at Canandaigua, N.Y., 28 Nov. 1893, d. at Sheffield Mass., 8 Sept. 1955 (see Chapter LIV).

3) HENRY CLAY TURNER, JR. (orginally named Ralston Turner), educated at Bordentown Military Academy, Bordentown, N.J., and Rutgers University, New Brunswick, N.J., b. at Wilmington, N.J., 9 July 1893, d. at Trenton, N.J., 19 Oct. 1951; m. at Ashton, R.I., 9 Aug. 1935, by the Rev. Sydney Peters, to Sara Kelsall Kirk, dau. of William Fell Kirk of Philadelphia and Holidaysburg, Penn., by his wife, Sally Krebs, dau. of Philip Krebs of Tamocqua, Penn., educated at Swarthmore College, Swarthmore, Penn., class of 1911, b. at Holidaysburg, Penn., 1 Nov. 1888, d. at Princeton, N.J., 26 May 1971.

Chapter LXXIX

WYCHE — POOLE — ADAMS — MOORE — CARTLAND

CHARLEMAGNE

(See Chapter LXX)

ARNULF I, Count of Flanders, b. 890, d. 27 Mar. 964; m. Alix de Vermandois, d. 958/60, dau. of Herbert II, Count de Vermandois (a descendant of Charlemagne, see Chapter LXVIII)

ELSTRUDE, of Flanders, m. Sigfred, Count of Guines, d. 965,

HALOISE DE GUINES, m. Crispin de Bec, d. 968, son of Grunald, Prince of Monaco,

GILBERT CRISPIN, Lord of Tillie, liv. 1030/1066; m. Gunnore d'Ainon, dau. of Baldrick, the Teuton,

HESILA (ELISA) CRISPIN, m. ca. 1044, Lord William Malet, follower of William the Conqueror,

GILBERT MALET, of Curry Malet, liv. 1078. 1086; m. a dau. of DeCorreole,

ROBERT MALET, Baron of Curry Malet, liv. 1130,

WILLIAM MALET, d. 1169; m. Maud Mortimer,

GILBERT MALET, of Curry Malet, d. 1194; m. Alice Picot, dau. of Ralph Picot, Sheriff of Kent,

SIR WILLIAM MALET, Lord of Curry and Shepton in Somersetshire, b. ca. 1174, d. 1217, served with King Richard in Normandy, 1195, served with King John in Poitou in campaign ended by defeat of King John at the Battle of Bouvines, 27 July

1214, 1211 Sheriff of Dorset and Somerset, 1215, Magna Charta Surety; m. Aliva (Alice) Basset d. 1220, dau. of Thomas Basset, of Headington,

HELEWISE (HAWISE) MALET, m. (first) ante 23 Mar. 1216/7, Sir Hugh Poyntz, Lord of Curry Malet, d. Apr. 1220, son of Nicholas Poyntz and his wife Julian Bardolf,

SIR NICHOLAS POYNTZ, Lord of Curry Malet, b. 1220, d. ante 7 Oct. 1273; m. Elizabeth Dyall, dau. of Timothy Dyall, Esq.,

HUGH POYNTZ, Knt., Lord of Curry Malet, First Baron Poyntz, b. 25 Aug. 1252, d. ante 4 Jan. 1307/8; fought in Wales 1277-94, M.P. 1295-1307; m. Margaret Paveley, dau. of Sir William Paveley,

SIR NICHOLAS POYNTZ, Knt., Second Baron Poyntz, b. ca. 1278, d. ante 12 July 1311; M.P. 1308-1311; m. (first) ante 20 Jan. 1287/8, Elizabeth LaZouche (See Chapter XIX, p 216)

NICHOLAS POYNTZ, of Hoo, co. Kent, 2nd son, d. ante 2 May 1337; m. ante 1 June 1330, Margaret Paynell, dau. of Sir Walter Paynell,

NICHOLAS POYNTZ, Esq., b. co. Kent, d. at North Okenden, co Essex, 1372,

PONTIUS POYNTZ, Esq., of North Okenden, co. Essex, liv. 1393; m. Eleanor Baldwin, liv. 1393,

SIR JOHN POYNTZ, Knt., of North Okenden, co. Essex, d. 1447 (w.d. 12 Mar. 1446/7); m. Eleanor dau. of Sir. John Deincote,

JOHN POYNTZ, of North Okenden, w.d. 15 Apr. 1469; m. Matilda Perth, dau. of William Perth of Aveley, Essex,

WILLIAM POYNTZ, Esq., of North Okenden, co. Essex, d. 1494; m. Elizabeth Shaw, dau. of Sir Edmund Shaw, Sheriff, 1474; Lord Mayor of London, 1484,

THOMAS POYNTZ, Esq., b. at North Okenden, co. Essex, d. at London, 5 May 1562; m. Ann Calva, dau. of John Calva (a German),

SUSANNA POYNTZ, w.d. 16 Nov. 1612, d. 1613, bur. at South Okenden; m. Sir Richard Saltonstall, Knt., Lord Mayor of London, 1597/8 (Sir Richard Saltonstall, one of the founders of the Massachusetts Bay Colony, was his nephew),

ELIZABETH SALTONSTALL, m. 18 Dec. 1583/4, Richard Wyche, Gent., b. in England, 1554, d. at London, England, 20 Nov. 1621,

THE REV, HENRY WYCHE I, b. in co. Surry, England, 7 Oct. 1604, d. prob. in Surry, England, Sept. 1678; m. Ellen Bennett, dau. of Ralph Bennett, of Old Palace Yard, Westminster,

HENRY WYCHE II, b. 27 Jan. 1648, in co. Surry, England, d. in Surry Co., Virginia, w.p. 18 Mar. 1714,

GEORGE WYCHE I, Gent., b. in Va., d. in Sussex Co., Va., w.p. 15 July 1757

GEORGE WYCHE II, b. in Va., d. in Greensville Co., Va., w.p. 20 June 1781; m. Sarah Peters, d. in Va.,

PETER WYCHE, b. in Greensville Co., Va., 30 Oct. 1748, d. in Brunswick Co., Va., 10 Dec. 1803; m. in Va., 27 Dec. 1775, Elizabeth Jenkins, b. in Greensville Co., Va. 1755, d. in Brunswick Co., Va., 17 June 1816,

JAMES WYCHE, b. in Greensville Co., Va., 25 Dec. 1785, d. at Raleigh, N.C., 28 Mar. 1845; m. in Va., 21 Apr. 1806, Pamela Evans, b. in Cumberland Co., Va., 28 Feb. 1789, d. in Vance Co., N.C., 28 Feb. 1869,

BENJAMIN WYCHE, b. in Granville Co., N.C., 22 Oct. 1829, d. in Vance Co., N.C., 9 July 1887; m. in Halifax Co., N.C., 21 Nov. 1854, Sarah Elizabeth Hunter, b. in Halifax Co., N.C., 28 Sept. 1832, d. in Vance Co., N.C., 22 July 1871,

SARAH ELIZABETH WYCHE, b. in Vance Co., N.C., 24 Feb. 1866, d. at Greensboro, N.C., 1 Nov. 1944; m. at Henderson, N.C.,

19 Dec. 1894, Ezekiel Poole, b. at Northampton, England, 17 Mar. 1867, d. at Greensboro, N.C., 14 June 1915,

1) ALICE HUNTER POOLE, b. at Greensboro, N.C., 21 Feb. 1897; grad.: University of N.C., at Greensboro; member: DAR, chapter registrar, sec'y.; U.C. Book Club, president; Gastonia Garden Club, sec'y; Women of First Presbyterian Church, treas., sec'y.; Order of the Crown of Charlemagne in the United States of America; m. at Greensboro, N.C., 3 July 1918, Edward Clarence Adams, b. in York Co., S.C., 26 Sept. 1887, d. at Gastonia, N.C., 19 Feb. 1956,

  a) JANE WYCHE ADAMS, b. 10 Mar. 1922, at Gastonia, N.C.; A.B., University of N.C., Greensboro, grad. studies, University of N.C., Chapel Hill, Appalachian State University, Boone, N.C., U.N.C., Charlotte, Columbia University, New York City; member: U.N.C. Alumni Assoc.; State and National Teachers Assocs.; DAR; Order of the Crown of Charlemagne in the United States of America; Gaston Country Club; River Hills Plantation Club, York Co., S.C.; m. 27 Aug. 1949, David Wyatt Moore, b. at Gastonia, N.C., 22 Apr. 1923.

    i) JANE WYATT MOORE, b. 23 Dec. 1950; 1971, grad., St. Mary's Jr. College, Raleigh, N.C., pres. of senior class; 1973, grad. U.N.C., Chapel Hill, A.B., pledged Chi Omega Sorority; 1976, Master in Ed., Florida Atlantic Univ., Boca Raton, Fla.; member: Order of the Crown of Charlemagne in the United States of America;

    ii) DAVID WYCHE MOORE, b. 19 Nov. 1954;

    iii) EDWARD ADAMS MOORE, b. 24 July 1957.

2) SARAH POOLE, b. 8 Apr. 1899, ed.: Univ. of N.C., Greensboro; charter member, Garden Makers; charter member, Twentieth Century Book Club; Chief Marshall,

American Contract Bridge League; member, Order of the Crown of Charlemagne in the United States of America; m. (first) at Greensboro, N.C., 12 Oct. 1922, Herbert Hardy Cartland, b. at Greensboro, N.C., 16 June 1897, d. at Miami, Fla., 6 Jan. 1956; m. (second) 6 Sept. 1963, Wilson Stuart Mitchell. Issue by first marriage.

a) WILLIAM HOUSTON CARTLAND, b. at Greensboro, N.C., 19 Mar. 1925; B.S., University of Miami, member: Order of the Crown of Charlemagne in the United States of America; m. in Dade Co., Fla., 6 Apr. 1950, Elizabeth A. Deming, b. at Cornish, N.H., 17 July 1924,

   i) CAROL ANNE CARTLAND, b. 17 May 1952; m. 30 Dec. 1976, at Cocoa Beach, Fla., Scott Busby;

   ii) JAMES POOLE CARTLAND, b. at Miami, Fla., 25 Sept. 1953; ed.: University of South Fla., Brevard Community College, Univ. of Calif. at Santa Barbara, (B.S. in Math., magnu cum laude) Fla. Technological Univ., grad. work in Math. at Univ. of Hawaii.; member; Order of the Crown of Charlemagne in the United States of America; m. at Seattle, Wash., 29 Dec. 1975, Marcia E. Muramatsu, b. at Renton, Wash., 24 Apr. 1954;

b) RICHARD WYCHE CARTLAND, b. at Greensboro, N.C., 11 Apr. 1929; B.S. Univ. of N.C., Chapel Hill; grad. Officers Training School, San Diego, Lt. j.g. U.S.N.; member; Alpha Kappa Fraternity, Order of the Crown of Charlemagne in the United States of America; m. at Greensboro, N.C., 27 June 1952, Kathleen Cousins Deans, b. at Greensboro, N.C., 21 Sept. 1929,

   i) LAURA LEE CARTLAND

ii) SARAH WYCHE CARTLAND, b. 24 Aug. 1957;

iii) KATHLEEN DEANS CARTLAND, b. 11 Aug. 1962.

3) JAMES WYCHE POOLE, b. at Greensboro, N.C., 24 Oct. 1903; grad.: Univ. of N.C., Chapel Hill; member: N.C. Bankers Conference, 1938/9; High Point Chamber of Commerce, past president; Greensboro Chamber of Commerce, director; Rotary Club of Greensboro; Emerywood Country Club, past president; Greensboro Country Club, director; Country Club of N.C. (Pinehurst); Southern Seniors Golf Assoc.; Tarheel State Seniors Golf Assoc.; International Seniors Amateur Golf Society; Three Score and Ten Club; Lt. Cmdr. U.S.N.(R);SAR; Order of the Crown of Charlemagne in the United States of America; m. at High Point, N.C., 8 June 1935, Alice Elizabeth Freeze, b. at High Point, N.C., 3 Nov. 1908.

Chapter LXXX

WYCHE

CHARLEMAGNE

(See Chapter LXXIX)

HENRY WYCHE II, b. in co. Surry, England, 27 Jan. 1648, d. in Surry Co., Va., w.p. 18 Mar. 1714, name of wife unknown,

JAMES WYCHE, b. in Va., d. in Albermarle Co., Va., 1749; m. Elizabeth — , d. in Va.,

NATHANIEL WYCHE, b. in Va.; d. in Sussex Co., Va., in May 1777; m. Mary — , b. in Va., d. prob. in Va.,

NATHANIEL WYCHE, b. in Va., d. in Madison Co., Ala., 1816; m. in Brunswick Co., Va., 3 Feb. 1790, Middleton Fletcher, b. in Brunswick Co., Va., 1778, d. in Madison Co., Ala., w.d. 26 Feb. 1851,

DR. JOHN FLETCHER WYCHE, b. in Va., 1794, bur. at Plain Dealing, Ala., 30 Oct. 1856; m. 15 Dec. 1818, in Ala., Lucinda Wright, b. in Ala., 30 Jan. 1803, d. at Huntsville, Ala., 11 June 1850,

JOHN FLETCHER WYCHE, b. in Va., 3 Jan. 1834, d. at Belmont Plantation, Iberia Parish, Louisiana, 29 Nov. 1901; m. at Raymond, Miss., or Hopkinsville, Ky., in 1853, Mary Robinson Peebles, b. in Miss. or Ala., 12 Feb. 1838; d. at Belmont Plantation, Iberia Parish, La., 16 Nov. 1911,

JAMES WRIGHT WYCHE, b. at Peebles Plantation, Iberia Parish, La., 14 Apr. 1859, d. at Belmont Plantation, Iberia Parish, La., 30 Apr. 1937; m. 5 Apr. 1900, at New Iberia, La., Lucy

Malone Harrison, b. at New Orleans, La., 5 July 1874, d. at Port Arthur, Texas, 25 Aug. 1962,

JAMES WRIGHT WYCHE, JR., b. at Belmont Plantation, Iberia Parish, La., 2 Sept. 1906; B.A. in Engineering, University of Southwestern La.; Consulting Engineer; member of the Board of the Iberia Sugar Co-operative Sugar Mill, New Iberia, La.; formerly on the Board of the Federal Land Bank, New Iberia; member: Royal Arch Masons; SAR; Order of the Crown of Charlemagne in the United States of America; m. at Swarthmore, Pa., 26 Nov. 1932, Arleen Louise Snyder, b. at Pittsburgh, Pa., 12 Apr. 1905,

1) BARBARA FRANCES WYCHE, b. 11 July 1936; m. 7 July 1962, Paul J. Qualey;

2) MARY MALONE WYCHE, b. 7 Apr. 1939, member of the Order of the Crown of Charlemagne in the United States of America, DAR; m. at New Iberia, La., 29 July 1961, Glen Dale Estes, b. 15 Nov. 1936, in Oklahoma, d. at Huntsville, Ala., 26 Dec. 1972;

3) JAMES WRIGHT WYCHE III, b. 14 Aug. 1949; m. 10 Aug. 1974, Judith Jay.

Chapter LXXXI

WYCHE — BURGESS

C<small>HARLEMAGNE</small>

(See Chapter LXXIX)

J<small>AMES</small> W<small>YCHE</small>, b. in Greensville Co., Va. 25 Dec. 1785, d. at Raleigh, N.C., 28 Mar. 1845; m. in Virginia, 21 Apr. 1806, Pamela Evans, b. in Cumberland Co., Va., 28 Feb. 1789, d. in Vance Co., N.C., 28 Feb. 1869,

W<small>ILLIAM</small> E<small>VANS</small> W<small>YCHE</small>, b. in Brunswick Co., Va., 29 July 1810, d. in Henderson Co., N.C.; m. 25 June 1833, Sarah Thomas Reavis, b. in Granville Co., N.C., 8 Apr. 1818,

C<small>YRIL</small> T<small>HOMAS</small> W<small>YCHE</small>, b. at Henderson, N.C., 26 May 1837, d. at Prosperity, S.C., 3 May 1930; m. at Prosperity, S.C., in July 1884, Carrie Varina Sease, b. in Newberry Co., S.C., 2 July 1865, d. at Columbia, S.C., 4 Feb. 1958,

C<small>YRIL</small> G<small>RANVILLE</small> W<small>YCHE</small>, b. at Prosperity, S.C., 3 Sept. 1890; m. 16 June 1914, at Newberry, S.C., Mary Wheeler, b. 24 Feb. 1893, d. at New York, N.Y., 5 Jan. 1939,

M<small>ARY</small> W<small>YCHE</small>, b. 6 Nov. 1916, B.A. Randolph-Macon Woman's College, Lynchburg, Va.; M.A., Furman Univ., Greenville, S.C.; member: OBK; Junior League of Greenville, past treasurer; Greenville Symphony Association, Board; violinist with the Symphony 1948-1975; Order of the Crown of Charlemagne in the United States of America; m. 25 June 1938, Alfred Franklin Burgess, b. 1 June 1906, at Greer, S.C.,

    1) M<small>ARY</small> W<small>YCHE</small> B<small>URGESS</small>, b. 2 Oct. 1939, at Greenville, S.C.; m. 25 Aug. 1962, at Greenville, S.C., Arthur Ervin Lesesne, b. 26 April 1939, at Greenville, S.C.;

2) CAROLINE CUNNINGHAM BURGESS, b. 23 Sept. 1941, at Greenville, S.C.; m. 7 Sept. 1968, at Greenville, S.C., Benjamin R. Ansbacher, b. 12 May 1937, at Burlington, Vt.;

3) ALFRED FRANKLIN BURGESS, Jr., b. 15 Mar. 1943, at Greenville, S.C.; m. 5 June 1976 at Cambridge, Mass., Diana Martin, b. 2 Sept. 1949, at Washington, D.C.;

4) GRANVILLE WYCHE BURGESS, b. 8 Feb. 1947, at Greenville, S.C.;

5) VICTORIA WHEELER BURGESS, b. 9 Nov. 1948, at Greenville, S.C., m. Anthony Richard Pitman, b. 11 Jan. 1948, at Cambridge, England.

Chapter LXXXII

WYCHE — CLARK

CHARLEMAGNE

(See Chapter LXXIX)

JAMES WYCHE, b. in Greensville Co., Va., 25 Dec. 1785, d. at Raleigh, N.C., 28 Mar. 1845; m. in Va., 21 Apr. 1806, Pamela Evans, b. in Cumberland Co., Va., 28 Feb. 1789, d. in Vance Co., N.C., 28 Feb. 1869,

PARRY WAYNE WYCHE, b. at Brunswick, Va., 22 Dec. 1813, d. at Henderson, N.C., in 1888; m. at Henderson, N.C., 19 July 1854, Rebecca James Southall, b. at Henderson, N.C., 3 Mar. 1840, d. at Roanoke Rapids, N.C., 22 May 1915,

CLARENCE ADOLPHUS WYCHE, b. at Henderson, N.C., 14 Mar. 1878, d. at Roanoke Rapids, N.C., 19 July 1947; m. at Henderson, N.C., 20 Nov. 1902, Lemme Mae Kenzie Jordan, b. at Petersburg, Va., 9 Oct. 1878, liv. 1975,

TRAYNHAM WYCHE, b. at Roanoke Rapids, N.C., 23 Aug. 1903; B.A., Converse College, Spartanburg, S.C., grad. work University of Va., University of California, Berkeley; member: Roanoke Womens Club; Sunnyside Garden Club, past President; Order of the Crown of Charlemagne in the United States of America; m. at Roanoke Rapids, N.C., 10 June 1933, David Crockett Clark, b. at Enfield, N.C., 3 Feb. 1904,

1) DAVID CROCKETT CLARK, JR., b. 2 July 1935; m. Sally Ray Draper;

2) CLARENCE WYCHE CLARK, b. 3 Apr. 1940; grad.: Va. Technical Institute, 1962; biography in OUTSTANDING YOUNG MEN OF AMERICA, 1970; member of

the Order of the Crown of Charlemagne in the United States of America; m. 8 July 1967, at Jacksonville, Fla., Joanne Lorraine Bennett, b. at Jacksonville, Fla., 8 Nov. 1942, and has issue:

    a)   TIMOTHY WYCHE CLARK, b. 30 June 1969;

    b)   ROBIN LORRAINE CLARK, b. 29 July 1972.

Chapter LXXXIII

WYCHE — FLORY

CHARLEMAGNE

(See Chapter LXXIX)

JAMES WYCHE, b. in Greensville Co., Va., 25 Dec. 1785, d. at Raleigh, N.C., 28 Mar. 1845; m. in Va., 21 Apr. 1806, Pamela Evans, b. in Cumberland Co., Va., 28 Feb. 1789, d. in Vance Co., N.C., 28 Feb. 1869,

IRA THOMAS WYCHE, b. in Brunswick Co., Va., 14 Feb. 1816, d. at LaGrange, N.C., 24 Oct. 1880; m. at Aspen Grove, N.C., 10 Nov. 1842, Martha F. Pierce, b. at Aspen Grove, N.C., ca. 1820, d. at Thomasville, N.C., in June 1897,

IRA THOMAS WYCHE, b. at Oracoke, N.C., 16 Oct. 1887; m. at Ft. Sam Houston, Texas, 15 Dec. 1917, Mary Louise Dunn, b. at Washington, D.C., 29 Nov. 1894,

1) ELIZABETH WYCHE, b. at Washington, D.C., 15 Nov. 1919; ed.: Stephens College, Columbia, Mo.; member: Junior League of Washington, D.C., 1949-1963; Order of the Crown of Charlemagne in the United States of America; m. at Pinehurst, N.C., 13 Feb. 1954, Henry Cyril Flory, b. at Wrexham, Wales, 28 Aug. 1910,

    a) PETER CYRIL WYCHE FLORY, b. 16 Oct. 1955;

    b) ELIZABETH ALEXANDRA FLORY, b. 25 Oct. 1957;

    c) EDITH CHRISTINA FLORY, b. 8 Jan. 1959;

    d) JANET LOUISE FLORY, b. 8 Jan. 1959.

Chapter LXXXIV

YALE — IVES — BLAKESLEE — BROOKS

CHARLEMAGNE

(See Chapter LVII)

HUGH OF KEVELIOC, Earl of Chester, b. 1147, d. 1181; m. 1169, Bertrade d'Evreux de Montfort, dau. of Simon, Count of Montfort,

MABEL OF CHESTER, m. William d'Aubigny, d. Mar. 1220/1, Crusader, Earl of Arundel, (See Chapter XLIV, p. 152)

NICHOLE D'AUBIGNY, m. (first) Roger Somery, son of John Somery and Hawise de Paynell,

JOAN DE SOMERY, d. 1282; m. John LeStrange IV, of Knockin, d. 26 Feb. 1275/6,

JOHN LE STRANGE V, d. 8 Aug. 1309; m. (second) Maud de Walton,

ELIZABETH LE STRANGE, m. 8 July 1304, Gruffyd ap Madog ap Gruffyd Maelor of Rhudal and Glyndyfrdwy, b. 23 Nov. 1298,

GRUFFYDD FYCHAN, m. Helen (Ellen) dau. of Thomas ap Llewllyn ap Owen,

TWDR AP GRUFFYD FYCHAN, m. Maud. dau. of Ienaf ap Adda,

LOWRI, m. Gruffyd ap Einion of Gwyddelwern ap Gruffyd ap Llewellyn ap Gruffyd Lloyd,

EISSAU AP GRUFFYD, m. Margaret, dau. and coh. of Jenkyn of Allt Lwyn ap Ienan ap Llewellyn ap Gruffyd Lloyd,

305

DAVID LLOYD, m. Gwenhywyfar Lloyd, dau. of Richard Lloyd ap Robert Lloyd of Llwyn y Maen,

JOHN WYNN or Ial of Plas yn Ital, m. Elizabeth Mostyn (not mother of David. David's mother was Agnes Lloyd)

REV. DAVID YALE, D.L.C., nat. son, d. 1626; m. Frances, dau. of John Lloyd ap David Lloyd,

THOMAS YALE, b. at Plas Grono, Wales, d. 1619; m. Ann Lloyd, b. at Chester, England, dau. of Rt. Rev. George Lloyd, d. 1615, Bishop of Chester. She m. (second) Theophilus Eaton, Gov. of the New Haven Colony and came with him and her children to New England,

THOMAS YALE, b. at Plas Grono, Wales, 1616, d. at New Haven, Conn., 27 Mar. 1683; m. Mary Turner, d. at New Haven, 15 Oct. 1704,

MARY YALE, b. at New Haven, Conn., 26 Oct. 1650, d. at New Haven, Conn.; m. at New Haven, 2 Jan. 1672, Joseph Ives, b. at New Haven, 1648, d. at New Haven, 17 Nov. 1694,

EBENEEZER IVES, b. at New Haven, Conn., 6 Apr. 1692, d. at North Haven, Conn., 7 July 1759; m. at New Haven, 17 Jan. 1714/5, Mary Atwater, b. at New Haven, 12 Mar. 1694/5, d. at North Haven, 13 Feb. 1772,

EUNICE IVES, b. at New Haven, Conn., 4 May 1732, d. at North Haven, Conn., 27 Apr. 1801; m. at New Haven, 1757, Zophar Blakeslee, b. at New Haven, 21/22 Apr. 1730, d. at North Haven, 2 Feb. 1798,

MELIA BLAKESLEE, b. at New Haven, Conn., 4 Dec. 1764, d. at Morris, N.Y., 13 Apr. 1831; m. at North Haven, Conn., 9 Nov. 1786, Lemuel Brooks, b. at Bristol, Conn., 1758, d. at Butternuts, N.Y., 26 Nov. 1856,

BELA BROOKS, b. at North Haven, Conn., 30 Dec. 1799, d. at Superior, Wisc., 9 Mar. 1873; m. (second) at Butternuts, N.Y., Sarah Chase (Shaw) Williams b. at Butternuts, N.Y., 4 Sept. 1812, d. at Morris, N.Y., 1 Aug. 1855,

GEORGE LE MONT BROOKS, b. at Butternuts, N.Y., 21 May 1846, d. at Superior, Wisc., 15 Mar. 1917; m. 9 Aug. 1892, at Superior, Wisc., Clara Louise Berwick, b. at Norwalk, Conn., 2 Nov. 1863, d. at Rochester, Minn., 9 Jan. 1947,

HERBERT BERWICK BROOKS, m. Ella Tatum Rowland,
    (See Chapter LXXI)

CHAPTER LXXXV

WARREN — MARRIOTT — DAVIS

After evaluating surviving records in England and Virginia, Noel Currer-Briggs, the well-known English genealogist, had made a valid conclusion that Thomas Warren of Ripple, Kent, England, and Thomas Warren of James City County, whose land was later in Surry County, Virginia, were one and the same person. He feels that there is little doubt that Thomas Warren who was baptised at Ripple, Kent, 30 January 1624/25, the son of William and Katherine (Gookin) Warren, was the Thomas Warren who arrived in Virginia with Daniel Gookin in 1641.

Mr. Currer-Briggs examined the original parish records of Ripple from 1571 to 1645 which contain many entries for the Gookin and Warren families who were notable in this parish and whose coats of arms are described in Edward Hasted's *History . . . of the County of Kent* 2nd Ed [Canterbury 1800] Val. 9, pp 564-573. The marriage of William Warren and Katherine Gookin on 1 June 1619, and the baptisms of their four children; Edward Warren (born and died in 1621), Albertus Warren (baptised 22 April 1622), Thomas Warren (baptised 30 January 1624/25) and Mary Warren (baptised 21 October 1627) are entered in the parish register. Mr. Currer-Briggs also examined numerous Warren wills and administrations in the Consistory Court of Canterbury and the Prerogative Court of Canterbury (including the will of John Sewall of Halstead, Essex, PCC 10 Evelyn, the step-father of Thomas Warren), as well as various depositions and port records. In addition he studied the original Virginia Land Patent Books and surviving Surry County, Virginia records, and with the mass of information that he gleaned, gave his opinion that the circumstatial evidence is strongly in favor of the identification. A brief synopsis of the evidence follows.

After Thomas Warren's father died in 1631, his mother remarried, had further children and died before 1641, the year of the death of her second husband, John Sewall. It was logical that

Thomas Warren would become part of the family of Capt. Daniel Gookin, one of his older male relatives. The Gookin family had had interests in Virginia, since the 1620's. A good account of the family appears in *Adventurers of Purse and Person* (second edition 1964, pp. 181-185) co-authored by Annie L. Jester and Martha W. Hidden, and sponsored by the Order of the First Families of Virginia, 1607-1624. Capt. Daniel Gookin had returned to England and married just about the time of the death of Thomas Warren's mother. In 1641 when he returned to Virginia, Thomas Warren went along and was listed as a headright immediately following the names of Goodkin's wife and infant son in a patent to Daniel Gookin the following year. From what is known of the position and the finances of the Warren, Sewall and Gookin families, it was likely that Thomas Warren had received enough money from the estates of his parents to purchase the 450 acres in James City County (later in Surry County) which were granted to him not long after his arrival. It has been shown in Nell Marion Nugent's *Cavaliers and Pioneers . . .* (Richmond, Va., 1934-1977. v.1 pp. 138-139, 176 v.2 pp. 30, 276) that the Thomas Warren who arrived in 1641 received the above patent and confirmation of 290 acres of this grant in 1648. Moreover, there are additional land entries in the same vicinity to him, and a later patent to his son, Thomas Warren, Jr., refers back to the 1648 grant. An erroneuos entry in Miss Nugent's work to a Thomas Warren in 1635, actually concerns one Thomas Markham (v.1 p. 34)

The lineages from Thomas Warren in this volume have been accepted by the Order. Any additional material concerning Thomas Warren and the Warren and Gookin family which may be in the hands of the readers of this volume would be of interest to the Order and the descendants of Thomas Warren.

CHARLEMAGNE

(See Chapters X, XXXII, XXXIX, XLIII, LXVIII)

ISABEL DE VERMANDOIS, Countess of Leicester, d. ante 1147; m. (second) William de Warenne, 2nd Earl of Surrey, b. at Rouen, d. 11 May 1138,

ADA DE WARENNE, d. 1178; m. 1139, Henry de Huntingdon, Prince of Scotland, Earl of Huntingdon and Northumberland, d. 12 June 1152, 3rd and only surviving son of David I, King of Scotland,

DAVID, Earl of Huntingdon, b. 1144, d. at Yardley, Northants., younger brother of Kings Malcolm IV and William I of Scotland; m. 26 Aug. 1190, Maud, b. in 1171, d. ca. 2 Jan. 1233/4, eldest dau. of Hugh, Earl of Chester,

ADA OF HUNTINGDON, liv. 2 Nov. 1241; m. ante 7 June 1237, Sir Henry de Hastings of Ashill, co. Norfolk, d. ante 12 Aug. 1250,

HILARIA DE HASTINGS of Ashill, co. Norfolk; m. (his second) ca. 1254, Sir William de Harcourt of Stanton-Harcourt, Oxfordshire, b. ca. 1237, d. 1258,

RICHARD DE HARCOURT of Stanton-Harcourt, Oxfordshire, b. 9 Dec. 1256, d. in 1293; m. ca. 1278, Margaret, d. ca. 1303/4, dau. of John Beke, Lord of Eresby, Lincolnshire,

SIR JOHN DE HARCOURT, Knt., of Stanton-Harcourt, b. ca. 1280, d. 1330; m. ca. 1305, Ellen la Zouche, of Haryngworth, Northants., b. ca. 1278,

MATILDA DE HARCOURT of Stanton-Harcourt, b. ca. 1323; m. ca. 1345, Henry Crispe of Standlake, Oxfordshire, d. ca. 1389,

JOHN CRISPE of Kingston, Oxfordshire, b. ca. 1348, d. aft. 1404; m. ca. 1375, Anne, dau. of William Phettiplace of Kingsley, Bucks.,

HENRY CRISPE, of Cobcote, Oxfordshire, b. ca. 1378, d. ca. 1426; m. ca. 1405, Joan, dau. of Nicholas Dyer of Rotherfield Oxfordshire,

JOHN CRISPE, of Whitstable, co. Kent, b. ca. 1415, d. ca. 1475; m. Joan, dau. of John Sevenoaks, of Sevenoaks, co. Kent,

JOHN CRISPE, of Canterbury and Quekes, co. Kent, b. ca. 1440, d. 1503; m. ca. 1464, Agnes, dau. of John Quekes, of Quekes in Thanet, co. Kent,

JOHN CRISPE, of Quekes in Thanet, co. Kent, b. ca. 1466, d. ca. 1534; m. ca. 1488, Avice, dau. of Thomas Denne, of Kingstone, co. Kent,

MARGARET CRISPE, of Quekes in Thanet, co. Kent, b. ca. 1509; m. ca. 1527, John Crayford of Great Mongeham, co. Kent, d. ca. 1535,

EDWARD CRAYFORD, of Great Mongeham, co. Kent, b. ca. 1529, d. 1558; m. ca. 1550, Mary, dau. of Henry Atsea, of Herne, co. Kent,

SIR WILLIAM CRAYFORD, of Great Mongeham, co. Kent, b. ca. 1554, d. 15 Aug. 1623; m. ca. 1574, Anne, dau. of John Norton, of London, Eng., d. 26 May 1624,

ANNE CRAYFORD, b. ca. 1579/80, bapt. at Great Mongeham, co. Kent, 21 May 1581; m. at Great Mongeham, 2 Aug. 1591, John Warren, of Ripple Court, b. prob. at Dover, Eng., ca. 1551, d. 21 Jan. 1612/3,

WILLIAM WARREN, bapt. at Ripple Court, co. Kent, 7 Mar. 1596/7, d. in 1631; m. 4 June 1619, Catherine, dau. of Thomas Gookin, b. at Ripple Court, co. Kent,

CAPT. THOMAS WARREN, bapt. at Ripple Court, co. Kent, Eng., 30 Jan. 1624, came to Surry Co., Va., ante 3 Feb. 1640/1, d. at Smith's Fort Plantation, Surry Co., Va. 1669/70; m. (first) in Surry Co., Va., ca. 1644, Jane — , d. in Surry Co., Va., ca. 1652,

ALICE WARREN, b. in Surry Co., Va., ca. 1645, d. ca. 1707; m. in Va., ca. 1670, Matthias Marriott, d. in 1707,

WILLIAM MARRIOTT, of Surry Co., Va., b. ca. 1688, d. in 1766; m. in Va., ca. 1710, Sarah Collier, dau. of Thomas Collier. She d. ante 1705,

MARY MARRIOTT, b. in Surry Co., Va., ca. 1712, d. ca. 1764; m. ca. 1732, Henry Davis of Surry Co., Va., b. ca. 1712, d. ca. 1767,

MAJ. BENJAMIN DAVIS, of Brunswick, Ga., b. ca. 1742, d. in Apr. 1817; m. ca. 1770, Tabitha Rose, d. ante 1810, dau. of John Rose,

THOMAS DAVIS, b. at Clarkesville, Va., 26 July 1782, resided for a time at Shelbyville, Tenn., d. 9 Sept. 1846; m. 20 Nov. 1828, Eliza Stevenson, b. in Ireland, 25 Dec. 1799, d. at Peoria, Ill., 8 Oct. 1878,

WILLIAM HENRY DAVIS, b. 20 Jan. 1830, d. at Peoria, Ill., 9 June 1880; m. at Peoria, Ill., 25 Dec. 1855, Elizabeth Julia Gosling, b. at Tournay, France or Tournay, Belgium, 12 Sept. 1831, d. at Peoria, Ill., 23 June 1908,

GEORGE HENRY DAVIS, b. at Peoria, Ill., 10 Nov. 1864, d. at Peoria, Ill., 25 Jan. 1953; m. at Berkeley, Cal., 4 Feb. 1903, Julia Mabel Cullom, b. at Juliet, Ill., 27 Sept. 1877, d. at Peoria, Ill., 12 Mar. 1928,

THE HONORABLE SHELBY CULLOM DAVIS, b. at Peoria, Ill., 1 Apr. 1909; ed.: Lawrenceville School; Princeton Univ., A.B.; Columbia Univ., M.A.; University of Geneva, Switzerland, Docteures Sciences Politiques; First Deputy Superintendent of Insurance, State of N.Y., 1943-47; United States Ambassador to Switzerland 1969-75; member: Society of Colonial Wars, Governor General 1978-80; Sons of the Revolution in the State of New York, past President; The Society of Mayflower Descendants (N.Y.) past Governor; Order of Founders and Patriots of America (N.Y.) past Governor; Baronial Order of Magna Charta; Order of the Crown of Charlemagne in the United States of America; m. 4 June 1932 at New York, N.Y., Kathryn Edith Waterman, b. at Philadelphia, Penn., 25 Feb. 1907,

1) SHELBY M. CULLOM DAVIS, b. 20 Mar. 1937, m. Wendy Adams;

2) DIANA CULLOM DAVIS, b. 10 Sept. 1938, m. John Means Spencer.

CHAPTER LXXXVI

WARREN — WEST — MacLAMROC — HOGE — DAINE

CHARLEMAGNE

(See Chapter LXXXV)

CAPT. THOMAS WARREN, bapt. at Ripple Court, co. Kent, England, 30 Jan. 1624, came to Surry Co., Virginia, ante 3 Feb. 1640/1, d. at Smith's Fort Plantation, Surry Co., Va., 1669/70; m. (his third, her second) in Surry Co., Va., ca. 1658, Jane — , d. in Surry Co., Va., aft. 1669,

ALLEN WARREN I (or Sr.) b. in Surry Co., Va., in 1663, d. in 1738; m. Elizabeth Clements, dau. of John Clements of Surry Co., Va.,

ALLEN WARREN II (or Jr.) b. in Surry Co., Va., ca. 1690, w.p. in Surry Co., 15 Aug. 1733; m. ca. 1715, Anne Hart, b. and d. in Surry Co., Va., a granddau. of Capt. Charles Barham, a descendant of the Emperor Charlemagne (See Vol. II of PEDIGREES, p. 29),

ALLEN WARREN III, b. in Surry Co., Va., w.p. in Surry Co., 28 Mar. 1780; m. in Surry Co., ca. 1740, Mary Phillips, b. in Surry Co., d. in Surry Co.,

LIEUT. JESSE WARREN, officer in Surry Co. militia against the British in the Revolutionary War, b. in Surry Co., Va. ca. 1745, d. in Surry Co., ca. 1794; m. in Surry Co., ca 1770, Martha Thompson, b. and d. in Surry Co., Va.,

JESSE PHILLIPS WARREN, b. in Surry Co., Va., ca. 1770, w.d. 28 Aug. 1829; m. in Surry Co., Va., 25 Jan. 1814, Sarah Caroline Bell, b. in Surry Co., Va., ca. 1793, d. in Surry Co., ca. 1836,

LUCY CAROLINE WARREN, b. in Surry Co., Va., in 1817, d. in Surry Co., Va., in Jan. 1873; m. (his second) in Surry Co., 26 Sept. 1836, William Major West, b. in Surry Co., 25 Dec. 1806, d. in Surry Co., 26 Jan. 1866,

SAMUEL EDWIN WEST, served in Confederate Army in the War Between the States (1861-65) b. at Surry, Va., in 1838, d. in Surry Co., Va., 1879; m. in Isle of Wight Co., Va., 27 Jan. 1859, Oceana Winifred Gwaltney, b. in Isle of Wight Co., Va., 1 Aug. 1840, d. in Surry Co., Va., 1 Jan. 1877,

GRACE WEST, b. in Surry Co., Va., 7 Sept. 1874, d. at Greensboro, N.C., 17 July 1960; m. at Newport News, Va., 22 Feb. 1901, James Robbins MacLamroc, b. at Mocksville, N.C., 17 Nov. 1870, d. at Greensboro, N.C., 16 Dec. 1935,

   1) JAMES GWALTNEY WESTWARREN MAC LAMROC, lawyer, financier, philanthropist, b. at Greensboro, N.C.; ed.: Univ. of N.C., B.A.; Yale Univ., J.D.; member: American Bar Assoc.; N.C. Bar Assoc., first V.P.; Bar of U.S. Supreme Court; Sigma Chi, Phi Delta Phi; N.C. State Highway Comm.; Sons of Confederate Veterans, Comdr. N.C. Div.: Soc. of War of 1812; SAR, past pres. N.C. Soc.; S.R.; Jamestowne Society; Society of Colonial Wars, first Gov. of N.C. Society; Society of Descendants of Colonial Clergy, Chancellor; Order of Americans of Armorial Ancestry; National Society Americans of Royal Descent; Order of the Crown in America; Baronial Order of Magna Charta, surety; Order of Three Crusades; Military Order of the Crusades; Order of the Crown of Charlemagne in the United States of America, Chancellor; Yale Club of N.Y.; Guilford Co. American Rev. Bicentenial Comm.; Historic Preservation Society of N.C.; Greensboro Country Club; donor with Mrs. MacLamroc of the MacLamroc Collection of Ancestral Family Portraits (Baliol-Scott family — Elizabethan) to the N.C. Museum of Art, Raleigh; author of newspaper, magazine, radio and television articles on history, genealogy, law, transportation, resources, pollution etc.; m. at Palm Beach, Florida, 19 Jan. 1954, Maxine Pugh,

a) ALAN GWALTNEY WESTWARREN MACLAMROC, b. Dec. 26, 1954, at Greensboro, N.C.; member: Children of the Confederacy; C.A.R.; Jamestowne Society; Military Order of the Crusades; Baronial Order of Magna Charta; Order of the Crown of Charlemagne in the United States of America;

b) BRIAN GWALTNEY WESTWARREN MACLAMROC, b. Feb. 24, 1956, at Greensboro, N.C.; C.A.R. member: Children of the Confederacy; Jamestowne Society; Military Order of the Crusades; Baronial Order of Magna Charta; Order of the Crown of Charlemagne in the United States of America; etc.

2.) VIRGINIA MACLAMROCH, b. at Greensboro, N.C.; ed.: Hollins College, B.A.; member: Junior League of N.Y., Admissions Com.; Colony Club of N.Y.; Protestant Council of N.Y.; YWCA in New York, Bd. of Directors; Bd. of Trustees Hollins College; Delta Delta Delta; U.D.C.; D.A.R.; Jamestowne Soc.; Nat. Soc. of Colonial Dames in N.Y., Bd. of Mgrs.; Soc. of Descendants of the Colonial Clergy; Order of Americans of Armorial Ancestry; Nat. Soc. Americans of Royal Descent; Order of the Crown in America; Nat. Soc. Daughters of the Barons of Runnemede; Other of Three Crusades; Order of the Crown of Charlemagne in the United States of America, etc., m. James Fulton Hoge, J.D., LL.D., at Greensboro, N.C., 26 March 1932, and have issue:

a) BARBARA HUME HOGE, b. 19 January 1934, at New York, N.Y.; grad.: Chapin School, N.Y.; Hollins College; B.S. Adelphi College; member: Junior League of N.Y.; Nat. Soc. of Colonial Dames in N.Y.; Jamestowne Soc.; Order fo the Crown of Charlemagne in the United States of America; m. on 16 June 1956, at New York, N.Y., Robert Armand Daine, and has issue:

i VIRGINIA FORD DAINE, b. 24 January 1959, at Easton, Pa., student Duke Univ.;

    ii JAMES HOGE DAINE (adopted), b. 7 May 1969.

b) JAMES FULTON HOGE, JR., b. 25 December 1935, at New York, N.Y.; grad.: Buckley School; Exeter Academy; Yale Univ., B.A.; Univ. of Chicago, M.A.; Editor, Chicago Sun Times; selected 1969 as one of ten outstanding young men of the U.S. by Nat. Jaycees; member: Jamestowne Soc.; Order of the Crown of Charlemagne in the United States of America; m. at Chicago Ill., 2 June 1962, Alice Patterson (Reeve) Albright, gr. dau. of Capt. Joseph Medill Patterson, co-publisher of the Chicago Tribune and founder of the New York Daily News, and have issue:

    i ALICIA MACLAMROCH HOGE, b. at Chicago, Ill., 6 March 1963;

    ii JAMES PATRICK HOGE, b. at Chicago, Ill., 26 December 1964;

    iii ROBERT WARREN HOGE, b. at Chicago, Ill., 11 April 1965;

c) WARREN MACLAMROCH HOGE, b. at New York, N.Y., 13 April 1941; grad.: Buckley School, Trinity School, N.Y.; Yale Univ., B.A.; George Washington Univ. Graduate School; City Editor of the New York Post, former Washington Correspondent; Metropolitan Staff N.Y. Times; member: Jamestowne Soc.; Order of the Crown of Charlemagne in the United States of America;

d) VIRGINIA HOWE HOGE, b. at New York, N.Y., 23 September 1945, ed.: Chapin School, Boston Conservatory of Music, Hunter College; member: Jamestowne Soc.; Order of the Crown of Charlemagne in the United States of America.

CORRECTIONS TO VOLUME II

PEDIGREES OF SOME OF THE EMPEROR CHARLEMAGNE'S DESCENDANTS

Pages	Lines	
xviii	16	read Jacobus instead of Joacobus
xxi	8	add London after Stanford
xlvi	21	read Jacobson instead of Jackson
xcii	26	read foreword instead of forward
11	5	*le Debonnaire* instead of le Debonnaire
20	9	read 1665 instead of 1685
21	39	read 1907 instead of 1910
25	27	read 1665 instead of 1685
29	29	read MacLamroc instead of McLamroch
30	20	read Historic Preservation Society of N.C. instead of N.C. Soc. for the Preservation of Antiquitie
62	18	read LXXII instead of LXXIV
72	5	read ca. 1095 instead of ca. 1058
92	15	read Pittsgrove Township, N.J. instead of Pittstown Township, Pa.
105	3	read named in Magna Charta instead of Magna Charta Surety
109	14	read Mauduit instead of Maudit
111	21,22	read ca. 12 Jan. 1818 instead of bef. Mar. 15, 1823
111	23	read Dec. 2, 1817 instead of in 1817
111	24	read 26 instead of 27
111	25	read Oct. 2, instead of ca. Oct. 1
111	27	Norfolk, Va., Nov. 4, 1905 instead of in Northampton Co., Va. 1905
116	34	read of Charlemagne instead of on Charlemagne
130	2	King James III
130	36	read Maxwellton parish of Gleneairn, Dumfries
154	33	read Order of Three Crusades 1096-1192 instead of Order of the Three Crusades
156		Delete last generation on the page.
160	19	read DIANE instead of DIANA
165		Delete last generation on the page.
183	5	read Henry III instead of Henry II
194	21,22,23	Omit generation "Francis Mapes etc."
220	36	read MARIAM instead of MARIAN
227	6	read ELIZA instead of Elizabeth
227	6	read Pitt Co. instead of near Greenville
227	7	read 17 instead of 27
227	10	read 1940 instead of 1949
238	18	1230 is date of death of Sir Gilbert Lacy not of Isabel Bigod

317

246	27,28	omit all after the name Mary. Her identity is unknown (Mary Ann Bickley m. a cousin of Solomon, Dale Carter. In the will of Solomon Carter ex. 7 Feb. 1784, pr. 2 Oct. 1786, his wife is named as Maryann.)
247	10	read 1863 instead of 1836
274	17	Sarah Beard born Sept. 14 not 12
288	22	read 1915 instead of 1918
311	15	read Jan. instead of June
353	40	(second column) read Hugh instead of High

INDEX

Aasa Salmundsdatter, 256
Aasulf Skuleson, 256
Acton, Joan, 249
  Thomas, 249
Adalbert, King of Italy, 18
Adalbert of Ivrea, 18, 182
Adams, Edward C., 295
  Helen, 272
  Jane W., 295
  Lydia Ann, 87
  Mary, 230, 271
  William, 87
Adela of Dagsbourg, 151
Adelaide, 55
Adelaide of Burgundy, 6, 35, 125,
  151, 206
Adelaide of France, 145
Adelaide of Lorraine, 56
Adelaide of Maurienne, 265
Adelaide of Orlamunda, 151
Adelaide of Poitou, 34, 130, 158
Adele (See Adela) 6, 206
Adele of France, 7, 117, 125, 136,
  158, 183, 246
Adele of Normandy, 34, 158
Adele of Vexin, 98, 146, 247
Adeliza of Brabant, 152
Aelfthryth of Wessex, 116, 255
Affeton, Katherine, 174
Agatha, 183
Agatha of Hungary, 7
Agnes of Bavaria, 266
Agnes d'Evreux, 125
Agnes of Poitou, 265
Alan, Lord of Galloway, 280
Alberada of Mons, 151
Albert I of Braunschweig, 19
Albert I, Count of Namur, 56
Albert II, Ct. of Namur, 56
Albert III, Ct. of Namur, 56
Albred, Eve, 65
Albright, Alice P., 316
Alcock, Anne, 232
  Dr. John, 232
Alessina of Montferrat, 19
Alf Erlingsson, 256

Alfonso IV, King of Aragon, 266
Alfonson VI, King of Castile, 104
Alfonso VII, King of Castile, 104,
  105
Alfonso VIII, Kg. of Castile, 104
Alfonso IX, King of Leon, 104
Alfonso I, Kg. of Portugal, 105
Alfred the Great, 55, 116, 152, 255
Alix of Burgundy, 19
Allen, Achsah, 111
  Elizabeth, 205
  Jane, 68, 79
  James, 205
  Sylvia, 69
Allerton, Remember, 177
Allison, Sarah, 149
Allyn, Mary, 217, 222
  Matthew, 217, 222
Alphonso (See Alfonso)
Alvord, Abigail, 217
Amadeus IV of Savoy, 19
Amice of Gloucester, 202
Amund Rolfsson, 257
Anderson, Adrian W., 290
  Christopher T., 290
  Craig M., 290
  George, 94
  John, 134
  Mary, 95
  Roland W., 290
  Susanna, 134
Andrews, Hannah, 114
Angell, Mary, 94
Angelom, 1, 2, 3, 4, 5
Angharad ferch David, 191
Angharad ferch Llewelyn, 190
Angharad ferch Owen, 190
Angus, Malcolm Earl of
Anna of Bohemia, 267
Anna Marie, 268
Anna Sofie, 268
Annabel, Joan, 262
Anne Anversdatter Berge, 258
Anne of Burgundy, 19
Anne, Queen of England, 285
Anne of Kiev, 35, 131, 146, 247

Barron, Alice E., 77
  Susie E., 14
Barta, Agnes D., 270
  Jennifer A., 270
  John B., 270
  John J., 270
  Rev. F. Kenneth, 269
  Cdr. Louis J., 269
Bartholow, Lester C. Jr., 279
Bartlett, Elizabeth, 222, 224
  Samuel, 224
Baskerville, Sir John, 16
Basset, Aliva (Alice) 293
  Edward, 114
  Jane, 114
  Thomas, 293
Bates, Charles T. R., 144, 157
  Daniel M. 144, 157
Bauder, Doris T., 84
  Paul F., 84
  Paul F., Jr., 84
  Diana C. E., 40
  Otto S., 40
Baxter, Brook A., 230
  Edwin O., 230
  Erskine, 230
  Francis H., 230
  Greenberry H., 27
  Lee R., 230
  Mourning, 27
  Robert B., 230
Bayley, Richard de, 248
Baynham, Sir Alexander, 160
  Margaret, 160
Beal, Susannah, 175
Beall, Amelia Jane, 41
  Charles Edward, 45
  Col. George, 44
  Col. George, Jr., 44
  John, 44
  Ens. Levin C., 44
  Lillie Ora, 42
  Mary E., 45
  Col. Samuel, Jr., 41
  Sarah, 204
  Thaddeus, 4
  Thaddeus, Jr., 42
  Thaddeus S., 42
  William Rufus, 44

Beals, Ann F., 194
  Thomas, 194
  Samuel, 194
Beane, Barbara M., 77
Beard, Anne Stuart-Menteth, 195
  Dr. Cornelius C., 194
  Henry Sudler, 195
  James S., 196
  Maximillian C., 194
  Philadelphia, 196
  Sarah, 196
  Stuart-Menteth, II, 195, 290
  Stuart-Menteth, III, 195
  Stuart-Menteth, IV, 196
  Timothy Field, 196
  Walter J., 196
Beasley, Barbara L., 220
  Dorothy A., 220
  William Neiter, 220
Beatrice of Macon, 125
Beatrice of Savoy, 7, 266
Beatrice of Silesia-Glogan, 19
Beatrice of Vienne, 19
Beatrix of Burgundy, 266
Beauchamp, Anne de, 114
  Beatrice de, 7
  Elizabeth de, 28, 89, 118
  Sir Giles de, 23, 113
  Isabel de, 100, 184, 237
  John de, 163
  Sir John de, 24, 113, 114, 164
  Margaret de, 24
  Mary, 164
  Maud de, 56, 280
  Richard de, 118
  Sir Richard de, 114
  Robert, IV, 164
  Roger de, 23
  Thomas de, 280
  Sir Walter de, 23, 113
  William de, 7, 100, 164, 236
  Sir William de, 113
Beaufort, Joan, 29, 86, 105, 118
  John, 105
Beaumont, Elizabeth de, 163
  Hawise de, 85, 131, 202
  Isabel de, 100, 163, 173, 215, 236
  Margaret de, 35, 146

322

326

Cocke, Anne, 8, 11
  Richard, 8
  Lt. Col. Richard, 8
Cockrell, Nancy S., 239
Codd, Col. St. Leger, 285
Coe, Mary, 194
Cokeworthy, Thomasine, 174
Colburn, Hannah, 278
Colby, Susanna, 71
Cole, Priscilla, 165
  Sarah, 165
  Thomas, 165
Coleman, Sarah, 81
Coleville, Alice de, 159
  Roger de, 159
Coley, Sandra Faye, 33
Collier, Sarah, 311
  Thomas, 311
Collins, Christopher R., 187
  Pamela C., 187
  William W., 186
  William W., Jr., 187
  Wortham A., 186
Colville, Isabel de 261
  Sir John, 261
  Rebecca, 262
  Sir Tobert, 86
  Sir William de, 261
Comyn, Alexander, 36
  Elizabeth, 36
  William, 36
Conan I, Duke of Burgundy, 6,
  206, 283
Coney, Nathaniel, 177
  Samuel, 177
  Susanna, 177
Conrad I, King of Burgundy, 265
Conrad II, Emperor, 265
Constable, Frances, 242
  Marmaduke, 242
  Sir Robert, 242
  Sir William, 242
Constance of Brittany, 190
Constance of Burgundy, 104
Constance of Sicily, 266
Constance of Toulouse, 34, 130,
  158
Converse, Capt. Edward, 97

  Ens. Edward, 97
  Elisha, 98
  Lucy C., 98
  Samuel, 97
  Samuel David, 97
  Sergt. Samuel, 97
Conway, Elizabeth, 27
  Joseph, 27
  Louisa, 28
  Samuel, 27
Conwy, Hugh, 191
  Janet, 191
  Reynold, 191
Conyers, Agnes, 122
  Christopher, 97
  Edward, 97
  Sir John, 97
  Leonard, 122
  Reginald, 97
  Richard, 97
Coolidge, Catherine, 275
Cook, Hazel, 289
Cooke, Joseph, R. G., 209
  Mary-Alice, 210
  Robert George, 209
Cooper, Elizabeth, 97
Copelan, Leila, 251
Copley, Eleanor, 101, 184, 237
  Sir Roger, 184, 237
Corbet, Jane, 212
  Mary, 62
  Sir Roger, 212
  Robert, 62
Cornell, Alyce, 142
  Cornelius, 142
  Jacob C., 142
  John, 142
  Phoebe, 142
  William R., 142
Corson, Benjamin, 143
  Frances S., 144, 156
  Hiram, M. D., 143, 156
  Joseph, 143
Cornwallis, Affra, 165
  Elizabeth, 262
Cotton, Audrey, 90
Cotter, Ellen H., 102
  Sir Charles, 102

327

Davenport, Anne, 169
  Henry, 207
  Hugh, 168
  John, 168, 169
  John de, 168
  Rev. John, 192
  Margery, 168
  Mary, 207
  Mary E., 244
  Ralph, 168
David ap Evan, 191
David, Earl of Huntingdon, 310
David I, King of Scots, 24, 310
David Lloyd ap David, 153
David Lloyd ap Howell, 153
Davidson, Eunice, 272
  Oliver, 271
Davis, Maj. Benjamin, 312
  Diana C., 312
  Eldred B., 50
  George Henry, 312
  Henry, 311
  Capt. John, 110
  Lilian G., 50
  Margaret, 111
  Mary, 97, 111
  Nathaniel, 111
  Philip, 110
  Hon. Shelby Cullom, 312
  Shelby M. C., 312
  Thomas, 312
  William Henry, 312
Dawkins, Anne, 46
Dawson, Benoni, 39
  Benoni, II, 39
  George, 197
  Ruth, 39
Day, Bertha C., 144, 156
  Richard H., 144, 156
Dean, Constance, 259
Deans, Kathleen C., 296
DeBonneson, Judith E., 106
DeCorreale, 292
Deighton, Jane, 114
  John, 114
Deincote, Eleanor, 293
  John, 293
Deincourt, John, 242

Margaret, 242
William, 242
Deinville, Adele V., 39
Deitz, Delta, 61, 95
  Emerson E., 95
  John, 95
  Joseph D., 95
Delamere, Joan, 216
  Sir John, 216
de la Warre, Catherine, 199
  Joan, 101, 184, 237
  John, 198
  Roger, 101, 184, 237
  Sir Roger, 198
Delves, Elizabeth, 8
Deming, Elizabeth A., 296
Denbigh, Robert de, 168
Denne, Avice, 311
  Thomas, 311
Dent, Barbara, 44, 46
Despencer, Anne de, 96
  Sir Edward le, 118
  Sir Hugh le, 118
  Isabel le, 118
  Margery le, 242
  Sir Philip le, 242
  Thomas le, 118
Devorgilla of Galloway, 198
d'Evreux, Bertrade, 167, 207, 305
Dewey, Electa, 217
  Israel, 217
  Noble, 217
Deyvill, Maud deW., 152
Dhu, Gladys, 15
Dickenson, Hannah, 143
  Theresa A., 135
Digby, Elizabeth, 199
  Everard, 199
  Sir John, 199
  Simon, 199
  William, 199
Digges, Sir Dudley, 119
  Gov. Edward, 119
  Eliza, 119
  Leonard, 119
  Thomas, 119
  Col. William, 119
Dinham, Elizabeth, 110

Disney, Emlyn, 284
  Richard, 284
Dixon, Henry, 9
  Lillian, 31
  Mary, 9
  Mary B., 9
Dodge, Abigail, 213
Donnell, Harry E., 233
  Sarah D., 233
Dorothe Mattson, 257
Dorothea verch Evan, 153
Dorsey, Martha A., 47
  Philip, Jr., 46
Dosher, Anne P., 67
Douglas Emma J., 244
  Erskine, 243
  George, 224
  James, 86, 106
  Janet, 86, 106
  Pamela C., 224
  Sperry, II, 224
Dow, Lydia R., 213
  Waldo H., 213
Downes, Grace, 83
Dowrish, Grace, 174
  Thomas, 174
Drake, Elizabeth, 123
  Henry, 123
  Mary, 123, 143
  Robert, 123
Draper, Sally R., 302
Driby, Alice de, 62
  John de, 62
Drummond, Andrew, 204
  Ann, 286
  Annabella, 106
  Capt. John, 123
  Sir John, 106
  Capt. Richard, 123, 124, 286
Drogo, Archbishop, 2, 3
Dubini, Cecilia, 110
Dudley, Anna, 193, 194
  Ann, 134
  Caleb, 193
  Christopher, 134
  Dea. David, 193
  Edward, 127, 133, 134
  James, 128, 134

  Dr. Jeptha, 128
  John, 127, 133, 134, 192
  Mary J., 128
  Col. Richard, 127
  Robert, 127, 128, 133
  Sir Robert, 127, 133
  Thomas, 134
  William, 128, 134
  Col. William, 128
Dulin, Gwynne, 139
Dungan, Frances, 138
  Sir John, 138
  Joseph, 143
  Mary, 138
  Sarah, 141, 143
  Thomas, 138
  Thos., Jr., 143
  Rev. Thomas, 141, 143
  William, 138, 141, 143
Dunham, Louisa W., 272, 273
Dunn, Clyde M., 179
  Mary L., 304
Dunning, Arden, 273
DuPuy, Alfred C., 31
  Catherine Ann, 31
  Catherine B., 33
  David C., 33
  David N., 32
  Elbert N., 31
  Elbert S., M. D., 31
  James D., 32
  James N., 31
  John Stuart, 32
  Karl F. G., 32
  Laura Kay, 33
  Nancy Lee, 32
  Richard S., 31
  Samuel S., 32
  Samuel S., Jr., 32
  William Edwin, 32
Dutch, Samuel, 212
  Susanna, 212
Dutton, Sir Geoffrey de, 168
  Margaret de, 168
Dyer, Joan, 310
Dyneley, Anne, 16

Eadgifu of England, 55

330

Eberhard of Friuli, 18
Ebles Mancer, 130, 158
Eaton, Hannah, 192
　Rev. Richard, 192
　Gov. Theophilus, 192, 306
Edson, Daniel S., 227
　Dorothy A., 227
　Col. Josiah, 226
Edward the Aethling, 7
Edward the Elder, 55
Edward the Exile, 183
Edward ap David, 153
Edward I, King of England, 7, 89,
　105, 110, 113, 117, 126, 137,
　231
Edward II, King of England, 105
Edward III, King of England, 105,
　110, 118, 132
Edwards, Mary R., 279
Edmund, Earl of Lancaster, 184
Edmunds, Charlotte, 11
Eells, Elva S., 58
　Ralph S., 58
　Samuel R., 58
　Walter G., 58
Egeleiv Olavsdatter, 257
Egendorf, Janet M., 31
Eissau ap Gruffyd, 305
Ela, Countess of Salisbury, 280
Eldridge, Judith, 13
Eleanore of Albuquerque, 267
Eleanor of Aquitaine, 7, 104, 117,
　126, 136, 159, 183
Eleanor of Castile, 89, 105, 117,
　126, 231
Eleanor of England, 104
Eleanor of Normandy, 255
Eleanor of Provence, 7, 117, 126,
　137, 183
Eleanore of Sicily, 267
Eleanor verch Hugh, 153
Eleanore of Wurtemberg, 20
Elias ap Rees, 148
Elinor of Castile, 89, 105, 117,
　126, 231
Elinor ferch Meredith, 191
Elizabeth of Aragon, 19
Elizabeth of Bavaria, 20

Elizabeth of England, 89
Elizabeth I, of England, 185
Elizabeth II, of England, 123
Elizabeth, Queen Mother, 123
Elizabeth of Scotland, 86
Elizabeth, Countess von
　Zweibrucken-Bitsch, 20
Ellen ferch Maelgwyn, 190
Ellen ferch Thomas, 191
Ellen ferch Robert 191
Ellen of Mar, 86
Elliott, Edward, 24
　Jane, 24, 187
　Jane A., 238
Ellis, Daniel, 149
　Francis A., 149
　Howard, 149
　Howard R., 150
　Jacquelle, 199
　Jane D., 150
　Sir John, 199
　John Pell, 150
　Rowland, 148
　Rowland, II, 149
　Rowland, III, 149
　Rowland, IV, 149
　Rowland, V, 150
　Rowland, VI, 150
　Ruldoph P., 149
　Virginia, 95
Elmeden, Joan de, 36
　Sir William de, 36
Eloff, Carla Jane, 32
Elstrude of Flanders, 292
Emerson, Andrew W., 65
　Bradford M., 179
　David M., 179
　Ebeneezer, 65
　George D., 178
　Helen E., 66
　Howard, 178
　James, 65
　Jane H., 179
　John P., 178
　Rev. Joseph, 65
　Joseph Platt, 65
　June A., 179
　Kendall, 65

332

Fetherstonehaugh, Mary, 36
Field, Abigail, 194
    Alfred B., 194
    Ens. David, 193
    Rev. David, D.D., 193
    Louise F., 194
    Capt. Timothy, 193, 194
    Rev. Timothy, 193
    Virginia Warren, 28
Fienes, Margaret, 15
Fiennes, Maud de, 109
Filley, Abigail, 226, 229
Finkle, Linda, 77
Finlay, Carol J., 214
    Christopher A., 214
    Susan C., 214
Finley, Gertrude F., 194
    Horace M., 194
    Marshall, 194
Fisk, James E., 32
Fitler, Edwin H., 59
    Edwin H., Jr., 59
    Kimberly D., 59
    Ralston B., 59
    Ralston B., Jr., 59
    Ralston B., III, 59
    Susanna R., 59
    Tamsin L., 59
    Walter E., 59
    Walter E., Jr., 59
FitzAkaris, Hervey, 283
FitzAlan, Alice, 105
    Sir Edmund, 93, 147
    Elizabeth, 93, 147, 231
    Joan (Joanne) 110, 281
    John, 93
    Richard, 105
    Sir Richard, 93, 147, 231, 281
FitzBardolf, Akaris, 283
FitzGeoffrey, Sir John, 100, 236
FitzHammon, Maud, 167
    Robert, 167
FitzHamon, Mable, 131
    Maud, 207
    Robert, 131, 207
FitzHenry, Sir Hugh, 284
    Randolph, 283
FitzHerbert, Piers, 247, 261

FitzHervey, Henry, 283
FitzHugh, Annabel, 284
    Eustache, 247
    Sir Henry, 284
    Ralph, 247
FitzJohn, Maud, 100, 236
FitzMaurice, Juliane, 132
    Maurice, 132
FitzOsbern, Emma, 35, 85, 131, 146
    William, 35, 131, 146, 202
FitzOtes, Thomas, 7
FitzPeter, Roger, 174
FitzPiers, Lucy, 247, 261
    Reginald, 173
    Reynold, 173
FitzRandolph, Sir Henry 284
FitzReginald, Peter, 174
FitzRobert, Amice, 85, 131
    Maud, 167
    William, 85, 131, 202
FitzRoger, Alice, 174, 261
    Elizabeth, 174
    John, 174
FitzThomas, Maud, 7
FitzWalter, Alice, 283
    Randolf, 283
Fleckenstein, Anne L., 289
    William O., 289
Fleet, Ann, 128
    William, 128
Fleming, Margaret, 106
Fletcher, Middleton, 298
Flint, Albert M., 279
    James P., 279
    Lida I., 279
    Luther, 279
    Porter, 278
Flory, Edith C., 304
    Elizabeth A., 304
    Henry C., 304
    Janet L., 304
    Peter C. W., 304
Floyd, Berry, 286
    Kesiah, 286
Forster, Margaret, 138
    Sir Roger, 36
    Sir Thomas, 36
    Walter, 138

Foster, Carl DeKalb, 250
  Elizabeth, 9
  Gareth A., 250
  Jonathan, 250
  Jonathan E., 250
  Mary L., 251
  Michael, 250
  Nancy (Bab) Gulley, 251
  Peter M., 250
  Samuel, 91
  Susan, 36
  Thomas, 36
Foulke ap Thomas, 153
Foulke, Amos, 156
  Ann Jones, 144, 156
  Edward, 153, 156
  Hugh, 154
  Israel, 154
  Letitia, 154
  Samuel, 154
  Thomas, 154, 156
Fowke, Ann B., 161
  Gerard, 161
  Col. Gerard, 160
  John, 160
  Richard, 161
  Roger, 160,161
France, Adam, Jr., 175, 180
  Christian, 175
  Jacob, 180
  Louise, 175
  Maude C., 180
  Thomas B., 180
Frederick I, Emperor, 266
Frederick I. Duke, 168
Frederick II, Emperor, 266
Frederick of Bavaria, 20
Frederick, Duke of Lower
  Lorraine, 56
Frederick, Count of Luxemburg,
  117
Freeborn, Mary, 141
Freeze, Alice E., 297
Freville, Alexander de, 56
  Baldwin de, 56, 57
  Sir Baldwin, 8, 56
  Margaret de, 57
Freyville, Joyce de, 8

Frink, Ermina, 218
Frisbie, Henrietta, 69
Fritchett, Thomas H., 50
  Margaret G., 50
Frost, Frances, 16
Frowick, Elizabeth, 164
  Isabel, 164
  Sir Thomas, 164
Fox, David, Sr., 285
  Nancy, 225
Fulford, Andrew, 110
  Eleanor, 110
  Faith, 110
  John, 110
Fulk II, County of Anjou, 125,
  206
Fulk III, Ct. of Anjou, 125
Fulk IV, Ct. of Anjou, 125
Fulk V, Ct. of Anjou, 125
Fullthorpe, Joan, 242
Fulton, Dr. Brown, 39
  Jane B. Evans, 40
Fychen, Lowri, 122

Gale, Joyce, 128
Gamble, Lydia, 87
  Nancy A., 14
Gantt, Anne, 46
  Thomas, 46
Garcia V, King of Navarre, 104
Gardiner, Catherine W., 37
  Mary S. P., 139
  Walter C., 138
Gardner, Geoffrey L., 273
  Henry P., 273
  Leland G., 273, 274
  Louanna J., 250
  Nancy E., 274
Garland, Nattie A. V., 31
Garrett, Sophia, 243
  Thomas J., 243
Garrison, Archibald, 286
  Jonathan, 286
  Mary A., 286
Gates, John, 275
  Jonathan, 275
Gaunt, John of, 105, 118

Gavaston, Amy de, 62
    Piers de, 62
Gawton, Joan, 123
    Thomas, 123
Gedge, James, 24
    Jane, 24
Geneville, Joan de, 15, 132, 280
Geoffrey I Grisgonelle, 125, 206
Geoffrey III, Ct. of Gatinais, 125
Geoffrey, Ct. of Brittany, 283
Gerard, Ct. of Auverne, 130, 158
Gerberga, 99
Gerberga of Anjou, 206
Gerberga of Lorraine, 99, 145,
    151, 245
Gerberga of Macon, 18
Gerberga of Saxony, 55, 145, 246,
    265
Gerloc of Normandy, 130, 158
Gernon, Sir John, 159
    Margaret, 159
Gernons, Ranulph de, 167
Gerold I, Ct. of Vinzgau, 116, 255
Gervaise, Ct. of Rethel, 56
Gethin, Margaret, 191
    Maurice, 191
Gibbons, Ambrose, 249
    Rebecca, 249
Giles, Mary, 24
Gillen, Mary T., 189
Gillison, Karen, 25
Ginleik Torson Nordgarden, 158
Gisela (Volsea), 18
Gisela of Italy, 18, 182
Gisela of Swabia, 265
Giselbert, Count, 99
Giselbert, Ct. of Burgundy, 125,
    206
Giselbert of Lorraine, 99, 145, 246
Giselbert, Ct. of Maasgau, 151
Gisele of France, 18
Glass, Mollie, 107
    William Wood, Jr., 107
Glemham, Anne, 232
    John, 232
Glendower, Owen, 122
Glenn, Mourning, 27
Glover, Hugh W., 201
    Janet R., 201

Godfrey I, Ct. of Lorraine, 152
Godfrey the Old, 55
Goff, Henry A., 273
    Lillie B., 273
Gonard, Aurora M. B., 149
Goodell (Goodale), Dorothy, 227
Gookin, Catherine, 311
    Daniel, 308, 309
    Thomas, 311
Gordon, Margaret, 204
Goronwy ap Gruffud, 152
Gorsuch, Charles, 165
    Eleanor, 165
    John, 165
    Rev. Peter, 165
    Thomas, 165
Gosling, Elizabeth J., 312
Gothelo I (Gothelon) of Lorraine,
    56, 151
Gough, Margaret, 37
Goushill (Gousell), Elizabeth, 94,
    232
    Joan, 147
    Sir Robert de, 93, 147, 231
Gove, Abel R., 72
    Eva Cole, 72
    George E., 72
    Nettie A., 72
Gradidge, Rosina, 210
Graham, Elizabeth, 106
    Margaret, 203
Grandison, Mabel de, 23
Grantmesnil, Hugh de, 35, 146
    Pernell (Petronilla), 35, 146
Gratney, Earl of Mar, 86
Greasley, Ann, 154
Green, Edward, 127, 133
    Eliza A., 11
    Mary, 79
    Richard, 127
    Robert, 133
Greene, Joan, 57
    Sir Thomas, 57
Greenfield, Martha, 30
Greenhalghe, Elizabeth, 169
    John, 169, 170
    Orlando, 169
    Rachel, 170
    Richard, 169

336

338

Howel ap Penllyn, 153
Howell, Benjamin P., 276
  Rev. Frank M., 276
  Nannie E., 276
Howland, Elizabeth C., 178
Hubbell, Dorothy, 218
  Edward Parmelee, 218
  William Butler, 218
Huddleston, Annette K., 197
  William E., Jr., 197
Huey, Margo W., 59
Huff, Esther, 72
  George, 72
Hugh Capet, Kg. of France, 34,
  130, 158
Hugh Magnus, Duke of France,
  35, 100, 131, 146, 247
Hugh Magnus, Count of Paris, 34
Hugh, Earl of Chester, 159, 198,
  310
Hugh II of Burgundy, 19
Hugh II, Count of Orleans, 99,
  151
Hugh III of Burgundy, 19
Hugh of Kevlioc, 167, 207, 305
Hugh, Eleanor, 156
  Sibill, 148
Hughes, John B., 128
  Mary A., 128
Hugo, Nicholas F., 175
Hugo- Smith, Annie T., 176
  Trevanion, 176
Hull, Edward, 233
  Jane, 233
  Robert, 233
  Tiddeman, 233
Humphrey, Ann, 148, 185
Humphrey ap Hugh, 148
Humphrey, John 185
Hungerford, Katherine, 101, 184,
  237
  Sir Robert, 184, 237
Hunt, Christian, 212
  Thomas, 123
Hunter, 294
Huntingdon, Ada de, 211, 310
  David de, 198, 211
  Henry de, 109, 198, 211, 247,
  310

Margaret de, 109, 198
Hussey, Joan, 36
Hutchins, John, 249
  Love, 249

Ida of Namur, 152
Ida of Saxony, 56
Ienaf ap Adda, 305
Ingalls, David W., 253
  Maria, 253
Ingebjor Baardsdatter, 256
Ingegard of Sweden, 131
Ingerman, Count of Hasbaye, 99,
  182
Irby, Olive, 71, 73, 271
Irmgard (Ermengarde) of Bar, 246
Irmingard, Empress, 2, 3
Isabel verch Gruffudd, 152
Isabella of Angouleme, 7, 117,
  126, 137, 183
Isabel, Queen of Castile, 267
Isabella of France, 105
Isabel of Scotland, 247
Ives, Ebeneezer, 306
  Eunice, 306
  Joseph, 306
Jackson, Mary, 253
Jacobs, Isabel deL., 287
  Marie Louise, 268
  Dr. William S., 268
Jacobson, Gustave, 290
  Oscaria, 290
James I, King of England, 133,
  285
James I, King of Scots, 86, 105,
  106
James II, of Aragon and Sicily,
  266
James, Mary, 73
Jamieson, Daniel, 141
  Elizabeth, 141
Jaroslav I, of Kiev, 35, 131,
  146, 247
Jason, Elizabeth, 243
  Simon, 243
Jay, Judith, 299
Jeanne of Pouthieu, 126, 231
Jenkins, Elizabeth, 294

339

Kumblad, Ruth V., 129
Kuser, Harry C., 244
Kvaale, Einar S., 240
Kyrton, Thomas, 216

Lachard, 102
Lacy, Alice de, 168
  Idonia de, 168
  John de, 167
  Maude de, 132
  Roger de, 167
Lambert I, Count of Louvain,
  151
Lambert II, Ct. of Louvain, 151
Lambert, Julia Glenn, 52
  Kimberly M., 51
  Louis E., 50
  Margaret G., 50
  Nancy C., 52
  Nancy M., 51
  Robert F., 51
  Robert Louis, 51
  Thomas R., 52
Lancaster, Eleanor de, 93
  Sarah, 154
Landon, David M., 252
  Rev. Harold, 252
Lane, Hannah, 57
  Isaac, 56, 60
  Sarah, 60
Lang, Janet R., 201
  Laurence C., 201
  Laurence C., III, 201
  Dr. Nathaniel H., 201
  Stephen G., 201
Langton, Joan, 248
  Henry de, 248
Lanvellei, Hawise de, 198
  William de, 198
l'Arcedeckne, Eleanor, 212
  Sir Warin, 212
Lascelles, Elizabeth, 243
  Sir George, 243
Latham, Frances, 138, 141, 143
Lathrop, Elijah, 200
  Eunice, 200
Latimer, Elizabeth de, 199

Thomas, Lord, 199
  Sir Warin de, 199
Laubenthal, Lt. Col. Gerard J.,
  9
Lawrence, Emerald, 47
  Dr. Thomas J., 47
Lawrenson, Sara P., 102
Layfield, Priscilla, 286
Leaper, Carrie L., 210
  Laura M., 210
  Col. Percy J., 210
  Percy F., 210
  Scott R. F., 210
Learned, Hannah, 275, 278
Lee, Eleanor, 122
  Geoffrey, 122
  Mary, 123
  Richard, 122
  Sir Richard, 122
Lees, Edith M. B., 150
Lemek, Bonita Ann, 240
Leo III, Pope, 18 130
Leonard, Pamela, 250
LeRus, Alice, 159
  William, 159
Lesesne, Arthur E., 300
Lesh, Marie L., 228
Lestrange (see Strange)
  Elizabeth, 152, 305
  John, IV, 152, 305
  John, V, 152, 305
Levin, Dorothy M., 42
Lewis, Anne, 165
  Mary, 134
  William, 134
Leycester, Elizabeth, 168, 207
  John, 207
  Nicholas, 168, 207
  Sir Nicholas, 168
  Roger, 168
Liegarde, 6, 206
Liegarde of France, 125, 246
Lille, Baldwin V de, 7
Lindsay, David, 86
  Elizabeth, 86
Linton, Benjamin, 111
  Elizabeth, 111
  John, 111

341

Lionel of Antwerp, 132
Lisle, Anne, 184, 237
Litchfield, Mary Scott, 263
Littell, Abraham A., 111
  Gregory S., 112
  Harry E., 111
  Pamela S., 112
  Robert Burgess, 112
  Vicki S., 112
Liv Ranesdatter i Tunsberg, 256
Liv Torsteinsdatter, 257
Livingston, Edward, 106
  Isabelle, 279
  Margaret, 106
  William, 106
Llencu ferch Llewelyn, 191
Llewelyn ap Jorwerth, 15, 159, 190
Llewellyn, Margaret, 159
Llewelyn ap Owen, 151
Lloyd, Agnes, 306
  Anne (Ann) 192, 306
  David, 306
  Frances, 306
  Rt. Rev. George 192, 306
  Gwenhywyfar, 306
  John, 191, 306
  Meredith, 191
  Richard, 306
Locke, Margaret, 281
Loker, George Clinton, 37
  Katie, 38
  Thomas, 37
Lomax, Mary, 169
Longespee, Emmeline de, 132
Lord, Hon. Richard 200
  Susanna, 200
Lothair I, Emperor, 1, 2, 3, 4, 5, 99, 151, 182
Lothair II, King of Lorraine, 182
Louis the German, 1
Louis I, Emperor, 1, 2, 18, 55, 99, 116, 130, 145, 151, 158, 182, 255
Louis IV, King of France, 55, 265
Louis VII, King of France, 136, 159, 183

Louise Henriette, 268
Louthe, Anne, 262
  Edmund, 262
  Thomas, 262
Lovel, Maude, 241
Lovelace, Anne, 165
  William, 165
  Sir William, 165
Lowe, Col. Henry, 120*
  Mary, 120
Lowell, Anna G., 227
  George W., 227
Lowman, Elizabeth R., 235
  Roy M., 235
Lowri, 305
Lowri ferch Griffith, 191
Lucas, Eleanor J., 166
  James, 166
Lucy, Eleanor, 212
  Sir Walter, 212
Ludlow, Elizabeth, 102
  Henry, 101
  Sir Henry, 101
  Stephen, 102
Ludwig IV of Bavaria, 19
Ludwig Friedrich I, 268
Lusignan, Alice de, 147
  Maud de, 109
Lygon, Elizabeth, 114
  Henry, 114
  Sir Richard, 114
Lyman, Lt. Daniel, 223
  Lauren D., 223
  Sarah E., 223
Lynde, Elizabeth, 200
  Enoch, 199
  Hon. Nathaniel, 200
  Hon. Simon, 199, 282
Lyttleton, Joan, 8

Mable of Chester, 152, 305
Mackall, Benjamin, 39
  James, 37, 39
  Capt. John, 37
  Rebecca, 37, 39
MacLamroc, Alan G. W., 315
  Brian G. W., 315
  James G. W., 314

James R., 314
Virginia, 315
MacLean, Sally H., 51
MacMurrough, Dermot, 100, 163, 173, 215, 236
Eva, 100, 173, 215, 236
Macomber, Fannie H., 178
MacRae, Jean, 252
Maelgwyn ap Rhys, 190
Maelgwyn Fycham, 190
Magdelene Sibylle, 268
Magruder, Alexander, 204
Eleanor, 204
John, 204
Ninian, 204
Samuel, 204
Sarah, 204
Mahone, Geraldine S., 9
James S., 9
Marion D., 9
Stephen W., 9
Mainwaring (Manwaring)
Elizabeth, 62
George, 208
Joan, 168
Mary, 37, 49, 54, 208
Mercy, 208
Oliver, 208
Ralph, 208
Randle, 168, 208
Roger, 207
William, 62, 168, 207, 208
Malcolm III, King of Scots, 7, 117, 136, 183
Malcolm IV, King of Scots, 310
Malet, Gilbert, 292
Helewise (Hawise) 293
Mabel, 163
Robert, 292
William, 163, 292
Sir William, 292
Malory, Sir Anketil, 62
Margaret, 62
Sir William, 62
Margaret of Buchan, 36
Margaret of France, 137
Margaret verch Jenkin, 305
Margaret ferch Maelgwn, 190

Margaret ot Norfolk, 137
Margaret of Scotland, St., 7, 117, 183
Marguerite of Austria, 20
Marguerite of Savoy, 19
Maria of Champagne, 19
Marie Eleanor, 267
Marjory of Scotland, 203
Marmion, Robert II, 56
Robert III, 56
Robert IV, 56
Robert V, 56
Mazera, 56
Phillip, 56
Marquis, (Marquiss)
Mary, 204
William Kidd, 204
Marriott, Mary, 311
Matthias, 311
William, 311
Marshall, Eva, 109, 215, 241
Isabel, 85, 131, 202
Maud, 100, 236
Sibyl, 163, 173
William, 85, 167, 202
Sir William, 100, 131, 163, 173, 215, 236, 241
Marsham, Katherine, 30, 53
William, 30
Martel, Ela, 174
Roger, 174
Martin, Allen, 28
Ann Field, 28
Diana, 301
Martinez-Hernandez, Minette, 149
Mary verch Reinallt, 152
Mandeville, Maud FitzGeoffrey de, 109
Mantfield, Elianore, 160
Robert, 160
Manfred Lancia, 266
Manrow, Mahala, 82
Mansfield, Hannah, 68
Masnilwaring, Sir Ralph de, 207
Mason, Glen M., 14
John R., 13
Lt. Col. John R., 14
Kent W., 14

344

Midbøn, Ann T., 240
Middleton, Anne, 191
  David, 191
Migne, J. P., 5
Milburn, Barbara, 16
Miller, Hercules, 170
  John W., 107
  Laura P., 107
  Mary, 95
Millet, Dr. Charles S., 178
  Mary B., 178
Mills, Dea, Ezekiel, 229
  Isaac, 229
  Isaac E., 230
  Martha G., 230
Mitchell, Cora M., 209
  Elizabeth F., 161
  George B., 209
  George M., 209
  Gerard P., 161
  Ignatius S., 161
  Wilson S., 296
Mobberly, Mary de, 168
  Sir Raufe de, 168
  William de. 168
Montagu, William de, 132
  Phillippa de, 132
Montfort, Alice de, 131
  Amice (Amicia) 35, 85, 146,
  202, 207
  Elizabeth de, 56
  Ralph, 131
  Ralph de Gael, 35, 85, 146, 202
  Simon de, 167
Montgomery, Roger de, 167, 207
  Sybil de, 167, 207
Mohun, Alice de, 164
Moore, Ann H., 195
  David W., 295
  Edward A., 295
  Elva L., 205
  Jane W., 295
  Mary, 278
Montifex, Mary, 204
More, Jasper, 212
  Katherine, 212
  Richard, 212
  Samuel, 212
  Susanna, 212

Thomas, 212
Thomas, 212
Morewike, Sir Hugh de, 284
  Tiphaine de, 284
Morgan ap Jenkins, 24
Morgan, Nettie C., 213
  William Carroll, 213
Morgan, Anna, 185
  Solomon, 185
Morley, James, 123
Morris, Mildred J., 9
Morrison, Anna, 193
  Andrew, 193
  Dorothy L., 251
Morsell, Arthur L., III, 259
Mortimer, 292
  Edmund, 132
  Edmund, Lord, 132
  Edmund de, 126, 231
  Sir Edmund de, 15
  Elizabeth, 132
  Isabella, 93
  Isolt de, 126
  Joyce, 8
  Katherine de, 280
  Joan de, 15
  Margaret, 15
  Ralph de, 15
  Roger de, 15
  Sir Roger de, 15, 132, 280
Morton, Alan W., 51
  Bruce Alan, 51
  Daphne G., 51
  Elizabeth, 101, 184, 237
  Sir Robert, 184, 237
  Rosalie M., 51
  Stuart S., 51
Moseley, Cecily, 217
  John, 217
  Joseph, 217
  Rachel, 217
  Rhoda, 224
Moses, Mary, 71
Mostyn, Elizabeth, 306
Mowbray, Alianore de, 101, 184,
  237
  Eleanor de, 137
  John de, 101, 184, 237

345

Moon, Mary, 111
Mottrom, Anne, 285
　Col. John, 285
Muirhead, Rebecca, 106
Mullery, Helen M., 209
　Valentine J., 209
Mulso, Anne, 262
　William, 262
Muramatsu, Marcia, 296
Mure, Elizabeth, 203
Mumford, Bathsheba, 63
Murfey, Julia A., 189
Muscegros, Hawise de, 23
　Sir Robert de, 23

Naile, Ann Paulding, 88
　Frederick I, 87
　Frederick R., 87
Namur, Elizabeth de, 56
　Godfrey, Count of, 56
Nason, Joyce, 8
Neale, Anthony, 120
　Edward, 120
　Martha, 120
Needham, Dorothy, 90
　Robert, 90
　Thomas, 90
Negus, Alexander, 115
　Estelle C., 115, 154
　Hannah, 114
　Capt. Isaac, 114
　Isaac, Jr., 114
　John, 115
　Jonathan, 114
　Stephen West, 115
　Thomas, 114
　William Steel, 115
Nevell, Anne, 24
　Thomas, 24
Neville, Alice, 97
　Sir Edward, 118
　George de, 29
　Sir George, 119
　Sir Henry, 29
　John, 29
　Margaret, 29

Phillipa, 132
　Ralph, 29, 132
　Ralph de, 118
　Sir Richard, 29
　Ursula, 119
Nevsteinsdatter, Gudrun, 256
Newberry, Benjamin, 217
　Capt. Benjamin, 222
　Mary, 217, 226, 229
　Richard, 216
　Sarah, 222
　Thomas, 217, 222, 226, 229
Newburgh (Newborough)
　Alice, 216
　Alice de, 113
　John, 216
　Sir John, 216
　Richard, 216
　Roger de, 113
　Thomas, 216
　Waleran de, 113
Newdigate, Hannah, 282
　Margaret, 164
Newgate, Hannah, 200
Newman, Dieter Eby, 245
　George F., 244
　George H., 244
Niblock, Andrea P., 32
　William P., 32
Nicholson, Barbara J., 72
　John B., M.D., 72
　John R., 72
Niebell, Nancy, 221
　Paul M., 220
　Paul M., Jr., 221
　Paula, 221
Noble, Joanna, 217
Norris, Abell A., 45
　Abell A., Jr., 45
　Abell A., III, 45
　James Edward, 45
　Janet A., 45
　Dr. William V., 161
　William V., Jr., 161
　William V., III, 161
Norton, Anne, 311
　John, 311
Norwich, Anna, 97

346

347

Pease, Dorothy G., 227
Peebles, Mary R., 298
Pelham, Elizabeth, 185
  Herbert, 185, 238
  Penelope, 238
Pennewill, David, 286
  Simeon S., 286
Pepin, Emperor, 6, 34
Pepin, King of Italy, 206, 246
Pepin, Count of Senlis, 6, 34, 206,
  246
Percy, Alice, 283
  Eleanor de, 119
  Elizabeth de, 119, 132
  Henry, 29, 119
  Sir Henry de, 132
  Maud de, 29
  William, 283
Perry, Eleanor B., 54, 120
  Elton H., 54, 120
Perth, Matilda, 293
  William, 293
Peter III of Aragon and Sicily, 266
Peter IV, King of Aragon, 267
Peter Jakobsson, 256
Peters, Sarah, 294
Rev. Sydney, 291
Peto, Audrey, 160
  Edward, 160
  John, 160
  John de, 160
  William de, 160
Pheatt, Ermina C., 218
  Isaac T., 218
  Zubulon C., 217
Phelps, Ann Naile, 88
  Asahel, 229
  Charles M., 88
  Susannah, 226
  Ursula, 229
Phettiplace, Anne, 310
  William, 310
Philip, Archduke of Austria, 267
Philippa of Hainault, 105
Phillippe III, King of France, 105,
  137
Phillippe IV, King of France, 105
Phillips, Alice, 65
  Mary, 313

Picot, Alice, 292
  Ralph, 292
Pidgeon, Barbara, 84
  Geo. Henry, 84
Pierce, Lewis H., 107
  Martha F., 304
  Mary R., 107
Pilkington, Ann, 170
  James Penn, 251
  Sir John, 199
  George H., 251
  Louise Penn, 252
  Margaret, 199
Pinney, Anne (Anna) 229
  Isaac, 226, 229
  Isaac, II, 226, 229
  Isaac, III, 226
  Sarah, 226
Pistell, Anne E., 290
  Clarence K., 289
  John C., 289
  Joseph K. 289
  Laurence T., 289
Pitman, Anthony R., 301
Plantagenet, Anne, 110
  Constance, 118
  Edmund, 101, 105, 118, 237
  Eleanor, 147, 231
  Elizabeth, 110
  Geoffrey V, 7, 117, 125, 136,
  159, 183
  Henry, 100, 147, 184, 237
  Joan, 101, 105, 118, 126, 184,
  237
  Philippa, 132
  Thomas, 110
Plumley, Sarah, 87
Plumpton, Alice de, 248
  Sir Robert, 247
  Sir William, 248
Plunket, Christopher, 137
  Janet, 137
Poitou, Adelaide of, 34, 130, 158
  Agnes of, 265
  Ranulf I, 130, 158
  Ranulf II, 130, 158
  William I of, 158
  William II of, 158, 265
  William VII of, 7

348

Pomeroy, Daniel, 217
  Ebenezer, 217
  Eleanor, 217
Poole, Alice H., 295
  Ethel L., 171
  Ezekiel, 294
  Sarah, 295
Pope, John A., 176
  Robert T., 176
Potter, Susanne, 213
Potts, Andrew E., 43
  Charles W., 42
  Daniel C., 42
  James Webb, 43
  Jas. Webb, Jr., 43
  Luken Wm., 42
Poultney, Sir Thomas, 199
Pond, Abigail, 193
Powell, Elizabeth, 148
  John, 148
Poyntz, Aliandra, 193
  Hugh, 293
  Hugh de, 216
  Sir Hugh, 293
  John, 293
  Sir John, 293
  Margaret, 216
  Nicholas de, 216, 293
  Sir Nicholas, 293
  Pontius, 293
  Susanna, 294
  Thomas, 293
  William, 293
Pratt, Elizabeth, 65
  Charles C., 273
  Helen L., 273
Prescott, Dorothy, 90
  Elizabeth, 63
  Dr. Jonathon, 63
Preston, Abigail, 213
  Benjamin, 213
Prestwick, Rose, 199
  William, 199
Price, Ellis, 148
Pringle, Jean, 87
Pritchard, Elizabeth, 133
Provence, Harold, 279
Pryor, Ann L., 171
  Robert W., 170

  Thomas, 170
  William, 170
  Wm. Brand, 171
  Wm. Walsh, 170
  Wm. Young, 170
Pugh, Maxine, 314
Puleston, Angharad, 122
  Jane, 148
  John, 191
  Margaret, 191
  Robert, 122, 191
Purcell, Mary, 102
Purnell, Maj. John, 286
  Martha, 286

Qualey, Cornelius S., 240
  Paul J., 299
  Steinar E., 240
Qualley, George T., 240
Quarles, Margery, 94
Quant, Barbara A., 260
  Burton E., 259
  Robert S., 259
  Wendy Sue, 260
Quekes, Agnes, 310
  John, 310
Quincy, Elena de, 280
  Elizabeth de, 36
  Hawise de, 146
  Margaret de, 23, 96, 167
  Robert de, 167
  Saher de, 146, 167
  Roger de, 23, 25, 96, 280

Radcliffe, Thomas, 16
Ragnfrid Erlingsdatter, 156
Rainier I, of Lorraine, 151
Rainier II, Ct. of Hainault, 151
Rainier III, Ct. of Hainault, 151
Ralph, Lord Bulmer, 261
Ralph, Earl of Norfolk, 131
Ralston, John, 286
  Sarah B., 286
Randes, Rt. Rev. Henry, D.D., 285
  Mary, 285
  Thomas, 285

349

352

Weaver, Sgt. Clement, 141
Elizabeth, 141, 143
Webb, David, 90
Elizabeth, 90
Webber, Mary C., 238
Webster, Catherine, 101
Weeden, Mary, 233
Weeks, Lucille A., 144
Welby, Olive, 271, 275, 278
Richard, 171
Welf, Ct. of Alamannia, 145
Welford, Bridget, 119
Weller, Nathan, 224
Rhode, 224
Solomon, 224
Welles, Anne, 89
Cicely de, 281
Elizabeth, 137
Eudo de, 137, 281
Sir John de, 137
Sir Lionel de, 281
William de, 137
Wells, Annie M., 175
Willoughby, 175
Wensley, Sarah, 238
Wentworth, Agnes, 242
Sir Roger, 242
West, Elizabeth, 185
Sir George, 101, 184, 237
Grace, 314
Lavina, 114
Letitia, 101
Penelope, 238
Sir Reginald, 184
Sir Reynold, 101, 184, 237
Sir Richard, 101, 184, 237
Samuel E., 314
Sir Thomas, 101, 184, 185, 237,
238
Maj. William, 314
Sir William, 101, 185, 237
Westall, Robert, 170
Sarah A., 170
Westbury, John, 216
Wetzel, Jason, 221
Wheeler, Betty, 275
Buford M., 205
Christopher, 205

Howard R., 205
Janice R., 205
Mary, 300
White, Elizabeth, 111
Priscilla, 286
Sarah, 134
William, 111
Whitener, Susan A., 273
Whitmore, Eunice A., 259
Whitsett, Minerva J., 25
Whyte, Margaret, 138
Patrick, 138
Wickham, Elizabeth, 138
Thomas, 138
Samuel, 138
Wier, Cdr. Richard A., 220
Jean Stuart, 220
Margaret A., 220
Wiggin, Mercy, 253
Wigglesworth, Frances, 205
Wilfong, Beatrice L., 92
Wilhelm, Duke of Julich, 267
Wilhelm Ludwig, Prince, 268
Wilkinson, Ann, 192
John, 192
Rebecca, 194
Willa, 182
Willa of Arles, 18
Willa of Tuscany, 18
Willes, Elizabeth, 272
Sylvanus, 272
William of Aquitaine, 183
William I, of Burgundy, 19, 104
William the Conqueror, 7, 117,
131, 136, 159, 183, 207, 215,
283, 292
William ap Griffith, 191
William III, of Hainault, 105
William the Lion, 247
William I, of Poitou, 158
William II, of Poitou, 158, 265
William VII, of Poitou, 7
William I of Scotland, 310
Williams, Ann, 154
Benjamin, 134
Dorothy S., 228
Eunice, 188
Howard Joseph, 227

James W., III, 299
John F., 298
Dr. John F., 298
Mary, 298, 300
Mary M., 299
Nathaniel, 298
Parry W., 302
Peter, 294
Richard, 294
Sarah E., 294
Traynham, 302
William E., 300
Wydville, Richard, 164
John, 164
Joan, 164
Wynn, John, 306

Yale, Rev. David, 306
Thomas, 192, 285, 306
Yarbrough, Elizabeth H., 9
James, 9
Yaraslov I, of Kiev, 35, 131, 146, 247
Yelverton, Margaret, 232
Yerger, Sarah E., 150
Yerkes, Deborah A., 42

Yorke, Mary, 285, 306
Young, Anna P., 225
Annie Mae, 170
Britton D., 225
Britton D., Jr., 225
Britton D., III, 225
David, 170
David W., 128
Don J., IV, 225
Margaret A., 128
Matthew, 225
Ross R., 225
Sarah, 49
Stephen M., IV, 225

Zeller, Dr. Julius C., 75
Margaret L. 75
Zouche, Sir Alan la, 280
Elizabeth la, 216, 293
Ellen la, 310
Eudo la, 216, 241, 280
Eva la, 280
Milicent la, 241
Sir William la, 241
Zulauf, Janet, 179

360